Computing Meaning

TEXT, SPEECH AND LANGUAGE TECHNOLOGY

VOLUME 47

For further volumes:
www.springer.com/series/6636

Harry Bunt · Johan Bos · Stephen Pulman

Editors

Computing Meaning

Volume 4

 Springer

Editors
Harry Bunt
Tilburg Center for Cognition
  & Communication
Tilburg University
Tilburg, The Netherlands

Stephen Pulman
Department of Computer Science
Oxford University
Oxford, UK

Johan Bos
Center for Language and Cognition (CLCG)
Rijksuniversiteit Groningen
Groningen, The Netherlands

ISSN 1386-291X   Text, Speech and Language Technology
ISBN 978-94-017-7999-9   ISBN 978-94-007-7284-7 (eBook)
DOI 10.1007/978-94-007-7284-7
Springer Dordrecht Heidelberg New York London

Printed on acid-free paper

Springer is part of Springer Science+Business Media (www.springer.com)

Contents

Part III   Semantic Resources and Annotation

Contributors

Theodore Alexandrov University of Bremen, Bremen, Germany

Hiyan Alshawi Google, Mountain View, CA, USA

Olga Batiukova Department of Spanish Philology, Autonomous University of Madrid, Cantoblanco, Madrid, Spain

Raffaella Bernardi University of Trento, Trento, Italy

Johan Bos Center for Language and Cognition (CLCG), University of Groningen, Groningen, The Netherlands

Susan Windisch Brown Universita degli Studi di Firenze, Florence, Italy

Harry Bunt Tilburg Center for Cognition and Communication (TiCC) and Department of Philosophy, Tilburg University, Tilburg, The Netherlands

Diego Calvanese Free University of Bozen-Bolzano, Bolzano, Italy

Pi-Chuan Chang Google, Mountain View, CA, USA

Stephen Clark Computer Laboratory, University of Cambridge, Cambridge, UK

Bob Coecke Department of Computer Science, Oxford University, Oxford, UK

Dmitriy Dligach Boston Children's Hospital, Harvard Medical School, Boston, MA, USA

Katrin Erk University of Texas at Austin, Austin, USA

Dan Garrette University of Texas at Austin, Austin, USA

Edward Grefenstette Department of Computer Science, Oxford University, Oxford, UK

Jerry R. Hobbs Information Sciences Institute, University of Southern California, Marina del Rey, CA, USA

Bill MacCartney Stanford University, Stanford, CA, USA

Christopher D. Manning Stanford University, Stanford, CA, USA

Michael C. McCord Ossining, NY, USA

Niloofar Montazeri Information Sciences Institute, University of Southern California, Marina del Rey, CA, USA

Raymond Mooney University of Texas at Austin, Austin, USA

Jessica L. Moszkowicz Department of Computer Science, Brandeis University, Waltham, MA, USA

Rutu Mulkar-Mehta San Diego Supercomputer Center, University of California in San Diego, La Jolla, CA, USA

Ekaterina Ovchinnikova Information Sciences Institute, University of Southern California, Marina del Rey, CA, USA

Martha Palmer Department of Linguistics, University of Colorado at Boulder, Boulder, CO, USA

Volha Petukhova Department of Spoken Language Systems, Saarland University, Saarbrücken, Germany

Stephen Pulman Department of Computer Science, Oxford University, Oxford, UK

James Pustejovsky Department of Computer Science, Brandeis University, Waltham, MA, USA

Michael Ringgaard Google, Aarhus, Denmark

Anna Rumshisky Department of Computer Science, University of Massachusetts, Lowell, MA, USA; Computer Science and Artificial Intelligence Laboratory, Massachusetts Institute of Technology, Cambridge, MA, USA

Mehrnoosh Sadrzadeh School of Electronic Engineering and Computer Science, Queen Mary University of London, London, UK

Camilo Thorne Free University of Bozen-Bolzano, Bolzano, Italy

Computing Meaning: Annotation, Representation, and Inference

Harry Bunt, Johan Bos, and Stephen Pulman

Abstract This chapter introduces the subsequent chapters in the book and how they are related, against the background of a discussion of the nature and the complexity of processes that compute the meanings of natural language expressions. The discussion focuses on three aspects of the computation of meanings that play an important part in later chapters: (1) the nature of meaning representations; (2) the integration of inferencing with compositional interpretation; and (3) the construction of semantically annotated corpora and their use in machine learning of meaning computation.

1 Introduction

While computers are very good at computing in general, they are not very good at computing meaning. There are at least three reasons why this may be so: (R1) the very notion of meaning, as expressed in natural language, is something extremely complex, and therefore difficult to compute; (R2) the process of computing meanings is extremely complex, because it requires the effective use of a variety of extremely rich information sources (linguistic knowledge, general knowledge of the world, specific knowledge of the domain of discourse, knowledge of interactive settings, ...); and (R3) the very notion of meaning is not well enough understood to

H. Bunt (✉)
Tilburg Center for Cognition and Communication (TiCC) and Department of Philosophy, Tilburg University, P.O. Box 90153, 5000 LE Tilburg, The Netherlands
e-mail: harry.bunt@uvt.nl

J. Bos
Center for Language and Cognition (CLCG), University of Groningen, Groningen, The Netherlands
e-mail: johan.bos@rug.nl

S. Pulman
Department of Computer Science, Oxford University, Oxford, UK
e-mail: stephen.pulman@cs.ox.ac.uk

H. Bunt et al. (eds.), *Computing Meaning*, Text, Speech and Language Technology 47,
DOI 10.1007/978-94-007-7284-7_1,

effectively program and/or teach computers what it is and how it can be computed for a given natural language expression, occurring in a given context.

Most of the work in formal as well as in computational semantics tacitly assumes, different from (R3), that we do have a clear understanding of what we mean by meaning, and different from (R1), that natural language meanings are simple enough to be represented by very simple structures, such as formulas in first-order logic (or, equivalently, Discourse Representation Structures). Assuming that such structures are adequate representations of meaning, computing the meaning of a given natural language expression comes down to syntactic parsing of it and composing the semantic representations of the parts to form the meaning representation, which itself has a semantics defined by the representation formalism.

Since computational semantics started to develop, in the last two decades of the twentieth century (see Blackburn and Bos 2005), it has become clear that the dream of computing meaning representations by syntactic/semantic (de-)composition, made popular especially through the work of Richard Montague (see Thomason 1974), cannot become reality, simply because natural language expressions much of the time do not contain sufficiently much information to construct such a representation. Other information sources are indispensable. This insight has inspired the introduction of the notion of an underspecified meaning representation, which represents the semantic information that is present in the sentence without disambiguating those aspects for which the sentence does not contain sufficient information. It also became very clear that relying solely on linguistic information for computing meanings would lead to impossibly complex interpretation processes, due to the astronomical number of readings that ordinary sentences have when considered in isolation (see Bunt and Muskens 1999). Again, underspecified meaning representations offer solace here, as they obviate the need to fully disambiguate. Several of the chapters in this book, in particular in Part I, witness the ongoing search for appropriate forms of meaning representation and for methods of exploiting linguistic as well as other information in their computation.

A problematic aspect of the use of underspecified semantic representations is that they do not allow straightforward application of logic-based inference methods, since different resolutions of underspecifications may result in interpretations that allow different inferences (see e.g. van Deemter 1996; Blackburn et al. 2001). This is indeed problematic on the traditional view of meaning representations as unambiguously supporting a specific set of inferences, thereby explaining differences in meaning and relations between different meanings. One way to deal with this problem is to move away from strictly deductive approaches to inferencing, and instead turn to abductive methods (Hobbs et al. 1993) or to textual entailment, where inferencing is performed directly on natural language expressions, rather than on their interpretations, and logical proof is replaced by psychological plausibility (see e.g. Dagan et al. 2008 and Bos 2013). One way or another, the use of inference processes involving natural language expressions and/or their interpretations is needed, since nonlinguistic information must be exploited in order to arrive at intended and contextually appropriate interpretations; methods for combining pieces of information therefore have to be applied in order to arrive at a appropriate interpretations.

The chapters in Part II of this book are all concerned with forms of inferencing (or combining pieces of information) in the computation of meanings.

Related to the limitations of effectively following strictly logic- and rule-based methods in the computation of meaning is the exploration of statistical and machine learning techniques that have been successfully applied in other areas of computational linguistics. These techniques presuppose the availability of large corpora, and can benefit in particular from semantically annotated resources. The development of such corpora (e.g. Basile et al. 2012), and of well-founded semantic annotation methodologies (see Bunt 2013), have supported the use of these new methods in computational semantics research (see e.g. Clark and Pulman 2007), as reflected in several of the chapters in this book, both in Part I and in Part III.

2 About This Book

The chapters in this book are organized into three parts. A first cluster of four chapters is focused on aspects of the representation of meaning and the computation of these representations. A second group of four chapters is concerned with issues of inferencing and its role in language understanding. The chapters in the third and final cluster of four deal with resources for meaning computation and their use.

2.1 Semantic Representation and Compositionality

In the opening chapter of this part of the book, entitled *Deterministic Statistical Mapping of Sentences to Underspecified Semantics*, the authors Hiyan Alshawi, Pi-Chuan Chang and Michael Ringgaard present a method for training a statistical model for mapping natural language sentences to semantic expressions. The semantics are expressions of an underspecified logical form that has properties making it particularly suitable for statistical mapping from text. An encoding of the semantic expressions into dependency trees with automatically generated labels allows application of existing methods for statistical dependency parsing to the mapping task (without the need for separate traditional dependency labels or parts of speech). The encoding also results in a natural per-word semantic-mapping accuracy measure.

The authors report on the results of training and testing statistical models for mapping sentences of the Penn Treebank into the semantic expressions, for which per-word semantic mapping accuracy ranges between 79 % and 86 % depending on the experimental conditions.

The particular choice of algorithms used also means that the trained mapping is deterministic (in the sense of deterministic parsing), paving the way for large-scale text-to-semantics mapping.

In the next chapter, *A Formal Approach to Linking Logical Form and Vector-Space Lexical Semantics*, the authors Dan Garrette, Katrin Erk and Raymond

Mooney argue that first-order logic provides a powerful and flexible mechanism for representing natural language semantics, but that it is an open question of how best to integrate it with uncertain, weighted knowledge, for example regarding word meaning. They describe a mapping between predicates of logical form and points in a vector space. This mapping is used to project distributional inferences to inference rules in logical form. The authors then describe the first steps of an approach that uses this mapping to recast first-order semantics into the probabilistic models that are part of Statistical Relational AI. Specifically, they show how Discourse Representation Structures can be combined with distributional models for word meaning inside a Markov Logic Network and used to successfully perform inferences that take advantage of logical concepts such as negation and factivity, as well as weighted information on word meaning in context.

In the chapter *Annotations that Effectively Contribute to Semantic Interpretation*, Harry Bunt presents a new perspective on the use of semantic annotations. He argues that semantic annotations should capture semantic information that is supplementary to the information that is expressed in the source text, and should have a formal semantics. If the latter condition is satisfied then the information in semantic annotations can be effectively combined with information extracted by a compositional semantic analysis. This can be used (1) for making semantic relations explicit which are not expressed in the text as such, such as coreference relations and implicit discourse relations, and (2) for specializing an interpretation to one that is contextually appropriate.

Bunt shows how such uses of semantic annotations can be optimally facilitated by defining a semantics of annotations in the form of a compositional translation of annotations into a formalism that is also suitable for underspecified semantic representations as commonly built by compositional semantic analyzers, allowing a unification-like combination of pieces of information from different sources. He shows that slightly modified Discourse Representation Structures, where discourse referents are paired with annotation markables, are particularly convenient for this purpose.

The approach is illustrated with examples from recent efforts concerning the annotation of information about time and events, about coreference, about semantic roles, and about discourse relations.

In the last chapter of this part of the book, entitled *Concrete Sentence Spaces for Compositional Distributional Models of Meaning*, a group of authors consisting of Edward Grefenstette, Mehrnoosh Sadrzadeh, Stephen Clark, Bob Coecke, and Stephen Pulman describe a compositional model of meaning that they have developed for distributional semantics, in which each word in a sentence has a meaning vector and the distributional meaning of the sentence is a function of the tensor products of the word vectors. Abstractly speaking, this function is the morphism corresponding to the grammatical structure of the sentence in the category of finite dimensional vector spaces.

The authors provide a concrete method for implementing this linear meaning map by presenting an algorithm for computing representations for various syntactic classes which have functional types; this algorithm results in assigning concrete corpus-based vector spaces to the abstract type of 'sentence'. The construction method is based on structured vector spaces whose basis vectors are pairs of words and grammatical roles. The concrete sentence spaces only depend on the types of the verbs of sentences; the authors use an embedding of these spaces and compare meanings of sentences with different grammatical structures by simply taking the inner product of their vectors in the bigger space. The constructions are exemplified on a toy corpus.

2.2 Inference and Understanding

In the first of the four chapters forming the second part of the book, entitled *Recognising Textual Entailment and Computational Semantics*, Johan Bos notes that recognising textual entailment (RTE)—deciding whether one piece of text contains new information with respect to another piece of text—remains a big challenge in natural language processing.

One attempt to deal with this problem is combining deep semantic analysis and logical inference, as is done in the Nutcracker RTE system. In doing so, various obstacles will be met on the way: robust semantic interpretation, designing interfaces to state-of-the-art theorem provers, and acquiring relevant background knowledge. The coverage of the parser and semantic analysis component is high (nearly reaching 100 %). Yet the performance on RTE examples yields high precision but low recall.

An empirical study of the output of Nutcracker reveals that the true positives are caused by sophisticated linguistic analysis such as coordination, active-passive alternation, pronoun resolution and relative clauses; the small set of false positives are caused by insufficient syntactic and semantic analyses. Most importantly, the false negatives are produced mainly by lack of background knowledge.

The next chapter, entitled *Abductive Reasoning with a Large Knowledge Base for Discourse Processing*, presents a discourse processing framework based on weighted abduction. The authors, Ekaterina Ovchinnikova, Niloofar Montazeri, Theodore Alexandrov, Jerry Hobbs, Michael C. McCord, and Rutu Mulkar-Mehta, elaborate on ideas concerning abduction in language understanding described in Hobbs et al. (1993) and implement the abductive inference procedure in a system called *Mini-TACITUS*. Particular attention is paid to constructing a large and reliable knowledge base for supporting inferences. For this purpose such lexical-semantic resources are exploited as WordNet and FrameNet. English Slot Grammar (McCord 1990) is used to parse text and produce logical forms.

The proposed procedure and the resulting knowledge base are tested on the Recognizing Textual Entailment task using the data sets from the RTE-2 challenge for evaluation. In addition, an evaluation is provided of the semantic role labeling produced by the system taking the Frame-Annotated Corpus for Textual Entailment as a gold standard.

In the chapter *Natural Logic and Natural Language Inference* Bill MacCartney and Christopher Manning propose a model of natural language inference which

identifies valid inferences by their lexical and syntactic features, without full semantic interpretation. They extend past work in *natural logic*, which has focused on
semantic containment and monotonicity, by incorporating both semantic exclusion
and implicativity. The proposed model decomposes an inference problem into a sequence of atomic edits linking premise to hypothesis; predicts a lexical entailment
relation for each edit; propagates these relations upward through a semantic composition tree according to properties of intermediate nodes; and joins the resulting
entailment relations across the edit sequence.

A computational implementation of the model achieves 70 % accuracy and 89 %
precision on the FRACAS test suite (Cooper et al. 1996). Moreover, including this
model as a component in an existing system is shown to yield significant performance gains on the Recognizing Textual Entailment challenge.

In the final chapter of this part of the book, *Designing Efficient Controlled Languages for Ontologies*, the authors Raffaella Bernardi, Diego Calvanese, and Camilo
Thorne describe a methodology to recognize *efficient* controlled natural languages
that compositionally translate into ontology languages, and as such are suitable for
using in natural language front-ends to ontology-based systems. Efficiency in this
setting is defined as the tractability (in the sense of computational complexity theory) of logical reasoning in such fragments, measured in the size of the data they
aim to manage.

In particular, to identify efficient controlled languages, fragments are considered
which correspond to the *DL-Lite* family of description logics, known to underpin
data intensive ontologies and systems. The proposed methodology exploits the link
between syntax and semantics of natural language captured by categorial grammars, controlling the use of lexical terms that introduce logical structure outside the
allowed fragments. A major role is played by the control of function words introducing logical operators in first-order meaning representations.

Bernardi et al. present a preliminary analysis of semantically parsed English written corpora, which was carried out in order to show how empirical methods may be
useful in identifying CLs that provide good trade-offs between coverage and efficiency.

2.3 Semantic Resources and Annotation

Part III of the book opens with a chapter entitled *A Context-Change Semantics for
Dialogue Acts* where Harry Bunt presents an update semantic for dialogue acts, defined in terms of combinations of very simple 'elementary update functions' for
updating the information state of an addressee of a dialogue act. This approach,
which is rooted in Dynamic Interpretation Theory (Bunt 1995; 2000) is motivated
by the observation that related types of dialogue acts such as answers, confirmations,
and disconfirmations give rise to similar but slightly different information state updates, which can be described elegantly in terms of overlapping sets of elementary
update functions. This makes fine-grained distinctions between types of dialogue

acts explicit and explains semantic relations like entailment and exclusion between dialogue acts.

The approach is applied to dialogue act representations as defined in the Dialogue Act Markup Language (DiAML), which forms part of the recently established ISO standard 24617-2 (ISO 2012) for dialogue annotation, and to the varieties of dialogue act types defined in this standard and in the DIT^{++} taxonomy of dialogue acts.

Next is a chapter by Susan Windisch Brown, Dmitriy Dligach, and Martha Palmer on the semantic classification of verb senses, entitled *VerbNet Class Assignment as a WSD Task*. The VerbNet lexical resource classifies English verbs based on semantic and syntactic regularities and has been used for a variety of NLP tasks, most notably, semantic role labeling. Since, in addition to thematic roles, it also provides semantic predicates, it can serve as a foundation for further inferencing. Many verbs belong to multiple VerbNet classes, with each class membership corresponding roughly to a different sense of the verb. A VerbNet token classifier is essential for current applications using the resource and could provide the basis for a deep semantic parsing system, one that made full use of VerbNet's extensive syntactic and semantic information. The authors describe their VerbNet classifier, which uses rich syntactic and semantic features to label verb instances with their appropriate VerbNet class. It is shown to achieve an accuracy of 88.67 % with multiclass verbs, which is a 49 % error reduction over the most frequent class behaviour as a baseline.

In the chapter *Annotation of Compositional Operations with GLML* James Pustejovsky, Jessica Moszkowics, Olga Batiukova, and Anna Rumshisky introduce a methodology for annotating compositional operations in natural language text and describe the Generative Lexicon Mark-up Language (GLML), a mark-up language inspired by the Generative Lexicon model, for identifying such relations. While most annotation systems capture surface relationships, GLML captures the "compositional history" of the argument selection relative to the predicate. The chapter provides a brief overview of GL before moving on to the proposed methodology for annotating with GLML.

Three main tasks are described in this chapter. The first one is based on atomic semantic types and the other two exploit more fine-grained meaning parameters encoded in the Qualia Structure roles: (i) argument selection and coercion annotated for the SemEval-2010 competition; (ii) qualia in modification constructions; (iii) type selection in modification constructions and verb-noun combinations involving dot objects. The authors explain what each task comprises and include the XML format for annotated sample sentences. It is shown that, by identifying and subsequently annotating the typing and subtyping shifts in these constructions, an insight is gained into the workings of the general mechanisms of composition.

In the closing chapter of this book, entitled *Incremental Recognition and Prediction of Dialogue Acts*, by Volha Petukhova and Harry Bunt, is concerned with incremental machine-learned recognition of the communicative functions of dialogue utterances. Language use in human conversation is fundamentally incremental, and human language processing is continuously sensitive to multiple partial constraints, where contextual ones play a very important role. The question arises whether dialogue systems can be enabled to access and use various sources of information well enough and fast enough to interpret incoming spoken utterances from its users in real time. This chapter focuses on the on-line recognition of the communicative functions of user utterances, more specifically on the question of how the intended (multi-)functionality of dialogue utterances can be recognized on the basis of observable features of communicative behaviour in a data-oriented way.

The authors discuss and examine an incremental approaches to dialogue utterance interpretation. A token-based approach combining the use of local classifiers, which exploit local utterance features, and global classifiers which use the outputs of local classifiers applied to previous and subsequent tokens, is shown to result in excellent dialogue act recognition scores for unsegmented spoken dialogue. This can be seen as a significant step forward towards the development of fully incremental, on-line methods for computing the meaning of utterances in spoken dialogue.

References

ISO (2012). ISO 24617-2: *Semantic annotation framework, Part 2: Dialogue acts. International standard*. Geneva: ISO, September 2012.

Basile, V., Bos, J., Evang, K., & Venhuizen, N. (2012). Developing a large semantically annotated corpus. In *Proceedings of the eight international conference on language resources and evaluation* (LREC 2012), Istanbul, Turkey (pp. 3196–3200).

Blackburn, P., & Bos, J. (2005). *Representation and inference for natural language. A first course in computational semantics*. Stanford: CSLI.

Blackburn, P., Bos, J., Kohlhase, M., & De Nivelle, H. (2001). Inference and computational semantics. In H. Bunt, R. Muskens, & E. Thijsse (Eds.), *Computing meaning* (Vol. 2, pp. 11–28). Dordrecht: Kluwer Academic.

Bos, J. (2013). Recognising textual entailment and computational semantics. In H. Bunt, J. Bos, & S. Pulman (Eds.), *Computing meaning* (Vol. 4, pp. 89–105). Dordrecht: Springer.

Bunt, H. (1995). Dynamic interpretation and dialogue theory. In M. Taylor, F. Neél, & D. Bouwhuis (Eds.), *The structure of multimodal dialogue II* (pp. 139–166). Amsterdam: Benjamins.

Bunt, H. (2000). Dialogue pragmatics and context specification. In H. Bunt & W. Black (Eds.), *Abduction, belief and context in dialogue. Studies in computational pragmatics* (pp. 81–150). Amsterdam: Benjamins.

Bunt, H. (2013). *A methodology for designing semantic annotations* (TiCC Technical Report TR 2013-001). Tilburg University.

Bunt, H., & Muskens, R. (1999). Computational semantics. In H. Bunt & R. Muskens (Eds.), *Computing meaning* (Vol. 1, pp. 1–32). Dordrecht: Kluwer Academic Publishers.

Clark, S., & Pulman, S. (2007). Combining symbolic and distributional models of meaning. In *Proceedings AAAI spring symposium on quantum interaction*, Stanford (pp. 52–55).

Cooper, R., Crouch, D., van Eijck, J., Fox, C., van Genabith, J., Jaspars, J., Kamp, H., Milward, D., Pinkal, M., Poesio, M., & Pulman, S. (1996). *The FRACAS consortium: Using the framework*. Project FraCaS, a framework for computational semantics. Deliverable D16, University of Edinburgh.

Dagan, I., Bar-Haim, R., Szpektor, I., Greental, I., & Shnarch, E. (2008). Natural language as the basis for meaning representation and inference. In A. Gelbukh (Ed.), *Lecture notes in computer science: Vol. 4949. Computational linguistics and intelligent text processing* (pp. 151–170). Berlin: Springer.

Hobbs, J., Stickel, M., Appelt, D., & Martin, P. (1993). Interpretation as abduction. *Artificial Intelligence, 63*, 69–142.

McCord, M. (1990). Slot grammar: A system for simpler construction of practical natural language grammars. In *Natural language and logic: International scientific symposium* (pp. 118–145). Berlin: Springer.

Thomason, R. H. (Ed.) (1974) *Formal philosophy: Selected papers of Richard Montague*. New Haven: Yale University Press.

van Deemter, K. (1996). Towards a logic of ambiguous expressions. In K. van Deemter & S. Peters (Eds.), *Semantic ambiguity and underspecification* (pp. 203–237). Stanford: CSLI.

Part I
Semantic Representation
and Compositionality

Deterministic Statistical Mapping of Sentences to Underspecified Semantics

Hiyan Alshawi, Pi-Chuan Chang, and Michael Ringgaard

Abstract We present a method for training a statistical model for mapping natural language sentences to semantic expressions. The semantics are expressions of an underspecified logical form that has properties making it particularly suitable for statistical mapping from text. An encoding of the semantic expressions into dependency trees with automatically generated labels allows application of existing methods for statistical dependency parsing to the mapping task (without the need for separate traditional dependency labels or parts of speech). The encoding also results in a natural per-word semantic-mapping accuracy measure. We report on the results of training and testing statistical models for mapping sentences of the Penn Treebank into the semantic expressions, for which per-word semantic mapping accuracy ranges between 79 % and 86 % depending on the experimental conditions. The particular choice of algorithms used also means that our trained mapping is deterministic (in the sense of deterministic parsing), paving the way for large-scale text-to-semantic mapping.

1 Introduction

Producing semantic representations of text is motivated not only by theoretical considerations but also by the hypothesis that semantics can be used to improve automatic systems for tasks that are intrinsically semantic in nature such as question answering, textual entailment, machine translation, and more generally any natural language task that might benefit from inference in order to more closely approximate human performance. Since formal logics have formal denotational semantics,

H. Alshawi (✉) · P.-C. Chang
Google, 1600 Amphitheatre Pkwy, Mountain View, CA 94043, USA
e-mail: hiyan@google.com

P.-C. Chang
e-mail: pichuan@google.com

M. Ringgaard
Google, Åbogade 15, 8200 Aarhus, Denmark
e-mail: ringgaard@google.com

H. Bunt et al. (eds.), *Computing Meaning*, Text, Speech and Language Technology 47,
DOI 10.1007/978-94-007-7284-7_2,
© Springer Science+Business Media Dordrecht 2014

and are good candidates for supporting inference, they have often been taken to be the targets for mapping text to semantic representations, with frameworks emphasizing (more) tractable inference choosing first order predicate logic (Stickel 1985) while those emphasizing representational power favoring one of the many available higher order logics (van Benthem 1995).

It was later recognized that in order to support some tasks, fully specifying certain aspects of a logic representation, such as quantifier scope, or reference resolution, is often not necessary. For example, for semantic translation, most ambiguities of quantifier scope can be carried over from the source language to the target language without being resolved. This led to the development of underspecified semantic representations, such as QLF (Alshawi and Crouch 1992) and MRS (Copestake et al. 2005), which are easier to produce from text without contextual inference but which can be further specified as necessary for the task being performed.

While traditionally mapping text to formal representations was predominantly rule-based, for both the syntactic and semantic components (Montague 1974; Pereira and Shieber 1987; Alshawi 1992), good progress in statistical syntactic parsing (Collins 1999; Charniak 2000) led to systems that applied rules for semantic interpretation to the output of a statistical syntactic parser (e.g. Bos et al. 2004). More recently researchers have looked at statistical methods to provide robust and trainable methods for mapping text to formal representations of meaning (Zettlemoyer and Collins 2005).

In this paper we further develop the two strands of work mentioned above, i.e. mapping text to underspecified semantic representations and using statistical parsing methods to perform the analysis. Here we take a more direct route, starting from scratch by designing an underspecified semantic representation (Natural Logical Form, or NLF) that is purpose-built for statistical text-to-semantics mapping. An underspecified logic whose constructs are motivated by natural language and that is amenable to trainable direct semantic mapping from text without an intervening layer of syntactic representation. In contrast, the approach taken by Zettlemoyer and Collins (2005), for example, maps into traditional logic via lambda expressions, and the approach taken by Poon and Domingos (2009) depends on an initial step of syntactic parsing.

In this paper, we describe a supervised training method for mapping text to NLF, that is, producing a statistical model for this mapping starting from training pairs consisting of sentences and their corresponding NLF expressions. This method makes use of an encoding of NLF expressions into dependency trees in which the set of labels is automatically generated from the encoding process (rather than being pre-supplied by a linguistically motivated dependency grammar). This encoding allows us to perform the text-to-NLF mapping using any existing statistical methods for labeled dependency parsing (Eisner 1996; Yamada and Matsumoto 2003; McDonald et al. 2005). A side benefit of the encoding is that it leads to a natural per-word measure for semantic mapping accuracy which we use for evaluation purposes. By combing our method with deterministic statistical dependency models together with deterministic (hard) clusters instead of parts of speech, we obtain a deterministic statistical text-to-semantics mapper, opening the way to feasible mapping of text-to-semantics at a large scale, for example the entire web.

This paper concentrates on the text-to-semantics mapping which depends, in part, on some properties of NLF. We will not attempt to defend the semantic representation choices for specific constructions illustrated here. NLF is akin to a variable-free variant of QLF or an MRS in which some handle constraints are determined during parsing. For the purposes of this paper it is sufficient to note that NLF has roughly the same granularity of semantic representation as these earlier underspecified representations.

We outline the steps of our text-to-semantics mapping method in Sect. 2, introduce NLF in Sect. 3, explain the encoding of NLF expressions as formal dependency trees in Sect. 4, and report on experiments for training and testing statistical models for mapping text to NLF expressions in Sect. 5.

2 Direct Semantic Mapping

Our method for mapping text to natural semantics expressions proceeds as follows:

1. Create a corpus of pairs consisting of text sentences and their corresponding NLF semantic expressions.
2. For each of the sentence-semantics pairs in the corpus, align the words of the sentence to the tokens of the NLF expressions.
3. "Encode" each alignment pair as an ordered dependency tree in which the labels are generated by the encoding process.
4. Train a statistical dependency parsing model with the set of dependency trees.
5. For a new input sentence S, apply the statistical parsing model to S, producing a labeled dependency tree D_S.
6. "Decode" D_S into a semantic expression for S.

For step 1, the experiments in this paper (Sect. 5) obtain the corpus by converting an existing constituency treebank into semantic expressions. However, direct annotation of a corpus with semantic expressions *is* a viable alternative, and indeed we are separately exploring that possibility for a different, open domain, text corpus.

For steps 4 and 5, any method for training and applying a dependency model from a corpus of labeled dependency trees may be used. As described in Sect. 5, for the experiments reported here we use an algorithm similar to that of Nivre (Nivre 2003).

For steps 2, 3 and 6, the encoding of NLF semantic expressions as dependency trees with automatically constructed labels is described in Sect. 4.

3 Semantic Expressions

NLF expressions are by design amenable to facilitating training of text-to-semantics mappings. For this purpose, NLF has a number of desirable properties:

Fig. 1 Example of an NLF
semantic expression

```
[acquired
  /stealthily
   :[in, ^, 2002],
 Chirpy+Systems,
 companies.two
   :profitable
   :[producing,
     ^,
     pet+accessories]]
```

1. Apart from a few built-in logical connectives, all the symbols appearing in NLF expressions are natural language words.
2. For an NLF semantic expression corresponding to a sentence, the word tokens of the sentence appear exactly once in the NLF expression.
3. The NLF notation is variable-free.

Technically, NLF expressions are expression of an underspecified logic, i.e. a semantic representation that leaves open the interpretation of certain constructs (for example the scope of quantifiers and some operators and the referents of terms such as anaphora, and certain implicit relations such as those for compound nominals). NLF is similar in some ways to Quasi Logical Form, or QLF (Alshawi 1992), but the properties listed above keep NLF closer to natural language than QLF, hence *natural* logical form.[1] There is no explicit formal connection between NLF and Natural Logic (van Benthem 1986), though it may turn out that NLF is a convenient starting point for some Natural Logic inferences.

In contrast to statements of a fully specified logic in which denotations are typically taken to be *functions* from possible worlds to truth values (Montague 1974), denotations of a statement in an underspecified logic are typically taken to be *relations* between possible worlds and truth values (Alshawi and Crouch 1992; Alshawi 1996). Formal denotations for NLF expressions are beyond the scope of this paper and will be described elsewhere.

3.1 Connectives and Examples

A NLF expression for the sentence *In 2002, Chirpy Systems stealthily acquired two profitable companies producing pet accessories* is shown in Fig. 1.

The NLF constructs and connectives are explained in Table 1. For variable-free abstraction, an NLF expression [p, ^, a] corresponds to $\lambda x.p(x,a)$. Note that some common logical operators are not built-in since they will appear directly as words such as *not*.[2]

---

[1]The term QLF is now sometimes used informally (e.g. Liakata and Pulman 2002; Poon and Domingos 2009) for any logic-like semantic representation without explicit quantifier scope.

[2]NLF does include Horn clauses, which implicitly encode negation, but since Horn clauses are not part of the experiments reported in this paper, we will not discuss them further here.

Table 1 NLF constructs and connectives

Operator	Example	Denotation	Lang. constructs
[...]	[sold, Chirpy, Growler]	predication tuple	clauses, prepositions, ...
:	company:profitable	intersection	adjectives, relative clauses, ...
.	companies.two	(unscoped) quantification	determiners, measure terms
^	[in, ^, 2005]	variable-free abstract	prepositions, relatives, ...
_	[eating, _, apples]	unspecified argument	missing verb arguments, ...
{...}	and{Chirpy, Growler}	collection	noun phrase coordination, ...
/	acquired/stealthily	type-preserving operator	adverbs, modals, ...
+	Chirpy+Systems	implicit relation	compound nominals, ...
@	meeting@yesterday	temporal restriction	bare temporal modifiers, ...
&	[...] & [...]	conjunction	sentences, ...
|...|	|Dublin, Paris, Bonn|	sequence	paragraphs, fragments, lists, ...
%	met%as	uncovered op	constructs not covered

We currently use the unknown/unspecified operator, %, mainly for linguistic constructions that are beyond the coverage of a particular semantic mapping model. An example that includes % in our converted WSJ corpus is *Other analysts are nearly as pessimistic* for which the NLF expression is

```
[are, analysts.other, pessimistic%nearly%as]
```

In Sect. 5 we give some statistics on the number of semantic expressions containing % in the data used for our experiments and explain how it affects our accuracy results.

4 Encoding Semantics as Dependencies

We encode NLF semantic expressions as labeled dependency trees in which the label set is generated automatically by the encoding process. This is in contrast to conventional dependency trees for which the label sets are presupplied (e.g. by a linguistic theory of dependency grammar). The purpose of the encoding is to enable training of a statistical dependency parser and converting the output of that parser for a new sentence into a semantic expression. The encoding involves three aspects: Alignment, headedness, and label construction.

4.1 Alignment

Since, by design, each word token corresponds to a symbol token (the same word type) in the NLF expression, the only substantive issue in determining the alignment is the occurrence of multiple tokens of the same word type in the sentence. Depending on the source of the sentence-NLF pairs used for training, a particular word in the sentence may or may not already be associated with its corresponding word position in the sentence. For example, in some of the experiments reported in this paper, this correspondence is provided by the semantic expressions obtained by converting a constituency treebank (the well-known Penn WSJ treebank). For situations in which the pairs are provided without this information, as is the case for direct annotation of sentences with NLF expressions, we currently use a heuristic greedy algorithm for deciding the alignment. This algorithm tries to ensure that dependents are near their heads, with a preference for projective dependency trees. To guage the importance of including correct alignments in the input pairs (as opposed to training with inferred alignments), we will present accuracy results for semantic mapping for both correct and automatically infererred alignments.

4.2 Headedness

The encoding requires a definition of headedness for words in an NLF expression, i.e., a head-function h from dependent words to head words. We define h in terms of a head-function g from an NLF (sub)expression e to a word w appearing in that (sub)expression, so that $g(w) = w$, and, recursively:

$$g([e_1, \ldots, e_n]) = g(e_1)$$
$$g(e_1 : e_2) = g(e_1)$$
$$g(e_1.e_2) = g(e_1)$$
$$g(e_1/e_2) = g(e_1)$$
$$g(e_1 @ e_2) = g(e_1)$$
$$g(e_1 \& e2) = g(e_1)$$
$$g(|e_1, \ldots, e_n|) = g(e1)$$
$$g(e_1\{e_2, \ldots, e_n\}) = g(e_1)$$
$$g(e_1 + \cdots + e_n) = g(e_n)$$
$$g(e_1 \% e_2) = g(e_1).$$

Then a head word $h(w)$ for a dependent w is defined in terms of the smallest (sub)expression e containing w for which

$$h(w) = g(e) \neq w.$$

For example, for the NLF expression in Fig. 1, this yields the heads shown in Table 3. (The labels shown in that table will be explained in the following section.)

This definition of headedness is not the only possible one, and other variations could be argued for. The specific definition for NLF heads turns out to be fairly close to the notion of head in traditional dependency grammars. This is perhaps not surprising since traditional dependency grammars are often partly motivated by semantic considerations, if only informally.

4.3 Label Construction

As mentioned, the labels used during the encoding of a semantic expression into a dependency tree are derived so as to enable reconstruction of the expression from a labeled dependency tree. In a general sense, the labels may be regarded as a kind of formal semantic label, though more specifically, a label is interpretable as a sequence of instructions for constructing the part of a semantic expression that links a dependent to its head, given that part of the semantic expression, including that derived from the head, has already been constructed. The string for a label thus consists of a sequence of atomic instructions, where the decoder keeps track of a current expression and the parent of that expression in the expression tree being constructed. When a new expression is created it becomes the current expression whose parent is the old current expression. The atomic instructions (each expressed by a single character) are shown in Table 2.

A sequence of instructions in a label can typically (but not always) be paraphrased informally as "starting from head word w_h, move to a suitable node (at or above w_h) in the expression tree, add specified NLF constructs (connectives, tuples, abstracted arguments) and then add w_d as a tuple or connective argument."

Continuing with our running example, the labels for each of the words are shown in Table 3.

Algorithmically, we find it convenient to transform semantic expressions into dependency trees and vice versa via a derivation tree for the semantic expression in which the atomic instruction symbols listed above are associated with individual nodes in the derivation tree.

The output of the statistical parser may contain inconsistent trees with formal labels, in particular trees in which two different arguments are predicated to fill the same position in a semantic expression tuple. For such cases, the decoder that produces the semantic expression applies the simple heuristic of using the next available tuple position when such a conflicting configuration is predicated. In our experiments, we are measuring per-word semantic head-and-label accuracy, so this heuristic does not play a part in that evaluation measure.

Table 2 Atomic instructions in formal label sequences

Instruction	Decoding action
[, {, |	Set the current expression to a newly created tuple, collection, or sequence.
:, /, ., +, &, @, %	Attach the current subexpression to its parent with the specified connective.
*	Set the current expression to a newly created symbol from the dependent word.
0, 1, …	Add the current expression at the specified parent tuple position.
^, _	Set the current subexpression to a newly created abstracted-over or unspecified argument.
–	Set the current subexpression to be the parent of the current expression.

Table 3 Formal labels for an example sentence

Dependent	Head	Label
in	acquired	[:^1-*0
2002	in	-*2
Chirpy	Systems	*+
Systems	acquired	-*1
stealthily	acquired	*/
acquired		[*0
two	companies	*.
profitable	companies	*:
companies	acquired	-*2
producing	companies	[:^1-*0
pet	accessories	*+
accessories	producing	-*2

5 Experiments

5.1 Data Preparation

In the experiments reported here, we derive our sentence-semantics pairs for training and testing from the Penn WSJ Treebank. This choice reflects the lack, to our knowledge, of a set of such pairs for a reasonably sized publicly available corpus, at least for NLF expressions. Our first step in preparing the data was to convert the WSJ phrase structure trees into semantic expressions. This conversion is done by programming the Stanford treebank toolkit to produce NLF trees bottom-up from the phrase structure trees. This conversion process is not particularly noteworthy in itself (being a traditional rule-based syntax-to-semantics translation process) except

Table 4 Datasets used in experiments

Dataset	Null labels?	Auto align?	WSJ sections	Sentences
Train+Null-AAlign	yes	no	2–21	39213
Train-Null-AAlign	no	no	2–21	24110
Train+Null+AAlign	yes	yes	2–21	35778
Train-Null+AAlign	no	yes	2–21	22611
Test+Null-AAlign	yes	no	23	2416
Test-Null-AAlign	no	no	23	1479

perhaps to the extent that the closeness of NLF to natural language perhaps makes the conversion somewhat easier than, say, conversion to a fully resolved logical form.

Since our main goal is to investigate trainable mappings from text strings to semantic expressions, we only use the WSJ phrase structure trees in data preparation: the phrase structure trees are not used as inputs when training a semantic mapping model, or when applying such a model. For the same reason, in these experiments, we do not use the part-of-speech information associated with the phrase structure trees in training or applying a semantic mapping model. Instead of parts-of-speech we use word cluster features from a hierarchical clustering produced with the unsupervised Brown clustering method (Brown et al. 1992); specifically we use the publicly available clusters reported by Koo et al. (2008).

Constructions in the WSJ that are beyond the explicit coverage of the conversion rules used for data preparation result in expressions that include the unknown/unspecified (or 'Null') operator %. We report on different experimental settings in which we vary how we treat training or testing expressions with %. This gives rise to the data sets in Table 4 which have +Null (i.e., including %), and -Null (i.e., not including %) in the data set names.

Another attribute we vary in the experiments is whether to align the words in the semantic expressions to the words in the sentence automatically, or whether to use the correct alignment (in this case preserved from the conversion process, but could equally be provided as part of a manual semantic annotation scheme, for example). In our current experiments, we discard non-projective dependency trees from training sets. Automatic alignment results in additional non-projective trees, giving rise to different effective training sets when auto-alignment is used: these sets are marked with +AAlign, otherwise -AAlign. The training set numbers shown in Table 4 are the resulting sets after removal of non-projective trees.

5.2 Parser

As mentioned earlier, our method can make use of any trainable statistical dependency parsing algorithm. The parser is trained on a set of dependency trees with

Table 5 Per-word semantic accuracy when training with the correct alignment

Training	Test	Accuracy (%)
+Null-AAlign	+Null-AAlign	81.2
-Null-AAlign	+Null-AAlign	78.9
-Null-AAlign	-Null-AAlign	86.1
+Null-AAlign	-Null-AAlign	86.5

Table 6 Per-word semantic accuracy when training with an auto-alignment

Training	Test	Accuracy (%)
+Null+AAlign	+Null-AAlign	80.4
-Null+AAlign	+Null-AAlign	78.0
-Null+AAlign	-Null-AAlign	85.5
+Null+AAlign	-Null-AAlign	85.8

formal labels as explained in Sects. 2 and 4. The specific parsing algorithm we use in these experiments is a deterministic shift reduce algorithm (Nivre 2003), and the specific implementation of the algorithm uses a linear SVM classifier for predicting parsing actions (Chang et al. 2010). As noted above, hierarchical cluster features are used instead of parts-of-speech; some of the features use coarse (6-bit) or finer (12-bit) clusters from the hierarchy. More specifically, the full set of features is:

- The words for the current and next input tokens, for the top of the stack, and for the head of the top of the stack.
- The formal labels for the top-of-stack token and its leftmost and rightmost children, and for the leftmost child of the current token.
- The cluster for the current and next three input tokens and for the top of the stack and the token below the top of the stack.
- Pairs of features combining 6-bit clusters for these tokens together with 12-bit clusters for the top of stack and next input token.

5.3 Results

Tables 5 and 6 show the *per-word semantic accuracy* for different training and test sets. This measure is simply the percentage of words in the test set for which both the predicted formal label and the head word are correct. In syntactic dependency evaluation terminology, this corresponds to the labeled attachment score.

All tests are with respect to the correct alignment; we vary whether the correct alignment (Table 5) or auto-alignment (Table 6) is used for training to give an idea of how much our heuristic alignment is hurting the semantic mapping model. As shown by comparing the two tables, the loss in accuracy due to using the automatic alignment is only about 1 %, so while the automatic alignment algorithm can probably be improved, the resulting increase in accuracy would be relatively small.

Table 7 Per-word semantic accuracy after pruning label sets in Train-Null+AAlign (and testing with Test-Null-AAlign)

# Labels	# Train sents	Accuracy (%)
151 (all)	22611	85.5
100	22499	85.5
50	21945	85.5
25	17669	83.8
12	7008	73.4

As shown in the Tables 5 and 6, two versions of the test set are used: one that includes the 'Null' operator %, and a smaller test set with which we are testing only the subset of sentences for which the semantic expressions do not include this label. The highest accuracies (mid 80's) shown are for the (easier) test set which excludes examples in which the test semantic expressions contain Null operators. The strictest settings, in which semantic expressions with Null are not included in training but included in the test set effectively treat prediction of Null operators as errors. The lower accuracy (high 70's) for such stricter settings thus incorporates a penalty for our incomplete coverage of semantics for the WSJ sentences. The less strict Test+Null settings in which % is treated as a valid output may be relevant to applications that can tolerate some unknown operators between subexpressions in the output semantics.

Next we look at the effect of limiting the size of the automatically generated formal label set prior to training. For this we take the configuration using the TrainWSJ-Null+AAlign training set and the TestWSJ-Null-AAlign test set (the third row in Table refPerWordSemanticAccuracyAAlign for which auto-alignment is used and only labels without the NULL operator % are included). For this training set there are 151 formal labels. We then limit the training set to instances that only include the most frequent k labels, for $k = 100, 50, 25, 12$, while keeping the test set the same. As can be seen in Table 7, the accuracy is unaffected when the training set is limited to the 100 most frequent or 50 most frequent labels. There is a slight loss when training is limited to 25 labels and a large loss if it is limited to 12 labels. This appears to show that, for this corpus, the core label set needed to construct the majority of semantic expressions has a size somewhere between 25 and 50. It is perhaps interesting that this is roughly the size of hand-produced traditional dependency label sets. On the other hand, it needs to be emphasized that since Table 7 ignores beyond-coverage constructions that presently include Null labels, it is likely that a larger label set would be needed for more complete semantic coverage.

6 Conclusion and Further Work

We've shown that by designing an underspecified logical form that is motivated by, and closely related to, natural language constructions, it is possible to train a direct statistical mapping from pairs of sentences and their corresponding semantic expressions, with per-word accuracies ranging from 79 % to 86 % depending on the strictness of the experimental setup. The input to training does not require any traditional syntactic categories or parts of speech. We also showed, more specifically, that we can train a model that can be applied deterministically at runtime (using a deterministic shift reduce algorithm combined with deterministic clusters), making large-scale text-to-semantics mapping feasible.

In traditional formal semantic mapping methods (Montague 1974; Bos et al. 2004), and even some recent statistical mapping methods (Zettlemoyer and Collins 2005), the semantic representation is overloaded to performs two functions: (i) representing the final meaning, and (ii) composing meanings from the meanings of subconstituents (e.g. through application of higher order lambda functions). In our view, this leads to what are perhaps overly complex semantic representations of some basic linguistic constructions. In contrast, in the method we presented, these two concerns (meaning representation and semantic construction) are separated, enabling us to keep the semantics of constituents simple, while turning the construction of semantic expressions into a separate structured learning problem (with its own internal prediction and decoding mechanisms).

Although in the experiments we reported here we *do* prepare the training data from a traditional treebank, we are encouraged by the results and believe that annotation of a corpus with only semantic expressions is sufficient for building an efficient and reasonably accurate text-to-semantics mapper. Indeed, we have started building such a corpus for a question answering application, and hope to report results for that corpus in the future. Other further work includes a formal denotational semantics of the underspecified logical form and elaboration of practical inference operations with the semantic expressions. This work may also be seen as a step towards viewing semantic interpretation of language as the interaction between a pattern recognition process (described here) and an inference process.

References

Alshawi, H. (Ed.) (1992). *The core language engine.* Cambridge: MIT Press.

Alshawi, H. (1996). Underspecified first order logics. In K. van Deemter & S. Peters (Eds.), *Semantic ambiguity and underspecification* (pp. 145–158). Stanford: CSLI.

Alshawi, H., & Crouch, R. (1992). Monotonic semantic interpretation. In *Proceedings of the 30th annual meeting of the association for computational linguistics*, Newark, Delaware (pp. 32–39).

Bos, J., Clark, S., Steedman, M., Curran, J. R., & Hockenmaier, J. (2004). Wide-coverage semantic representations from a ccg parser. In *Proceedings of the 20th international conference on computational linguistics*, Geneva, Switzerland (pp. 1240–1246).

Brown, P., Pietra, V., Souza, P., Lai, J., & Mercer, R. (1992). Class-based n-gram models of natural language. *Computational Linguistics*, *18*(4), 467–479.

Chang, Y.-W., Hsieh, C.-J., Chang, K.-W., Ringgaard, M., & Lin, C.-J. (2010). Training and testing low-degree polynomial data mappings via linear svm. *Journal of Machine Learning Research*, *11*, 1471–1490.

Charniak, E. (2000). A maximum entropy inspired parser. In *Proceedings of the 1st conference of the North American chapter of the association for computational linguistics*, Seattle, Washington (pp. 132–139).

Collins, M. (1999). *Head driven statistical models for natural language parsing.* Ph.D. thesis, University of Pennsylvania.

Copestake, A., Flickinger, D., & Sag, C. P. I. (2005). Minimal recursion semantics, an introduction. *Research on Language and Computation*, *3*, 281–332.

Eisner, J. (1996). Three new probabilistic models for dependency parsing: An exploration. In *Proceedings of the 16th international conference on computational linguistics*, Sydney (pp. 340–345).

Koo, T., Carreras, X., & Collins, M. (2008). Simple semisupervised dependency parsing. In *Proceedings of the annual meeting of the association for computational linguistics*, Columbus, Ohio (pp. 595–603).

Liakata, M., & Pulman, S. (2002). From trees to predicate-argument structures. In *Proceedings of the 19th international conference on computational linguistics*, Taipei, Taiwan (pp. 563–569).

McDonald, R., Crammer, K., & Pereira, F. (2005). Online large-margin training of dependency parsers. In *Proceedings of the 43rd annual meeting of the association for computational linguistics*, Ann Arbor, Michigan (pp. 91–98).

Montague, R. (1974). The proper treatment of quantification in ordinary English. In R. Thomason (Ed.), *Formal philosophy: Selected papers of Richard Montague* (pp. 247–270). New Haven: Yale University Press.

Nivre, J. (2003). An efficient algorithm for projective dependency parsing. In *Proceedings of the 8th international workshop on parsing technologies*, Nancy, France (pp. 149–160).

Pereira, F., & Shieber, S. (1987). *Prolog and natural language analysis*. Stanford: CSLI.

Poon, H., & Domingos, P. (2009). Unsupervised semantic parsing. In *Proceedings of the 2009 conference on empirical methods in natural language processing*, Singapore (pp. 1–10).

Stickel, M. (1985). Automated deduction by theory resolution. *Journal of Automated Reasoning*, *1*, 333–355.

van Benthem, J. (1986). *Essays in logical semantics*. Dordrecht: Reidel.

van Benthem, J. (1995). *Language in action: Categories, lambdas, and dynamic logic*. Cambridge: MIT Press.

Yamada, H., & Matsumoto, Y. (2003). Statistical dependency analysis with support vector machines. In *Proceedings of the 8th international workshop on parsing technologies*, Nancy, France (pp. 195–206).

Zettlemoyer, L. S., & Collins, M. (2005). Learning to map sentences to logical form: Structured classification with probabilistic categorial grammars. In *Proceedings of the 21st conference on uncertainty in artificial intelligence*, Edinburgh, Scotland (pp. 658–666).

A Formal Approach to Linking Logical Form and Vector-Space Lexical Semantics

Dan Garrette, Katrin Erk, and Raymond Mooney

Abstract First-order logic provides a powerful and flexible mechanism for representing natural language semantics. However, it is an open question of how best to integrate it with uncertain, weighted knowledge, for example regarding word meaning. This paper describes a mapping between predicates of logical form and points in a vector space. This mapping is then used to project distributional inferences to inference rules in logical form. We then describe first steps of an approach that uses this mapping to recast first-order semantics into the probabilistic models that are part of Statistical Relational AI. Specifically, we show how Discourse Representation Structures can be combined with distributional models for word meaning inside a Markov Logic Network and used to successfully perform inferences that take advantage of logical concepts such as negation and factivity as well as weighted information on word meaning in context.

1 Introduction

Logic-based representations of natural language meaning have a long history (Montague 1970; Kamp and Reyle 1993). Representing the meaning of language in a first-order logical form is appealing because it provides a powerful and flexible way to express even complex propositions. However, systems built solely using first-order logical forms tend to be very brittle as they have no way of integrating uncertain knowledge. They therefore tend to have high precision at the cost of low recall (Bos and Markert 2005).

Recent advances in computational linguistics have yielded robust methods that use statistically-driven weighted models. For example, distributional models of

D. Garrette (✉) · K. Erk · R. Mooney
University of Texas at Austin, Austin, USA
e-mail: dhg@cs.utexas.edu

K. Erk
e-mail: katrin.erk@mail.utexas.edu

R. Mooney
e-mail: mooney@cs.utexas.edu

H. Bunt et al. (eds.), *Computing Meaning*, Text, Speech and Language Technology 47,   27
DOI 10.1007/978-94-007-7284-7_3,
© Springer Science+Business Media Dordrecht 2014

word meaning have been used successfully to judge paraphrase appropriateness by representing the meaning of a word in context as a point in a high-dimensional semantics space (Erk and Padó 2008; Thater et al. 2010; Reisinger and Mooney 2010; Dinu and Lapata 2010; Van de Cruys et al. 2011). However, these models only address word meaning, and do not address the question of providing meaning representations for complete sentences. It is a long-standing open question how best to integrate the weighted or probabilistic information coming from such modules with logic-based representations in a way that allows for reasoning over both. See, for example, Hobbs et al. (1993).

The goal of this work is to establish a formal system for combining logic-based meaning representations with weighted information into a single unified framework. This will allow us to obtain the best of both situations: we will have the full expressivity of first-order logic and be able to reason with probabilities. We believe that this will allow for a more complete and robust approach to natural language understanding.

While this is a large and complex task, this chapter proposes first steps toward our goal by presenting a mechanism for injecting distributional word-similarity information from a vector space into a first-order logical form. We define a mapping from predicate symbols of logical form to points in vector space. Our main aim in linking logical form to a vector space in this chapter is to project inferences from the vector space to logical form. The inference rules that we use are based on substitutability. In a suitably constructed distributional representation, distributional similarity between two words or expressions A and B indicates that B can be substituted for A in text (Lin and Pantel 2001). This can be described through an inference rule $A \rightarrow B$. Distributional information can also be used to determine the degree η to which the rule applies in a given sentence context (Szpektor et al. 2008; Mitchell and Lapata 2008; Erk and Padó 2008; Thater et al. 2010; Reisinger and Mooney 2010; Dinu and Lapata 2010; Van de Cruys et al. 2011). This degree η can be used as a weight on the inference rule $A \rightarrow B$.

In this chapter, we first present our formal framework for projecting inferences from vector space to logical form. We then show how that framework can be applied to a real logical language and vector space to address issues of ambiguity in word meaning. Finally, we show how the weighted inference rules produced by our approach interact appropriately with the first-order logical form to produce correct inferences.

Our implementation uses Markov Logic Networks (MLN) (Richardson and Domingos 2006) as the underlying engine for probabilistic inference. We are able to demonstrate that an MLN is able to properly integrate the first-order logical representation and weighted inference rules so that inferences involving correct word sense are assessed as being highly probable, inferences involving incorrect word sense are determined to be low probability, and inferences that violate hard logical rules are determined to have the lowest probability.

2 Background

Textual Entailment   Recognizing Textual Entailment (RTE) is the task of determining whether one natural language text, the *premise*, implies another, the *hypothesis*. For evaluation of our system, we have chosen to use a variation on RTE in which we assess the relative probability of entailment for a of set of hypotheses.

We have chosen textual entailment as the mode of evaluation for our approach because it offers a good framework for testing whether a system performs correct analyses and thus draws the right inferences from a given text. As an example, consider (1) below.

(1)   *p*: The spill left a stain.
  h1: The spill resulted in a stain.
  h2*: The spill fled a stain.
  h3*: The spill did not result in a stain.

Here, hypothesis *h1* is a valid entailment, and should be judged to have high probability by the system. Hypothesis *h2* should have lower probability since it uses the wrong sense of *leave* and *h3* should be low probability because the logical operator *not* has reversed the meaning of the premise statement.

While the most prominent forum using textual entailment is the Recognizing Textual Entailment (RTE) challenge (Dagan et al. 2005), the RTE datasets do not test the phenomena in which we are interested. For example, in order to evaluate our system's ability to determine word meaning in context, the RTE pair would have to specifically test word sense confusion by having a word's context in the hypothesis be different from the context of the premise. However, this simply does not occur in the RTE corpora. In order to properly test our phenomena, we construct hand-tailored premises and hypotheses based on real-world texts.

Logic-Based Semantics   Boxer (Bos et al. 2004) is a software package for wide-coverage semantic analysis that provides semantic representations in the form of Discourse Representation Structures (Kamp and Reyle 1993). It builds on the C&C CCG parser (Clark and Curran 2004).

Bos and Markert (2005) describe a system for Recognizing Textual Entailment (RTE) that uses Boxer to convert both the premise and hypothesis of an RTE pair into first-order logical semantic representations and then uses a theorem prover to check for logical entailment.

Distributional Models for Lexical Meaning   Distributional models describe the meaning of a word through the context in which it appears (Landauer and Dumais 1997; Lund and Burgess 1996), where contexts can be documents, other words, or snippets of syntactic structure. Based on the hypothesis that words that are similar in meaning will occur in similar contexts (Harris 1954; Firth 1957), distributional models predict semantic similarity between words based on distributional similarity. They can be learned in an unsupervised fashion. Recently distributional models have been used to predict the applicability of paraphrases in context (Erk and Padó 2008; Thater et al. 2010; Reisinger and Mooney 2010; Dinu and Lapata 2010;

Van de Cruys et al. 2011). For example, in "The spill left a stain", *result in* is a better paraphrase for *leave* than *flee*, because of the context of *spill* and *stain*. In the sentence "The suspect left the country", the opposite is true: *flee* is a better paraphrase. Usually, the distributional representation for a word mixes all its usages (senses). For the paraphrase appropriateness task, these representations are then reweighted, extended, or filtered to focus on contextually appropriate usages.

Markov Logic   In order to perform logical inference with weights, we draw from the large and active body of work related to Statistical Relational AI (Getoor and Taskar 2007). Specifically, we make use of Markov Logic Networks (MLNs) (Richardson and Domingos 2006) which employ weighted graphical models to represent first-order logical formulas. MLNs are appropriate for our approach because they provide an elegant method of assigning weights to first-order logical rules, combining a diverse set of inference rules, and performing probabilistic inference.

An MLN consists of a set of weighted first-order clauses. It provides a way of softening first-order logic by making situations in which not all clauses are satisfied less likely, but not impossible (Richardson and Domingos 2006). More formally, if X is the set of all propositions describing a world (i.e. the set of all ground atoms), $\mathcal{F}$ is the set of all clauses in the MLN, w_i is the weight associated with clause $f_i \in \mathcal{F}$, $\mathcal{G}_{f_i}$ is the set of all possible groundings of clause f_i, and $\mathcal{Z}$ is the normalization constant, then the probability of a particular truth assignment $\mathbf{x}$ to the variables in X is defined as:

$$P(X = \mathbf{x}) = \frac{1}{\mathcal{Z}} \exp\left(\sum_{f_i \in \mathcal{F}} w_i \sum_{g \in \mathcal{G}_{f_i}} g(\mathbf{x}) \right) = \frac{1}{\mathcal{Z}} \exp\left(\sum_{f_i \in \mathcal{F}} w_i n_i(\mathbf{x}) \right)$$

where $g(\mathbf{x})$ is 1 if g is satisfied and 0 otherwise, and $n_i(\mathbf{x}) = \sum_{g \in \mathcal{G}_{f_i}} g(\mathbf{x})$ is the number of groundings of f_i that are satisfied given the current truth assignment to the variables in X. This means that the probability of a truth assignment rises exponentially with the number of groundings that are satisfied.

Markov Logic has been used previously in other NLP applications (e.g. Poon and Domingos (2009)). However, this chapter differs in that it is an attempt to represent deep logical semantics in an MLN.

While it is possible to learn rule weights in an MLN directly from training data, our approach at this time focuses on incorporating weights computed by external knowledge sources. Weights for word meaning rules are computed from the distributional model of lexical meaning and then injected into the MLN. Rules governing implicativity are given infinite weight (hard constraints).

We use the open source software package Alchemy (Kok et al. 2005) to perform MLN inference.

3 Linking Logical Form and Vector Spaces

In this section we define a link between logical form and vector space representations through a mapping function that connects predicates in logical form to points in vector space. Gärdenfors (2004) uses the interpretation function for this purpose, such that logical formulas are interpreted over vector space representations. However, the *conceptual spaces* that he uses are not distributional. Their dimensions are qualities, like the hue and saturation of a color or the taste of a fruit. Points in a conceptual space are, therefore, potential entities. In contrast, the vector spaces that we use are distributional in nature, and, therefore, cannot be interpreted as potential entities. A point in such a space is a potential word, defined through its observed contexts. For this reason, we define the link between logical form and vector space through a second mapping function independent of the interpretation function, which we call the *lexical mapping* function.

3.1 Lexical Mapping and Inference Projection

Let V be a vector space whose dimensions stand for elements of textual context. We also write V for the set of points in the space. We assume that each word is represented as a point in vector space.[1] The central relation in vector spaces is semantic similarity. We represent this through a *similarity function*

$$\text{sim} : V \times V \rightarrow [0, 1]$$

that maps each pair of points in vector space to their degree of similarity. While most similarity functions in the literature are symmetric, such that $\text{sim}(\vec{v}, \vec{w}) = \text{sim}(\vec{w}, \vec{v})$, our definition also accommodates asymmetric similarity measures like Kotlerman et al. (2010).

We link logical form and a vector space through a function that maps every predicate symbol to a point in space. Let $\mathcal{L}$ be a logical language. For each $n \geq 0$, let the set of n-ary predicate symbols of $\mathcal{L}$ be $\mathcal{P}^n_{\mathcal{L}}$, and let $\mathcal{P}_{\mathcal{L}} = \cup_{n \geq 0} \mathcal{P}^n_{\mathcal{L}}$. Let V be a vector space. Then a *lexical mapping function* from $\mathcal{L}$ to V is a function $\ell : \mathcal{P}_{\mathcal{L}} \rightarrow V$.

A central property of distributional vector spaces is that they can predict similarity in meaning based on similarity in observed contexts (Harris 1954). Lin and Pantel (2001) point out that in suitably constrained distributional representations, distributional similarity indicates substitutability in text. If two words v and w are similar in their observed contexts, then w can be substituted for v in texts. This can be written as an inference rule $v \rightarrow w$, weighted by $\text{sim}(\vec{v}, \vec{w})$.

We use this same idea to project inference rules from vector space to logical form through the lexical mapping function. If the lexical mapping function maps the n-ary predicate P to $\vec{v}$ and the n-ary predicate Q to $\vec{w}$, and $\text{sim}(\vec{v}, \vec{w}) = \eta$, then we obtain the weighted inference rule $\forall x_1, \ldots, x_n [P(x_1, \ldots, x_n) \rightarrow Q(x_1, \ldots x_n)]$

---

[1] The assumption of a single vector per word is made for the sake of simplicity. If we want to cover models in which each word is represented through multiple vectors (Reisinger and Mooney 2010; Dinu and Lapata 2010), this can be done through straightforward extensions of the definitions given here.

with weight η. More generally, let $\mathcal{L}$ be a logical language with lexical mapping ℓ to a vector space V. Let sim be the similarity function on V. For all $Q \in \mathcal{P}_\mathcal{L}$ and $\mathcal{Q} \subseteq \mathcal{P}_\mathcal{L}$, let $\zeta(Q, \mathcal{Q}) \subseteq \mathcal{Q}$. Then the *inference projection* for the predicate $P \in \mathcal{P}_\mathcal{L}^n$ is

$$\Pi_{\text{sim},\zeta,\ell}(P) = \{(F, \eta) \mid \exists Q \in \zeta(P, \mathcal{P}_\mathcal{L}^n)[$$
$$F = \forall x_1, \ldots, x_n [P(x_1, \ldots, x_n) \to Q(x_1, \ldots, x_n)],$$
$$\eta = \text{sim}(\ell(P), \ell(Q))]\}$$

That is, the inference projection for P is the set of all weighted inference rules (F, η) predicted by the vector space that let us infer some other predicate Q from P. Additionally, we may have information on the inferences that we are willing to project that is not encoded in the vector space. For example we may only want to consider predicates Q that stand for paraphrases of P. For this reason, the function ζ can be used to limit the predicates Q considered for the right-hand sides of rules. If $\zeta(P, \mathcal{P}_\mathcal{L}^n) = \mathcal{P}_\mathcal{L}^n$, then a rule will be generated for every $Q \in \mathcal{P}_\mathcal{L}^n$.

3.2 Addressing Polysemy

When a word is polysemous, this affects the applicability of vector space-based inference rules. Consider the rule $\forall e[fix(e) \to correct(e)]$ (any fixing event is a correcting event): this rule applies in contexts like "fix a problem", but not in contexts like "fix the date". We therefore need to take context into account when considering inference rule applicability. We do this by computing vector representations for word meaning in context, and predicting rule applicability based on these context-specific vectors. We follow the literature on vector space representations for word meaning in context (Erk and Padó 2008; Thater et al. 2010; Reisinger and Mooney 2010; Dinu and Lapata 2010; Van de Cruys et al. 2011) in assuming that a word's context-specific meaning is a function of its out-of-context representation and the context. The context may consist of a single item or multiple items, and (syntactic or semantic) relations to the target word may also play a role (Erk and Padó 2008; Thater et al. 2010; Van de Cruys et al. 2011).

We first define what we mean by a context. Given a vector space V and a finite set R of semantic relations, the set $C(V, R)$ of *contexts over V and R* consists of all finite sets of pairs from $V \times R$. That is, we describe the context in which a target word occurs as a finite set of pairs $(\vec{v}, r)$ of a context item $\vec{v}$ represented as a point in vector space, and the relation r between the context item and the target. For a word w in a context $c \in C(V, R)$, the context-specific meaning $\vec{w}_c$ of w is a function of the out-of-context vector $\vec{w}$ for w and the context c:

$$\vec{w}_c = \alpha(\vec{w}, c)$$

The function α is a *contextualization function* with signature $\alpha : V \times C(V, R) \to V$.

This definition of contextualization functions is similar to the framework of Mitchell and Lapata (2008), who define the meaning $\vec{p}$ of a two-word phrase $p = vw$ as a function of the vectors for v and w, and their syntactic relation r in the text: $\vec{p} = f(\vec{v}, \vec{w}, r, K)$, where f is some function, and K is background knowledge. However, we use contextualization functions to compute the meaning of a word in context, rather than the meaning of a phrase. We map predicate symbols to points in space, and predicate symbols need to map to word meanings, not phrase meanings. Also, Mitchell and Lapata only consider the case of two-word phrases, while we allow for arbitrary-size contexts.

In existing approaches to computing word meaning in context, bag-of-words representations or syntactic parses of the sentence context are used to compute the contextualization. In contrast, we use the logical form representation, through a function that maps a logic formula to a context in $C(V, R)$. Given a logical language $\mathcal{L}$, a vector space V, and set R of semantic relations, a *context mapping* is a function that computes the context $c \in C(V, R)$ of a predicate P in a formula G as

$$c = \kappa(P, G)$$

The signature of a context mapping function is $\kappa : \mathcal{P}_{\mathcal{L}} \times \mathcal{L} \to C(V, R)$.

We can now compute a context-specific vector space representation $\vec{w}_{P,G}$ for a predicate P in a formula G from the context-independent vector $\ell(P)$ and the context $\kappa(P, G)$. It is

$$\vec{w}_{P,G} = \alpha(\ell(P), \kappa(P, G))$$

To obtain an inference projection for P that takes into account its context in the formula G, we adapt the lexical mapping function. Given a lexical mapping ℓ, let $\ell_{[Q/\vec{v}]}$ be the function that is exactly like ℓ except that it maps Q to $\vec{v}$. Let $\Pi_{\text{sim},\zeta,\ell}$ be an inference projection for vector space V and logical language $\mathcal{L}$, let α be a contextualization function on V and R, and κ a context mapping from $\mathcal{L}$ to $C(V, R)$. Then the *contextualized inference projection* for predicate $P \in \mathcal{P}_{\mathcal{L}}^n$ in formula $G \in \mathcal{L}$ is

$$\Pi_{\text{sim},\zeta,\ell}^{G}(P) = \Pi_{\text{sim},\zeta,\ell_{[P/\alpha(\ell(P),\kappa(P,G))]}}(P)$$

In this contextualized inference projection, any rule $\forall x_1, \ldots, x_n [P(x_1, \ldots, x_n) \to Q(x_1, \ldots, x_n)]$ is weighted by similarity $\text{sim}(\alpha(\ell(P), \kappa(P, G)), \ell(Q))$ between the context-specific vector for P and the vector for Q. This follows common practice in vector space models of word meaning in context of computing a context-specific representation of the target, but not the paraphrase candidate. But if the paraphrase candidate is polysemous, it may be useful to compute a representation for it that is also specific to the sentence context at hand (Erk and Padó 2010). We can do this by defining a lexical mapping $\gamma^{P,G}$ specific to predicate P and formula G by $\gamma^{P,G}(Q) = \alpha(\ell(Q), \kappa(P, G))$. Then we can compute the contextualized inference projection of P as $\Pi_{\text{sim},\zeta,\ell}^{G}(P) = \Pi_{\text{sim},\zeta,\gamma^{P,G}}(P)$.

In computational semantics, polysemy is mostly addressed by using multiple predicates. For example, for the noun "bank" there would be predicates bank_1, bank_2 to cover the financial and riverside senses of the word. In contrast, we use a separate predicate for each word token, but these predicates are not associated with any particular fixed senses. Instead, we vary the lexical mapping of a predicate based on the formula that it appears in: a predicate P in a formula G is mapped to the vector $\alpha(\ell(P), \kappa(P, G))$, which depends on G. We make this change for two reasons. First, a system that uses distinct predicates $bank_1$, $bank_2$ has to rely on an external word sense disambiguation system that decides, during semantics construction, which of the senses to use. In contrast, we determine lexical meaning based on the overall semantic representation of a sentence, directly linking sentence semantics and lexical semantics. Second, in the case of polysemy, the senses to distinguish are not always that clear. For example, for a noun like "onion", should the vegetable sense and the plant/bulb sense be separate (Krishnamurthy and Nicholls 2000)? Through the vector space model, we can model word meaning in context without ever referring to distinct dictionary senses (Erk 2010). But if we do not want to consider a fixed list of senses for a word w, then we also cannot represent its meanings through a fixed list of predicates.

4 Transforming Natural Language Text to Logical Form

In transforming natural language text to logical form, we build on the software package Boxer (Bos et al. 2004). Boxer is an extension to the C&C parser (Clark and Curran 2004) that transforms a parsed discourse of one or more sentences into a semantic representation. Boxer outputs the meaning of each discourse as a Discourse Representation Structure (DRS) that closely resembles the structures described by Kamp and Reyle (1993).

We chose to use Boxer for two main reasons. First, Boxer is a wide-coverage system that can deal with arbitrary text. Second, the DRSs that Boxer produces are close to the standard first-order logical forms that are required for use by the MLN software package Alchemy. Our system interprets discourses with Boxer, augments the resulting logical forms by adding inference rules, and outputs a format that the MLN software Alchemy can read.

5 Ambiguity in Word Meaning

In order for our system to be able to make correct natural language inferences, it must be able to handle paraphrasing. For example, in order to license the entailment pair in (2), the system must recognize that "owns" is a valid paraphrase for "has", and that a "car" is type of "vehicle":

(2) p: Ed owns a car.
     h: Ed has a vehicle.

We address this problem as described in Sect. 3: we use distributional information to generate inferences stating, for example, that "has" can be substituted for "owns". This inference is weighted by the degree to which "owns", in the context in which it is used in (2), is similar to "has". To integrate these inference rules with the logical form representations of sentences like (2), we use the formalism introduced in Sect. 3. We now describe how we instantiate it in the current chapter.

First, we generate a vector space V. We have chosen to implement a very simple vector space based on a bag-of-words representation of context. To ensure that the entries in the vector space correspond to the predicates in our logical forms, we first lemmatize all sentences in our corpus using the same lemmatization process as Boxer. The features used by V are the N most frequent lemmas, excluding stopwords. To calculate the vector in V for a lemma, we count the number of times the lemma appears in the same sentence as each feature, and then calculate the pointwise mutual information (PMI) between the lemma and each feature. The resulting PMI values for each feature are used as the vector for the lemma.

As the *similarity function* sim on our vector space, we use cosine similarity. For two vectors $\vec{v}$ and $\vec{w}$, their similarity is

$$\text{sim}(\vec{v}, \vec{w}) = cosine(\vec{v}, \vec{w}) = \frac{\vec{v} \cdot \vec{w}}{\|\vec{v}\| \|\vec{w}\|}$$

Logical forms in our system are generated by Boxer, so our logical language $\mathcal{L}$ is the set of formulas that may be returned from Boxer (modulo some modifications described in Sect. 6). Likewise, the set of predicate symbols $\mathcal{P}_{\mathcal{L}}$ are the predicates generated by Boxer. Boxer's predicates, as represented by the `pred` relation in Boxer's Prolog output,[2] consist of a word lemma and a token index indicating the original token that generated that predicate. Our *lexical mapping* function maps each predicate symbol to the vector that represents the lemma portion of the predicate.

In order to assess the similarity between a word's context and a possible replacement word, we must define a *context mapping* that generates a context from a predicate $P \in \mathcal{P}_{\mathcal{L}}$ and a formula $G \in \mathcal{L}$. For the current chapter we use the simplest possible definition for κ, which ignores semantic relations. We define the context of P as the vectors of all predicates Q that occur in the same sentence as P. Since every predicate in a logical form returned by Boxer is indexed with the sentence from which it was generated, we can define a simple context mapping that defines a predicate's context solely in terms of the other predicates generated by Boxer for that sentence.

$$\kappa(P, G) = \{(same\text{-}sentence, \ell(Q)) \mid Q \text{ is a predicate found in } G,$$

$$Q\text{'s sentence index} = P\text{'s sentence index, and}$$

$$Q \neq P\}$$

Note that the only predicates Q that are used are those derived from the lemmas of words found in the text. Meta-predicates representing relations such as *agent*, *patient*, and *theme* are not included.

---

[2]See http://svn.ask.it.usyd.edu.au/trac/candc/wiki/DRSs for the detailed grammar of Boxer DRS output.

The context mapping κ computes a context for a predicate P occurring in a formula G. Next we require a *contextualization function* that uses the context returned by κ to compute a context-specific vector for P. Again we use the simplest instantiation possible. Our contextualization function just computes the sum of the vectors for each lemma in the context

$$\alpha(\vec{v}, c) = \sum_{(r_i, \vec{w}_i) \in c} \vec{w}_i$$

Other, more complex instantiations of κ and α are possible. We comment on this further in Sect. 8.

Based on these definitions, we compute the *contextualized inference projection* $\Pi^G_{\text{sim}, \zeta, \ell}(P)$, the set of weighted inference rules mapping predicate P to its potential replacements, as described in Sect. 3.

Finally, in order to limit the number of inference rules generated in the inference projection, we define a restriction function ζ that specifies, for a predicate $P \in \mathcal{P}^n_{\mathcal{L}}$, which of the predicates in $\mathcal{P}^n_{\mathcal{L}}$ may serve as replacements. Our system uses WordNet (Miller 2009) to restrict substitutions only to those predicates representing synonyms or hypernyms of the lemma underlying P. So, for a predicate $P \in \mathcal{P}^n_{\mathcal{L}}$ and a set of predicates $\mathcal{Q} \subseteq \mathcal{P}^n_{\mathcal{L}}$, we define ζ as

$$\zeta(P, \mathcal{Q}) = \{Q \in \mathcal{Q} \mid Q\text{'s lemma is a synonym of, a hypernym of, or equal to } P\text{'s}\}$$

5.1 A Lexical Ambiguity Example

Assume we have sentence (3), which is parsed by C&C and translated into DRT by Boxer, as shown in Fig. 1.

(3) p: A stadium craze is sweeping the country.
       $h1$: A craze is covering the nation.
       $h2$*: A craze is brushing the nation.

The DRS in Fig. 1b, a formula of logical language $\mathcal{L}$, shall be denoted by G. Formula G contains a unary predicate $sweep_{1005}$. In order to generate weighted substitution rules for $sweep_{1005}$, we calculate the *contextualized inference projection* of $sweep_{1005}$: the set of inference rules mapping $sweep_{1005}$ to each (unary) predicate $Q \in \mathcal{P}^1_{\mathcal{L}}$, with each rule weighted by the similarity of the vector representing the context of $sweep_{1005}$ in G to the vector representing the replacement Q. This is

$$\Pi^G_{\text{sim}, \zeta, \ell}(sweep_{1005})$$

$$= \{(F, \eta) \mid \exists Q \in \zeta(P, \mathcal{P}^1_{\mathcal{L}})[$$

$$F = \forall x.[sweep_{1005}(x) \rightarrow Q(x)] \text{ and}$$

$$\eta = \text{sim}(\alpha(\ell(sweep_{1005}), \kappa(sweep_{1005}, G)), \ell(Q))]\}$$

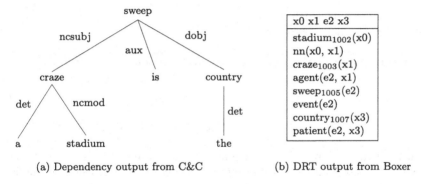

(a) Dependency output from C&C   (b) DRT output from Boxer

Fig. 1 Dependency parse tree and DRT interpretation of the premise in (3)

Let us assume that our logical language $\mathcal{L}$ also includes unary predicates $cover_{2004}$ and $brush_{3004}$ and that the lemmas $cover$ and $brush$ are known to be synonyms of $sweep$ (though from different senses). In other words,

$$\{cover_{2004}, brush_{3004}\} \in \zeta(sweep_{1005}, \mathcal{P}_{\mathcal{L}}^1)$$

So, in the calculation of $\Pi^G_{\text{sim},\zeta\ell}(sweep_{1005})$, we will generate weighted inference rules (F, η) for both $cover_{2004}$ and $brush_{3004}$. This will allow us to calculate the probability of inference for both hypotheses in (3).

We look first at $cover_{2004}$. The rule formula F is instantiated simply as

$$\forall x.[sweep_{1005}(x) \rightarrow cover_{2004}(x)]$$

The weight η is the similarity between the context of $sweep_{1005}$ in G, and $cover_{2004}$. The context vector for $sweep_{1005}$ is calculated as

$$\alpha(\ell(sweep_{1005}), \kappa(sweep_{1005}, G))$$

Since we defined the lexical mapping $\ell(P)$ to simply return the vector from V for the lemma portion of the predicate P, $\ell(sweep_{1005}) = \overrightarrow{sweep}$ and $\ell(cover_{2004}) = \overrightarrow{cover}$.

The context of P in G, $\kappa(P, G)$ is the set of a set of predicates and their relations to P, so

$$\kappa(sweep_{1005}, G) = \{(\ell(stadium_{1002}), same\text{-}sentence)\}$$
$$(\ell(craze_{1003}), same\text{-}sentence),$$
$$(\ell(country_{1007}), same\text{-}sentence),$$
$$= \{(\overrightarrow{stadium}, same\text{-}sentence),$$
$$(\overrightarrow{craze}, same\text{-}sentence),$$
$$(\overrightarrow{country}, same\text{-}sentence)\}$$

We defined our contextualization function $\alpha(\vec{v}, c)$ to be the vector sum of word vectors from the context c, so

$$\alpha(\ell(sweep_{1005}), \kappa(sweep_{1005}, G)) = \alpha(\overrightarrow{sweep}, \{(\overrightarrow{stadium}, same\text{-}sentence),$$
$$(\overrightarrow{craze}, same\text{-}sentence),$$
$$(\overrightarrow{country}, same\text{-}sentence)\})$$
$$= \overrightarrow{stadium} + \overrightarrow{craze} + \overrightarrow{country}$$

Finally, since we have the vector representing the context of $sweep_{1005}$ in G and the vector representing the replacement predicate $cover_{2004}$, we can compute the weight, η for our inference rule $\forall x.[sweep_{1005}(x) \to cover_{2004}(x)]$ as

$$\text{sim}(\alpha(\ell(sweep_{1005}), \kappa(sweep_{1005}, G)), \ell(Q))$$
$$= \text{sim}(\overrightarrow{stadium} + \overrightarrow{craze} + \overrightarrow{country}, \overrightarrow{cover})$$
$$= cosine(\overrightarrow{stadium} + \overrightarrow{craze} + \overrightarrow{country}, \overrightarrow{cover})$$

Likewise, the rule for replacing $sweep_{1005}$ by $brush_{3004}$ would be $\forall x.[sweep_{1005}(x)$ $\to brush_{3004}(x)]$ weighted by $cosine(\overrightarrow{stadium} + \overrightarrow{craze} + \overrightarrow{country}, \overrightarrow{brush})$.

Since, $cosine(\overrightarrow{stadium} + \overrightarrow{craze} + \overrightarrow{country}, \overrightarrow{cover}) > cosine(\overrightarrow{stadium} + \overrightarrow{craze} + \overrightarrow{country}, \overrightarrow{brush})$, $cover$ is considered to be a better replacement for $sweep$ than $brush$ in the sentence "A stadium craze is sweeping the country". Thus, the rule $\forall x.[sweep_{1005}(x) \to cover_{2004}(x)]$ will be given more consideration during inference, and hypothesis $h1$ will be determined to be more probable than $h2$.

5.2 Hypernymy

According to our definition of ζ above, we construct inference rules of the form $\forall x_1, \ldots, x_n[P(x_1, \ldots, x_n) \to Q(x_1, \ldots x_n)]$ where Q is a synonym or hypernym of P. Thus, for two synonyms A and B, we will generate rules $A \to B$ and $B \to A$. However, for hypernym relationships, we only construct the inference rule entailing *up* the hierarchy: from the hyponym to the hypernym. This is important for licensing correct inferences. Consider example (4).

(4) p: Ed owns a car.
     h: Ed has a vehicle.

Here the inference is valid since a *car* is a type of *vehicle*. For this pair, our system will generate the rule $\forall x[car(x) \to vehicle(x)]$ and assign a weight based on the similarity of the lemma *vehicle* to the context of *car* in the premise sentence. However, an inference in the reverse direction of (4) would be invalid, which is why we do not generate the reverse inference rule.

With hypernymy, we can see how our system naturally integrates logical phenomena with distributional information. In example (4), the distributional similarity between *vehicle* and the context of *car* affects the overall probability of inference for the pair. However, it does not override the logical requirements imposed by the hypernym relationship: if the premise and hypothesis were reversed then it would not matter how similar the words were since the inference would be impossible.

The logical rules generated for hypernyms work properly with other logical aspects as well. For example, in (5) below we can see that the direction of entailment along the hypernym hierarchy is reversed when the words appear in negative contexts. Our system handles this correctly.

(5) *p*: Ed does not own a vehicle.
     h: Ed does not have a car.

6 Implicativity

Implicativity and factivity are concerned with analyzing the truth conditions of nested propositions (Nairn et al. 2006). For example, in the premise of the entailment pair shown in example (6) below, the *locking* is the event that Ed *forgot to* do, meaning that it did not happen. In example (7), *build* is the main verb of the complement of *hope*, so we cannot infer that the *building* event occurred, nor can we infer that it did not occur. Correctly recognizing nested propositions and analyzing their contexts is necessary for preventing the licensing of entailments like (6) and rejecting those like (7).

(6) *p*: Ed forgot to lock the door.[3]
     h: Ed did not lock the door.

(7) *p*: The mayor hoped to build a new stadium.[4]
     h: *The mayor built a new stadium.

Nairn et al. (2006) presented an approach to the treatment of inferences involving implicatives and factives. Their approach identifies an "implication signature" for every implicative or factive verb. This signature specifies the truth conditions for the verb's nested proposition, depending on whether the verb occurs in a positive or negative environment. Following MacCartney and Manning (2009), we write implication signatures as "x/y" where x represents the entailment to which the speaker commits in a positive environment and y represents entailment in a negative environment. Both x and y have three possible values: "+" for positive entailment, meaning the nested proposition is entailed, "-" for negative entailment, meaning the negation of the proposition is entailed, and "o" for "null" entailment, meaning that neither the proposition nor its negation is entailed. Figure 2 gives concrete examples.[5]

---

[3] Example (6) is derived from examples by MacCartney and Manning (2009).

[4] Example (7) is adapted from document wsj_0126 from the Penn Treebank.

[5] Note that *forget to* and *forget that* have different implication signatures. As such, in order to select the right signature, it is necessary to examine not simply the verb but the entire subcategorization frame. To do this, we make use of the dependency parse generated by the C&C parser that is input to Boxer.

	Signature	Example
forgot that	+/+	he forgot that Dave left ⊨ Dave left he did not forget that Dave left ⊨ Dave left
managed to	+/-	he managed to escape ⊨ he escaped he did not manage to escape ⊨ he did not escape
forgot to	-/+	he forgot to pay ⊨ he did not pay he did not forget to pay ⊨ he paid
refused to	-/o	he refused to fight ⊨ he did not fight he did not refuse to fight ⊭ {he fought, he did not fight}

Fig. 2 Implication signatures

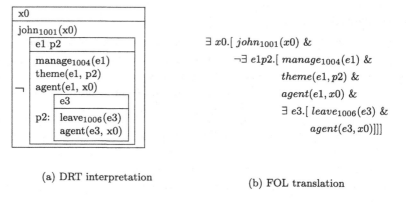

$\exists\, x0.[\, john_{1001}(x0)\ \&$
$\quad\neg\exists\, e1p2.[\, manage_{1004}(e1)\ \&$
$\qquad theme(e1, p2)\ \&$
$\qquad agent(e1, x0)\ \&$
$\qquad \exists\, e3.[\, leave_{1006}(e3)\ \&$
$\qquad\qquad agent(e3, x0)]]]$

(a) DRT interpretation

(b) FOL translation

Fig. 3 Boxer's DRT interpretation of "John did not manage to leave."

6.1 Inferences with Nested Propositions

The standard conversion from DRT to first-order logic (FOL) (the one used by Boxer) falls short in its analysis of nested propositions. Consider the entailment pair "John did not manage to leave" and "John left". The DRT interpretation of the premise and its corresponding FOL conversion are shown in Fig. 3.

It should be clear that "John did not manage to leave" does *not* entail "John left" (and, in fact, entails the opposite). Unfortunately, the FOL formula shown in Fig. 3b *does* entail the FOL representation of "John left", which is

$$\exists x0\, e1.[john_{1001}(x0)\ \&\ leave_{1006}(e1)\ \&\ agent(e1, x0)]$$

The incorrect inference occurs here because the standard DRT-to-FOL translation loses some information. DRT expressions are allowed to have *labeled subexpressions*, such as $p2$ in Fig. 3a that is used to reference the *theme* of the *manage* event: the *leave* event. The FOL expression, on the other hand, shows that $p2$ is the theme of event $e1$, but has no way of stating what $p2$ refers to.

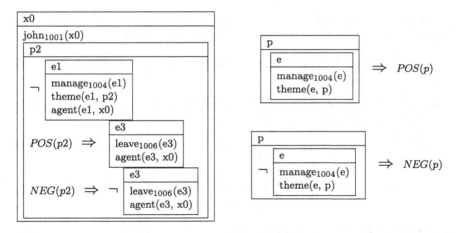

(a) DRT interpretation with subexpression triggers

(b) Subexpression-triggering inference rules for implicative "manage to" with signature +/-

Fig. 4 First (insufficient) attempt at correcting for the loss of labeled sub-expression information

In order to capture the information that the DRT labels provide, we modify the DRT expression to contain explicit *subexpression triggers*. That is, for a sub-DRS A labeled by p, we replace A with two new expressions in the same scope: $POS(p) \rightarrow A$ and $NEG(p) \rightarrow \neg A$. The result of such a replacement on the DRS in Fig. 3a can be see in Fig. 4a.

Now that our labeled subexpression has triggers, we can introduce inference rules to activate those triggers. The purpose of these inference rules is to capture the behavior dictated by the implication signature of the implicative or factive verb for which the relevant subexpression is the theme. For example, according to the implication signature in Fig. 2, the implicative *manage to* is positively entailing in positive contexts and negatively entailing in negative contexts. This means that if John *managed to* do what is described by p, then the event described by p occurred, or in other words, the subexpression of p is *true*. Likewise, if John *did not manage to* do what is described by p, then the event described by p *did not* occur, meaning that the subexpression of p is *false*.

The triggering inference rules for *managed to* are shown in Fig. 4b. The first rule, for positive contexts, says that for all propositions p, if p is "managed", then p's subexpression is *true*, so trigger the "positive entailment" subexpression which, in our example, says that the *leaving* event occurred. The second rule, for negative contexts, says that for all propositions p, if there is *no* "managing" of p, then p's subexpression is *false*, so trigger the "negative entailment" subexpression to say that there is *no* event of *leaving*.

While this approach works for positive contexts, there is a subtle problem for negative contexts. The negative context rule in Fig. 4b can be translated to FOL as

$$\forall p.[\neg \exists e.[manage_{1004}(e) \wedge theme(e, p))] \rightarrow NEG(p)]$$

This expression is stating that for all propositions p, p is *false* if there is no "managing" of p. Now, we want this inference rule to be used in cases where it is stated that "managing" did not occur, such as in the expression of Fig. 4a, where we see that is the case that

$$\neg \quad \boxed{\begin{array}{l} e1 \\ \hline manage_{1004}(e1) \\ theme(e1, p2) \\ agent(e1, x0) \end{array}}$$

which is equivalent to the FOL expression

$$\neg \exists e1[manage_{1004}(e1) \wedge theme(e1, p2) \wedge agent(e1, x0)]$$

stating that there is no "managing" of $p2$ by $x0$. However, the antecedent of our negative context rule states that there is *no* "managing" of the proposition, so the rule would only be used if it could be proven that there is no "managing" event at all. Unfortunately, stating that $p2$ is not "managed" *by* $x0$ does *not* entail that $p2$ is not "managed" at all since $p2$ could be managed by someone other than $x0$.

To overcome this problem, we modify our representation of a negated event. Instead of representing an event, such as the "managing" event, that *did not* occur as $\neg \exists e.[manage(e)]$, we represent it explicitly as an event of *non-occurrence*: $\exists e.[$**not_manage**$(e)]$. Applying this change to the DRS and inference rules in Fig. 4, we arrive at our final form in Fig. 5.

Using this strategy, we can see that the negative context rule is active when there exists a "not-managing" state, and the representation of "John did not manage to leave" explicitly requires that there is such an state, meaning that the rule will be used in the inference. With all of these pieces in place, the inference works as expected.

Thus, we transform the output of Boxer in two ways. First, we identify any labeled propositions and replace them with pairs of proposition triggers. Then, we modify any negated DRSs by extracting the verb and theme atoms, changing the verb predicate to a "not_" predicate,[6] and finally ensuring that all other expressions under the negated DRS (aside from the labeled proposition itself), remain under a negated DRS.

Once the sentence representations have been modified, we generate inference rules for each implicative verb. If the verb is positively entailing in positive contexts, we generate a rule of the form

$$\forall p.[\exists e.[\langle verb \rangle(e) \wedge theme(e, p))] \rightarrow POS(p)]$$

---

[6]The lexical mapping for these new predicates ignores the negation, i.e. $\ell(not\_manage) = \ell(manage)$.

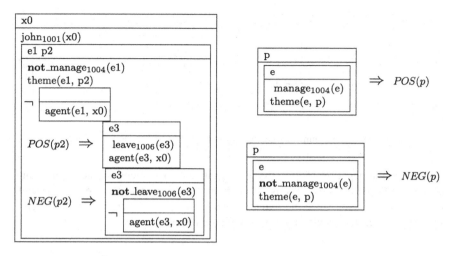

(a) DRT interpretation with subexpression triggers

(b) Subexpression-triggering inference rules for implicative "manage to" with signature $+/-$

Fig. 5 Explicit capturing of sub-expression information

but if it is negatively entailing in positive contexts, we instead generate a rule of the form

$$\forall p.[\exists e.[\langle verb \rangle(e) \land theme(e, p))] \to NEG(p)]$$

If the verb is positively entailing in *negative* contexts, we generate a rule of the form

$$\forall p.[\exists e.[\mathbf{not\_}\langle verb \rangle(e) \land theme(e, p))] \to POS(p)]$$

but if it is negatively entailing in negative contexts, we instead generate a rule of the form

$$\forall p.[\exists e.[\mathbf{not\_}\langle verb \rangle(e) \land theme(e, p))] \to NEG(p)]$$

If the verb is non-entailing in either positive or negative contexts, then we do not generate a rule for that context polarity.

This approach works for arbitrarily long chains of nested implicatives and factives. For example, consider the entailment in (8).

(8)   Dave managed to fail to not forget to leave $\vDash$ Dave did not leave

Our approach is able to predict this entailment by correctly handling the three nested implicatives along with the negation. Figure 6 shows the nested polarity environments and how the implicative verbs and negations modify the polarity. The top-level verb *managed to* maintains its same polarity and predicts a positive environment for the *fail to* event. The *fail to* reverses the polarity for the *not forget to*

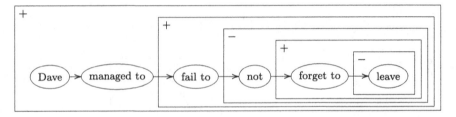

Fig. 6 Nested polarity environments showing how implicative verbs and negation modify polarity

state. Since the negation of *forget* is in a negative environment, the negations cancel, putting *forget* in a positive environment, thus predicting a negative environment for the *leaving* event. Since the *leaving* event is in a negative environment, we can say that the sentence entails that the leaving did not occur.

6.2 Interaction with Other Phenomena

MacCartney and Manning (2009) extended the work by Nairn et al. (2006) in order to correctly treat inference involving monotonicity and exclusion. Our approach to implicativity and factivity combines naturally with hypernymy to ensure correct entailment judgements. For example, no additional work is required to license the entailments in (9).

(9) (a) John refused to dance ⊨ John didn't tango
     (b) John did not forget to tango ⊨ John danced

Likewise, no further work is needed for our implicativity and factivity approach to interact correctly with our approach to ambiguity in word meaning. For example, consider example (10). Here the premise contains the verb *prevent* in a positive context, which is negatively entailing. It also contains the word *leave* which is synonymous with both *result in* and *flee* through different senses. As the example shows, our approach is able to correctly handle the interaction between the lexical ambiguity and the implicative verb.

(10)   *p*:   He prevented the spill from leaving a stain.
       h1: The spill did not result in a stain.
       h2*: The spill did not flee a stain.
       h3*: The spill resulted in a stain.

In example (11), the *prevent* event is nested under the null-entailing verb *try*. As such, neither alternate sense of *leave* is entailed since *try* says nothing about the truth or falsity of its nested proposition.

(11)   *p*:   He tried to prevent the spill from leaving a stain.
       h1*: The spill did not result in a stain.
       h2*: The spill did not flee a stain.
       h3*: The spill resulted in a stain.

7 Preliminary Evaluation

As a preliminary evaluation of our system, we constructed the set of demonstrative examples included in this paper to test our system's ability to handle the previously discussed phenomena and their interactions. We ran each example with both a standard first-order theorem prover and Alchemy to ensure that the examples work as expected. Note that since weights are not possible when running an example in the theorem prover, any rule that would receive a non-zero weight in an MLN is simply treated as a "hard clause" following Bos and Markert (2005). For the experiments, we generated a vector space from the entire New York Times portion of the English Gigaword corpus (Graff and Cieri 2003).

The example entailments evaluated were designed to test the interaction between the logical and weighted phenomena. For example, in (12), "fail to" is a negatively entailing implicative in a positive environment, so according to the theorem prover, p entails both $h1$ and $h2$. However, using our weighted approach, Alchemy outputs that $h1$ is more probable than $h2$.

(12) p: The U.S. is watching closely as South Korea fails to honor U.S. patents.[7]
     $h1$: South Korea does not **observe** U.S. patents.
     $h2$*: South Korea does not **reward** U.S. patents.

The first-order approach, which contains inference rules for both paraphrases as hard clauses, cannot distinguish between good and bad paraphrases, and considers both of them equally valid. In contrast, the weighted approach can judge the degree of fit of the two potential paraphrases. Also, it does so in a context-specific manner, choosing the paraphrase *observe* over *reward* in the context of *patents*.

Our ability to perform a full-scale evaluation is currently limited by problems in the Alchemy software required to perform probabilistic inference. This is discussed more in Sect. 8.

8 Future Work

Our plans for continued work can be divided into two categories: work on the theoretical side and work on implementation and evaluation.

From a theoretical perspective, we have used a simplistic bag-of-words approach for computing a context-specific vector for a predicate based on its formula context (functions α and κ). We plan to move to a more informative construction that takes semantic relations into account. This will be interesting in particular because the relations that can be read off a logical form differ from those available in a dependency parse. For example, we can check whether two predicates occur within the same DRS, or whether they apply to a common variable. We can also ask what influence different logical connectives have on perceived word meaning.

---

[7] Sentence adapted from Penn Treebank document wsj_0020.

Additionally, up to this point we have only addressed word-level paraphrasing with weighted lexical ambiguity rules that connect individual words. However, our framework could easily be extended to allow for weighted paraphrase rules for higher-order phrases such as noun-noun compounds, adjective-noun compounds, or full noun phrases.

We would also like to extend our formalism to address a wider range of linguistic phenomena. Many phenomena are better described using weights than through categorial analyses, and first-order representations do not correctly address this. By extending our framework, we hope to be able to apply weights derived from distributional information to a wide variety of modeled concepts. The inference rules generated by our approach to factivity might be good candidates for this extension. Nairn et al. (2006) proposed that there may be "degrees of factivity" based on the context of the verb. Because the inference rules that we use to activate the presupposition triggers are externalized, they can be weighted independently of the rest of the semantic analysis. Right now the rules are either generated or not, which is equivalent to assigning a weight of either 1 or 0, but a weighted approach could be taken instead.

From an implementation perspective, we would like to run a large-scale evaluation of our techniques. However, the major barrier to scaling up is that the Alchemy software has severe inefficiencies in terms of memory requirements and speed. This prevents us from executing larger and more complex examples. There is on-going work to improve Alchemy (Gogate and Domingos 2011), so we hope to be able to make use of new probabilistic inference tools as they become available.

9 Conclusion

In this paper, we have defined a link between logical form and vector spaces through a lexical mapping of predicate symbols to points in space. We address polysemy not through separate predicate symbols for different senses of a word, but by using a single predicate symbol with a lexical mapping that gets adapted to the context in which the predicate symbol appears. We use the link to project weighted inferences from the vector space to the logical form.

We showed how these weighted first-order representations can be used to perform probabilistic first-order inferences using Markov Logic. We have shown how our approach handles three distinct phenomena, word meaning ambiguity, hypernymy, and implicativity, as well as allowing them to interact appropriately. Most importantly our approach allows us to model some phenomena with hard first-order techniques and other phenomena with soft weights, and to do all of this within a single, unified framework. The resulting approach is able to correctly solve a number of difficult textual entailment problems that require handling complex combinations of these important semantic phenomena.

Acknowledgements This work was supported by the U.S. Department of Defense through a National Defense Science and Engineering Graduate Fellowship (NDSEG) Fellowship for the first author, National Science Foundation grant IIS-0845925 for the second author, Air Force Contract FA8750-09-C-0172 under the DARPA Machine Reading Program and NSF grants IIS-0712097 and IIS-1016312 for the third author, and a grant from the Texas Advanced Computing Center (TACC), The University of Texas at Austin.

We would like to thank Gemma Boleda, Louise McNally, Karl Pichotta, and Yinon Bentor for their helpful comments.

References

Bos, J., & Markert, K. (2005). Recognising textual entailment with logical inference. In *Proceedings of EMNLP 2005*, Vancouver, Canada (pp. 628–635).

Bos, J., Clark, S., Steedman, M., Curran, J. R., & Hockenmaier, J. (2004). Wide-coverage semantic representations from a CCG parser. In *Proceedings of COLING 2004*, Geneva, Switzerland (pp. 1240–1246).

Clark, S., & Curran, J. R. (2004). Parsing the WSJ using CCG and log-linear models. In *Proceedings of ACL 2004*, Barcelona, Spain (pp. 104–111).

Dagan, I., Glickman, O., & Magnini, B. (2005). The PASCAL recognising textual entailment challenge. In *Proceedings of the PASCAL challenges workshop on recognising textual entailment*.

Dinu, G., & Lapata, M. (2010). Measuring distributional similarity in context. In *Proceedings of EMNLP 2010*, Cambridge (pp. 1162–1172).

Erk, K. (2010). What is word meaning, really? (and how can distributional models help us describe it?). In *Proceedings of the 2010 workshop on geometrical models of natural language semantics*, Uppsala, Sweden (pp. 17–26).

Erk, K., & Padó, S. (2008). A structured vector space model for word meaning in context. In *Proceedings of EMNLP 2008*, Honolulu (pp. 897–906).

Erk, K., & Padó, S. (2010). Exemplar-based models for word meaning in context. In *Proceedings of ACL 2010*, Uppsala, Sweden (pp. 92–97).

Firth, J. R. (1957). A synopsis of linguistic theory 1930–1955. In *Studies in linguistic analysis* (pp. 1–32). Oxford: Blackwell Publishers.

Gärdenfors, P. (2004). *Conceptual spaces*. Cambridge: MIT Press.

Getoor, L. & Taskar, B. (Eds.) (2007). *Introduction to statistical relational learning*. Cambridge: MIT Press.

Gogate, V., & Domingos, P. (2011). Probabilistic theorem proving. In *27th conference on uncertainty in artificial intelligence (UAI)*.

Graff, D., & Cieri, C. (2003). *English Gigaword*. Philadelphia: Linguistic Data Consortium.

Harris, Z. (1954). Distributional structure. *Word, 10*, 146–162.

Hobbs, J. R., Stickel, M., Appelt, D., & Martin, P. (1993). Interpretation as abduction. *Artificial Intelligence, 63*(1–2), 69–142.

Kamp, H., & Reyle, U. (1993). *From discourse to logic; An introduction to modeltheoretic semantics of natural language, formal logic and DRT*. Dordrecht: Kluwer Academic.

Kok, S., Singla, P., Richardson, M., & Domingos, P. (2005). *The alchemy system for statistical relational AI* (Technical report). Department of Computer Science and Engineering, University of Washington. http://www.cs.washington.edu/ai/alchemy.

Kotlerman, L., Dagan, I., Szpektor, I., & Zhitomirsky-Geffet, M. (2010). Directional distributional similarity for lexical inference. *Natural Language Engineering, 16*(04), 359–389.

Krishnamurthy, R., & Nicholls, D. (2000). Peeling an onion: The lexicographers' experience of manual sense-tagging. *Computers and the Humanities, 34*(1–2).

Landauer, T., & Dumais, S. (1997). A solution to Platos problem: The latent semantic analysis theory of acquisition, induction, and representation of knowledge. *Psychological Review, 104*(2), 211–240.

Lin, D., & Pantel, P. (2001). Discovery of inference rules for question answering. *Natural Language Engineering, 7*(4), 343–360.

Lund, K., & Burgess, C. (1996). Producing high-dimensional semantic spaces from lexical co-occurrence. *Behavior Research Methods, Instruments, and Computers*, *28*, 203–208.

MacCartney, B., & Manning, C. D. (2009). An extended model of natural logic. In *Proceedings of the eighth international conference on computational semantics* (IWCS-8) (pp. 140–156).

Miller, G. A. (2009). Wordnet—about us. http://wordnet.princeton.edu.

Mitchell, J., & Lapata, M. (2008). Vector-based models of semantic composition. In *Proceedings of ACL* (pp. 236–244).

Montague, R. (1970). Universal grammar. *Theoria*, *36*, 373–398. Reprinted in Thomason (1974), pp. 7–27.

Nairn, R., Condoravdi, C., & Karttunen, L. (2006). Computing relative polarity for textual inference. In *Proceedings of inference in computational semantics* (ICoS-5), Buxton.

Poon, H., & Domingos, P. (2009). Unsupervised semantic parsing. In *Proceedings of EMNLP 2009* (pp. 1–10).

Reisinger, J., & Mooney, R. J. (2010). Multi-prototype vector-space models of word meaning. In *Proceedings of NAACL 2010*.

Richardson, M., & Domingos, P. (2006). Markov logic networks. *Machine Learning*, *62*, 107–136.

Szpektor, I., Dagan, I., Bar-Haim, R., & Goldberger, J. (2008). Contextual preferences. In *Proceedings of ACL 2008*, Columbus (pp. 683–691).

Thater, S., Fürstenau, H., & Pinkal, M. (2010). Contextualizing semantic representations using syntactically enriched vector models. In *Proceedings of ACL 2010*, Uppsala, Sweden (pp. 948–957).

Thomason, R. H. (Ed.) (1974). *Formal philosophy. Selected papers of Richard Montague*. New Haven: Yale University Press.

Van de Cruys, T., Poibeau, T., & Korhonen, A. (2011). Latent vector weighting for word meaning in context. In *Proceedings of EMNLP 2011*, Edinburgh, Scotland (pp. 1012–1022).

Annotations that Effectively Contribute to Semantic Interpretation

Harry Bunt

Abstract This chapter presents a new perspective on the use of semantic annotations. It is argued that semantic annotations should themselves have a semantics in order to be really useful. It is shown that, when this is the case, the information in a semantic annotation can be effectively combined with the results of compositional semantic analysis, with the effect of removing some of the underspecification in a compositional interpretation, or narrowing the interpretation down to one that is appropriate in a given context.

1 Introduction: Functions of Semantic Annotations

Annotations add information to a primary text. In the pre-digital age, annotations took the form of bibliographical, historical, or interpretative notes in the margin or in footnotes. In the digital age, annotations take on a different form, but their function is essentially the same: they add information to a given text.

An annotation that does not add any information would seem not make much sense, but consider the following example of the annotation of a temporal expression using TimeML (Pustejovsky et al. 2003):[1]

```
(1)  <timeml>
     The CEO announced that he would resign as of
     <TIMEX3 tid="t1" type="date" value="2008-12-01"/>
      the first of December 2008
     </TIMEX3>
     </timeml>
```

---

[1] For simplicity, the annotations of the events that are mentioned in this sentence and the way they are linked to the date that is mentioned, are suppressed here.

H. Bunt (✉)
Tilburg Center for Cognition and Communication (TiCC) and Department of Philosophy, Tilburg University, P.O. Box 90153, 5000 LE Tilburg, The Netherlands
e-mail: harry.bunt@uvt.nl

H. Bunt et al. (eds.), *Computing Meaning*, Text, Speech and Language Technology 47, DOI 10.1007/978-94-007-7284-7_4,

In this annotation, the subexpression (2) adds to the noun phrase *the first of December 2008* the information that his phrase describes the date "2008-12-01".

(2) `<TIMEX3 tid="t1" type="date" value="2008-12-01"/>`

This does not add any information; it rather paraphrases the noun phrase in TimeML. This could be useful if the expression in the annotation language had a formally defined semantics, which could be used directly by computer programs for applications like information extraction or question answering. Unfortunately, TimeML is just a particular form of XML, and as such does not have a semantics.

A case where the annotation of a date as in (1) *does* add something, is the following.

(3) Mr Brewster called a staff meeting today.

In the absence of context information we do not know which date *today* refers to; in this case the annotation (4) would be informative.

(4) `<timeml>`
      Mr Brewster called a staff meeting
      `<TIMEX3 tid=t1 type=date value="2012-05-14"/>`
      today
      `</TIMEX3>`
      `</timeml>`

Note that the annotations in TimeML (1) and (4) are 'old-fashioned' in the sense that the `TIMEX3` element is wrapped around the annotated string, so the annotations are inserted in the primary text, similar to the annotations in pre-digital times that were inserted in the same printed text. Modern annotation methods prefer a 'stand-off' approach, where annotations are contained in a separate file and point to locations in the primary text. For example, instead of the TIMEX3 element in (1), an element is used as in (5), where the attribute `@target` points to the sequence `#w10...#w14` of word tokens that form the string *the first of December 2008*. In addition to respecting the integrity of the original text, this has the advantage of allowing multiple annotations linked to the same primary text.

(5) `<TIMEX3 xml:id="t1" target="#w10...#w14" type="date"`
      `value="2008-12-01"/>`

The examples in (1) and (4) illustrate two different functions that semantic annotations may have: *recoding* information contained in a natural language expression in a formal annotation language, and *interpreting* a context-dependent natural language expression. This is for instance also the function of coreference annotations, as illustrated in (6), and of the markup of discourse connectives in the Penn Discourse Treebank (PDTB, Prasad et al. (2008)), illustrated in (7).[2]

---

[2]The annotation in (7) uses a modified version of the PDTB representation, following Bunt et al. (2012b).

(6)   a.   Robin looked at Chris. She seems happy, he thought.

    b.
```
<refml>
   <refEntity xml:id="r1" target="#w1" name="robin"/>
   <refEntity xml:id="r2" target="#w4" name="chris"/>
   <refEntity xml:id="r3" target="#w5" natGender="female"/>
   <refEntity xml:id="r4" target="#w8" natGender="male"/>
   <refLink anchor="#r3" antecedent="#r2"
    relType="identity"/>
   <refLink anchor="#r4" antecedent="#r1"
    relType="identity"/>
</refml>
```

This annotation provides the information that *She* is interpreted as indicating Chris (and thus that Chris is a female person; from which it follows that *he* does not refer to Chris but rather to Robin, and that Robin is a male person).

The annotations (4), (5) and (6) are especially useful if the information which they contain about the interpretation of deictic and anaphoric expressions can be combined effectively with the interpretation of the rest of the sentence. Applying a syntactic parser and a compositional semantic analyzer to the sentence (3), for example, will lead to a semantic representation which leaves the date indicated by *today* unspecified. Such a representation is underspecified in the sense that it does not contain sufficient information to compute its truth value. The information in an underspecified semantic representation (USR) and that in a semantic annotation can be effectively combined if the annotation has a well-defined semantics of its own, so once again we see that the usefulness of a semantic annotation depends on whether it has a formal semantics.

There is a third function that semantic annotations may have, namely to make explicit how two subexpressions of a natural language expression are semantically related, or what is the function of a subexpression. This is illustrated in (7) for the function of a discourse connective (temporal or causal sense of *since*); in (8) (discussed in Sect. 3.3.2) for the implicit coherence relation connecting two sentences in a discourse; in (9) (discussed in more detail in Sect. 3.3) for the function of a temporal expression (*at six o'clock* indicating the time of occurrence of the *set*-event or the time at which the alarm is to sound); and in (10) for the semantic role of the referent of a noun phrase.

(7)   a.   1.   *since* as a temporal discourse connective:
           The Mountain View, Calif., company has been receiving 1,000 calls a day about the product <u>since</u> *it was demonstrated at a computer publishing conference several weeks ago.*
      2.   *since* as a causal discourse connective:
           It was a far safer deal for lenders <u>since</u> *NWA had a healthier cash flow and more collateral on hand.*

b. Annotation of (7a1):

```
<dRelML>
<discourseRelation xml:id="dr1"
  arg1="#a1" arg2="#a2" rel="#r1"/>
<dRelArgument xml:id="a1"target="#w1...#w14"/>
<dRelArgument xml:id="a2" target="#w16...#w26"/>
<explRel xml:id="r1" target="#w15"
  sense="succession"/>
</dRelML>
```

(8) Some have raised their cash positions to record levels. [Implicit=because] High cash positions help buffer a fund when the market falls.

(9) Henry set the alarm at six o'clock.

(10) a. He drew a gun.
    b. First interpretation (a gun is taken out of its holster):

```
<xml>
<refEntity xml:id="p1" target="#w1" natGender="male"/>
<event xml:id="e1" target="#w2" pred="draw1"/>
<refEntity xml:id="p2" target="#w3 #w4" pred="gun"/>
<semRole event="#e1" participant="#p1"
  relType="agent"/>
<semRole event="#e1" participant="#p2"
  relType="theme"/>
</xml>
```

    c. Second interpretation (a drawing is made of a gun):

```
<xml>
<refEntity xml:id="p1" target="#w1" natGender="male"/>
<event xml:id="e1" target="#w2" pred="draw2"/>
<refEntity xml:id="p2" target="#w3 #w4" pred="gun"/>
<semRole event="#e1" participant="#p1"
  relType="agent"/>
<semRole event="#e1" participant="#p2"
  relType="result"/>
</xml>
```

The annotation in (10b) represents the interpretation where a gun was taken out of its holster; the one in (10c) where a drawing was made of a gun.

In sum, a semantic annotation of an expression E in a primary text may have the following functions:

a. **Recoding**: re-expression of the meaning of E in the annotation language;
b. **Contextualization**: specification of the interpretation of a context-specific deictic or anaphoric expressions E;
c. **Explicitation**: representation of an implicit semantic relation or function of one or more subexpressions of E.

Semantic annotations nearly always have the second or third function; this is where their usefulness mainly lies, and what the rest of this chapter will focus on. We have seen that semantic annotations that have the first function do not make much sense if they don't have a semantics, and that the usefulness of semantic annotations having the second or third function also depends on having a formal semantics (see also Bunt and Romary (2002)).

The combination of annotations and USRs is optimally facilitated when the semantics of annotation structures is defined via a translation into the same format as that used in USRs. Bunt (2007a) has shown that an 'interpretation-by-translation' semantics can be defined for TimeML, by means of a systematic, compositional translation of TimeML expressions into Discourse Representation Structures (DRSs, Kamp and Reyle 1993). In Sect. 3 of this chapter we will show how DRSs interpreting semantic annotations can effectively be combined with under-specified DRSs constructed by a compositional semantic analyzer.

In Sect. 2 we first consider some work concerned with the design of semantic annotation languages that have a formal semantics.

2 The Semantics of Semantic Annotations

2.1 Interpreting Annotations Expressed in XML

Attempts to provide a semantics for semantic annotations include the Interval Temporal Logic semantics for TimeML by Pratt-Hartmann (2007); the event-based semantics for TimeML by Bunt and Overbeeke (2008a), and other attempts to formally interpret temporal annotations by Katz (2007) and Lee (2008). The most elaborate proposal for a semantics of semantic annotation is formulated in Bunt (2007a) and Bunt and Overbeeke (2008a,b), where a semantic annotation language is presented with a formal semantics, that integrates temporal information, semantic roles, and coreference relations. These proposals all involve a translation of semantic annotations into first-order logic; however it has been shown to be very hard to achieve this in a satisfactory, compositional manner, where the translation of an annotation structure would be systematically constructed from the translations of its components (see Lee (2008), Bunt (2011)).

Bunt (2011) provides a DRS-based semantics for (a revised version of) ISO-TimeML, the annotation language that forms part of the ISO 24617-1 standard for the annotation of time and events (ISO 2012a). While formally equivalent to first-order logic, the representation formalism of DRSs offers an attractive alternative, since it was designed to facilitate the incremental construction of semantic representations. For annotations which are expressed in XML, as is the case for ISO-TimeML annotations, a semantic interpretation via translation into DRSs can exploit the existence of certain structural correspondences between XML expressions and DRSs. Semantic annotations such as (6b), (7b), (10b) and (10c), consist of XML elements of two kinds: (A) those which associate semantic information with a stretch of primary text, that is identified by the value of the @target attribute; and (B) those which contain semantic information about an implicit relation (hence having no @target attribute) between two stretches of primary data.[3] These two kinds of elements can be translated into DRSs as follows.

A. An XML element of the form <ENTITY xml:id="id1" target="#m1 attribute_1="val_1" ...attribute_n="val_n"/> can be translated into a DRS which introduces a discourse referent that corresponds to the value of the attribute @xml:id, and for every feature specification attribute_i="val_i" contains a corresponding condition of the form $a_i'(x, v_i')$, where a_i' translates $attribute_i$, x is the newly introduced discourse referent, and v_i' translates val_i.

For example, <refEntity xml:id="#r1" target="#m1"

name="robin"> ⤳ $\boxed{\begin{array}{l} x \\ \hline \text{NAME}(x, \text{robin}) \end{array}}$.

B. An XML element of the form <RELATION attribute_1="val_1" ... attribute_n="val_n"/> can be translated into a DRS which introduces two discourse referents, and for each feature specification attribute_i = "val_i" contains a condition of the form $a_i'(x, y)$, where a_i' is the translation of $attribute_i$, and x and y are the two newly introduced discourse referents.[4]

For example, <TIME_ANCHORING eventID="#e1"

relatedToTime="#t1" relType="before"/> ⤳ $\boxed{\begin{array}{l} e, t \\ \hline \text{BEFORE}(e, t) \end{array}}$.

These correspondences make it attractive to interpret annotations expressed in XML via a translation into DRSs. According to the Linguistic Annotation Framework (LAF, ISO 24616; see ISO (2012c)), however, an annotation standard should not be defined at the level of representation formats, like XML, but at a more abstract level. The semantics of a annotations should therefore be defined likewise at a more abstract level than that of XML. In the next subsection we will see that systematic correspondences can also be established between abstract annotation structures and DRSs.

---

[3] A relation between two stretches of primary data which is explicitly expressed in the primary text corresponds to an XML element of type A. Here we consider only XML elements of type A which have an XML identifier as value of the attribute @xml:id, and elements of type B which have no such identifier. For other cases see Bunt (2013a).

[4] For certain attributes which have a particular status the DRS interpretation of a specification attribute_i ="val_i" has to be stipulated separately. An example is the TimeML attribute @polarity, of which a specification of the value negative gives rise to the negation of the DRS interpreting the rest of the XML element in which it occurs.

2.2 The Design of Semantic Annotation Languages

2.2.1 The CASCADES Design methodology

The Linguistic Annotation Framework draws a distinction between the concepts of *annotation* and *representation*. The term 'annotation' refers to the linguistic information that is added to segments of primary data, independent of the format in which the information is represented, while the term 'representation' refers to the format in which an annotation is rendered, independent of its content. According to LAF, *annotations* are the proper level of standardization, rather than representations.

In order to (a) comply with the Linguistic Annotation Framework, and (b) satisfy the requirement that semantic annotations should have a semantics, we have developed a methodology for defining languages for semantic annotation, called 'CASCADES' (Conceptual analysis, Abstract syntax, Semantics, and Concrete syntax for Annotation language DESign); Bunt (2010, 2013a). This approach introduces in the definition of an annotation language a component which specifies the categories of linguistic information that can be used to build semantic annotations, and their possible combinations. This component is called an *abstract syntax*; it specifies the set of possible annotations in abstract, set-theoretical terms. To avoid overloading the term 'annotation', we will use the term 'annotation structure' for the set-theoretical constructs defined by an abstract syntax. Following this approach, the annotation language definition has three parts: (1) an abstract syntax, defining annotation structures; (2) the specification of a representation format for annotation structures, called a 'concrete syntax'; and (3) a semantics. The semantics is defined for the *abstract* rather than the concrete syntax; this has the important advantage that any concrete syntax which specifies a way of representing the annotation structures defined by the abstract syntax inherits the same semantics, from which it follows that alternative representation formats are semantically equivalent, and hence convertible from one to another (see Bunt (2010, 2013a) for formal definitions and proofs).

The distinction between abstract and concrete syntax, which is at the heart of the CASCADES approach, with the definition of a semantics for an abstract syntax, was developed during the project of defining an ISO standard for the annotation of time and events, in order to make this standard compatible with the Linguistic Annotation Framework. More recently, the CASCADES method was developed further (Bunt 2013a) by specifying in some detail the steps of (1) defining an abstract syntax given a conceptual analysis of the annotation task; (2) defining the semantics of a given abstract syntax; (3) and specifying a XML-based concrete syntax given an abstract syntax. Moreover, steps backward were defined for feedback loops in this process, as visualized in Fig. 1. Using these steps, the CASCADES method has been applied in the development of ISO standard 24617-2 for dialogue act annotation, resulting in the 3-part definition of the Dialogue Act Markup Language DiAML (see ISO (2012b); Bunt et al. (2010, 2012a); and Bunt (2013b)). The approach is currently applied in ISO projects for defining standards for the annotation of discourse relations (see Bunt et al. (2012b)), semantic roles (see Bunt and Palmer (2013)), and spatial information (Pustejovsky et al. (2012)).

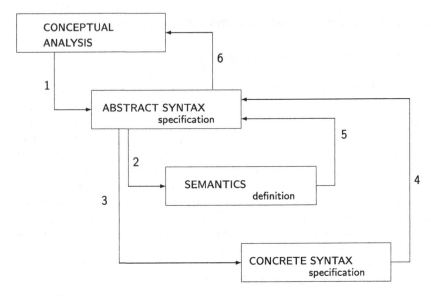

Fig. 1 Steps in the CASCADES model

In the rest of this section we summarize the application of CASCADES to the definition of an abstract syntax and its semantics for the ISO-TimeML language (Bunt and Pustejovsky 2012; Pustejovsky et al. 2010a,b).

2.2.2 The Case of ISO-TimeML

Abstract Syntax   An abstract syntax specification consists of two parts, a *conceptual inventory*, specifying the elements from which annotation structures are built up, and a specification of the possible ways of combining these elements into annotation structures.

The conceptual inventory for ISO-TimeML consists of finite sets of elements called '*event types*', '*time points*', '*tenses*', '*aspects*', '*temporal relations*', '*temporal units*', '*aspectual relations*', and '*event-subordination relations*'.

An annotation structure is a set of two kinds of structures, built up from elements of the conceptual inventory: *entity structures* and *link structures*. An entity structure contains information about a segment of primary text; a link structure contains information about the relation between two (or more) segments of primary text. An entity structure is formally a pair $\langle s, a \rangle$, where s identifies a segment of source text[5] and a is a set-theoretical construct whose elements belong to the conceptual

---

[5] Segments of source text may be identified directly (see TEI (2009)) or via the output of another layer of processing, such as a tokeniser.

inventory. In the case of ISO-TimeML, a is simply an n-tuple of such concepts.[6] A link structure is formally a triple $\langle \epsilon, E, \rho \rangle$, consisting of an entity structure ϵ, a non-empty set E of entity structures, and a relation ρ, which may itself be a structured object.

Four types of entity structure are distinguished and five types of link structure:[7]

(11) a. Types of entity structure:

    1. event structure;
    2. time point structure;
    3. temporal interval structure;
    4. time-amount structure.

  b. Types of link structure:

    1. temporal anchoring structure, anchoring an event (or state; more generally, an eventuality) in time;
    2. temporal relation structure, relating a time point or interval to another time point or interval;
    3. event-duration structure, relating an event or state to its duration;
    4. aspectual structure, describing an aspectual relation between two events;
    5. subordination structure, capturing a subordination relation between two events.

Note that, while in general a link structure may relate an entity structure to a set of other entity structures, in ISO-TimeML a link structure always relates an entity structure to a single other entity structure; moreover, the relational component of a link structure in ISO-TimeML is not a structured object but simply a relation.

Semantics It was noted above that certain correspondences between XML and DRS representations can be used to define a semantics for annotation representations. The same is true for defining a semantics of abstract annotation structures, for the simple reason that both entity structures and link structures are n-tuples, similar to the sequence of attribute-value pairs in an XML element, the significance of an element in an n-tuple being encoded by its position rather than by an XML at-

---

[6]See Bunt (2013b) for more complex entity structures.

[7]The four types of entity structure correspond to four different XML elements in the concrete syntax; the five types of link structure correspond to three relational tags in the concrete syntax, where, following the original TimeML representation format, the TLINK tag is used for each of the first three kinds of relation listed in (11b), as well as for representing temporal relations between events. This forms a mismatch between the abstract and the concrete syntax of ISO-TimeML, which should be remedied in the future. In TimeML TLINK was also used for relating a temporal interval to its length; ISO-TimeML has the separate MLINK tag for this purpose.

tribute.[8] Similar to the XML-DRS translation sketched in Sect. 2.1, a mapping from annotation structures to DRSs can be defined as follows:[9]

1. An entity structure $\langle m, s \rangle$, with $s = \langle a_1, \ldots, a_n \rangle$ is mapped into a DRS which introduces a discourse referent x and which contains for each ϵ-component a_i a condition $\pi(x, a_i')$, where π_i is a predicate that interprets the position of a_i and a_i' is the translation of a_i;
2. A link structure $\langle \epsilon_1, \{\epsilon_2\}, R \rangle$ is interpreted as a DRS that introduces two discourse referents, x_1 and x_2, and which contains a condition of the form $R'(x_1, x_2)$, where R' is a predicate translating the relation R.

For example, ISO-TimeML annotation of the temporal information in the sentence

(12) *John called at midnight*

uses in its abstract annotation structure an entity structure ϵ_1 for the *call* event and an entity structure ϵ_2 for the time point *midnight*, while the temporal anchoring relation between the event and the time point gives rise to a link structure L_1 connecting the two.

The entity structure for an event contains an n-tuple $\langle a_1, \ldots, a_n \rangle$, with $1 \leq n \leq 6$, depending on the types of information which are available or relevant about the event. In this example only an event type and a tense are relevant, so the n-tuple is a pair $\langle event\ type, tense \rangle$.

The entity structure for the time specification is a pair $\langle s, time\ zone, clock\ time \rangle$; in this chapter we will suppress the use of time zones, which is not relevant here. The semantics maps the entity and link structures to mini-DRSs as follows:

(13) $\epsilon_1 \rightsquigarrow$

e_1
type(e_1, *call*)
tense(e_1, *past*)

$\epsilon_2 \rightsquigarrow$

t_1
clocktime(t_1, 2400)

$L_1 \rightsquigarrow$

e_2, t_2
at-time(e_2, t_2)

Merging these DRSs results in (14) for the annotation structure $\langle \{\epsilon_1, \epsilon_2\}, \{L_1\} \rangle$:

---

[8]In defining a semantics for the above abstract syntax, it was found (Bunt 2011) that finer distinctions need to be made in the conceptual inventory than those listed in (11). *Date structures* were added as a type of entity structure, and two types of link structure were added: one for linking an interval to its length (*interval measurement structure*) and one for expressing temporal relations between events (*event-temporal relation structures*); the latter two were necessary in order to avoid the semantically problematic overloading that occurs in TimeML of the TLINK relation.

[9]For more details see Bunt (2011, 2013a).

$$
(14) \quad
\begin{array}{|l|}
\hline
e, t \\
\hline
\text{type}(e, call) \\
\text{tense}(e, past) \\
\text{clocktime}(t, 2400) \\
\text{at-time}(e, t) \\
\hline
\end{array}
$$

This says that a call event occurred in the past, at 24:00 o'clock.

Concrete Syntax   The XML-based ISO-TimeML-ics representation format, defined by the concrete syntax, is an *ideal* format (Bunt 2010) in the sense that (a) every annotation structure, defined by the abstract syntax, can be represented in that format; and (b) every ISO-TimeML-ics expression represents only one annotation structure, defined by the abstract syntax. The semantics of an ISO-TimeML-ics representation is therefore defined simply as the semantics of the abstract annotation structure that it represents.

3 Combining Semantic Annotations and Semantic Representations

In this section we consider the use of semantic annotations for making the interpretation of a given sentence or text more specific than its purely compositional semantic analysis, by specifying the interpretation of a deictic or an anaphoric expression, or by adding disambiguating information, or by specifying semantic relations between textual elements.

For the representation of ambiguous or underspecified meanings, as the result of purely compositional semantic analysis, we will use an extended form of DRSs. In an overview of representation techniques, Bunt (2007b) shows that underspecified representation of a wide range of semantic phenomena is possible by using *labels* with scope constraints, as in UDRT (Reyle 1993), or *hole variables* or *handles* as in Hole Semantics (Bos 1996) and in Minimal Recursion Semantics (Copestake et al. 1996), in combination with *metavariables*, as proposed e.g. by Pinkal (1999). Labels, holes and handles are particularly useful for the representation of structural ambiguities, like relative quantifier scoping, while metavariables are suitable for representing local ambiguities, like anaphora, deixis, metonymy, and sense ambiguities. DRSs with labels and metavariables therefore form a powerful formalism for underspecified semantic representation. The usefulness of DRSs for defining the semantics of semantic annotations having been noted already, we will in the rest of this chapter use (extended) DRSs for both purposes.

3.1 Contextualization

The annotation of coreference relations can be used to effectively reduce the underspecificity in an semantic representation due to the occurrence of anaphoric expressions. Example (15) illustrates this. The USR in (15b) representing the result of compositional semantic analysis of the sentence *John saw Bill when he left the house* introduces a discourse referent (z) as the individual who left the house, allowing z to denote John or Bill. The annotation, in the form of an abstract annotation structure in (15c1) and in concrete XML representation form in (15c2), stipulates that the referential entities corresponding to *Bill* and *he* are identical.

(15) a. John saw Bill when he left the house.

b. Underspecified semantic representation:

$x, y, z, e_1, e_2, t_1, t_2$
name($x, john$)
name($y, bill$)
see(e_1, x, y, t_1)
lefthouse(e_2, z, t_2)

c. Annotation of coreference, with its representation and interpretation:

c1. *Annotation structure*: $a = \langle\{\epsilon_1, \epsilon_2, \epsilon_3\}, \{L_2\}\rangle$, where

- $\epsilon_1 = \langle m_1, a_1 \rangle$: markable m_1 identifies the word token w1 (*John*); a_1 is an individual named "John";
- $\epsilon_2 = \langle m_2, a_2 \rangle$: markable m_2 identifies the word token w3 (*Bill*); a_2 is an individual named "Bill";
- $\epsilon_3 = \langle m_3, a_3 \rangle$: markable m_3 identifies the word token w5 (*he*); a_3 is an individual indicated by "he";
- $L_2 = \langle \epsilon_2, \{\epsilon_3\}, R_{ID} \rangle$: R_{ID} is the identity relation between individuals.

c2. *Representation of annotation structure:*
```
<xml>
 <refEntity xml:id="r1" target="#w1" name="john"/>
 <refEntity xml:id="r2" target="#w3" name="bill"/>
 <refEntity xml:id="r3" target="#w5"
  natGender="male"/>
 <refLink anchor="#r3" ante="#r2"
  relType="identity"/>
</xml>
```

d. *Interpretation* of annotation structure:

x, y, z
name($x, john$)
name($y, bill$)
gender($z, male$)
$y = z$

Unification of this interpretation of the coreference annotation with the semantic representation (15b) gives the following fully specified representation:

(16)

$x, y, z, e_1, e_2, t_1, t_2$
$name(x, john)$
$name(y, bill)$
$see(e_1, x, y, t_1)$
$gender(z, male)$
$lefthouse(e_2, z, t_2)$
$y = z$

3.2 Semantic Alignment

The example of contextualization in the previous subsection may suggest that the combination of the information in an annotation with that in a USR is simply a matter of DRS merging. This is not quite true, however. This subsection forms an intermezzo in which we show that things may be more complicated, and that a process is required that keeps track of exactly to which segment of source text a component of a semantic annotation applies.

Consider the text fragment (17a), which contains four occurrences of the pronoun *he* and one of *him*, used anaphorically, that are all ambiguous between having Chris or Robin as their antecedent. An underspecified semantic representation of the text is shown in (17b) on the left; on the right the DRS-interpretation of a coreference annotation is shown.

(17) a. Chris saw Robin when he left the house. He was happy. He had phoned him last week and warned that he might be unable to come.

b. Underspecified representation (USR) and representation of annotation interpretation (AIR):

USR	AIR
$x, y, z, u, v, w, r,$ e_1, e_2, e_3, e_4	a, b, c, d, f, g, h
$name(x, chris)$	$name(a, chris)$
$name(y, robin)$	$name(b, robin)$
$see(e_1, x, y, t_1)$	$c = b$
$gender(z, male)$	$gender(c, male)$
$lefthouse(e_2, z, t_2)$	$gender(d, male)$
$when(e_1, e_2)$	$d = a$
$gender(u, male)$	$gender(f, male)$
$be(u, happy)$	$f = b$
$gender(v, male)$	$gender(g, male)$
$gender(w, male)$	$g = a$
$phone(e_3, v, w, t_3)$	$gender(h, male)$
$in\text{-}time(e_3, last\_week)$	$h = b$
$(\ldots)$	
$gender(r, male)$	
$come(e_4, r)$	

The alignment of the elements in the USR and those in the AIR immediately suggest a possible merge of the two DRSs by unifying a with x, b with y, c with z, d with us, and so on, corresponding to the reading:

(18) Chris saw Robin when Robin left the house. Chris was happy. Robin had phoned Chris last week and warned that he [Robin] might be unable to come.

Let us assume that this is the intended reading. From a technical point of view, however, the AIR variable c might just as well unify with (for example) the USR variable u, rather than with z, and similarly the variables d, f, g and h could unify with any of the variables in the USR, giving rise to a different (possibly inconsistent) interpretation of the USR variables that were introduced for anaphoric expressions. These unifications are all possible because the only information about the variables $c, d, \ldots, h$ in the AIR is that they are either equal to the discourse referent a or to the discourse referent b, but that doesn't impose any constraints on how they may unify with the USR variables $z, u, \ldots, r$. This reveals an inadequacy in the AIR: the interpretation of the anaphoric links in the annotation has lost the information concerning which token of *he/him* corresponds to which discourse referent; in that sense the AIR is not well 'aligned' with the source text.

This can be remedied by treating the information in semantic annotations about their textual anchoring as semantically significant, and taking it along in their interpretation. This information can then be exploited when combining the AIR with the USR, if the USR components are likewise anchored to the source text segments that they interpret. This can be accomplished by replacing discourse referent introductions by pairs, consisting of an identifier of the text segment which gives rise to its introduction, and the discourse referent itself—see (19), which corresponds to the first part of (17).

(19) a. Chris saw Robin when he left the house. He was happy.

b. Tokenization:
```
m1="Chris" m2="saw" m3="Robin" m4="when" m5="he"
m6="left the house" m7="he" m8="was happy"
```

c. Underspecified semantic representation and representation of annotation interpretation:

USR	AIR
$\langle m1, x \rangle$, $\langle m3, y \rangle$, $\langle m5, z \rangle$, $\langle m7, u \rangle$, $\langle m2, e1 \rangle$, $\langle m6, e2 \rangle$, $\langle m2, t1 \rangle$, $\langle m6, t2 \rangle$	$\langle m1, a \rangle$, $\langle m3, b \rangle$, $\langle m5, c \rangle$, $\langle m9, d \rangle$
name(x, *chris*)	name(a, *chris*)
name(y, *robin*)	name(b, *robin*)
see(e_1, x, y, t_1)	$c = b$
gender(z, *male*)	gender(c, *male*)
lefthouse(e_2, z, t_2)	gender(d, *male*)
when(e_1, e_2)	$d = a$
gender(u, *male*)	gender(f, *male*)
be(u, *happy*)	$f = b$

By unifying markable-variable pairs $\langle m, \alpha \rangle$ rather than just the variables, we ensure that effectively only those AIR and USR discourse referents unify that correspond to the same source text segments. Once the unification has been performed, and the anaphors have been resolved, the markables in the conditions can be eliminated, having done their duty, leading to a standard type of DRS as in (20):

(20)

$$\begin{array}{|l|}
\hline
x, y, z, u, e_1, e_2, t_1, t_2 \\
\hline
\text{name}(a, chris) \\
\text{name}(b, robin) \\
\text{see}(e_1, x, y, t_1) \\
\text{gender}(z, male) \\
z = x \\
\text{lefthouse}(e_2, z, t_2) \\
\text{when}(e_1, e_2) \\
\text{gender}(u, male) \\
\text{be}(u, happy) \\
u = x \\
\hline
\end{array}$$

3.3 Explicitation

In this section we show how a semantic annotation can be used to make an implicit semantic relation between parts of a sentence or text fragment explicit. Two cases are considered: (a) the semantic role of a prepositional temporal phrase, as either anchoring an event in time or as specifying a time-related participant in the event; (b) the semantic relation between the contents of two sentences in a coherent discourse, when this relation is not expressed in the text.

3.3.1 Semantic Roles

In example (21a) the prepositional phrase *at six o'clock* can be understood as specifying the time that Henry set an alarm clock for waking him up the next morning (as in *Before switching off his bed light, Henry set the alarm clock*), or as specifying the time that the alarm will sound (as in *Henry set the alarm to wake him up at six o'clock*). In order to distinguish the two interpretations, we make use of semantic roles in DRS conditions both in the annotation and in the compositional semantic interpretation (rather than multi-argument event predicates). The semantic role annotation is inspired by the proposals for semantic roles annotation in the LIRICS project (see LIRICS (2006)) and in ISO project 24617-5 (ISO 2013; Bunt and Palmer 2013; Bonial et al. 2011).

The USR in (21b) represents the *set* event and its three participants, identifying Henry as the agent and the alarm as the theme, but leaving the semantic role of the time unspecified.

(21) a. Henry set the alarm at six o'clock.

b. Underspecified semantic representation:

$\langle m1,x \rangle$, $\langle m3,y \rangle$, $\langle m4,t \rangle$, $\langle m2, e \rangle$
name(x, *henry*)
type(e, *set*)
type(y, *alarm*)
clocktime(t, 600)
agent(e, x)
theme(e, y)

c. Annotation of time and events, with its representation and interpretation:

c1. *Annotation structure*: $\alpha = \langle \{\epsilon_1, \epsilon_2\}, \{L_1\} \rangle$, where

- $\epsilon_1 = \langle m_1, \langle et_2, past \rangle \rangle$: markable m_1 identifies the word token w2 (*set*); et_2 is an event type;
- $\epsilon_2 = \langle m_2, ct_{600} \rangle$: markable m_2 identifies token sequence [w6,w7] (*six o'clock*); ct_{600} identifies a clock time;

if *at six o'clock* is interpreted as a temporal specifier of the *set*-event, then

- $L_1 = \langle \epsilon_1, \epsilon_2, R_{at} \rangle$ (relation R_{at} anchoring events in time);

else *at six o'clock* is interpreted as specifying a temporal participant in the *set*-event, and

- $L_1 = \langle \epsilon_1, \epsilon_2, R_{goal} \rangle$ (semantic role relation R_{goal}).

c2. *Representation of annotation structure:*

a. For *at six o'clock* as specification of event-time:
```
<xml>
<event xml:id="e1" target="#w2" pred="set"/>
<instant xml:id="t1" target="#w6 #w7" `
 clockTime="600"/>
<timeAnchoring event="#e1" time="#t1"
 relType="at"/>
</xml>
```

b. For *at six o'clock* as description of event participant:
```
<xml>
<event xml:id="e1" target="#w2" pred="set"/>
<instant xml:id="t1" target="#w6 #w7"
 clockTime="600"/>
<semRole event="#e1" participant="#t1"
 relType="goal"/>
</xml>
```

c3. *Semantic interpretation* of annotation structure:

a. For *at six o'clock* as specification of event-time:

$\langle m2,e \rangle$, $\langle m4,t \rangle$
type(e, *set*) clocktime(t, 600) at-time(e, t)

b. For *at six o'clock* as description of event participant:

$\langle m1,e \rangle$, $\langle m2,t \rangle$
type(e, *set*) clocktime(t, 600) goal(e, t)

Merging the URS in (21b) with either of the AIRs in (21c3) gives the fully specified semantic representation of either interpretation, as shown in (22):

(22) a.

x, y, t, e
name(x, *henry*) type(e, *set*) type(y, *alarm*) clocktime(t, 600) agent(e, x) theme(e, y) at-time(e, t)

b.

x, y, t, e
name(x, *henry*) type(e, *set*) type(y, *alarm*) clocktime(t, 600) agent(e, x) theme(e, y) goal(e, t)

3.3.2 Implicit Discourse Relations

Example (23), from the Penn Discourse Treebank, illustrates the use of a semantic annotation for interpreting the relation between sentences in a coherent discourse, when not expressed explicitly. The intended interpretation is that the second sentence provides a reason why the event mentioned in the first sentence occurs.

The underspecified representation shown in (23b) is simply the combined semantic representations of the two sentences in (23a). The annotation in (23c) applies the ISO standard for discourse relation annotation under development as ISO 24617-8 (see Bunt et al. (2012b)). The attribute @aoType is used to represent an 'abstract object type' in the sense of Asher (1993), and the attribute @attribution is used to represent the source to whom statements in the annotated text are attributed. Semantically, a discourse relation which connects two sentences by establishing a relation between an event expressed in the first sentence and another event expressed in the second, requires the annotation to indicate exactly which events are related, since each of the sentences may mention several events. The attributes @headID and @headPred are introduced for this purpose; the first specifies the relevant markable, the second the event type. This information is used to construct a representation of the interpretation as shown in (23c3).

(23) a. Some have raised their cash positions to record levels. Implicit=because
High cash positions help buffer a fund when the market falls.

b. Underspecified semantic representation:

$\langle m1, x\rangle, \langle m3,y\rangle, \langle m4,z\rangle, \langle m5,u\rangle, \langle m8,v\rangle, \langle m9,w\rangle,$ $\langle m2,e_1\rangle, \langle m6,e_2\rangle, \langle m7,e_3\rangle, \langle m10,e_4\rangle$
type(e_1, *raise*),   some(x), agent(e_1, x),   cashposition(y), theme(e_1, y),   recordlevel(z), goal(e_1, z),   type(e_2, *help*),   hicashposition(u), instrument(e_2, u),   type(e_3, *buffer*), theme(e_2, e_3),   fund(v), theme(e_3, v),   type(e_4, *fail*), when(e_4, e_3),   market(w), theme(e_4, w)

c. Annotation of discourse relations, with representation and interpretation:

c1. *Annotation structure*: $\alpha = \langle\{\epsilon_1, \epsilon_2\}, \{L_1\}\rangle$, where

- $\epsilon_1 = \langle m_1, \langle et_3, past\rangle\rangle$ (event type et_3);
- $\epsilon_2 = \langle m_2, \langle et_4\rangle\rangle$ (event type et_4);
- $L_1 = \langle\epsilon_1, \epsilon_2, R_{reason}\rangle$; R_{reason} is the 'reason' relation between events).

c2. *Representation of annotation structure:*
```
<dRelML>
<discourseRelation xml:id="dr1"
 arg1="#a1" arg2="#a2" rel="#r1"/>
<dRelArgument xml:id="a1" target="#w1...#w9"
 aoType="event" headID="#w3"
 headPred="raise" attribution="#at1"/>
<dRelArgument xml:id="a2" target="#w10...#w20"
 aoType="event" headID="#w13"
 headPred="help" attribution="#at1"/>
<implRel xml:id="r1" discRel="reason"
 attribution="#at1"/>
<attributionRep xml:id="at1" aSource="author"/>
</dRelML>
```
c3. *Semantic interpretation* of annotation structure:

$\langle m_2, e_1\rangle, \langle m_6, e_2\rangle$
type(e_1, *raise*)   type(e_2, *help*)   reason(e_1, e_2)

Unification of the semantic representations of the two sentences, construed as a
single DRS in (23b), with the interpretation of the annotation (and dropping the

markables associated with the discourse referents) leads to the representation (24) of the discourse fragment as a whole.

(24)

$x, y, z, u, v, w, e_1, e_2, e_3, e_4$
type(e_1, *raise*),   some(x), agent(e_1, x),   cashposition(y), theme(e_1, y),   recordlevel(z), goal(e_1, z),   type(e_2, *help*),   hicashposition(u), instrument(e_2, u),   type(e_3, *buffer*), theme(e_2, e_3),   fund(v), theme(e_3, v),   type(e_4, *fail*), when(e_4, e_3),   market(w), theme(e_4, w),   reason(e_2, e_3)

4 Conclusions and Perspectives

In this paper we have indicated how the information, contained in semantic annotations, may effectively be used to resolve ambiguities and to narrow down underspecified meanings. This is possible if the annotations are expressed in an annotation language that has a formal semantics. This is often not the case, but under the influence of efforts of the international organisation for standards ISO, projects are under way that do indeed aim to define such annotation languages. Studies by Pratt-Hartmann, Katz, Lee, and the author have demonstrated the feasibility of doing so for substantial fragments of semantic annotation languages, as illustrated by the annotation language ISO-TimeML of ISO standard 24617-1 (Time and Events) and annotation language DiAML of ISO standard 24617-2 (Dialogue Acts).

This approach opens the possibility to exploit semantic annotations in a computational interpretation process, as we have shown by casting the interpretation of semantic annotations in a DRS-based representation format that is suitable for underspecified semantic representation, allowing a unification-based process for combining the information in semantic annotations with that obtained through compositional semantic analysis.

This is potentially very useful, since semantic annotations are constructed using quite different techniques (machine learning from corpora, exploitation of domain ontologies, searching metadata, ...) than the compositional syntactic-semantic analysis techniques that make sentential semantic content explicit. The approach that we have described here therefore makes it possible to effectively combine heterogeneous processes and information sources in order to arrive at maximally specific and contextually appropriate interpretations.

References

Asher, N. (1993). *Reference to abstract objects in discourse*. Dordrecht: Kluwer Academic.

Bonial, C., Corvey, W., Petukhova, V., Palmer, M., & Bunt, H. (2011). A hierarchical unification of LIRICS and VerbNet thematic roles. In *Proceedings workshop on semantic annotation for computational linguistic resources*, Stanford.

Bos, J. (1996). Predicate logic unplugged. In *Proceedings 10th Amsterdam colloquium* (pp. 133–143).

Bunt, H. (2007a). The semantics of semantic annotation. In *Proceedings of the 21st Pacific Asia conference on language, information and computation* (PACLIC21), Korean Society for Language and Information (pp. 13–29).

Bunt, H. (2007b). Underspecified semantic representation: Which technique for what purpose? In H. Bunt, & R. Muskens (Eds.), *Computing meaning, vol. 3* (pp. 55–85). Dordrecht: Springer.

Bunt, H. (2010). A methodology for designing semantic annotation languages exploiting semantic-syntactic ISO-morphisms. In *Proceedings of the second international conference on global interoperability for language resources* (ICGL 2010), Hong Kong.

Bunt, H. (2011). Introducing abstract syntax + semantics in semantic annotations, and its consequences for the annotation of time and events. In E. Lee & A. Yoong (Eds.), *Recent trends in language and knowledge processing* (Vol. 2). Seoul: Hankukmunhwasa.

Bunt, H. (2013a). *A methodology for designing semantic annotations* (TiCC Technical Report TR 2013-001). Tilburg University.

Bunt, H. (2013b). A context-change semantics for dialogue acts. In H. Bunt, J. Bos & S. Pulman (Eds.), *Computing meaning* (Vol. 4, pp. 177–201). Dordrecht: Springer.

Bunt, H., & Overbeeke, C. (2008a). An extensible, compositional semantics of temporal annotation. In *Proceedings of LAW-II: The second linguistic annotation workshop*, Marrakech.

Bunt, H., & Overbeeke, C. (2008b). Towards formal interpretation of semantic annotation. In *Proceedings 6th international conference on language resources and evaluation* (LREC 2008), Marrakech. Paris: ELRA.

Bunt, H., & Palmer, M. (2013). Conceptual and representational choices in defining an ISO standard for semantic role annotation. In *Proceedings ninth joint ISO – ACL SIGSEM workshop on interoperable semantic annotation* (ISA-9), Potsdam, March 19–20.

Bunt, H., & Pustejovsky, J. (2012). Annotating temporal and event quantification. In *Proceedings of ISA-5, 5th international workshop on interoperable semantic annotation, workshop at the second international conference on global interoperability for language resources* (ICGL-2), Hong Kong, City University of Hong Kong.

Bunt, H., & Romary, L. (2002). Towards multimodal content representation. In K. S. Choi (Ed.), *Proceedings of LREC 2002, workshop on international standards of terminology and language resources management*, Las Palmas (pp. 54–60). Paris: ELRA.

Bunt, H., Alexandersson, J., Choe, J.-W., Fang, A., Hasida, K., Lee, K., Petukhova, V., Popescu-Belis, A., Romary, L., Soria, C., & Traum, D. (2010). Towards an ISO standard for dialogue act annotation. In *Proceedings of LREC 2010*, Malta. Paris: ELDA.

Bunt, H., Alexandersson, J., Choe, J.-W., Fang, A., Hasida, K., Petukhova, V., Popescu-Belis, A., & Traum, D. (2012a). A semantically-based standard for dialogue annotation. In *Proceedings of LREC 2012*, Istanbul. Paris: ELRA.

Bunt, H., Prasad, R., & Joshi, A. (2012b). First steps toward an ISO standard for the annotation of discourse relations. In *Proceedings of ISA-7, seventh joint ISO-ACL SIGSEM workshop on interoperable semantic annotation, workshop at LREC 2012*, Istanbul. Paris: ELRA.

Copestake, A., Fllickinger, D., & Sag, I. (1996). *Minimal recursion semantics: An introduction*. Cambridge: Cambridge University Press.

ISO (2012a). *Language resource management – semantic annotation framework (SemAF) – part 1: Time and events. International organisation for standardisation ISO*. ISO International Standard 24617-1:2012(E).

ISO (2012b). *Language resource management – semantic annotation framework (SemAF) – part 2: Dialogue acts. International organisation for standardisation ISO*. ISO International Standard 24617-2:2012(E).

ISO (2012c). *Linguistic annotation framework (LAF). International organisation for standardisation ISO*. ISO International Standard 24612-2:2012(E).

ISO (2013). *Language resource management – semantic annotation framework (SemAF) – part 5: Semantic roles. International organisation for standardisation ISO*. ISO Committee Draft, CD 24612-5:2013.

Kamp, H., & Reyle, U. (1993). *From discourse to logic*. Dordrecht: Kluwer Academic.

Katz, G. (2007). Towards a denotatial semantics for TimeML. In F. Schilder, G. Katz, & J. Pustejovsky (Eds.), *Annotation, extraction, and reasoning about time and events*. Dordrecht: Springer.

Lee, K. (2008). Formal semantics for interpreting temporal annotation. In *Unity and diversity of languages: Special lectures for the 18th international conference of linguists*. Amsterdam: Benjamins.

LIRICS (2006). Project LIRICS deliverable D4.3, Documented compilation of semantic data categories. http://lirics.loria.fr.

Pinkal, M. (1999). On semantic underspecification. In H. Bunt & R. Muskens (Eds.), *Computing meaning, vol. 1* (pp. 33–56). Dordrecht: Kluwer Academic Publishers.

Prasad, R., Dinesh, N., Lee, E., Miltsakaki, E., Robaldo, L., Joshi, A., & Webber, B. (2008). The Penn Discourse Treebank 2.0. In *Proceedings of LREC 2008, 6th international conference on language resources and evaluation*, Marrakech, Morocco.

Pratt-Hartmann, I. (2007). From TimeML to Interval temporal logic. In *Proceedings of the seventh international workshop on computational semantics* (IWCS-7), Tilburg, Netherlands (pp. 166–180).

Pustejovsky, J., Castano, J., Ingria, R., Gaizauskas, R., Katz, G., Saurí, R., & Setzer, A. (2003). TimeML: Robust specification of event and temporal expressions in text. In *Proceedings of the fifth international workshop on computational semantics* (IWCS-5), Tilburg, Netherlands (pp. 337–353).

Pustejovsky, J., Bunt, H., & Lee, K. (2010a). ISO-TimeML. In *Proceedings of LREC 2010*, Malta. Paris: ELDA.

Pustejovsky, J., Bunt, H., Lee, K., & Romary, L. (2010b). ISO-TimeML: An international standard for semantic annotation. In *Proceedings 7th international conference on language resources and evaluation* (LREC 2010), Malta. Paris: ELDA.

Pustejovsky, J., Moszkowics, J., & Verhagen, M. (2012). The current status of ISO-space. In *Proceedings of ISA-7, seventh joint ISO-ACL SIGSEM workshop on interoperable semantic annotation, workshop at LREC 2012*, Istanbul. Paris: ELRA.

Reyle, U. (1993). Dealing with ambiguities by underspecification. *Journal of Semantics, 10*(2), 123–179.

TEI (2009). *TEI P5: Guidelines for electronic text encoding and interchange*. Oxford: Text Encoding Initiative Consortium.

Concrete Sentence Spaces for Compositional Distributional Models of Meaning

Edward Grefenstette, Mehrnoosh Sadrzadeh, Stephen Clark, Bob Coecke, and Stephen Pulman

Abstract Coecke et al. (2010) developed a compositional model of meaning for distributional semantics, in which each word in a sentence has a meaning vector and the distributional meaning of the sentence is a function of the tensor products of the word vectors. Abstractly speaking, this function is the morphism corresponding to the grammatical structure of the sentence in the category of finite dimensional vector spaces. In this chapter, we provide a concrete method for implementing this linear meaning map by presenting an algorithm for computing representations for various syntactic classes which have functional types; this algorithm results in assigning concrete corpus-based vector spaces to the abstract type of 'sentence'. Our construction method is based on structured vector spaces whose basis vectors are pairs of words and grammatical roles. The concrete sentence spaces only depend on the types of the verbs of sentences; we use an embedding of these spaces and compare meanings of sentences with different grammatical structures by simply taking the inner product of their vectors in the bigger space. Our constructions are exemplified on a toy corpus.

E. Grefenstette (✉) · B. Coecke · S. Pulman
Department of Computer Science, Oxford University, Wolfson Building, Parks Road, Oxford OX1 3QD, UK
e-mail: edward.grefenstette@cs.ox.ac.uk

B. Coecke
e-mail: bob.coecke@cs.ox.ac.uk

S. Pulman
e-mail: sgp@clg.ox.ac.uk

M. Sadrzadeh
School of Electronic Engineering and Computer Science, Queen Mary University of London, Mile End Road, London E1 4NS, UK
e-mail: mehrnoosh.sadrzadeh@eecs.qmul.ac.uk

S. Clark
Computer Laboratory, University of Cambridge, William Gates Building, 15 JJ Thomson Avenue, Cambridge CB3 0FD, UK
e-mail: stephen.clark@cl.cam.ac.uk

H. Bunt et al. (eds.), *Computing Meaning*, Text, Speech and Language Technology 47,
DOI 10.1007/978-94-007-7284-7_5,
© Springer Science+Business Media Dordrecht 2014

1 Introduction

Representing the meanings of words and sentences in a form suitable for use by a computer is a central problem in Computational Linguistics and Natural Language Processing (Jurafsky and Martin 2000). The problem is of theoretical interest—to linguists, philosophers, cognitive scientists and computer scientists—but also has practical implications: finding a suitable meaning representation can greatly improve the effectiveness of a Natural Language Processing system, whether it be for automatically translating sentences from one language to another, paraphrasing, answering questions, or summarising articles (to give just a few examples).

There have been two distinct approaches to the representation of meaning in Natural Language Processing. Distributional semantic models adapt geometric methods from information retrieval (Manning et al. 2008) to implement the philosophical view of semantics that meaning is determined by use. These models are often related to Wittgenstein's philosophy of language (Wittgenstein 1953), but the closer connection is with the work of structural linguists such as Firth (1957). In concrete terms, the meanings of words are equated with the distributions of contexts in which they occur, where 'context' is typically taken to mean 'tokens that occur near the target word' (Schuetze 1998). In practice, such distributions are modeled as vectors in high-dimensional Hilbert spaces, and existing geometric distance metrics are used to determine the semantic similarity of words by measuring the distance between their vector representations (Widdows 2004). This approach to natural language semantics has found applications in many areas of Natural Language Processing, e.g. Landauer and Dumais (1997) and Grefenstette (1994), demonstrating its power for modelling the meanings of individual words. However, this class of model does not naturally lend itself to modeling meanings of larger units of text, as such models do not explicitly define a canonical composition operation by which the meanings of words can be *composed* to form the meaning of the resulting phrase.

Formal semantic models exhibit almost opposite qualities to distributional semantic models. They are built as extensions of existing syntactic analysis models (typically generative grammars), and associate with each grammatical production rule a semantic composition rule (Montague 1970). Such composition rules generally involve the application of the semantic interpretation of one of the grammatical components to that of the semantic representation of the other grammatical component(s), thereby treating the semantic interpretation of some grammatical components as functions, and that of others as arguments. Concretely, formal semantic models implement a view popular in philosophy from Leibniz to Frege (1892) stating that natural language serves as an imperfect vehicle for the ideal rational language of the mind embodied by logic. The interpretations of functions and arguments in these models correspond to partial expressions of a predicate logic formed by predicates, relations and arguments enhanced by elements of a lambda calculus, and composition merely involves applying such partial expressions to one another to obtain the logical form of the sentence through β-reduction. While formal semantic models naturally support syntax-driven semantic compositionality—a feature distributional semantic models lack—they have their own shortcoming: the underlying semantic representation is a predicate logic. While the reduction of meaning to logical form may be appropriate for some tasks, it is unclear how this view of semantics might be adapted to deal with the language processing tasks that involve, for example, classification, search or summarisation, as the notion of semantic similarity at play in such cases is usually more topic driven than a matter of equivalence or closeness of logical form or truth value. Additionally, unlike distributional semantic models, the basic meanings of words are not learned, but stipulated by a logical model which must be provided, leaving open the question as to how formal semantic models may be constructed empirically.

Given that the weaknesses of formal semantic models seem to be addressed by distributional semantic models and vice-versa, several researchers such as Mitchell and Lapata (2008), Coecke et al. (2010), and Clark and Pulman (2007) have begun investigating the development of models of semantics that would exhibit the syntax-driven compositionality of formal semantics while retaining the empirical nature of distributional models: we call such models Compositional Distributional Models of Semantics. In this chapter, we introduce a concrete implementation of one such model. In Sect. 2, we present the mathematical foundations of an existing compositional distributional semantic framework (Coecke et al. 2010). In Sect. 3 we introduce the foundations for a concrete implementation of such a framework, and present an algorithm for computing representations for various syntactic classes which have functional types in Sect. 4. In Sect. 5, we discuss concrete sentence spaces and an embedding between them which allows the comparison of meanings of sentences with different grammatical structures, and in Sect. 6 we discuss how such models provide implicit disambiguation through composition. These concrete constructions are exemplified on a toy hand-made corpus, which provides a basis for further large-scale experimentation with this model. In Sect. 7, we present a brief overview of work in this field relating to the new approach to compositional distributional semantics presented here.

2 Background

Coecke et al. (2010) develop a mathematical framework for a compositional distributional model of meaning, based on the intuition that *syntactic analysis guides the semantic vector composition*. The setting consists of two parts: a formalism for a type-logical syntax and a formalism for vector space semantics. Each word is assigned a grammatical type and a meaning vector in the space corresponding to its type. The meaning of a sentence is obtained by applying the function corresponding to the grammatical structure of the sentence to the tensor product of the meanings of the words in the sentence. Based on the type-logic used, some words will have atomic types and some compound function types. The compound types live in a tensor space where the vectors are weighted sums (i.e. superpositions) of the tuples of basis vectors from each space. Compound types are "applied" to their arguments by taking inner products, in a similar manner to how predicates are applied to their arguments in Montague semantics.

For the type-logic we use Lambek's pregroup grammars (Lambek 2008). The use of pregoups is not essential, but leads to a more elegant formalism, given its proximity to the categorical structure of vector spaces (see Coecke et al. (2010)). A pregroup is a partially ordered monoid where each element has a right and left cancelling element, referred to as an *adjoint*. A pregroup can be seen as the algebraic counterpart to the cancellation calculus of Harris (1968). The operational difference between a pregroup and Lambek's original type-algebra, the Syntactic Calculus, is that in the latter, the monoid multiplication of the algebra (used to model juxtaposition of the types of the words) has a right and a left adjoint, whereas in the pregroup the elements themselves have adjoints. The adjoint types are used to denote functions, e.g. that of a transitive verb with a subject and object as input and a sentence as output. In the pregroup setting, these function types are still denoted by adjoints, but this time they are the adjoints of the elements themselves.

As an example, consider the sentence "dogs chase cats". We assign the type n (for noun phrase) to "dog" and "cat", and $n^r s n^l$ to "chase", where n^r and n^l are the right and left adjoints of n, and s is the type of a (declarative) sentence. The type $n^r s n^l$ expresses the fact that the verb is a predicate that takes two arguments of type n as input, on its right and left, and outputs the type s of a sentence. The parsing of the sentence is the following reduction:

$$n\left(n^r s n^l\right)n \leq 1s1 = s$$

This parse is based on the cancellation of n and n^r, and also n^l and n; i.e. $nn^r \leq 1$ and $n^l n \leq 1$ for 1 the unit of juxtaposition. The reduction expresses the fact that the juxtapositions of the types of the words reduce to the type of a sentence.

On the semantic side, we assign the vector space N to the type n, and the tensor space $N \otimes S \otimes N$ to the type $n^r s n^l$. Recall that a basis vector of the tensor space $A \otimes B$ is a pair of basis vectors of A and B. Recall also that any vector can be expressed as a weighted sum of basis vectors; e.g. if $\{\overrightarrow{v_i}\}_i$ is a basis of A then any vector $\overrightarrow{a} \in A$ can be written as $\overrightarrow{a} = \sum_i C_i \overrightarrow{v_i}$ where the $C_i \in \mathbb{R}$ are weighting factors. Now for $\{\overrightarrow{v_i}\}_i$ a basis of A and $\{\overrightarrow{v_i'}\}_i$ a basis of B, a vector $\overrightarrow{c}$ in the tensor space $A \otimes B$ can be expressed as follows:

$$\sum_{ij} C_{ij}\left(\overrightarrow{v_i} \otimes \overrightarrow{v_j'}\right)$$

where the tensor of basis vectors $\overrightarrow{v_i} \otimes \overrightarrow{v_j'}$ stands for their pair $(\overrightarrow{v_i}, \overrightarrow{v_j'})$. In general $\overrightarrow{c}$ is not separable into the tensor of two vectors, except for the case when $\overrightarrow{c}$ is not *entangled*. For non-entangled vectors we can write $\overrightarrow{c} = \overrightarrow{a} \otimes \overrightarrow{b}$ for $\overrightarrow{a} = \sum_i C_i \overrightarrow{v_i}$ and $\overrightarrow{b} = \sum_j C_j' \overrightarrow{v_j'}$; hence the weighting factor of $\overrightarrow{c}$ can be obtained by simply multiplying the weights of its tensored counterparts, i.e. $C_{ij} = C_i \times C_j'$. In the entangled case these weights cannot be determined as such and range over all the possible weights. We take advantage of this fact to encode meanings of verbs, and in general all words that have compound types and are interpreted as predicates, relations, or functions. For a brief discussion, see the last paragraph of this section. Finally, we use the Dirac notation to denote the dot or inner product of two vectors $\langle \vec{a} \mid \vec{b} \rangle \in \mathbb{R}$ defined by $\sum_i C_i \times C_i'$.

Returning to our example, for the meanings of nouns we have $\overrightarrow{dogs}, \overrightarrow{cats} \in N$, and for the meanings of verbs we have $\overrightarrow{chase} \in N \otimes S \otimes N$, i.e. the following superposition:

$$\sum_{ijk} C_{ijk}(\vec{n_i} \otimes \vec{s_j} \otimes \vec{n_k})$$

Here $\vec{n_i}$ and $\vec{n_k}$ are basis vectors of N and $\vec{s_j}$ is a basis vector of S. From the categorical translation method presented in Coecke et al. (2010) and the grammatical reduction $n(n^r s n^l)n \leq s$, we obtain the following linear map as the categorical morphism corresponding to the reduction:

$$\epsilon_N \otimes 1_s \otimes \epsilon_N : N \otimes (N \otimes S \otimes N) \otimes N \to S$$

Using this map, the meaning of the sentence is computed as follows:

$$\overrightarrow{dogs\ chase\ cats} = (\epsilon_N \otimes 1_s \otimes \epsilon_N)(\overrightarrow{dogs} \otimes \overrightarrow{chase} \otimes \overrightarrow{cats})$$

$$= (\epsilon_N \otimes 1_s \otimes \epsilon_N)\left(\overrightarrow{dogs} \otimes \left(\sum_{ijk} C_{ijk}(\vec{n_i} \otimes \vec{s_j} \otimes \vec{n_k}) \right) \otimes \overrightarrow{cats} \right)$$

$$= \sum_{ijk} C_{ijk} \langle \overrightarrow{dogs} \mid \vec{n_i} \rangle \vec{s_j} \langle \vec{n_k} \mid \overrightarrow{cats} \rangle$$

There are two key features to this operation. First, that the inner-products reduce dimensionality by 'consuming' tensored vectors and by virtue of the following linear map:

$$\epsilon_N : N \otimes N \to \mathbb{R} :: \vec{a} \otimes \vec{b} \mapsto \langle \vec{a} \mid \vec{b} \rangle$$

Thus the image of $\epsilon_N \otimes 1_s \otimes \epsilon_N$ on the tensored vector $\overrightarrow{dogs} \otimes \overrightarrow{chase} \otimes \overrightarrow{cats}$ is a vector in a sentence space S which is common to all sentences regardless of their grammatical structure or complexity. Second, note that the tensor product $\overrightarrow{dogs} \otimes \overrightarrow{chase} \otimes \overrightarrow{cats}$ does not need to be calculated, since all that is required for computation of the sentence vector are the noun vectors and the C_{ijk} weights for the verb. Note also that the inner product operations are simply picking out basis vectors in the noun space, an operation that can be performed in constant time. Hence this formalism avoids two problems faced by approaches in the vein of Smolensky and Legendre (2005) or Clark and Pulman (2007), which use the tensor product as a composition operation. The first problem is that the sentence meaning space is high dimensional and grammatically different sentences which even have the same type of verb have representations with different dimensionalities, preventing them from being compared directly using inner products. The second problem is that the space complexity of the tensored representation grows exponentially with the length and grammatical complexity of the sentence. In contrast, the model we propose does not require the combination of the tensored vectors, e.g. $\overrightarrow{\text{dogs}} \otimes \overrightarrow{\text{chase}} \otimes \overrightarrow{\text{cats}}$, to be represented explicitly.

Note that we have taken the vector of the transitive verb, e.g. $\overrightarrow{\text{chase}}$, to be an entangled vector in the tensor space $N \otimes S \otimes N$. If this was a separable vector, the meaning of the verb would be as follows:

$$\overrightarrow{\text{chase}} = \sum_i C_i \overrightarrow{n_i} \otimes \sum_j C'_j \overrightarrow{s_j} \otimes \sum_k C''_k \overrightarrow{n_k}$$

The meaning of the sentence would then become

$$\overrightarrow{\text{dogs chase cats}} = \sum_i C_i \langle \overrightarrow{\text{dogs}} \mid \overrightarrow{n_i} \rangle \times \sum_k C''_k \langle \overrightarrow{n_k} \mid \overrightarrow{\text{cats}} \rangle \times \sum_j C'_j \overrightarrow{s_j}$$

The problem is that here there is no interaction between meanings of subject and object: the verb consists of three independent entities: a subject part $\sum_i C_i \overrightarrow{n_i}$ that acts on the subject to produce a real number $\sum_i C_i \langle \overrightarrow{\text{dogs}} \mid \overrightarrow{n_i} \rangle$, an object part $\sum_k C''_k \overrightarrow{n_k}$ that acts on the object to produce another real number $\sum_k C''_k \langle \overrightarrow{n_k} \mid \overrightarrow{\text{cats}} \rangle$, and a sentence part, which is a vector $\sum_j C'_j \overrightarrow{s_j}$ that has not acted on anything. Whereas in the non-entangled case, the vector meanings of subject and object do interact with each other via the C_{ijk} weights to produce a vector on the sentence basis $\overrightarrow{s_j}$.

3 From Truth-Theoretic to Corpus-Based Meaning

The model presented above is compositional and distributional, but still abstract. To make it concrete, N and S have to be constructed by providing a method for determining the C_{ijk} weightings. Coecke et al. (2010) show how a truth-theoretic meaning can be derived in the compositional framework. For example, assume that N is spanned by all animals and S is the two-dimensional space spanned by $\overrightarrow{\text{true}}$ and $\overrightarrow{\text{false}}$. We use the weighting factor to define a model-theoretic meaning for the verb as follows:

$$C_{ijk} \overrightarrow{s_j} = \begin{cases} \overrightarrow{\text{true}} & chase(\overrightarrow{n_i}, \overrightarrow{n_k}) = \text{true} \\ \overrightarrow{\text{false}} & o.w. \end{cases}$$

The definition of our meaning map ensures that this value propagates to the meaning of the whole sentence. So $chase(\overrightarrow{\text{dogs}}, \overrightarrow{\text{cats}})$ becomes true whenever "dogs chase cats" is true and false otherwise. This is exactly how meaning is computed in the model-theoretic view on semantics. One way to generalise this truth-theoretic meaning is to assume that $chase(\overrightarrow{n_i}, \overrightarrow{n_k})$ has degrees of truth, for instance by defining *chase* as a combination of *run* and *catch*, such as:

$$chase = \frac{2}{3}run + \frac{1}{3}catch$$

Again, the meaning map ensures that these degrees propagate to the meaning of the whole sentence. For a worked out example see Coecke et al. (2010). But neither of these examples provide a *distributional* sentence meaning.

Here we take a first step towards a corpus-based distributional model, by attempting to recover a meaning for a sentence based on the meanings of the words derived from a corpus. But crucially this meaning goes beyond just composing the meanings of words using a vector operator, such as tensor product, summation or multiplication (Mitchell and Lapata 2008). Our computation of sentence meaning treats some vectors as functions and others as function arguments, according to how the words in the sentence are typed, and uses the syntactic structure as a guide to determine how the functions are applied to their arguments. The intuition behind this approach is that *syntactic analysis guides semantic vector composition*.

The contribution of this chapter is to introduce some concrete constructions for a compositional distributional model of meaning. These constructions demonstrate how the mathematical model of Coecke et al. (2010) can be implemented in a concrete setting which introduces a richer, not necessarily truth-theoretic, notion of natural language semantics which is closer to the ideas underlying standard distributional models of word meaning. We leave full evaluation to future work, in order to determine whether the following method in conjunction with word vectors built from large corpora leads to improved results on language processing tasks, such as computing sentence similarity and paraphrase evaluation.

Nouns and Transitive Verbs   We take N to be a *structured vector space*, as in Erk and Padó (2008) and Grefenstette (1992). The basis elements of N are annotated by 'properties' obtained by combining dependency relations with nouns, verbs and adjectives. For example, basis vectors might be associated with properties such as "arg-fluffy", denoting the argument of the adjective fluffy, "subj-chase" denoting the subject of the verb chase, "obj-buy" denoting the object of the verb buy, and so on. We construct the vector for a noun by counting how many times in the corpus a word has been the argument of 'fluffy', the subject of 'chase', the object of 'buy', and so on.

The framework of Coecke et al. (2010) offers no guidance as to what the sentence space should be. Here we take the sentence space S to be $N \otimes N$, so its basis elements are of the form $\overrightarrow{s_j} = (\overrightarrow{n_i}, \overrightarrow{n_k})$. The intuition is that, for a transitive verb, the meaning of a sentence is determined by the meaning of the verb together with its subject and object.[1] The verb vectors $C_{ijk}(\overrightarrow{n_i}, \overrightarrow{n_k})$ are built by counting how many times a word that is n_i (e.g. has the property of being fluffy) has been subject of the verb and a word that is n_k (e.g. has the property that it is bought) has

---

[1]Intransitive and ditransitive verbs are interpreted in an analogous fashion; see Sect. 5.

been its object, where the counts are moderated by the extent to which the subject and object exemplify each property (e.g. *how fluffy* the subject is). To give a rough paraphrase of the intuition behind this approach, the meaning of "dog chases cat" is given by: the extent to which a dog is fluffy and a cat is something that is bought (for the $N \otimes N$ property pair "arg-fluffy" and "obj-buy"), and the extent to which fluffy things *chase* things that are bought (accounting for the meaning of the verb for this particular property pair); plus the extent to which a dog is something that runs and a cat is something that is cute (for the $N \otimes N$ pair "subj-run" and "arg-cute"), and the extent to which things that run *chase* things that are cute (accounting for the meaning of the verb for this particular property pair); and so on for all noun property pairs.

Adjective Phrases Adjectives are dealt with in a similar way. We give them the syntactic type nn^l and build their vectors in $N \otimes N$. The syntactic reduction $nn^l n \to n$ associated with applying an adjective to a noun gives us the map $1_N \otimes \epsilon_N$ by which we semantically compose an adjective with a noun, as follows:

$$\overrightarrow{\text{red fox}} = (1_N \otimes \epsilon_N)(\overrightarrow{\text{red}} \otimes \overrightarrow{\text{fox}}) = \sum_{ij} C_{ij} \overrightarrow{n_i} \langle \overrightarrow{n_j} \mid \overrightarrow{\text{fox}} \rangle$$

We can view the C_{ij} counts as determining what sorts of properties the arguments of a particular adjective typically have (e.g. arg-red, arg-colourful for the adjective "red").

Prepositional Phrases We assign the type $n^r n$ to the whole prepositional phrase (when it modifies a noun), for example to "in the forest" in the sentence "dogs chase cats in the forest". The pregroup parsing is as follows:

$$n(n^r sn^l)n(n^r n) \le 1sn^l 1n \le sn^l n \le s1 = s$$

The vector space corresponding to the prepositional phrase will thus be the tensor space $N \otimes N$ and the categorification of the parse will be the composition of two morphisms: $(1_S \otimes \epsilon_N^l) \circ (\epsilon_N^r \otimes 1_S \otimes 1_N \otimes \epsilon_N^r \otimes 1_N)$. The substitution specific to the prepositional phrase happens when computing the vector for "cats in the forest" as follows:

$$\overrightarrow{\text{cats in the forest}} = (\epsilon_N^r \otimes 1_N)(\overrightarrow{\text{cats}} \otimes \overrightarrow{\text{in the forest}})$$

$$= (\epsilon_N^r \otimes 1_N)\left(\overrightarrow{\text{cats}} \otimes \sum_{lw} C_{lw} \overrightarrow{n_l} \otimes \overrightarrow{n_k}\right)$$

$$= \sum_{lw} C_{lw} \langle \overrightarrow{\text{cats}} \mid \overrightarrow{n_l} \rangle \overrightarrow{n_w}$$

Here we set the weights C_{lw} in a similar manner to the cases of adjective phrases and verbs with the counts determining what sorts of properties the noun modified by the prepositional phrase has, e.g. the number of times something that has attribute n_l has been in the forest.

Adverbs We assign the type $s^r s$ to the adverb, for example to "quickly" in the sentence "Dogs chase cats quickly". The pregroup parsing is as follows:

$$n(n^r s n^l) n(s^r s) \leq 1s1s^r s = ss^r s \leq 1s = s$$

Its categorification will be a composition of two morphisms $(\epsilon^r_S \otimes 1_S) \circ (\epsilon^r_N \otimes 1_S \otimes \epsilon^l_N \otimes 1_S \otimes 1_S)$. The substitution specific to the adverb happens after computing the meaning of the sentence without it, i.e. that of "Dogs chase cats", and is as follows:

$$\overrightarrow{\text{Dogs chase cats quickly}}$$

$$= (\epsilon^r_S \otimes 1_S) \circ (\epsilon^r_N \otimes 1_S \otimes \epsilon^l_N \otimes 1_S \otimes 1_S)(\overrightarrow{\text{Dogs}} \otimes \overrightarrow{\text{chase}} \otimes \overrightarrow{\text{cats}} \otimes \overrightarrow{\text{quickly}})$$

$$= (\epsilon^r_S \otimes 1_S) \left(\sum_{ijk} C_{ijk} \langle \overrightarrow{\text{dogs}} \mid \overrightarrow{n_i} \rangle \overrightarrow{s_j} \langle \overrightarrow{n_k} \mid \overrightarrow{\text{cats}} \rangle \otimes \overrightarrow{\text{quickly}} \right)$$

$$= (\epsilon^r_S \otimes 1_S) \left(\sum_{ijk} C_{ijk} \langle \overrightarrow{\text{dogs}} \mid \overrightarrow{n_i} \rangle \overrightarrow{s_j} \langle \overrightarrow{n_k} \mid \overrightarrow{\text{cats}} \rangle \otimes \sum_{lw} C_{lw} \overrightarrow{s_l} \otimes \overrightarrow{s_w} \right)$$

$$= \sum_{lw} C_{lw} \left\langle \sum_{ijk} C_{ijk} \langle \overrightarrow{\text{dogs}} \mid \overrightarrow{n_i} \rangle \overrightarrow{s_j} \langle \overrightarrow{n_k} \mid \overrightarrow{\text{cats}} \rangle \mid \overrightarrow{s_l} \right\rangle \overrightarrow{s_k}$$

The C_{lw} weights are defined in a similar manner to the above cases, i.e. according to the properties the adverb has, e.g. which verbs it has modified. Note that now the basis vectors $\overrightarrow{s_l}$ and $\overrightarrow{s_w}$ are themselves pairs of basis vectors from the noun space, $(\overrightarrow{n_i}, \overrightarrow{n_j})$. Hence, $C_{lw}(\overrightarrow{n_i}, \overrightarrow{n_j})$ can be set only for the case when $l = i$ and $w = j$; these counts determine what sorts of properties the verbs that happen quickly have (or more specifically what properties the subjects and objects of such verbs have). By taking the whole sentence into account in the interpretation of the adverb, we are in a better position to semantically distinguish between the meaning of adverbs such as "slowly" and "quickly", for instance in terms of the properties that the verb's subjects have. For example, it is possible that elephants are more likely to be the subject of a verb which is happening slowly, e.g. run slowly, and cheetahs are more likely to be the subject of a verb which is happening quickly.

4 Concrete Computations

In this section we first describe how to obtain the relevant counts from a parsed corpus, and then give some similarity calculations for some example sentence pairs.

Let C_l be the set of grammatical relations (GRs) for sentence s_l in the corpus. Define $verbs(C_l)$ to be the function which returns all instances of verbs in C_l, and $subj$ (and similarly obj) to be the function which returns the subject of an instance

$V_{instance}$ of a verb V, for a particular set of GRs for a sentence:

$$subj(V_{instance}) = \begin{cases} noun & \text{if } V_{instance} \text{ is a verb with subject } noun \\ \varepsilon_n & o.w. \end{cases}$$

where ε_n is the empty string. The question of what is the vector of the empty string is left open for now. We propose an answer in Sect. 5, when we treat intransitive verbs as transitive verbs with an empty object.

We express C_{ijk} for a verb V as follows:

$$C_{ijk} = \begin{cases} \sum_l \sum_{v \in verbs(C_l)} \delta(v, V) \langle \overrightarrow{subj(v)} \mid \overrightarrow{n_i} \rangle \langle \overrightarrow{obj(v)} \mid \overrightarrow{n_k} \rangle & \text{if } \overrightarrow{s_j} = (\overrightarrow{n_i}, \overrightarrow{n_k}) \\ 0 & o.w. \end{cases}$$

where $\delta(v, V) = 1$ if $v = V$ and 0 otherwise. Thus we construct C_{ijk} for verb V only for cases where the subject property n_i and the object property n_k are paired in the basis $\overrightarrow{s_j}$. This is done by counting the number of times the subject of V has property n_i and the object of V has property n_k, then multiplying the respective values, as prescribed by the inner products (which simply pick out the properties n_i and n_k from the noun vectors for the subjects and objects).

The procedure for calculating the verb vectors, based on the formulation above, is as follows:

1. For each GR in a sentence, if the relation is *subject* and the head is a verb, then find the complementary GR with *object* as a relation and the same head verb. If none, set the object to ε_n.
2. Retrieve the noun vectors $\overrightarrow{subject}, \overrightarrow{object}$ for the subject dependent and object dependent from previously constructed noun vectors.
3. For each $(n_i, n_k) \in basis(N) \times basis(N)$ compute the inner-product of $\overrightarrow{n_i}$ with $\overrightarrow{subject}$ and $\overrightarrow{n_k}$ with $\overrightarrow{object}$ (which involves simply picking out the relevant basis vectors from the noun vectors). Multiply the inner-products and add this to C_{ijk} for the verb, with j such that $\overrightarrow{s_j} = (\overrightarrow{n_i}, \overrightarrow{n_k})$.

We now give a number of example calculations. We first manually define the distributions for nouns, which in practice would be obtained from a corpus:

	bankers	cats	dogs	stock	kittens
1. arg-fluffy	0	7	3	0	2
2. arg-ferocious	4	1	6	0	0
3. obj-buys	0	4	2	7	0
4. arg-shrewd	6	3	1	0	1
5. arg-valuable	0	1	2	8	0

We aim to make these counts match our intuitions, in that bankers are shrewd and a little ferocious but not furry, cats are furry but not typically valuable, and so on.

We also define the distributions for the transitive verbs 'chase', 'pursue' and 'sell', again manually specified according to our intuitions about how these verbs are used. Since in the formalism proposed above, $C_{ijk} = 0$ if $\overrightarrow{s_j} \neq (\overrightarrow{n_i}, \overrightarrow{n_k})$, we can simplify the weight matrices for transitive verbs to two dimensional C_{ik} matrices as shown below, where C_{ik} corresponds to the number of times the verb has a subject with attribute n_i and an object with attribute n_k. For example, the matrix below encodes the fact that something ferocious ($i = 2$) chases something fluffy ($k = 1$) seven times in the hypothetical corpus from which we might have obtained these distributions.

$$C^{\text{chase}} = \begin{bmatrix} 1 & 0 & 0 & 0 & 0 \\ 7 & 1 & 2 & 3 & 1 \\ 0 & 0 & 0 & 0 & 0 \\ 2 & 0 & 1 & 0 & 1 \\ 1 & 0 & 0 & 0 & 0 \end{bmatrix} \qquad C^{\text{pursue}} = \begin{bmatrix} 0 & 0 & 0 & 0 & 0 \\ 4 & 2 & 2 & 2 & 4 \\ 0 & 0 & 0 & 0 & 0 \\ 3 & 0 & 2 & 0 & 1 \\ 0 & 0 & 0 & 0 & 0 \end{bmatrix}$$

$$C^{\text{sell}} = \begin{bmatrix} 0 & 0 & 0 & 0 & 0 \\ 0 & 0 & 3 & 0 & 4 \\ 0 & 0 & 0 & 0 & 0 \\ 0 & 0 & 5 & 0 & 8 \\ 0 & 0 & 1 & 0 & 1 \end{bmatrix}$$

These matrices can be used to perform sentence comparisons:

$$\langle \overrightarrow{\text{dogs chase cats}} \mid \overrightarrow{\text{dogs pursue kittens}} \rangle$$

$$= \left\langle \left(\sum_{ijk} C_{ijk}^{\text{chase}} \langle \overrightarrow{\text{dogs}} \mid \overrightarrow{n_i} \rangle \overrightarrow{s_j} \langle \overrightarrow{n_k} \mid \overrightarrow{\text{cats}} \rangle \right) \,\Big|\, \left(\sum_{ijk} C_{ijk}^{\text{pursue}} \langle \overrightarrow{\text{dogs}} \mid \overrightarrow{n_i} \rangle \overrightarrow{s_j} \langle \overrightarrow{n_k} \mid \overrightarrow{\text{kittens}} \rangle \right) \right\rangle$$

$$= \sum_{ijk} C_{ijk}^{\text{chase}} C_{ijk}^{\text{pursue}} \langle \overrightarrow{\text{dogs}} \mid \overrightarrow{n_i} \rangle \langle \overrightarrow{\text{dogs}} \mid \overrightarrow{n_i} \rangle \langle \overrightarrow{n_k} \mid \overrightarrow{\text{cats}} \rangle \langle \overrightarrow{n_k} \mid \overrightarrow{\text{kittens}} \rangle$$

The raw number obtained from the above calculation is 14844. Normalising it by the product of the length of both sentence vectors gives the cosine value of 0.979.

Consider now the sentence comparison $\langle \overrightarrow{\text{dogs chase cats}} \mid \overrightarrow{\text{cats chase dogs}} \rangle$. The sentences in this pair contain the same words but the different word orders give the sentences very different meanings. The raw number calculated from this inner product is 7341, and its normalised cosine measure is 0.656, which demonstrates the sharp drop in similarity obtained from changing sentence structure. We expect some similarity since there is some non-trivial overlap between the properties identifying cats and those identifying dogs (namely those salient to the act of chasing).

Our final example for transitive sentences is $\langle \overrightarrow{\text{dogs chase cats}} \mid \overrightarrow{\text{bankers sell stock}} \rangle$, as two sentences that diverge in meaning completely. The raw number for this inner product is 6024, and its cosine measure is 0.042, demonstrating the very low semantic similarity between these two sentences.

Next we consider some examples involving adjective-noun modification. The C_{ij} counts for an adjective A are obtained in a similar manner to transitive or intransitive verbs:

$$C_{ij} = \begin{cases} \sum_l \sum_{a \in adjs(C_l)} \delta(a, A) \langle \overrightarrow{arg\text{-}of(a)} \mid \overrightarrow{n_i} \rangle & \text{if } \overrightarrow{n_i} = \overrightarrow{n_j} \\ 0 & o.w. \end{cases}$$

where $adjs(C_l)$ returns all instances of adjectives in C_l; $\delta(a, A) = 1$ if $a = A$ and 0 otherwise; and $arg\text{-}of(a) = noun$ if a is an adjective with argument $noun$, and ε_n otherwise.

As before, we stipulate the C_{ij} matrices by hand (and we eliminate all cases where $i \neq j$ since $C_{ij} = 0$ by definition in such cases):

$$C^{\text{fluffy}} = [9\ 3\ 4\ 2\ 2] \qquad C^{\text{shrewd}} = [0\ 3\ 1\ 9\ 1] \qquad C^{\text{valuable}} = [3\ 0\ 8\ 1\ 8]$$

We compute vectors for "fluffy dog" as follows:

$$\overrightarrow{\text{fluffy dog}} = (3 \cdot 9)\ \overrightarrow{\text{arg-fluffy}} + (6 \cdot 3)\ \overrightarrow{\text{arg-ferocious}} + (2 \cdot 4)\ \overrightarrow{\text{obj-buys}}$$
$$+ (5 \cdot 2)\ \overrightarrow{\text{arg-shrewd}} + (2 \cdot 2)\ \overrightarrow{\text{arg-valuable}}$$

and "shrewd banker" as follows:

$$\overrightarrow{\text{shrewd banker}} = (0 \cdot 0)\ \overrightarrow{\text{arg-fluffy}} + (4 \cdot 3)\ \overrightarrow{\text{arg-ferocious}} + (0 \cdot 0)\ \overrightarrow{\text{obj-buys}}$$
$$+ (6 \cdot 9)\ \overrightarrow{\text{arg-shrewd}} + (0 \cdot 1)\ \overrightarrow{\text{arg-valuable}}$$

Vectors for $\overrightarrow{\text{fluffy cat}}$ and $\overrightarrow{\text{valuable stock}}$ are computed similarly. We obtain the following similarity measures:

$$cosine(\overrightarrow{\text{fluffy dog}},\ \overrightarrow{\text{shrewd banker}}) = 0.389$$

$$cosine(\overrightarrow{\text{fluffy cat}},\ \overrightarrow{\text{valuable stock}}) = 0.184$$

These calculations carry over to sentences which contain the adjective-noun pairings compositionally and we obtain an even lower similarity measure between sentences with dissimilar meanings:

$$cosine(\overrightarrow{\text{fluffy dogs chase fluffy cats}},\ \overrightarrow{\text{shrewd bankers sell valuable stock}}) = 0.016$$

To summarise, our example vectors provide us with the following similarity measures:

Sentence 1	Sentence 2	Degree of similarity
dogs chase cats	dogs pursue kittens	0.979
dogs chase cats	cats chase dogs	0.656
dogs chase cats	bankers sell stock	0.042
fluffy dogs chase fluffy cats	shrewd bankers sell valuable stock	0.016

5 Different Grammatical Structures

So far we have only presented the treatment of sentences with transitive verbs. For sentences with intransitive verbs, it suffices for the sentence space to be just N. To compare the meaning of a transitive sentence with an intransitive one, we embed the meaning of the latter from N into the former $N \otimes N$, by taking $\overrightarrow{\varepsilon_n}$ (the 'object' of an intransitive verb) to be $\sum_i \overrightarrow{n_i}$, i.e. the sum of all basis vectors of N.

Following the method for the transitive verb, we calculate C_{ijk} for an intransitive verb V and basis pair $\overrightarrow{s_j} = (\overrightarrow{n_i}, \overrightarrow{n_k})$ as follows, where l ranges over the sentences in the corpus:

$$\sum_l \sum_{v \in verbs(C_l)} \delta(v, V) \langle \overrightarrow{subj(v)} \mid \overrightarrow{n_i} \rangle \langle \overrightarrow{obj(v)} \mid \overrightarrow{n_k} \rangle$$

$$= \sum_l \sum_{v \in verbs(C_l)} \delta(v, V) \langle \overrightarrow{subj(v)} \mid \overrightarrow{n_i} \rangle \langle \overrightarrow{\varepsilon_n} \mid \overrightarrow{n_k} \rangle$$

and $\langle \overrightarrow{\varepsilon_n} \mid \overrightarrow{n_i} \rangle = 1$ for any basis vector n_i.

We can now compare the meanings of transitive and intransitive sentences by taking the inner product of their meanings (despite the different arities of the verbs) and then normalising by vector length to obtain the cosine measure. For example:

$$\langle \overrightarrow{dogs\ chase\ cats} \mid \overrightarrow{dogs\ chase} \rangle$$

$$= \left\langle \left(\sum_{ijk} C_{ijk} \langle \overrightarrow{dogs} \mid \overrightarrow{n_i} \rangle \overrightarrow{s_j} \langle \overrightarrow{n_k} \mid \overrightarrow{cats} \rangle \right) \mid \left(\sum_{ijk} C'_{ijk} \langle \overrightarrow{dogs} \mid \overrightarrow{n_i} \rangle \overrightarrow{s_j} \right) \right\rangle$$

$$= \sum_{ijk} C_{ijk} C'_{ijk} \langle \overrightarrow{dogs} \mid \overrightarrow{n_i} \rangle \langle \overrightarrow{dogs} \mid \overrightarrow{n_i} \rangle \langle \overrightarrow{n_k} \mid \overrightarrow{cats} \rangle$$

The raw number for the inner product is 14092 and its normalised cosine measure is 0.961, indicating high similarity (but some difference) between a sentence with a transitive verb and one where the subject remains the same, but the verb is used intransitively.

Comparing sentences containing nouns modified by adjectives to sentences with unmodified nouns is straightforward:

$$\langle \overrightarrow{fluffy\ dogs\ chase\ fluffy\ cats} \mid \overrightarrow{dogs\ chase\ cats} \rangle$$

$$= \sum_{ij} C_i^{fluffy} C_j^{fluffy} C_{ij}^{chase} C_{ij}^{chase} \langle \overrightarrow{dogs} \mid \overrightarrow{n_i} \rangle^2 \langle \overrightarrow{n_j} \mid \overrightarrow{cats} \rangle^2$$

$$= 2437005$$

From the above we obtain the following similarity measure:

$$cosine(\overrightarrow{fluffy\ dogs\ chase\ fluffy\ cats}, \overrightarrow{dogs\ chase\ cats}) = 0.971$$

For sentences with ditransitive verbs, the sentence space changes to $N \otimes N \otimes N$, on the basis of the verb needing two objects; hence its grammatical type changes to $n^r s n^l n^l$. The transitive and intransitive verbs are embedded in this larger space in a similar manner to that described above; hence comparison of their meanings becomes possible.

6 Ambiguous Words

The two different meanings of a word can be distinguished by the different properties that they have. These properties are reflected in the corpus, by the different contexts in which the words appear. Consider the following example from Erk and Padó (2008): the verb "catch" has two different meanings, "grab" and "contract". They are reflected in the two sentences "catch a ball" and "catch a disease". The compositional aspect of our meaning computation enables us to realise the different properties of the context words via the grammatical roles they take in the corpus. For instance, the word 'ball' occurs as argument of 'round', and so has a high weight for the base 'arg-round', whereas the word 'disease' has a high weight for the base 'arg-contagious' and as 'mod-of-heart'. We extend our example corpus from previously to reflect these differences as follows:

	ball	disease
1. arg-fluffy	1	0
2. arg-ferocious	0	0
3. obj-buys	5	0
4. arg-shrewd	0	0
5. arg-valuable	1	0
6. arg-round	8	0
7. arg-contagious	0	7
8. mod-of-heart	0	6

In a similar way, we build a matrix for the verb 'catch' as follows:

$$
C^{catch} = \begin{bmatrix}
3 & 2 & 3 & 3 & 3 & 8 & 6 & 2 \\
3 & 2 & 3 & 0 & 1 & 4 & 7 & 4 \\
2 & 4 & 7 & 1 & 1 & 6 & 2 & 2 \\
3 & 1 & 2 & 0 & 0 & 3 & 6 & 2 \\
1 & 1 & 1 & 0 & 0 & 2 & 0 & 1 \\
0 & 0 & 0 & 0 & 0 & 0 & 0 & 0 \\
0 & 0 & 0 & 0 & 0 & 0 & 0 & 0 \\
0 & 0 & 0 & 0 & 0 & 0 & 0 & 0
\end{bmatrix}
$$

The last three rows are zero because we have assumed that the words that can take these roles are mostly inanimate objects and hence cannot catch anything. Given these values, we compute the similarity measure between the two sentences "dogs catch a ball" and "dogs catch a disease" as follows:

$$\langle \overrightarrow{\text{dogs catch a ball}} \mid \overrightarrow{\text{dogs catch a disease}} \rangle = 0$$

In an idealised case like this where there is very little (or no) overlap between the properties of the objects associated with one sense of "catch" (e.g. a disease), and those properties of the objects associated with another sense (e.g. a ball), disambiguation is perfect in that there is no similarity between the resulting phrases. In practice, in richer vector spaces, we would expect even diseases and balls to share some properties. However, as long as those shared properties are not those typically held by the object of catch, and as long as the usages of catch play to distinctive properties of diseases and balls, disambiguation will occur by the same mechanism as the idealised case above, and we can expect low similarity measures between such sentences.

7 Related Work

Mitchell and Lapata introduce and evaluate a multiplicative model for vector composition (Mitchell and Lapata 2008). The particular concrete construction of this chapter differs from that of Mitchell and Lapata (2008) in that our framework subsumes truth-theoretic as well as corpus-based meaning, and our meaning construction relies on and is guided by the grammatical structure of the sentence. The approach of Erk and Padó (2008) is more in the spirit of ours, in that extra information about syntax is used to compose meaning. Similar to us, they use a structured vector space to integrate lexical information with selectional preferences. Finally, Baroni and Zamparelli (2010) model adjective-noun combinations by treating an adjective as a function from noun space to noun space, represented using a matrix, as we do in this chapter.

References

Baroni, M., & Zamparelli, R. (2010). Nouns are vectors, adjectives are matrices: Representing adjective-noun constructions in semantic space. In *Conference on empirical methods in natural language processing* (EMNLP-10), Cambridge.

Clark, S., & Pulman, S. (2007). Combining symbolic and distributional models of meaning. In *Proceedings of AAAI spring symposium on quantum interaction*. Menlo Park: AAAI Press.

Coecke, B., Sadrzadeh, M., & Clark, S. (2010). Mathematical foundations for a compositional distributional model of meaning. *Linguistic Analysis, 36*, 345–384 (Lambek Festschrift). arXiv:1003.4394v1 [cs.CL].

Erk, K., & Padó, S. (2008). A structured vector space model for word meaning in context. In *Conference on empirical methods in natural language processing* (EMNLP-08), Honolulu, Hawaii (pp. 897–906).

Firth, J. (1957). *Papers in linguistics, 1934–1951*. London: Oxford University Press.

Frege, G. (1892). Über Sinn und Bedeutung. *Zeitschrift fuer Philosophie un philosophische Kritik, 100*, 25–50.

Grefenstette, G. (1992). Use of syntactic context to produce term association lists for text retrieval. In N. J. Belkin, P. Ingwersen, & A. M. Pejtersen (Eds.), *SIGIR* (pp. 89–97). New York: ACM.

Grefenstette, G. (1994). *Explorations in automatic thesaurus discovery*. Boston: Kluwer Academic.

Harris, Z. (1968). *Mathematical structures of language*. New York: Wiley-Interscience.

Jurafsky, D., & Martin, J. H. (2000). *Speech and language processing: An introduction to natural language processing, computational linguistics, and speech recognition*. New York: Prentice Hall.

Lambek, J. (2008). *From word to sentence*. Monza: Polimetrica.

Landauer, T., & Dumais, S. (1997). A solution to Plato's problem: The latent semantic analysis theory of acquisition, induction, and representation of knowledge. *Psychological Review, 104*(2), 211–240.

Manning, C., Raghavan, P., & Schutze, H. (2008). *Introduction to information retrieval* (Vol. 1). Cambridge: Cambridge University Press.

Mitchell, J., & Lapata, M. (2008). Vector-based models of semantic composition. In *Proceedings of the 46th annual meeting of the association for computational linguistics*, Columbus (pp. 236–244).

Montague, R. (1970). English as a formal language. In *Linguaggi nella societae nella tecnica* (pp. 189–224).

Schuetze, H. (1998). Automatic word sense discrimination. *Computational Linguistics, 24*(1), 97–123.

Smolensky, P., & Legendre, G. (2005). *The harmonic mind: From neural computation to optimality-theoretic grammar. Vol. I: Cognitive architecture. Vol. II: Linguistic and philosophical implications*. Cambridge: MIT Press.

Widdows, D. (2004). *Geometry and meaning*. Stanford: CSLI.

Wittgenstein, L. (1953). *Philosophical investigations* (trans: Anscombe, G. E. M.). Oxford: Blackwell Sci.

Part II
Inference and Understanding

Recognizing Textual Entailment
and Computational Semantics

Johan Bos

Abstract Recognizing textual entailment (RTE)—deciding whether one piece of text contains new information with respect to another piece of text—remains a big challenge in natural language processing. One attempt to deal with this problem is combining deep semantic analysis and logical inference, as is done in the Nutcracker RTE system. In doing so, various obstacles will be met on the way: robust semantic analysis, designing interfaces to state-of-the-art theorem provers, and acquiring relevant background knowledge. The coverage of the parser and semantic analysis component is high, yet performance on RTE examples yields high precision but low recall. An empirical study of Nutcracker's output reveals that the true positives are caused by sophisticated linguistic analysis such as coordination, active-passive alternation, pronoun resolution and relative clauses; the small set of false positives are caused by insufficient syntactic and semantic analyses. But most importantly, the false negatives are produced mainly by lack of background knowledge that is only implicit in the RTE examples.

1 Introduction

Textual entailment has long been used as an illustrational device in formal semantics to show or convince scholars that certain natural language inferences hold or don't (as in popular textbooks such as Gamut 1991; Heim and Kratzer 1998, and Chierchia and McConnell-Ginet 1991). This has merely been a theoretical exercise, until the introduction of recognizing textual entailment (RTE) as a shared task in the area of natural language processing Dagan et al. (2006) in 2005, even though the idea of the computational variant was aired much earlier (Cooper et al. 1996; Monz and de Rijke 2001). The RTE challenge consists of predicting whether one (short) text entails another (short) text. The RTE data-sets are a collection of such text–hypothesis pairs, labelled with a gold standard tag. Here are two such examples, one labelled as

J. Bos (✉)
Center for Language and Cognition (CLCG), University of Groningen, Groningen,
The Netherlands
e-mail: johan.bos@rug.nl

H. Bunt et al. (eds.), *Computing Meaning*, Text, Speech and Language Technology 47,
DOI 10.1007/978-94-007-7284-7_6,
© Springer Science+Business Media Dordrecht 2014

FALSE (no entailment, i.e. hypothesis H contains new information with respect to text T), and one labelled as TRUE (entailment, i.e. no new information in H given T):

Example 1: FALSE
T: I recently took a round trip from Abuja to Yola, the capital of Adamawa State and back to Abuja, with a fourteen-seater bus.
H: Abuja is located in Adamawa State.

Example 2: TRUE
T: Bountiful arrived after war's end, sailing into San Francisco Bay 21 August 1945. Bountiful was then assigned as hospital ship at Yokosuka, Japan, departing San Francisco 1 November 1945.
H: Bountiful reached San Francisco in August 1945.

It soon became clear that RTE is an extremely difficult task: simple baseline systems based on textual surface features are hard to outperform by more sophisticated systems. Not only does one need a robust and accurate analysis of text, also the use of external resources to inform the inference process are essential.

Various approaches to RTE have been proposed, ranging from surface-oriented techniques to methods using sophisticated semantic analysis. This focus of this chapter is on a method belonging in the latter category, namely determining textual inferences on the basis of logical inference. The idea is simple and rooted in the formal approaches to natural language semantics mentioned before: we translate the texts into logical formulas, and then use (classical) logical inference to find out whether T entails H, whether T and H are consistent or contradictory, and so on.

Even though the idea itself is simple in theory, its practical execution isn't. In this chapter I describe a framework and implementation for textual inference based on first-order logic and formal theory. It comprises a system for RTE, Nutcracker, developed by myself over the years since the start of the RTE challenge (Bos and Markert 2005) and has been briefly described by others in a wider context (Balduccini et al. 2008), but never been the subject of publication itself. The aim is to find an answer to the question whether there is a significant role for computational semantics to play in the current state of RTE. From this "big" question several smaller questions arise, that are probably easier to answer, and I will concentrate on these first:

1. Can we use deep semantic analysis and logical inference, or are we lacking coverage?
2. Are the RTE data-sets suitable for black-box testing of systems claiming to performing natural language understanding?
3. And finally, given the knowledge that RTE is a hard (and yet unsolved) problem: can we identify a bottleneck—is it in semantic analysis, selecting background knowledge, or in theorem proving?

This chapter is organized as follows. First the framework and implementation of the logical approach to RTE, is presented in Sect. 2. This includes syntactic and semantic analysis, with a description of the parser (based on categorial grammar) and

```
                                                 El            Salvador
                                                 ------[lex] ---[lex]
                                                 n:nam/n:nam n:nam
                                                 ----------------[>]
                          a        crisis in            n:nam
                          ---[lex] --[lex] -----[lex] ----------------[*]
Alfredo     Cristiani     np/n:nom n:nom  (np\np)/np np
------[lex] ----[lex]     ------------[>] ------------------------[>]
n:nam/n:nam n:nam  caused np              np\np
----------------[>] --------[lex] ------------------------------------------[<]
n:nam              (s:dcl\np)/np np
----------------[*] ------------------------------------------------------[>]
np                 s:dcl\np
------------------------------------------------------------------------[<] ------[lex]
s:dcl                                                                        s:dcl\s:dcl
------------------------------------------------------------------------------------[<]
s:dcl
```

Fig. 1 Output of the C&C parser, a CCG derivation, as displayed by Boxer

the semantic interpretation component (Boxer, implementing a version of Discourse Representation Theory), and the use of off-the-shelf theorem provers to perform inferences on the textual analyses of RTE examples. In Sect. 3 I look critically at the performance of the logical approach to RTE, and show where it acts well and on what examples it fails to deliver the goods.

2 The Logical Method

2.1 Robust Semantic Analysis

With "semantic analysis" I mean the process of mapping text into logical formula. Traditionally, this is performed by a syntactic analysis (with the help of a parser) followed by a semantic analysis that produces a logical form based on the output of the syntactic parser. For the purposes of RTE based on logical inference, the linguistic analysis needs to be reasonably sophisticated and at the same time offer large coverage. It needs to be sophisticated in analysis because a shallow analysis would not support the logical inferences that need to be drawn and hence sacrifice precision in performance. It needs to be robust and offer large coverage to achieve a high recall in performance. As a practical rule of thumb, the loss in coverage should still outweigh the gain in performance using deep linguistic analysis.

Nowadays there are several (statistical) parsers available that offer broad coverage syntactic analysis on news-wire texts. The parser of our choice, the C&C parser (Clark and Curran 2004), combines speed and robustness with detailed syntactic analyses in the form of derivations of combinatory categorial grammar (Fig. 1).

Categorial grammar offers a principled way to construct formal meaning representations with the help of the λ-calculus. In a nutshell, it works as follows. Each basic syntactic category is associated with a basic semantic type, and using the recursive definition of categories and types, this also fixes the semantic types of complex syntactic categories. This results in a strongly lexically-driven approach, where only the semantic representations have to be provided for the lexical categories. Function application will take care of the rest and produce meaning representations for phrases beyond the token level and eventually for the entire sentence.

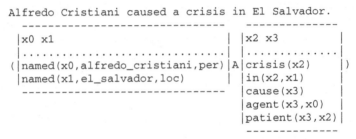

Fig. 2 Boxer output for a simple text, a DRS (Discourse Representation Structure)

As for choice of meaning representation language, it needs to be something that supports logical inference as well as adequately describe natural language meaning. There is an uneasy and unsolved tension here between expressiveness on the one hand and efficiency on the other. The formalisms proposed by linguists and philosophers are usually not computationally attractive—most of them exceed the expressive power of first-order logic, and theorem proving for first-order logic is already undecidable (more precisely, first-order logic is known to be *semi-decidable* (Blackburn and Bos 2005)). Yet, there are powerful theorem provers for first-order logic available developed by the automated deduction research community, and it seems a good compromising choice as language to perform logical inference given the current state-of-the-art.

However, we won't use standard first-order formula syntax, but adopt a variant of Discourse Representation Theory's DRSs, Discourse Representation Structures, graphically visualized as boxes (Fig. 2). DRT (Kamp and Reyle 1993) offers a way to deal with many linguistic phenomena in a principled way, including quantifiers, pronouns, presupposition and events. Diverging slightly from standard DRT, I adopt a neo-Davidsonian way for describing events (rather than the Davidsonian approach employed in classical DRT), because this results in a lower number of background knowledge rules (meaning postulates) required to draw correct inferences. Turning to implementation, the meaning representations are produced by the semantic parser Boxer (Bos 2008), which works on the output of the aforementioned C&C parser.

Boxer performs pronoun resolution, presupposition projection, thematic role labelling and assigns scope to quantifiers, negation and modal operators. It produces one semantic representations for each input, and its logical form is fully disambiguated. Note that semantic underspecification, a technique to pack several meanings into one compact representation, isn't a feasible option here, as it remains unclear how theorem provers would work with underspecified representations.

2.2 Applying Theorem Proving

In the previous section I showed how to produce a DRS for a text and hypothesis of a pair of the RTE data-set. The next step involves translating these DRSs into formulas of first-order logic, and pass on the result in a suitable way to a theorem prover. If the theorem prover then succeeds in finding a proof, we predict an entailment for this RTE pair. However, the standard translation from DRS to FOL (Muskens 1996; Kamp and Reyle 1993) gives wrong predictions to RTE problems because it doesn't take modalities and embedded propositions into account. The standard translation, for instance, would predict an entailment for the following example pair:

Example 3: FALSE
T: Leakey believed Kenya's wildlife, which underpins a tourist industry worth Dollars 450m a year, could be managed in a profitable and sustainable manner.
H: Kenya's wildlife is managed in a profitable manner.

Why is this? In the standard translation, it is impossible to connect the embedded proposition to a belief report (or other propositional attitude) or modal operator, because first-order terms can't be formulas. The modal translation, that I adopt, is based on a technique called reification. It translates a basic DRS condition with n terms into a first-order formula with $n + 1$ arguments, where the added term is a first-order variable ranging over entities. (I won't give the full translation from DRSs to modal FOL here for reasons of space, but instead refer the interested reader to Bos 2004.) One might want to refer to these entities as "possible worlds", "situations", or simply "propositions". Whatever you call them, this way it is possible to connect embedded propositions to attitudinal nouns and verbs or modal operators, and therefore prevents unwanted entailments such as in the example above. In cases with factive constructions (as in the sentence "Bill knows that Mary smokes" or "the fact that Mary smokes"), meaning postulates could specify the project content of the embedded clause to be interpreted as if it were in the main clause.

Theorem proving doesn't just play the role for checking entailment between T and H. We also need to check whether T and H are logically consistent. This is necessary because otherwise we might predict incorrect entailments. If T is inconsistent, anything would follow from that. Logically speaking that would be sound, but for natural language entailment this is (perhaps) an unwanted result. If H is inconsistent, then checking whether T entails H would boil down to checking whether T is consistent. Again, this is something we should be able to detect. And finally, if T and H taken together are inconsistent, then clearly T does not entail H (in fact, H is very informative in such a case!).

This brings us to the basic algorithm for applying first-order theorem proving to an RTE example with text T and hypothesis H. For convenience, we write X' to designate the FOL translation of natural language text X, derived from a DRS produced for X. The Boolean function *proof* has as input a formula, and returns true if it finds a proof (given certain time and space constraints), false otherwise. Figure 3 shows all the steps of the algorithm.

Note that in Fig. 3 we check for the consistency of a formula ϕ by trying to prove its negation—if we manage to do so, $\neg \phi$ is a theorem, and therefore ϕ has no model, in other words is inconsistent. Steps 1 and 2 apply to cases where—for whatever reason—the text or hypothesis is inconsistent itself. There isn't much point

```
IF proof(not(T')) THEN                           % STEP 1
    OUTPUT "unknown"
ELSE
    IF proof(not(H')) THEN                       % STEP 2
        OUTPUT "unknown"
    ELSE
        IF proof(not(and(T,H))) THEN             % STEP 3
            OUTPUT "informative"
        ELSE
            IF proof(not(and(T,not(H)))) THEN    % STEP 4
                OUTPUT "entailment"
            ELSE
                OUTPUT "informative"             % STEP 5
            ENDIF
        ENDIF
    ENDIF
ENDIF
```

Fig. 3 Core of the Nutcracker algorithm for recognizing textual entailment

to continue at this stage. Step 3 checks for a contradiction between T and H. If this is the case, there is no entailment. Step 4 is the moment of truth: the check whether T entails H, and applies only when both T and H are consistent. If a proof is found, then entailment is reported for this pair. Step 5, finally, is a fallback clause in case no proof was found in previous steps of the algorithm.

Any theorem prover for first-order logic could be used in theory. In practice, there is quite a lot of choice, thanks to the active area of automated deduction that offers various efficient state-of-the-art provers for research purposes, and a lot of variation in performance, too. The theorem prover used in our experiments reported later in this chapter is Vampire (Riazanov and Voronkov 2002), the currently highest ranked prover in CASC, the annual competition for inference engines (Sutcliffe and Suttner 2006). In addition to a theorem prover, we use the model builder Paradox to find counter models (Claessen and Sörensson 2003). Following Blackburn and Bos (2005), for each inference problem called in Fig. 3 the theorem prover and model builder work in parallel, where the model builder gets the negated input of the theorem prover. If a proof is found for problem $\neg\phi$, the model builder is halted because it would never be able to find a model for ϕ—if a model is found for ϕ, the theorem prover is halted because it would never be able to find a proof for $\neg\phi$.

The model builder searches for models up to a specified domain size n, and terminates if it can't construct a model for sizes $1 - n$. In theory, because first-order logic is semi-decidable, this setting always terminates with one of three results: (i) proof found, (ii) no proof found but finite countermodel constructed with domain size n, or (iii) no proof and no model for size n (for instance for inputs that have non-finite models). Case (i) succeeds if we give enough resources (time and space) to the theorem prover, but in practice we use a time-out. For case (ii) by specifying the maximum domain size as high as possible while maintaining reasonable response times. Case (iii) is one that we wish to avoid in practice.

Table 1 Coverage of the C&C parser and Boxer on RTE examples

Data-set	Pairs	Semantics	Coverage
RTE–2 dev	800	784	98.0 %
RTE–2 test	800	782	97.8 %
RTE–3 dev	800	780	97.5 %
RTE–3 test	800	786	98.3 %
Total	3,200	3,132	97.9 %

Table 2 Proofs found on RTE-2 and RTE-3 (3,132 pairs)

Data-set	Proofs	Precision	Recall
RTE-2 Dev	13	100 %	3.3 %
RTE-2 Test	14	86 %	3.0 %
RTE-3 Dev	14	93 %	3.3 %
RTE-3 Test	13	77 %	2.8 %

2.3 Implementation and Results

The approach to RTE as described above is implemented as the Nutcracker RTE system.[1] Nutcracker is basically a wrapper around a pipeline of NLP components, comprising a tokeniser, POS tagger, lemmatiser (Minnen et al. 2001) and named entity recognizer, followed by the C&C parser and Boxer. Nutcracker further coordinates the communication with the external theorem provers and model builders as designed in Fig. 3.

Coming back to one of the key questions posed at the beginning of this chapter, what is the coverage and quality of our NLP pipeline on RTE examples, and is it good enough? The coverage of the pipeline on RTE examples is shown in Table 1, from which we can conclude that the coverage for producing semantic representations is high (around 98 %), and therefore suitable for a task such as RTE, assuming we can recover from the loss of 2 % in recall by achieving a high precision. However, even though producing semantic representations in a robust way is a good start for performing well on the RTE task, it is merely a single step in the NLP pipeline. The ultimate success depends on the number and accuracy of the proofs that are found. As Table 2 shows in terms of precision and recall, the accuracy of proofs is high, but the number of proofs is very low.

As it stands, using simply logical inference would just about outperform the simplest baseline (flipping a coin, assuming an equal distribution between the TRUE and FALSE entailment pairs in the data-set, which is usually the case in RTE exercises). As a matter of fact, the Nutcracker system employs a slightly more sophisticated baseline system based on word overlap in the cases where it fails to find a

---

[1] The source code of the system can be downloaded via the website of the C&C tools Curran et al. (2007).

proof, a baseline that performs remarkably well. In the next section we try to find out why precision is not 100 %, explain why recall is low, and make suggestions for how to improve on this.

3 A Critical Evaluation of Performance

RTE is measured in terms of recall (how many instances of the total given to a system are correctly predicted) and precision (how many instances attempted by a system are correctly predicted). RTE systems based on logical inference tend to be low in recall and high in precision. Why is this so? In this section we would like to find an answer by inspecting the output of Nutcracker on the RTE-2 and RTE-3 data-sets.

The logical approach to RTE assumes there is no entailment for an T–H pair unless a proof is found. However, not every proof corresponds to an entailment in the RTE data-set, and not every entailment in the RTE data-set triggers a proof. Hence, we can evaluate and verify the performance of the system by dividing the data into four classes:

1. true positives (proofs found for an entailment);
2. false positives (proofs found for a non-entailment);
3. true negatives (no proof found for a non-entailment);
4. false negatives (no proof found for an entailment).

A moment of reflection informs us that it is not very interesting to discuss the true negatives, because, in a way, this can be viewed as a default behaviour of the system. It is however interesting to have a closer look at the remaining three classes of system output, and we will do so here.

3.1 Proofs Found for Entailment Pairs (True Positives)

In this class we can distinguish several semantic phenomena whose analyses in DRT correctly predict entailments. I will group them into various categories: conjunction elimination, coordination, active-passive altnernation, pronoun resolution, relative clauses, appositives, and control constructions.

3.1.1 Conjunction Elimination

The largest set of true positives is caught by conjunction elimination, a basic inference rule that says that from a conjunctive statement $\phi \wedge \psi$ one can infer ϕ and ψ. We encountered thirteen cases that were correctly classified by Nutcracker as entailment due to conjunction elimination in the RTE data. Some examples are shown below, where the relevant phrases in T and H are set in bold face. (In these and following examples, some are abbreviated versions of the original entry in the RTE data-set to save space. The gold-standard judgments (TRUE/FALSE) are taken from the RTE data-set.)

Example 4: TRUE
T: The Gurkhas come **from mountainous Nepal** and are extremely tenacious...
H: The Gurkhas come **from Nepal**.

Example 5: TRUE
T: At least eight people have been killed in a **suicide bomb attack** on Sri Lanka's...
H: People were killed in **suicide attacks**.

Example 6: TRUE
T: A male rabbit is called a buck **and** a female rabbit is called a doe, just like deer.
H: A female rabbit is called a doe.

Example 7: TRUE
T: Tom Cruise is **married to actress Nicole Kidman** and the couple has...
H: Tom Cruise is **married to Nicole Kidman**.

Example 8: TRUE
T: Spirou was **created in 1938 by Rob-Vel**, who sold the rights to...
H: Spirou was **created by Rob-Vel**.

As these examples illustrate, several syntactic constructions fall into this category of valid inferences: intersective adjectives ("X is from mountainous Y" entails "X is from Y"), noun-noun compounds (a suicide bomb attack is also a bomb attack), appositives ("X is the actress Nicole Kidman" entails that "X is Nicole Kidman"), and clauses ("X and Y" entails Y). The last example shows that the order of event modifiers is not sensitive to entailment ("created in X by Y" entails "created by Y"). Nutcracker makes corrected predictions for this type of examples, although, as we will see below, in some cases conjunction elimination doesn't always yield the desired result.

3.1.2 Verb Phrase Coordination

This category of examples shows that a correct syntactic and semantic analysis for verb phrase coordination can contribute to finding an entailment. Approaches based on surface features will likely run into problems for this class of examples. Consider the following examples that Nutcracker handled correctly:

Example 9: TRUE
T: Pibul was anti-communist as well as nationalistic.
H: Pibul was nationalistic.

Example 10: TRUE
T: Bush withheld judgment Monday on... Iraq, and said angry protests in Indonesia...
H: Bush said that protests in Indonesia...

Both examples are cases of verb phrase coordination ("X was P as well as Q" entails "X was Q", and "X did P and did Q" entails "X did Q"). These are non-trivial RTE examples because they require a sophisticated linguistic analysis; shallow RTE approach based on surface forms would have a hard time predicting these inferences. We found three cases of VP coordination entailment in the RTE data-set.

3.1.3 Active-Passive Alternation

In Boxer, verb phrases in passive form are semantically represented as their active paraphrase. Put differently, the Boxer system will produce the same semantic representation for the active sentence "Batman chased the Joker" and "The Joker was chased by Batman." This enables Nutcracker to make inferences of the following kind:

Example 11: TRUE
T: Initially the Bundesbank opposed the introduction of the euro but was...
H: The introduction of the euro has been opposed.

Example 12: TRUE
T: In India, carpets are made mostly in Uttar Pradesh, which adopted a "Child Labour Abolition and Regulation Act" in 1986.
H: The Child Labour Abolition and Regulation Act was adopted in 1986.

The Nutcracker system is able to deal with this because the C&C parser is able to detect verb phrases in passive mood, for which Boxer select the correct thematic roles. For instance, the active-passive alternation example above translates as "X opposed Y" entails "Y has been opposed". There were four cases of active-passive alternation in the studied RTE data-sets.

3.1.4 Past and Present Participles

Past and present participles that modify nouns are analysed in Boxer like events introduced by ordinary verb phrases. This ensures that Nutcracker predicts entailments as in the following examples:

Example 13: TRUE

T: Another factor in the **rising cost of paper** is the increased cost of wood pulp, from which paper is made.

H: The cost of paper is rising.

Example 14: TRUE

T: The provincial veterinarian with the Department of Forest Resources and Agrifoods, Dr. Hugh Whitney, confirmed today another case of rabies in Labrador, bringing the total number of **confirmed rabies cases** to nine in Labrador since November 2000.

H: A case of rabies was confirmed.

The two examples above were the only ones that I found in the RTE data. In the first example the present participle "rising" is analysed by Boxer as an event with the thematic roles for the corresponding intransitive verb. In the second example, the past participle "confirmed" is treated by Boxer as a passive verb.

3.1.5 Relative Clauses and Control Constructions

Relative clauses and control constructions invoke interesting semantic dependencies. Nutcracker is able to correctly predict entailments for the following examples, covering standard relative clauses, a reduced relative clause, and a control construction.

Example 15: TRUE

T: **Franz Liszt**, a Hungarian composer **who lived from 1811 to 1886** was the equivalent of a rock star in his day. His piano compositions were extremely popular and he often gave concerts to his multitude of fans. Liszt was also the pioneer of many musical techniques, including the symphonic poem and the technique of transforming themes.

H: Franz Liszt lived from 1811 to 1886.

Example 16: TRUE

T: The prize is named after **Alfred Nobel**, a pacifist and entrepreneur **who invented dynamite in 1866**. Nobel left much of his wealth to establish the award, which has honoured achievements in physics, chemistry, medicine, literature and efforts to promote peace since 1901.

H: Alfred Nobel invented dynamite in 1866.

Example 17: TRUE

T: **The Pharos**, a monumental **lighthouse built around 280 BC** and standing 330 ft high, lit the entrance to Alexandria harbour for centuries, but archeologists have never been able to identify positively any remains.

H: The Pharos Lighthouse was built around 280 BC.

Example 18: TRUE
T: **The 84-year-old pope** was wheeled to a hospital window, and blessed the crowd **by making the sign of the cross** in clear gestures, as a Vatican photographer snapped pictures.
H: The pope made the sign of the cross.

Note that the first three examples also interact with a proper analysis of appositives. Example 18 is correctly predicted thanks to the lexical semantics of "by", a VP modifiers sub-categorizing for a present participle, ensuring that the subject of the participle is the same as the subject of the VP it is modifying.

3.1.6 Pronouns

The current version of Boxer performs pronoun resolution using a simple rule-based algorithm that emphasizes precision at the cost of recall. This mean that not all pronouns are resolved, but when they are, they are usually associated with a correct antecedent. Consider the following examples that Boxer got correct and caused a correct entailment when running Nutcracker:

Example 19: TRUE
T: **Aeschylus** was born in 525 BC, and spent his youth as a soldier in the Athenian army. **He** wrote The Persians when he was 53 years old, but it is his earliest surviving work.
H: "The Persians" was written by Aeschylus.

Example 20: TRUE
T: **Yunus**, who shared the 1.4 million prize Friday with the Grameen Bank that **he** founded 30 years ago, pioneered the concept of "microcredit"...
H: Yunus founded the Grameen Bank 30 years ago.

Both examples demonstrate the need of pronoun resolution for RTE. We note in passing that the first example also shows active-passive alternation, and that the second example requires a proper treatment of object relative clauses, underlining that in real-world RTE there is often more than one complex phenomenon that one needs to get right to correctly predict entailments.

3.2 Incorrect Proofs Found (False Positives)

Assuming that the theorem prover that one uses is sound, any proof that is produced by it is mathematically correct. But in the RTE setting that we are examining, finding a proof doesn't automatically mean predicting a correct entailment. These cases, the *false positives*, are usually caused by a wrong semantic analysis of Boxer. Fortunately, this doesn't happen often. But when it does happen, it is interesting to find out why, because it informs you where semantic analysis (sometimes unexpectedly) failed and points out weak points in the semantic analysis. We will look at these cases in this section.

3.2.1 Incorrect Syntactic Analyses

An incorrect syntactic analysis automatically yields an incorrect semantic analysis. Sometimes this leads to incorrect entailment predictions. For the examples below Nutcracker predicted entailments, although they were tagged as non-entailments in the gold standard annotation:

Example 21: FALSE
T: Yunus, who was nominated for the peace prize at least twice before, is the first person from Bangladesh, a country of 147 million, to win a Nobel Prize.
H: Yunus is the first person to win a Nobel Prize.

Example 22: FALSE
T: Germany will pay more into the EU coffers than Britain had originally proposed—but still less than it had been prepared to pay at the last summit six months ago.
H: Germany will pay more into the EU coffers than Britain.

In Example 21, the set of alternatives for the superlative expression "first" comprises *persons from Bangladesh* (not just persons), blocking the entailment. Computing the alternative set of superlatives was recognized as an important problem in Bos and Nissim (2006), and the example above supports this once more. In Example 22 a wrong syntactic analysis of the comparative caused a false positive. The best remedy to deal with these kinds of problems is train the parser on more data or on revised gold-standard data, as in Honnibal et al. (2010).

3.2.2 Incorrect Semantic Analysis

This is a motley crew of examples, including unjustified conjunction elimination (Example 23), not covering certain downward entailing quantifiers (Example 24), wrongly resolved pronouns (Example 25), and not taking care of intensional adjectives (Example 26):

Example 23: FALSE
T: Boys and girls will be segregated during sex education in junior high school.
H: Boys and girls will be segregated in junior high school.

Example 24: FALSE

T: There are approximately 3.7 million European Citizens with intellectual disability.

H: There are approximately 3.7 million European Citizens.

Example 25: FALSE

T: The rhinestone-studded Nudie suit was invented by Nudie Cohn in the 1940s, an Americanization of the matador's "suit of lights".

H: The matador's "suit of lights" was invented by Nudie Cohn.

Example 26: FALSE

T: Belknap was impeached by a unanimous vote of the House of Representatives for allegedly having received money in return for post tradership appointments.

H: Belknap received money in return for post tradership appointments.

For some of these phenomena there are relatively easy fixes thinkable: equip Nutcracker with a better anaphora resolution component, and extend Boxer with a proper analysis of intensional adjectives. But such fixes probably won't have a high impact on the overall results of Nutcracker on the RTE data-sets, because they represent a long tail of various rare cases.

3.3 Missing Proofs (False Negatives)

A large class of predictions is formed by the false negatives: no proof was found by Nutcracker, but it should have. A great setting for the blame game to commence. Can you blame the parser? Boxer? The theorem prover? Where is the bottleneck?

As far as the RTE data-sets is concerned, none of the traditional pipeline components in Nutcracker is responsible for the majority of errors. To illustrate this point, I randomly picked a sequence of examples that had "missing proofs" (i.e. RTE examples that were labelled as TRUE but for which Nutcracker predicted no entailment) and examined them closely:

Example 27: TRUE

T: The Pentagon is rejecting demands by Kyrgyzstan to pay for the past use of Manas air base, a key military facility for US aircraft flying missions to Afghanistan.

H: Manas air base is located in Kyrgyzstan.

Example 28: TRUE

T: He also referred to the "illegal" arrest on 31 May of Mexican Professor Maria Eugenia Ochoa Garcia, whom the Salvadoran government accused of having connections with the Salvadoran guerrillas.

H: Maria Eugenia Ochoa Garcia was arrested in May.

Example 29: TRUE
T: Mercedes-Benz USA (MBUSA), headquartered in Montvale, New Jersey, is responsible for the sales, marketing and service of all Mercedes-Benz and Maybach products in the United States.
H: MBUSA is based in New Yersey.

Example 30: TRUE
T: Since joining the Key to the Cure campaign three years ago, Mercedes-Benz has donated over million toward finding new detection methods, treatments and cures for women's cancers.
H: Mercedez-Benz supports the Key to the Cure campaign.

Example 31: TRUE
T: ASCAP is a membership association of more than 200,000 U.S. composers, songwriters, lyricists and music publishers of every kind of music.
H: More than 200,000 U.S. composers, songwriters, lyricists and music publishers are members of ASCAP.

The inference in Example 27 can only be made with the knowledge that if a government of X demands someone to pay for the use of a facility Y, then Y is located in X. Similarly, the inference in Example 28 can only be made with the knowledge that if an arrest on time T of a person X takes place, then X was arrested on T. Likewise, the inference in Example 29 can only be made with the knowledge that if X is headquarted in Y, then X is based in Y. The inference in Example 30 can only be made with the knowledge that if X joins Y, then X supports Y. And finally, the inference in Example 31 can only be made with the knowledge that if X is a membership association of Y, then Y are members of X.

These aren't special cases, but are representative for a problem for logical approaches to RTE, and perhaps even for purely statistical approaches. These examples make clear that for the majority of the cases there is implicit knowledge required to make the requested inference. I don't think that this is knowledge that should be supplied by a dedicated component, rather than by the semantic analyzer (Boxer, in the case of the Nutcracker RTE system).

I am not aware of any resource that makes available background knowledge rules of the kind required by the class of false negatives represented above. Current lexical resources, such as WordNet and VerbNet, certainly do not offer such detailed information. Unsupervised knowledge mining approaches could be a future, partial answer to this problem; the current state-of-the-art in this area (Lin and Pantel 2001) shows interesting high-recall results, albeit with relatively low precision.

4 Discussion and Conclusion

Coverage for producing semantic representations is high (around 98 %), and therefore suitable for a task such as RTE. The number of proofs found is small. But when a proof is found, it is usually correct in playing a role for predicting entailment. The rare, incorrect proofs are due to insufficient syntactic and semantic analysis and usually of complex linguistic nature. However, the bottleneck for the logical approach to RTE isn't the current state of automated semantic analysis or theorem proving, but the lack of supporting background knowledge. The question is whether resources such as WordNet and VerbNet could play a role in filling this gap, or whether more elaborated knowledge bases are needed. This is an important question for future research on RTE and computational semantics.

References

Balduccini, M., Baral, C., & Lierler, Y. (2008). Knowledge representation and question answering. In V. Lifschitz, F. van Harmelen, & B. Porter (Eds.), *Handbook of knowledge representation* (pp. 779–819). Amsterdam: Elsevier.

Blackburn, P., & Bos, J. (2005). *Representation and inference for natural language. A first course in computational semantics*. Stanford: CSLI.

Bos, J. (2004). Computational semantics in discourse: Underspecification, resolution, and inference. *Journal of Logic, Language and Information, 13*(2), 139–157.

Bos, J. (2008). Wide-coverage semantic analysis with Boxer. In J. Bos & R. Delmonte (Eds.), *Research in computational semantics: Vol. 1. Semantics in text processing. STEP 2008 conference proceedings* (pp. 277–286). London: College Publications.

Bos, J., & Markert, K. (2005). Recognising textual entailment with logical inference. In *Proceedings of the 2005 conference on empirical methods in natural language processing* (pp. 628–635).

Bos, J., & Nissim, M. (2006). An empirical approach to the interpretation of superlatives. In *Proceedings of the 2006 conference on empirical methods in natural language processing*, Sydney, Australia (pp. 9–17).

Chierchia, G., & McConnell-Ginet, S. (1991). *Meaning and grammar. An introduction to semantics*. Cambridge: MIT Press.

Claessen, K., & Sörensson, N. (2003). New techniques that improve mace-style model finding. In P. Baumgartner & C. Fermüller (Eds.), *Model computation—principles, algorithms, applications* (Cade-19 Workshop), Miami, Florida, USA (pp. 11–27).

Clark, S., & Curran, J. R. (2004). Parsing the WSJ using CCG and log-linear models. In *Proceedings of the 42nd annual meeting of the association for computational linguistics* (ACL '04), Barcelona, Spain (pp. 104–111).

Cooper, R., Crouch, D., Van Eijck, J., Fox, C., Van Genabith, J., Jaspars, J., Kamp, H., Pinkal, M., Milward, D., Poesio, M., & Pulman, S. (1996). *Using the framework* (Technical report). FraCaS: A framework for computational semantics. FraCaS deliverable D16.

Curran, J., Clark, S., & Bos, J. (2007). Linguistically motivated large-scale NLP with C&C and Boxer. In *Proceedings of the 45th annual meeting of the association for computational linguistics companion volume proceedings of the demo and poster sessions*, Prague, Czech Republic (pp. 33–36).

Dagan, I., Glickman, O., & Magnini, B. (2006). The Pascal recognising textual entailment challenge. In *Lecture notes in computer science* (Vol. 3944, pp. 177–190).

Gamut, L. (1991). *Logic, language, and meaning. Volume II. Intensional logic and logical grammar*. Chicago: University of Chicago Press.

Heim, I., & Kratzer, A. (1998). *Semantics in generative grammar*. Oxford: Blackwell Sci.

Honnibal, M., Curran, J. R., & Bos, J. (2010). Rebanking ccgbank for improved np interpretation. In *Proceedings of the 48th meeting of the association for computational linguistics* (ACL 2010), Uppsala, Sweden (pp. 207–215).

Kamp, H., & Reyle, U. (1993). *From discourse to logic; An introduction to modeltheoretic semantics of natural language, formal logic and DRT.* Dordrecht: Kluwer Academic.

Lin, D., & Pantel, P. (2001). DIRT—discovery of inference rules from text. In *Proceedings of the ACM SIGKDD conference on knowledge discovery and data mining* (pp. 323–328).

Minnen, G., Carroll, J., & Pearce, D. (2001). Applied morphological processing of English. *Journal of Natural Language Engineering, 7*(3), 207–223.

Monz, C., & de Rijke, M. (2001). Light-weight entailment checking for computational semantics. In P. Blackburn & M. Kohlhase (Eds.), *Workshop proceedings ICoS-3* (pp. 59–72).

Muskens, R. (1996). Combining Montague semantics and discourse representation. *Linguistics and Philosophy, 19*, 143–186.

Riazanov, A., & Voronkov, A. (2002). The design and implementation of vampire. *AI Communications, 15*(2–3), 91–110.

Sutcliffe, G., & Suttner, C. (2006). The state of CASC. *AI Communications, 19*(1), 35–48.

Abductive Reasoning with a Large Knowledge Base for Discourse Processing

Ekaterina Ovchinnikova, Niloofar Montazeri, Theodore Alexandrov, Jerry R. Hobbs, Michael C. McCord, and Rutu Mulkar-Mehta

Abstract This chapter presents a discourse processing framework based on weighted abduction. We elaborate on ideas described in Hobbs et al. (1993) and implement the abductive inference procedure in a system called *Mini-TACITUS*. Particular attention is paid to constructing a large and reliable knowledge base for supporting inferences. For this purpose we exploit such lexical-semantic resources as WordNet and FrameNet. English Slot Grammar is used to parse text and produce logical forms. We test the proposed procedure and the resulting knowledge base on the recognizing textual entailment task using the data sets from the RTE-2 challenge for evaluation. In addition, we provide an evaluation of the semantic role labeling produced by the system taking the Frame-Annotated Corpus for Textual Entailment as a gold standard.

Michael C. McCord is an independent researcher.

E. Ovchinnikova (✉) · N. Montazeri · J.R. Hobbs
Information Sciences Institute, University of Southern California, 4676 Admiralty Way, Marina del Rey, CA 90292, USA
e-mail: katya@isi.edu

N. Montazeri
e-mail: niloofar@isi.edu

J.R. Hobbs
e-mail: hobbs@isi.edu

T. Alexandrov
University of Bremen, Bibliothekstr. 1, 28359 Bremen, Germany
e-mail: theodore@uni-bremen.de

M.C. McCord
112 Old Albany Post Rd, Ossining, NY 10562, USA
e-mail: mcmccord@member.ams.org

R. Mulkar-Mehta
San Diego Supercomputer Center, University of California in San Diego, 9500 Gilman Drive, La Jolla, CA 92093-0505, USA
e-mail: me@rutumulkar.com

H. Bunt et al. (eds.), *Computing Meaning*, Text, Speech and Language Technology 47,
DOI 10.1007/978-94-007-7284-7_7,
© Springer Science+Business Media Dordrecht 2014

1 Introduction

In this chapter, we elaborate on a semantic processing framework based on a mode of inference called *abduction*, or inference to the best explanation. In logic, abduction is a kind of inference which arrives at an explanatory hypothesis given an observation. Hobbs et al. (1993) describe how abductive reasoning can be applied to the discourse processing problem viewing the process of interpreting sentences in discourse as the process of providing the best explanation of why the sentence would be true. In this framework, interpreting a sentence means

- proving its logical form,
- merging redundancies where possible, and
- making assumptions where necessary.

As the reader will see later in this chapter, abductive reasoning as a discourse processing technique helps to solve many pragmatic problems such as reference resolution, the interpretation of noun compounds, and the resolution of some kinds of syntactic and semantic ambiguity as a by-product. We adopt this approach. Specifically, we use a system we have built called *Mini-TACITUS*[1] (Mulkar et al. 2007) that provides the expressivity of logical inference but also allows probabilistic, fuzzy, or defeasible inference and includes measures of the "goodness" of abductive proofs and hence of interpretations of texts and other situations.

The success of a discourse processing system based on inferences heavily depends on a knowledge base. This chapter shows how a large and reliable knowledge base can be obtained by exploiting existing lexical semantic resources and can be successfully applied to reasoning tasks on a large scale. In particular, we experiment with axioms extracted from WordNet (Fellbaum 1998), and FrameNet (Ruppenhofer et al. 2006). In axiomatizing FrameNet we rely on the study described in (Ovchinnikova et al. 2010; Ovchinnikova 2012).

We evaluate our inference system and knowledge base in recognizing textual entailment (RTE). As the reader will see in the following sections, inferences carried out by *Mini-TACITUS* are fairly general and not tuned for a particular application. We decided to test our approach on RTE because this is a well-defined task that captures major semantic inference needs across many natural language processing applications, such as question answering, information retrieval, information extraction, and document summarization. For evaluation, we have chosen the RTE-2 Challenge data set (Bar-Haim et al. 2006), because besides providing text-hypothesis pairs and a gold standard this data set has been annotated with FrameNet frame and role labels (Burchardt and Pennacchiotti 2008), which gives us the possibility of evaluating our frame and role labeling based on the axioms extracted from FrameNet.

This chapter is structured as follows. Section 2 introduces weighted abduction. In Sect. 3, we briefly describe our discourse processing pipeline and explain how abductive reasoning can be applied to discourse processing. Section 4 concerns unification in weighted abduction. In Sect. 5, we describe the obtained knowledge base.

---

[1]http://www.rutumulkar.com/tacitus.html

In Sect. 6, optimizations of the *Mini-TACITUS* system required to make the system able to handle large knowledge bases are described. Section 7 presents our procedure for recognizing textual entailment. In Sect. 8, we provide an evaluation of our discourse processing pipeline on the RTE-2 data set. The last section concludes the chapter and gives an outlook on future work and perspectives.

2 Weighted Abduction

Abduction is inference to the best explanation. Formally, logical abduction is defined as follows:

Given: Background knowledge B, observations O, where both B and O are sets of first-order logical formulas,

Find: A hypothesis H such that $H \cup B \models O$, $H \cup B \not\models \perp$, where H is a set of first-order logical formulas.

Typically, there exist several hypotheses H explaining O. To rank candidate hypotheses according to plausibility, we use the framework of *weighted abduction* as defined by Hobbs et al. (1993). In this framework, observation O is a conjunction of propositions existentially quantified with the widest possible scope

$$P_1 : c_1 \wedge \ldots \wedge P_n : c_n \qquad (1)$$

where P_i are propositions and c_i are positive real-valued costs ($i \in \{1, \ldots, n\}$). We use the notation $P : c$ to say that proposition P has cost c, and $cost(P)$ to represent the cost of P. The background knowledge B is a set of first-order logic formulas of the form

$$P_1^{w_1} \wedge \ldots \wedge P_n^{w_n} \rightarrow Q_1 \wedge \ldots \wedge Q_m \qquad (2)$$

where P_i, Q_j are propositions and w_i is a positive real-valued weight ($i \in \{1, \ldots, n\}, j \in \{1, \ldots, m\}$). We use the notation P^w to indicate that proposition P has weight w. All variables on the left-hand side of such axioms are universally quantified with the widest possible scope. Variables occurring on the right-hand side only are existentially quantified.[2]

The two main inference operations in weighted abduction are backward chaining and unification. *Backward chaining* is the introduction of new assumptions given an observation and background knowledge. For example, given $O = \exists x(q(x) : 10)$ and $B = \{\forall x(p(x)^{1.2} \rightarrow q(x))\}$, there are two candidate hypotheses: $H_1 = \exists x(q(x) : 10)$ and $H_2 = \exists x(p(x) : 12)$. In weighted abduction, a *cost function* f is used in order to calculate assumption costs. The function takes two arguments: costs of the propositions backchained on and weight of the assumption. Usually, a multiplication function is used, i.e. $f(c, w) = c \cdot w$, where c is the cost of

---

[2]In the rest of this chapter we omit quantification.

the propositions backchained on and w is the weight of the corresponding assumption. For example, if $q(x)$ costs 10 and w of p is 1.2 in the example above, then assuming p in H_2 costs 12.

Unification is the merging of propositions with the same predicate name by assuming that their arguments are the same and assigning the smallest cost to the result of the unification. For example, $O = \exists x, y(p(x) : 10 \wedge p(y) : 20 \wedge q(y) : 10)$. There is a candidate hypothesis $H = \exists x(p(x) : 10 \wedge q(x) : 10)$. The idea behind such mergings is that if an assumption has already been made then there is no need to make it again.

Both operations (backchaining and unification) can be applied any number of times to generate a possibly infinite set of candidate hypotheses. Weighted abduction defines the *cost* of hypothesis H as

$$cost(H) = \sum_{h \in H} cost(h) \tag{3}$$

where h is an atomic conjunct in H (e.g., $p(x)$ in the above H). In this framework, minimum-cost explanations are best explanations. The main idea of weighted abduction is to favor explanations involving fewer assumptions and more reliable assumptions.

3 Discourse Processing Pipeline and Abductive Reasoning

Our discourse processing pipeline produces interpretations of texts given an appropriate knowledge base. A text is first input to the English Slot Grammar (ESG) parser (McCord 1990, 2010; McCord et al. 2012). For each segment, the parse produced by ESG is a dependency tree that shows both surface and deep structure. The deep structure is exhibited via a word sense predication for each node, with logical arguments. These logical predications form a good start on a logical form (LF) for the whole segment. A component of ESG converts the parse tree into a LF in the style of Hobbs (1985).

The LF is a conjunction of predications, which have generalized entity arguments that can be used for showing relationships among the predications. Hobbs (1985) extends Davidson's approach (Davidson 1967) to all predications and posits that corresponding to any predication that can be made in natural language, there is an eventuality. Correspondingly, any predication in the logical notation has an extra argument, which refers to the "condition" in which that predication is true. Thus, in the logical form $John(e_1, j) \wedge run(e_2, j)$ for the sentence *John runs*, e_2 is a running event by John and e_1 is a condition of j being named "John".

In terms of weighted abduction, logical forms represent observations, which need to be explained by background knowledge. In the context of discourse processing, we call a hypothesis explaining a logical form an *interpretation* of this LF. In our pipeline, the interpretation of the text is carried out by an inference system called *Mini-TACITUS* (Mulkar-Mehta 2007). *Mini-TACITUS* tries to prove the logical form of the text, allowing assumptions where necessary. Where the system is able to prove parts of the LF, it is anchoring it in what is already known from the overall discourse or from a knowledge base. Where assumptions are necessary, it is gaining new information. Obviously, there are many possible proofs in this procedure. A cost function on proofs enables the system to chose the "best" (the cheapest) interpretation. The key factors involved in assigning a cost are the following.

1. Proofs with fewer assumptions are favored.
2. Short proofs are favored over long ones.
3. Plausible axioms are favored over less plausible axioms.
4. Proofs are favored that exploit the inherent implicit redundancy in texts.

Let us illustrate the procedure with a simple example. Suppose that we want to construct the best interpretation of the sentence *John composed a sonata*. As a by-product, the procedure will disambiguate between two readings of *compose*, namely between the "put together" reading instantiated, for example, in the sentence *The party composed a committee*, and the "create art" reading After being processed by the parser, the sentence will be assigned the following logical form, where the numbers (10) after every proposition correspond to the default costs of these propositions.[3] The total cost of this logical form is equal to 30:

$$John(e_1, x_1) : 10 \land compose(e_0, x_1, x_2) : 10 \land sonata(e_2, x_2) : 10$$

Suppose our knowledge base contains the following axioms:

(1) $put\_together(e, x_1, x_2)^{0.6} \land collection(e_2, x_2)^{0.6} \rightarrow compose(e, x_1, x_2)$
(2) $create\_art(e, x_1, x_2)^{0.6} \land work\_of\_art(e_2, x_2)^{0.6} \rightarrow compose(e, x_1, x_2)$
(3) $sonata(e, x)^{1.5} \rightarrow work\_of\_art(e, x)$

Axioms (1) and (2) correspond to the two readings of *compose*. Axiom (3) states that a sonata is a work of art. The propositions on the right hand side (*compose*, *work_of_art*) correspond to the given information, whereas the left hand side propositions will be assumed.

Two interpretations can be constructed for the LF above. The first one is the result of the application of Axiom (1). The costs of the backchained propositions (*compose*, *sonata*) are set to 0, because their costs are now carried by the newly introduced assumptions (*put_together*, *collection*). The total cost of the first interpretation **I1** is 32.

I1: $John(e_1, x_1) : 10 \land compose(e, x_1, x_2) : 0 \land sonata(e_2, x_2) : 10 \land$
$put\_together(e_0, x_1, x_2) : 6 \land collection(e_2, x_2) : 6$

The second interpretation is constructed in several steps. First, Axiom (2) is applied, so that *compose* is backchained on to *create_art* and *work_of_art* with the costs 6. Then, Axiom (3) is applied to *work_of_art*.

---

[3]The actual value of the default costs of the input propositions does not matter, because the interpretation costs are calculated using a multiplication function. The only heuristic we use here concerns setting all costs of the input propositions to be equal (all propositions cost 10 in the discussed example). This heuristic needs further investigation.

I2: $John(e_1, x_1) : 10 \wedge compose(e, x_1, x_2) : 0 \wedge sonata(e_2, x_2) : 10 \wedge$
   $create\_art(e_0, x_1, x_2) : 6 \wedge work\_of\_art(e_2, x_2) : 0 \wedge sonata(e_2, x_2) : 9$

The total cost of **I2** is 35. This interpretation is redundant, because it contains the predicate *sonata* twice. The procedure will unify propositions with the same predicate name, setting the corresponding arguments of these propositions to be equal and assigning the minimum of the costs to the result of merging. Thus, the final form of the second interpretation **I2** with the cost of 25 contains only one *sonata* with the cost of 9. The "create art" meaning of *compose* was chosen because it reveals implicit redundancy in the sentence.

Thus, on each reasoning step the procedure (1) applies axioms to propositions with non-zero costs and (2) merges propositions with the same predicate, assigning the lowest cost to the result of merging. Reasoning terminates when no more axioms can be applied. The procedure favors the cheapest interpretations. Among them, the shortest proofs are favored; i.e. if two interpretations have the same cost then the one that has been constructed with fewer axiom application steps is considered to be "better".

The described procedure provides solutions to a whole range of natural language pragmatics problems, such as resolving ambiguity and discovering implicit relations in noun compounds, prepositional phrases, or discourse structure; see (Hobbs et al. 1993) for detailed examples. Moreover, this account of interpretation solves the problem of where to stop drawing inferences, which could easily be unlimited in number; an inference is appropriate if it is part of the lowest-cost proof of the logical form.

4 Unification in Weighted Abduction

Frequently, the lowest-cost interpretation results from identifying two entities with each other, so that their common properties only need to be proved or assumed once. This feature of the algorithm is called "unification", and is one of the principal methods by which coreference is resolved.

However, this feature of the weighted abduction algorithm has a substantial potential for overmerging. Merging propositions with the same predicate names does not always give the intended solution. If we know $animal(e_1, x)$ and $animal(e_2, y)$, we do not want to assume x equals y if we also know $dog(e_3, x)$ and $cat(e_4, y)$. For *John runs and Bill runs*, with the logical form $John(e_1, x) \wedge run(e_2, x) \wedge Bill(e_3, y) \wedge run(e_4, y)$, we do not want to assume John and Bill are the same individual just because they are both running.

For the full treatment of the overmerging problem, one needs a careful analysis of coreference, including the complicated issue of event coreference. In this study, we adopt a heuristic solution.

The *Mini-TACITUS* system allows us to define non-merge constraints, which prevent undesirable mergings at every reasoning step. Non-merge constraints have the form $x_1 \neq y_1, \ldots, x_n \neq y_n$. These constraints are generated by the system at each reasoning step. Given the propositions $p(x_1)$ and $p(x_2)$ occurring in the input log-ical form and the non-merge constraint $x_1 \neq x_2$, *Mini-TACITUS* does not merge $p(x_1)$ and $p(x_2)$, because it would imply a conflict with the non-merge constraint. In the experiments described in this book, we used the following rule for generating non-merge constraints.

For each two propositions $p(e_1, x_1, \ldots, x_n)$ and $p(e_2, y_1, \ldots, y_n)$, which occur in the input, if

- e_1 is not equal to e_2,
- p is not a noun predicate, and
- $\exists i \in \{1, \ldots, n\}$ such that x_i is not equal to y_i, and both x_i and y_i occur as arguments of propositions other than $p(e_1, x_1, \ldots, x_n)$ and $p(e_2, y_1, \ldots, y_n)$,

then add $e_1 \neq e_2$ to the non-merge constraints.

This rule ensures that nouns can be merged without any restriction and other predicates can be merged only if all their non-first arguments are equal (due to the previous mergings) or uninstantiated. As seen from the statements above, the ar-gument merging restriction concerns first arguments only. First arguments of all predicates in the logical forms are treated by *Mini-TACITUS* as "handles" referring to conditions, in which the predicate is true of its arguments, i.e. referring to the predication itself, rather than to its semantic arguments.

The proposed non-merge rule is a heuristic, which corresponds to the intuition that it is unlikely that the same noun refers to different entities in a short discourse, while for other predicates this is possible. According to this rule the two *eat* propo-sitions can be merged in the sentence *John eats an apple and he eats the fruit slowly* having the following logical form:[4]

$$John(e_1, x_1) \wedge eat(e_2, x_1, x_2) \wedge apple(e_3, x_2) \wedge and(e_4, e_2, e_5) \wedge$$
$$he(e_1, x_1) \wedge eat(e_5, x_1, x_3) \wedge fruit(e_6, x_3) \wedge slowly(e_7, e_5)$$

In the logical form above, the propositions $eat(e_2, x_1, x_2)$ and $eat(e_5, x_1, x_3)$ can-not be merged, because they do not refer to nouns and their third arguments x_2 and x_3 are not equal. If the knowledge base contains the axiom $apple(e_1, x_1) \rightarrow fruit(e_1, x_1)$ then the logical form above can be expanded into the following:

$$John(e_1, x_1) \wedge eat(e_2, x_1, x_2) \wedge apple(e_3, x_2) \wedge and(e_4, e_2, e_5) \wedge$$
$$he(e_1, x_1) \wedge eat(e_5, x_1, x_3) \wedge fruit(e_6, x_3) \wedge apple(e_6, x_3) \wedge slowly(e_7, e_5)$$

After the expansion, the noun propositions $apple(e_3, x_2)$ and $apple(e_6, x_3)$ can be merged. Now, when all the arguments of the two *eat* propositions are equal, these propositions can be merged as well.

Concerning the sentence *John eats an apple and Bill eats an apple*, merging of two *eat* propositions is impossible, unless the system manages to prove that the predicates *John* and *Bill* can refer to the same individual.

---

[4]The anaphoric *he* in the logical form is already linked to its antecedent *John*.

There are cases when the proposed rule does not block undesired mergings. For example, given the sentence *John owns red apples and green apples*, it is wrong to merge both *apple* propositions, because "being red" and "being green" are incompatible properties that cannot be both assigned to the same entity. Thus, it seems to be reasonable to check whether two propositions to be merged have incompatible properties. A detailed study of coreference in an abductive framework is described in (Inoue et al. 2012).

5 Knowledge Base

The proposed discourse processing procedure is based on a knowledge base (KB) consisting of a set of axioms. In order to obtain a reliable KB with a large coverage we exploited existing lexical-semantic resources.

First, we have extracted axioms from WordNet (Fellbaum 1998), version 3.0., which has already proved itself to be useful in knowledge-intensive NLP applications. The central entity in WordNet (WN) is called a *synset*. Synsets correspond to word senses, so that every lexeme can participate in several synsets. We used the lexeme-synset mapping for generating axioms. For example, in the axioms below, the verb *compose* is mapped to *synset-X*, which represents one of its senses.

$$synset\text{-}X(s, e) \rightarrow compose(e, x_1, x_2)$$

Moreover, we have converted the following WordNet relations defined on synsets into axioms: hypernymy, instantiation, entailment, similarity, and meronymy. Hypernymy and instantiation relations presuppose that the related synsets refer to the same entity (the first axiom below), whereas other types of relations relate synsets referring to different entities (the second axiom below).

$$synset\text{-}1(e_0, e_1) \rightarrow synset\text{-}2(e_0, e_1)$$
$$synset\text{-}1(e_0, e_1) \rightarrow synset\text{-}2(e_2, e_3)$$

WordNet also provides morphosemantic relations, which relate verbs and nouns, e.g., *buy-buyer*. These relations can be used to generate axioms like the following one.

$$buyer(e_1, x_1) \rightarrow buy(e_2, x_1, x_2)$$

Additionally, we have exploited the WordNet synset definitions. In WordNet the definitions are given in natural language form. We have used the extended WordNet resource,[5] which provides logical forms for the definition in WordNet version 2.0. We have adapted logical forms from extended WordNet to our representation format and converted them into axioms; for example, the following axiom represents the meaning of the synset containing such lexemes as *horseback*.

$$on(e_1, e_2, x_1) \wedge back(e_3, x_1) \wedge of(e_4, x_1, x_2) \wedge horse(e_5, x_2) \rightarrow synset\text{-}X(e_0, x_0)$$

---

[5]http://xwn.hlt.utdallas.edu/

The second resource, which we have used as a source of axioms, is FrameNet, release 1.5, see Ruppenhofer et al. (2006). FrameNet has a shorter history in NLP applications than WordNet, but its potential to improve the quality of question answering (Shen and Lapata 2007) and recognizing textual entailment (Burchardt et al. 2009) has been demonstrated. The lexical meaning of predicates in FrameNet is represented in terms of frames, which describe prototypical situations spoken about in natural language. Every frame contains a set of roles corresponding to the participants of the described situation. Predicates with similar semantics are assigned to the same frame. For example, both *give* and *hand over* refer to the GIVING frame. For most of the lexemes FrameNet provides syntactic patterns showing the surface realization of these lexemes and their arguments. We used the patterns for deriving axioms. For example, the axiom below corresponds to phrases like *John gave a book to Mary.*

$$\text{GIVING}(e_1, x_1, x_2, x_3) \land \text{DONOR}(e_1, x_1) \land \text{RECIPIENT}(e_1, x_2) \land \text{THEME}(e_1, x_3)$$
$$\rightarrow give(e_1, x_1, x_3) \land to(e_2, e_1, x_2)$$

FrameNet also introduces semantic relations defined on frames such as inheritance, causation or precedence; for example, the GIVING and GETTING frames are connected with the causation relation. Roles of the connected frames are also linked, e.g. DONOR in GIVING is linked with SOURCE in GETTING. Frame relations have no formal semantics in FrameNet. In order to generate corresponding axioms, we used the previous work on axiomatizing frame relations and generating new relations from corpora (Ovchinnikova et al. 2010; Ovchinnikova 2012). An example of an axiomatized relation is given below.

$$\text{GIVING}(e_1, x_1, x_2, x_3) \land \text{DONOR}(e_1, x_1) \land \text{RECIPIENT}(e_1, x_2) \land \text{THEME}(e_1, x_3)$$
$$\rightarrow$$
$$\text{GETTING}(e_2, x_2, x_3, x_1) \land \text{SOURCE}(e_2, x_1) \land \text{RECIPIENT}(e_1, x_2) \land \text{THEME}(e_1, x_3)$$

Axiom weights are calculated using the frequency of the corresponding word senses in the annotated corpora. The information about frequency is provided both by WordNet and FrameNet. In our framework, axioms of the type *species* → *genus* should have weights greater than 1, which means that assuming *species* costs more than assuming *genus*, because there might be many possible *species* for the same *genus*. The weights of such axioms are heuristically defined as ranging from 1 to 2.

In order to assign a weight w_i to a sense i of a lexeme, we use information about the frequency f_i of the word sense in the annotated corpora. An obvious way of converting the frequency f_i to the weight w_i is the following equation:

$$w_i = 2 - \frac{f_i}{\sum_{1 \leq n \leq |S|} f_n} \qquad (4)$$

where S is a set of all senses of the lexeme. All axioms representing relations receive equal weights of 1.2.

Table 1 Statistics for extracted axioms

Axiom type	Source	Number of axioms
Lexeme-synset mappings	WN 3.0	207,000
Lexeme-synset mappings	WN 2.0	203,100
Synset relations	WN 3.0	141,000
Derivational relations	WN 3.0 (annotated)	35,000
Synset definitions	WN 2.0 (parsed, annotated)	115,400
Lexeme-frame mappings	FN 1.5	49,100
Frame relations	FN 1.5 + corpora	5,300

Both WordNet and FrameNet are manually created resources, which ensures a relatively high quality of the resulting axioms as well as the possibility of exploiting the linguistic information provided for structuring the axioms. Although manual creation of resources is a very time-consuming task, WordNet and FrameNet, being long-term projects, have an extensive coverage of English vocabulary. The coverage of WordNet is currently larger than that of FrameNet (155 000 vs. 12 000 lexemes). However, the fact that FrameNet introduces complex argument structures (roles) for frames and provides mappings of these structures makes FrameNet especially valuable for reasoning.

The complete list of axioms we have extracted from these resources is given in Table 1. The number of axioms is approximated to the nearest hundred.

6 Adapting *Mini-TACITUS* to a Large Knowledge Base

Mini-TACITUS (Mulkar et al. 2007) began as a simple backchaining theorem-prover intended to be a more transparent version of the original *TACITUS* system, which was based on Stickel's *PTTP* system (Stickel 1988). Originally, *Mini-TACITUS* was not designed for treating large amounts of data. A clear and clean reasoning procedure rather than efficiency was in the focus of its developers. In order to make the system work with the large knowledge base, we had to perform several optimization steps and add a couple of new features.

6.1 Time and Depth Parameters

For avoiding the reasoning complexity problem, we introduced two parameters. A time parameter t is used to restrict the processing time. After the processing time exceeds t the reasoning terminates and the best interpretation so far is output. The time parameter ensures that an interpretation will be always returned by the procedure even if reasoning could not be completed in a reasonable time.

Algorithm 1 *Mini-TACITUS* reasoning algorithm: interaction of the time and depth parameters

---

Require: a logical form LF of a text fragment, a knowledge base KB,
          a depth parameter D, a cost parameter C, a time parameter T
Ensure: the best interpretation I_{best} of LF
1: $I_{init} := \{p(e, x_1, \ldots, x_n, C, 0) | p(e, x_1, \ldots, x_n) \in LF\}$
2: $I\_set := \{I_{init}\}$
3: $apply\_inference(I_{init})$
4: $Cheapest\_I := \{I | I \in I\_set \text{ and } \forall I' \in I\_set : cost(I) \leq cost(I')\}$
5: $Best\_I := \{I | I \in Cheapest\_I \text{ and }$
                    $\forall I' \in Cheapest\_I : proof\_length(I) \leq proof\_length(I')\}$
6: **return** I_{best}, which is the first element of $Best\_I$

Subroutine *apply_inference*

Require: interpretation I
 1: **while** $processing\_time < T$ **do**
 2:   **for** $\alpha \in KB$ **do**
 3:     **for** $PropSubset \subseteq I$ such that $\forall p(e, x_1, \ldots, x_n, c, d) \in PropSubset : d < D$ **do**
 4:       **if** α is applicable to PS **then**
 5:         $I_{new} :=$ result of application of α to PS
 6:         $I\_set := I\_set \cup \{I_{new}\}$
 7:         $apply\_inference(I_{new})$
 8:       **end if**
 9:     **end for**
10:   **end for**
11: **end while**

A depth parameter d restricts the depth of the inference chain. Suppose that a proposition p occurring in the input has been backchained on and a proposition p' has been introduced as a result. Then, p' will be backchained on and so on. The number of such iterations cannot exceed d. The depth parameter reduces the number of reasoning steps.

The interaction between the time and depth parameters is shown in Algorithm 1.

6.2 Filtering out Axioms and Input Propositions

Since *Mini-TACITUS* processing time increases exponentially with the input size (sentence length and number of axioms), making such a large set of axioms work was an additional issue. For speeding up reasoning it was necessary to reduce both the number of the input propositions and the number of axioms. In order to reduce the number of axioms, the axioms that could never lead to any merging are filtered out. Suppose that the initial logical form contains the following propositions:

$$a(x_1, \ldots, x_n) \land b(y_1, \ldots, y_m) \land c(z_1, \ldots, z_k)$$

and the knowledge base consists of the following axioms:

(1) $d(x_1, \ldots, x_l) \rightarrow a(y_1, \ldots, y_n)$
(2) $b(x_1, \ldots, x_m) \rightarrow d(y_1, \ldots, y_l)$
(3) $e(x_1, \ldots, x_t) \rightarrow c(y_1, \ldots, y_k)$

Given the logical form above, Axiom (3) is obviously useless. It can be evoked by the input proposition $c(z_1, \ldots, z_k)$ introducing the new predicate e, but it can never lead to any merging reducing the interpretation cost. Thus, there is no need to apply this axiom.

Similarly, proposition $c(z_1, \ldots, z_k)$ in the input logical form can never be merged with any other proposition and can never evoke an axiom introducing a proposition, which can be merged with any other. Therefore, removing the proposition $c(z_1, \ldots, z_k)$ from the input for the reasoning machine and adding it to the best interpretation after the reasoning terminates (replacing its arguments with new variables if mergings took place) does not influence the reasoning process.

In logical forms, propositions that could not be linked to the rest of the discourse often refer to modifiers. For example, consider the sentence *Yesterday, John bought a book, but he has not started reading it yet.* The information concerning John buying a book is in the focus of this text fragment; it is linked to the second part of the sentence. However, the modifier *yesterday* just places the situation in time; it is not connected to any other part of the discourse.

7 Recognizing Textual Entailment

As the reader can see from the previous sections, the discourse processing procedure we have presented is fairly general and not tuned for any particular type of inference. We have evaluated the procedure and the KB derived from WordNet and FrameNet on the recognizing textual entailment (RTE) task, which is a generic task that seems to capture major semantic inference needs across many natural language processing applications. In this task, the system is given a text (T) and a hypothesis (H) and must decide whether the hypothesis is entailed by the text plus commonsense knowledge.

Our approach is to interpret both the text and the hypothesis using *Mini-TACITUS*, and then see whether adding information derived from the text to the knowledge base will reduce the cost of the best abductive proof of the hypothesis as compared to using the original knowledge base only. If the cost reduction exceeds a threshold determined from a training set, then we predict entailment.

A simple example would be the text *John gave a book to Mary* and the hypothesis *Mary got a book.* Our pipeline constructs the following logical forms for these two sentences.

T: *John*$(e_1, x_1) : 10 \wedge give(e_0, x_1, x_2) : 10 \wedge book(e_2, x_2) : 10 \wedge$
    $to(e_4, e_0, x_3) : 10 \wedge Mary(e_3, x_3) : 10$
H: *Mary*$(e_1, x_1) : 10 \wedge get(e_0, x_1, x_2) : 10 \wedge book(e_2, x_2) : 10$

These logical forms constitute the *Mini-TACITUS* input. *Mini-TACITUS* applies the axioms from the knowledge base to the input logical forms in order to reduce the overall cost of the interpretations. Suppose that we have the following FrameNet axioms in our knowledge base.

(1) $\text{GIVING}(e_1, x_1, x_2, x_3)^{0.9} \rightarrow give(e_1, x_1, x_3) \wedge to(e_2, e_1, x_2)$
(2) $\text{GETTING}(e_1, x_1, x_2, x_3)^{0.9} \rightarrow get(e_1, x_1, x_2)$
(3) $\text{GIVING}(e_1, x_1, x_2, x_3)^{1.2} \rightarrow \text{GETTING}(e_2, x_2, x_3, x_1)$

The first axiom maps *give to* to the GIVING frame, the second one maps *get* to GETTING and the third one relates GIVING and GETTING with the causation relation. As a result of the application of the axioms the following best interpretations will be constructed for T and H.

I(T): $John(e_1, x_1) : 10 \wedge give(e_0, x_1, x_2) : 0 \wedge book(e_2, x_2) : 10 \wedge$
$\quad to(e_2, e_0, x_3) : 0 \wedge Mary(e_3, x_3) : 20 \wedge \text{GIVING}(e_0, x_1, x_2, x_3) : 18$
I(H): $Mary(e_1, x_1) : 10 \wedge get(e_0, x_1, x_2) : 0 \wedge book(e_2, x_2) : 10 \wedge$
$\quad\quad \text{GETTING}(e_0, x_1, x_2) : 9$

The total cost of the best interpretation for H is equal to 29. Now the best interpretation of T will be added to H with the zero costs (as if T has been totally proven) and we will try to prove H once again. First of all, merging of the propositions with the same names will result in reducing costs of the propositions *Mary* and *book* to 0, because they occur in T:

I(I(T)+H): $John(e_1, x_1) : 0 \wedge give(e_0, x_1, x_2) : 0 \wedge book(e_2, x_2) : 0 \wedge$
$\quad\quad to(e_2, e_0, x_3) : 0 \wedge Mary(e_3, x_3) : 20 \wedge \text{GIVING}(e_0, x_1, x_2, x_3) : 0 \wedge$
$\quad\quad get(e_4, x_3, x_2) : 0 \wedge \text{GETTING}(e_4, x_3, x_2) : 9$

The only proposition left to be proved is GETTING. Using the GETTING-GIVING relation in Axiom (3) above, this proposition can be backchained on to GIVING, which will merge with GIVING coming from the T sentence. H appears to be proven completely with respect to T; the total cost of its best interpretation given T is equal to 0. Thus, using knowledge from T helped to reduce the cost of the best interpretation of H from 29 to 0.

In our framework, a full treatment of the logical structure of natural language would require a procedure for assessing the truth claims of a text given its logical form. Quantifiers and logical operators would be treated as predicates, and their principal properties would be expressed in axioms. However, we have not yet implemented this. Without a special account for the logical connectors *if*, *not* and *or*, given a text *If A then B* and a hypothesis *A and B*, our procedure will most likely predict entailment. Even worse, *not A* will entail *A*. Similarly, modality is not handled. Thus, *X said A* and *maybe A* both entail *A*. At the moment our RTE procedure mainly accounts for the informational content of texts, being able to detect the "aboutness" overlap of T and H, and does not reason about the truth or falsity of T and H.

8 Experimental Evaluation

We evaluated our procedure on the RTE-2 Challenge dataset[6] (Bar-Haim et al. 2006). The RTE-2 dataset contains the development and the test set, both including 800 text-hypothesis pairs. Each dataset consists of four subsets, which correspond to typical success and failure settings in different applications: information extraction (IE), information retrieval (IR), question answering (QA), and summarization (SUM). In total, 200 pairs were collected for each application in each dataset.

The main task in the RTE-2 challenge was entailment prediction for each pair in the test set. The evaluation criterion for this task was *accuracy*—the percentage of pairs correctly judged. The accuracy achieved by the 23 participating systems ranges from 53 % to 75 %. Two systems had 73 % and 75 % accuracy, two systems achieved 62 % and 63 %, while most of the systems achieved 55 %–61 % (cf. Bar-Haim et al. 2006).

Garoufi (2007) has performed a detailed study of the RTE-2 dataset investigating factors responsible for entailment in a significant number of text-hypothesis pairs. Surprisingly, Garoufi's conclusion is that such shallow features as lexical overlap (number of words from hypothesis, which also occur in text) seem to be more useful for predicting entailment than any sophisticated linguistic analysis or knowledge-based inference. This fact may have two explanations: Either the RTE-2 dataset is not properly balanced for testing advanced textual entailment technology, or the state-of-the-art RTE systems indeed cannot suggest anything more effective than simple lexical overlap.

Nevertheless, we chose the RTE-2 dataset for our experiments. First, none of the other RTE datasets has been studied in so much detail, therefore there is no guarantee that any other dataset has better properties. Second, the RTE-2 test set was additionally annotated with FrameNet semantic roles, which enables us to use it for evaluation of semantic role labeling.

8.1 *Weighted Abduction for Recognizing Textual Entailment*

We evaluated our procedure in RTE as described in Sect. 7. The RTE-2 development set was used to train the threshold for discriminating between the "entailment" and "no entailment" cases. Interpretation costs were normalized to the number of propositions in the corresponding H logical forms. This was done in order to normalize over the prediction of longer and shorter hypotheses. If hypothesis h_1 contains more propositions than h_2, then it can potentially contain more propositions not linked to propositions in the text.

As a baseline we processed the datasets with an empty knowledge base. The depth parameter was set to 3. Then, we did different runs, evaluating knowledge

---

[6]http://pascallin.ecs.soton.ac.uk/Challenges/RTE2/

Table 2 Evaluation results for the RTE-2 test set

KB	Accuracy	Number of axioms		Task	Accuracy
		T	H		
				SUM	75 %
No KB	57.3 %	0	0	IR	64 %
WN 3.0	59.6 %	294	111	QA	62 %
FN	60.1 %	1233	510	IE	50 %
Ext. WN 2.0	58.1 %	215	85		
WN 3.0 + FN	62.6 %	1527	521		

extracted from different resources separately.[7] Table 2 contains the results of our experiments.[8] The results suggest that the proposed method seems to be promising as compared to the other systems evaluated on the same task. Our best run gives 62.6 % accuracy.

The obtained baseline of 57.3 % is close to the lexical overlap baselines reported by the participants of RTE-2 (Bar-Haim et al. 2006). Although FrameNet has provided fewer axioms than WordNet in total (ca. 50 000 vs. 600 000), its application resulted in better accuracy than application of WordNet. The reason for this might be the confusing fine-grainedness of WordNet, which makes word sense disambiguation difficult. Moreover, the average number of WordNet axioms per sentence is smaller than the number of FrameNet axioms (cf. Table 1). This happens because the relational network of FrameNet is much more dense than that of WordNet.

The lower performance of the system using the KB consisting of axioms extracted from extended WordNet (Ext. WN 2.0) can be explained. The axioms extracted from the synset definitions introduce a lot of new lexemes into the logical form, since these axioms define words with the help of other words rather than abstract concepts. These new lexemes trigger more axioms. Finally, too many new lexemes are added to the final best interpretation, which can often be noisy. The WN 3.0 and FN axioms set do not cause this problem, because these axioms operate on frames and synsets rather than on lexemes.

For our best run (WN 3.0 + FN), we present the accuracy data for each application separately (Table 2). The distribution of the performance of *Mini-TACITUS* on the four datasets corresponds to the average performance of systems participating in RTE-2 as reported by Garoufi (2007). The most challenging task in RTE-2 appeared to be IE. QA and IR follow, and finally, SUM was titled the "easiest" task, with a performance significantly higher than that of any other task.[9]

---

[7] The computation was done on a High Performance Cluster (320 2.4 GHz nodes, CentOS 5.0) of the Center for Industrial Mathematics (Bremen, Germany).

[8] "Number of axioms" stands for the average number of axioms applied per sentence.

[9] In order to get a better understanding of which parts of our KB are useful for computing entailment and for which types of entailment, in future, we are planning to use the detailed annotation of the RTE-2 dataset describing the source of the entailment, which was produced by Garoufi (2007).

Experimenting with the time parameter t restricting processing time (see Sect. 6), we found that the performance of *Mini-TACITUS* increases with increasing time of processing. This is not surprising. The smaller t is, the fewer chances *Mini-TACITUS* has to apply all relevant axioms. Tracing the reasoning process, we found that given a long sentence and a short processing time *Mini-TACITUS* had time to construct only a few interpretations, and the "real" best interpretation was not always among them. For example, if the processing time is restricted to 30 minutes per sentence and the knowledge base contains some hundreds of axioms, then *Mini-TACITUS* has not enough time to apply all axioms up to depth 3 and construct all possible interpretations in order to select the best one, while processing a single sentence for 30 minutes is definitely not feasible in a realistic setting. This suggests that optimizing the system computationally could lead to producing significantly better results.

Several remarks should be made concerning our RTE procedure. First, measuring overlap of atomic propositions, as performed by most of the RTE systems (cf. Dagan et al. 2010), does not seem to be the perfect measure for predicting entailment. In the example below, H is fully lexically contained in T. Only one proposition *in* and its arguments pointing to the time of the described event actually make a difference in semantics of T and H and imply "no entailment" prediction.

T: *He became a boxing referee in 1964 and became most well-known for his decision against Mike Tyson, during the Holyfield fight, when Tyson bit Holyfield's ear.*

H: *Mike Tyson bit Holyfield's ear in 1964.*

As mentioned before, a much more elaborate treatment of logical connectors, quantification, and modality is required. In the example below, H is fully contained in T, but there is still no entailment.

T: *Drew Walker, NHS Tayside's public health director, said: "It is important to stress that this is not a confirmed case of rabies."*

H: *A case of rabies is confirmed.*

In order to address some of the problems mentioned above, one can experiment with more sophisticated classification methods (e.g., SVM or Decision Trees). The number of proven/unproven propositions for each part of speech can be used as a specific feature. This solution might reflect the intuition that an unproven verb, preposition, or negation is more likely to imply "no entailment" than an unproven adjective.

Obviously, WordNet and FrameNet alone are not enough to predict entailment. In the example below, our system inferred that *president* is related to *presidential*, Tehran is a part of Iran, *mayor* and *official* can refer to the same person, *runoff* and *election* can mean the same. However, all this information does not help us to predict entailment. We rather need to interpret the genitive *Iran's election* as *Iran*

We would like to thank one of the reviewers of our IWCS 2011 paper which is the basis of this chapter for giving us this idea.

holds election and be able to infer that if there is an election between A and B, then A faces B in the election.

T: *Iran will hold the first runoff presidential election in its history, between President Akbar Hashemi Rafsanjani and Tehran's hard-line mayor, election officials said Saturday.*

H: *Hashemi Rafsanjani will face Tehran's hard-line mayor in Iran's first runoff presidential election ever, officials said Saturday.*

The knowledge needed for RTE has been analysed, for example, in (Clark et al. 2007) and (Garoufi 2007). In both works, the conclusion is that lexical-semantic relations are just one type of knowledge required. Thus, our knowledge base requires significant extension.

8.2 Semantic Role Labeling

For the run using axioms derived from FrameNet, we have evaluated how well we do in assigning frames and frame roles. For *Mini-TACITUS*, semantic role labeling is a by-product of constructing the best interpretation. But since this task is considered to be important as such in the NLP community, we provide an additional evaluation for it. As a gold standard we have used the Frame-Annotated Corpus for Textual Entailment, FATE (Burchardt and Pennacchiotti 2008). This corpus provides frame and semantic role label annotations for the RTE-2 challenge test set.[10] It is important to note that FATE annotates only those frames that are relevant for computing entailment. Since *Mini-TACITUS* makes all possible frame assignments for a sentence, we provide only the recall measure for the frame match and leave the precision out.

The FATE corpus was also used as a gold standard for evaluating the *Shalmaneser* system (Erk and Pado 2006), which is a state-of-the-art system for assigning FrameNet frames and roles. In Table 3, we replicate results for *Shalmaneser* alone and *Shalmaneser* boosted with *WordNet Detour to FrameNet* (Burchardt et al. 2005). *WN-FN Detour* extended the frame labels assigned by *Shalmaneser* with the labels related via the FrameNet hierarchy or by the WordNet inheritance relation, cf. Burchardt et al. (2009). In frame matching, the number of frame labels in the gold standard annotation that can also be found in the system annotation (recall) was counted. Role matching was evaluated only on the frames that are correctly annotated by the system. The number of role labels in the gold standard annotation that can also be found in the system annotation (recall) as well as the number

---

[10]FATE was annotated with the FrameNet 1.3 labels, while we have been using version 1.5 for extracting axioms. However, in the new FN version the number of frames and roles increases and there is no message about removed frames in the General Release Notes R1.5, see http://framenet.icsi.berkeley.edu. Therefore we suppose that most of the frames and roles used for the FATE annotation are still present in FN 1.5.

Table 3 Evaluation of frames/roles labeling towards FATE

System	Frame match	Role match	
	Recall	Precision	Recall
Shalmaneser	0.55	0.54	0.37
Shalmaneser + Detour	0.85	0.52	0.36
Mini-TACITUS	0.65	0.55	0.30

of role labels found by the system that also occur in the gold standard (precision), were counted.[11] Table 3 shows that given FrameNet axioms, the performance of *Mini-TACITUS* on semantic role labeling is comparable with those of the system specially designed to solve this task.[12]

Unfortunately, FrameNet does not really provide any semantic typing for the frame roles. This type of information would be extremely useful for solving the SRL task. For example, consider the phrases *John took a bus* and *the meeting took 2 hours*. The lexeme *take* can be mapped both to the RIDE_VEHICLE and TAKING_TIME frame. Our system can use only the external context for disambiguation of the verb *take*. For example, if the phrase *John took a bus* is accompanied by the phrase *He got off at 10th street*, it is possible to use the relation between RIDE_VEHICLE evoked by *take* and DISEMBARKING evoked by *get off*. However, no information about possible fillers of the roles of the RIDE_VEHICLE frame (living being and vehicle) and the TAKING_TIME frame (activity and time duration) is provided by FrameNet itself. Future work on SRL using FrameNet should include learning semantic preferences for frame roles from corpora.

9 Conclusion and Future Work

This chapter presents a discourse processing framework including the abductive reasoner called *Mini-TACITUS*. We showed that interpreting texts using weighted abduction helps solve pragmatic problems in discourse processing as a by-product. In this chapter, particular attention was paid to reasoning with a large and reliable knowledge base populated with axioms extracted from such lexical-semantic resources as WordNet and FrameNet. The inference procedure as well as the knowledge base were evaluated in the recognizing textual entailment task. The data for evaluation were taken from the RTE-2 Challenge. First, we have evaluated the accuracy of the entailment prediction. Second, we have evaluated frame and role labeling using the Frame-Annotated Corpora for Textual Entailment as the gold standard. In

---

[11] We do not compare filler matching, because the FATE syntactic annotation follows different standards as the one produced by the ESG parser, which makes aligning fillers non-trivial.

[12] There exists one more probabilistic system labeling text with FrameNet frames and roles, called *SEMAFOR* (Das et al. 2010). We do not compare our results with the results of *SEMAFOR*, because it has not been evaluated against the FATE corpus yet.

both tasks our system showed performance comparable with those of the state-of-the art systems. Since the inference procedure and the axiom set are general and not tuned for a particular task, we consider the results of our experiments to be promising concerning possible manifold applications of the proposed discourse processing pipeline.

The experiments we have carried out have shown that there is still a lot of room for improving the procedure. First, for successful application of weighted abduction on a large scale the system needs to be computationally optimized. In its current state, *Mini-TACITUS* requires too much time for producing satisfactory results. As our experiments suggest, speeding up reasoning may lead to significant improvements in the system performance. Since *Mini-TACITUS* was not originally designed for large-scale processing, its implementation is in many aspects not effective enough. Recently, an alternative implementation of weighted abduction based on Integer Linear Programming (ILP) was developed (Inoue and Inui 2011). In this approach, the abductive reasoning problem is formulated as an ILP optimization problem. In a preliminary experiment the ILP-based system achieved a speed-up over *Mini-TACITUS* of two orders of magnitude (Inoue and Inui 2011).[13]

Second, in the future we plan to elaborate our treatment of natural language expressions standing for logical connectors such as implication *if*, negation *not*, disjunction *or* and others. Modality and quantifiers such as *all*, *each*, *some* also require a special treatment. This advance is needed in order to achieve more precise entailment inferences, which are at the moment based in our approach on the core information content ("aboutness") of texts. Concerning the heuristic non-merge constraints preventing undesired mergings (see Sect. 4), we have performed a detailed study of this issue that is published in Inoue et al. (2012).

Another future direction concerns the enlargement of the knowledge base. Handcrafted lexical-semantic resources such as WordNet and FrameNet provide both an extensive lexical coverage and a high-value semantic labeling. However, such resources still lack certain features essential for capturing some of the knowledge required for linguistic inferences. First of all, manually created resources are static; updating them with new information is a slow and time-consuming process. By contrast, commonsense knowledge and the lexicon undergo daily updates. This is especially true for proper names. Although some of the proper names have been already included in WordNet, new names appear regularly. In order to accommodate dynamic knowledge, we plan to make use of the distributional properties of words in large corpora. A similar approach is described, for example, in (Peñas and Ovchinnikova 2012).

Lexical-semantic resources as knowledge sources for reasoning have another shortcoming: They imply too little structure. WordNet and FrameNet enable some argument mappings of related synsets or frames, but they cannot provide a more detailed concept axiomatization. We are engaged in the manual encoding of abstract theories explicating concepts that pervade natural language discourse, such as

---

[13]The discourse processing pipeline including the ILP-based abductive reasoner is available at https://github.com/metaphor-adp/Metaphor-ADP.

causality, change of state, and scales, and the manual encoding of axioms linking lexical items to these theories. The core theories should underlie axiomatization of such highly frequent and ambiguous words as *have*. A selection of the core theories can be found at http://www.isi.edu/~hobbs/csk.html.

We believe that implementation of these improvements and extensions will make the proposed discourse processing pipeline a powerful reasoning system equipped with enough knowledge to solve manifold NLP tasks on a large scale. In our view, the experiments with the axioms extracted from the lexical-semantic resources presented in this chapter show the potential of weighted abduction for natural language processing and open new ways for its application.

References

Bar-Haim, R., Dagan, I., Dolan, B., Ferro, L., Giampiccolo, D., Magnini, B., & Szpektor, I. (2006). The second PASCAL recognising textual entailment challenge. In *Proc. of the second PASCAL challenges workshop on recognising textual entailment*.

Burchardt, A., & Pennacchiotti, M. (2008). FATE: A FrameNet-annotated corpus for textual entailment. In *Proc. of LREC'08*, Marrakech, Morocco.

Burchardt, A., Erk, K., & Frank, A. (2005). A WordNet detour to framenet. In *Sprachtechnologie, mobile Kommunikation und linguistische Resourcen* (Vol. 8).

Burchardt, A., Pennacchiotti, M., Thater, S., & Pinkal, M. (2009). Assessing the impact of frame semantics on textual entailment. *Natural Language Engineering*, *15*(4), 527–550.

Clark, P., Harrison, P., Thompson, J., Murray, W., Hobbs, J., & Fellbaum, C. (2007). On the role of lexical and world knowledge in RTE3. In *Proc. of the ACL-PASCAL workshop on textual entailment and paraphrasing* (pp. 54–59).

Dagan, I., Dolan, B., Magnini, B., & Roth, D. (2010). Recognizing textual entailment: Rational, evaluation and approaches – erratum. *Natural Language Engineering*, *16*(1), 105.

Das, D., Schneider, N., Chen, D., & Smith, N. A. (2010). *SEMAFOR 1.0: A probabilistic frame-semantic parser* (Technical Report CMU-LTI-10-001). Carnegie Mellon University, Pittsburgh, Pennsylvania.

Davidson, D. (1967). The logical form of action sentences. In N. Rescher (Ed.), *The logic of decision and action* (pp. 81–120). Pittsburgh: University of Pittsburgh Press.

Erk, K., & Pado, S. (2006). Shalmaneser – a flexible toolbox for semantic role assignment. In *Proc. of LREC'06*, Genoa, Italy.

Fellbaum, C. (Ed.) (1998). *WordNet: An electronic lexical database* (1st ed.) Cambridge: MIT Press.

Garoufi, K. (2007). *Towards a better understanding of applied textual entailment: Annotation and evaluation of the RTE-2 dataset*. Master's thesis, Saarland University.

Hobbs, J. R. (1985). Ontological promiscuity. In *Proc. of the 23rd annual meeting of the association for computational linguistics*, Chicago, Illinois (pp. 61–69).

Hobbs, J. R., Stickel, M., Appelt, D., & Martin, P. (1993). Interpretation as abduction. *Artificial Intelligence*, *63*, 69–142.

Inoue, N., & Inui, K. (2011). ILP-based reasoning for weighted abduction. In *Proc. of AAAI workshop on plan, activity and intent recognition*.

Inoue, N., Ovchinnikova, E., Inui, K., & Hobbs, J. R. (2012). Coreference resolution with ILP-based weighted abduction. In *Proc. of the 24th international conference on computational linguistics* (pp. 1291–1308).

McCord, M. C. (1990). Slot grammar: A system for simpler construction of practical natural language grammars. In *In natural language and Logic: International scientific symposium, lecture notes in computer science* (pp. 118–145). Berlin: Springer.

McCord, M. C. (2010). *Using slot grammar* (Technical report). IBM T. J. Watson Research Center. RC 23978 Revised.

McCord, M. C., Murdock, J. W., & Boguraev, B. K. (2012). Deep parsing in Watson. *IBM Journal of Research and Development, 56*(3/4), 3:1–3:15.

Mulkar, R., Hobbs, J. R., & Hovy, E. (2007). Learning from reading syntactically complex biology texts. In *Proc. of the 8th international symposium on logical formalizations of commonsense reasoning*, Palo Alto, USA.

Mulkar-Mehta, R. (2007). Mini-TACITUS. http://www.rutumulkar.com/tacitus.html.

Ovchinnikova, E. (2012). *Integration of world knowledge for natural language understanding.* Amsterdam: Atlantis Press.

Ovchinnikova, E., Vieu, L., Oltramari, A., Borgo, S., & Alexandrov, T. (2010). Data-driven and ontological analysis of FrameNet for natural language reasoning. In N. Calzolari, K. Choukri, B. Maegaard, J. Mariani, J. Odijk, S. Piperidis, M. Rosner, & D. Tapias (Eds.), *Proc. of LREC'10*. Valletta, Malta: European Language Resources Association (ELRA).

Peñas, A., & Ovchinnikova, E. (2012). Unsupervised acquisition of axioms to paraphrase noun compounds and genitives. In *LNCS. Proc. of the international conference on intelligent text processing and computational linguistics*, New Delhi, India (pp. 388–401). Berlin: Springer.

Ruppenhofer, J., Ellsworth, M., Petruck, M., Johnson, C., & Scheffczyk, J. (2006). *FrameNet II: Extended theory and practice*. Berkele: International Computer Science Institute.

Shen, D., & Lapata, M. (2007). Using semantic roles to improve question answering. In *Proc. of EMNLP-CoNLL* (pp. 12–21).

Stickel, M. E. (1988). A prolog technology theorem prover: Implementation by an extended prolog compiler. *Journal of Automated Reasoning, 4*(4), 353–380.

Natural Logic and Natural Language Inference

Bill MacCartney and Christopher D. Manning

Abstract We propose a model of natural language inference which identifies valid inferences by their lexical and syntactic features, without full semantic interpretation. We extend past work in *natural logic*, which has focused on semantic containment and monotonicity, by incorporating both semantic exclusion and implicativity. Our model decomposes an inference problem into a sequence of atomic edits linking premise to hypothesis; predicts a lexical entailment relation for each edit; propagates these relations upward through a semantic composition tree according to properties of intermediate nodes; and joins the resulting entailment relations across the edit sequence. A computational implementation of the model achieves 70 % accuracy and 89 % precision on the FraCaS test suite. Moreover, including this model as a component in an existing system yields significant performance gains on the Recognizing Textual Entailment challenge.

1 Introduction

Natural language inference (NLI) is the problem of determining whether a natural language hypothesis h can reasonably be inferred from a given premise p. For example:

(1) p: *Every firm polled saw costs grow more than expected, even after adjusting for inflation.*
     h: *Every big company in the poll reported cost increases.*

A capacity for open-domain NLI is clearly necessary for full natural language understanding, and NLI can also enable more immediate applications, such as semantic search and question answering. Consequently, NLI has been the focus of intense research effort in recent years, centered around the annual Recognizing Textual Entailment (RTE) competition (Dagan et al. 2006).

B. MacCartney (✉) · C.D. Manning
Stanford University, Stanford, CA, USA
e-mail: wcmac@cs.stanford.edu

C.D. Manning
e-mail: manning@cs.stanford.edu

H. Bunt et al. (eds.), *Computing Meaning*, Text, Speech and Language Technology 47,
DOI 10.1007/978-94-007-7284-7_8,

For a semanticist, the most obvious approach to NLI relies on full semantic interpretation: first, translate p and h into some formal meaning representation, such as first-order logic (FOL), and then apply automated reasoning tools to determine inferential validity. While the formal approach can succeed in restricted domains, it struggles with open-domain NLI tasks such as RTE. For example, the FOL-based system of Bos and Markert (2005) was able to find a proof for less than 4 % of the problems in the RTE1 test set. The difficulty is plain: truly *natural* language is fiendishly complex. The formal approach faces countless thorny problems: idioms, ellipsis, paraphrase, ambiguity, vagueness, lexical semantics, the impact of pragmatics, and so on. Consider for a moment the difficulty of fully and accurately translating example (1) to a formal meaning representation.

Yet example (1) also demonstrates that full semantic interpretation is often not necessary to determining inferential validity. To date, the most successful NLI systems have relied on surface representations and approximate measures of lexical and syntactic similarity to ascertain whether p subsumes h (Glickman et al. 2005; MacCartney et al. 2006; Hickl et al. 2006). However, these approaches face a different problem: they lack the precision needed to properly handle such commonplace phenomena as negation, antonymy, downward-monotone quantifiers, non-factive contexts, and the like. For example, if *every* were replaced by *some* or *most* throughout (1), the lexical and syntactic similarity of h to p would be unaffected, yet the inference would be rendered invalid.

In this paper, we explore a middle way, by developing a model of what Lakoff (1970) called *natural logic*, which characterizes valid patterns of inference in terms of syntactic forms which are as close as possible to surface forms. For example, the natural logic approach might sanction (1) by observing that: in ordinary *upward monotone* contexts, deleting modifiers preserves truth; in *downward monotone* contexts, inserting modifiers preserves truth; and *every* is downward monotone in its restrictor NP. Natural logic thus achieves the semantic precision needed to handle inferences like (1), while sidestepping the difficulties of full semantic interpretation.

The natural logic approach has a very long history,[1] originating in the syllogisms of Aristotle (which can be seen as patterns for natural language inference) and continuing through the medieval scholastics and the work of Leibniz. It was revived in recent times by van Benthem (1988, 1991) and Sánchez Valencia (1991), whose *monotonicity calculus* explains inferences involving semantic containment and inversions of monotonicity, even when nested, as in *Nobody can enter without a valid passport* $\models$ *Nobody can enter without a passport*. However, because the monotonicity calculus lacks any representation of semantic exclusion, it fails to license many simple inferences, such as *Stimpy is a cat* $\models$ *Stimpy is not a poodle*.

Another model which arguably belongs to the natural logic tradition (though not presented as such) was developed by Nairn et al. (2006) to explain inferences involving implicatives and factives, even when negated or nested, as in *Ed did not forget to force Dave to leave* $\models$ *Dave left*. While the model bears some resemblance

---

[1] For a useful overview of the history of natural logic, see van Benthem (2008). For recent work on theoretical aspects of natural logic, see (Fyodorov et al. 2000; Sukkarieh 2001; van Eijck 2005).

to the monotonicity calculus, it does not incorporate semantic containment or explain interactions between implicatives and monotonicity, and thus fails to license inferences such as *John refused to dance* $\models$ *John didn't tango*.

We propose a new model of natural logic which extends the monotonicity calculus to incorporate semantic exclusion, and partly unifies it with Nairn et al.'s account of implicatives. We first define an inventory of *basic entailment relations* which includes representations of both containment and exclusion (Sect. 2). We then describe a general method for establishing the entailment relation between a premise p and a hypothesis h. Given a sequence of *atomic edits* which transforms p into h, we determine the *lexical entailment relation* generated by each edit (Sect. 4); project each lexical entailment relation into an *atomic entailment relation*, according to properties of the context in which the edit occurs (Sect. 5); and join atomic entailment relations across the edit sequence (Sect. 3). We have previously presented an implemented system based on this model (MacCartney and Manning 2008); here we offer a detailed account of its theoretical foundations.

2 An Inventory of Entailment Relations

The simplest formulation of the NLI task is as a binary decision problem: the relation between p and h is to be classified as either *entailment* ($p \models h$) or *non-entailment* ($p \not\models h$). The *three-way* formulation refines this by dividing non-entailment into *contradiction* ($p \models \neg h$) and *compatibility* ($p \not\models h \wedge p \not\models \neg h$).[2] The monotonicity calculus carves things up differently: it interprets entailment as a *semantic containment* relation $\sqsubseteq$ analogous to the set containment relation $\subseteq$, and thus permits us to distinguish forward entailment ($p \sqsubseteq h$) from reverse entailment ($p \sqsupseteq h$). Moreover, it defines $\sqsubseteq$ for expressions of every semantic type, including not only complete sentences but also individual words and phrases. Unlike the three-way formulation, however, it lacks any way to represent contradiction (semantic exclusion). For our model, we want the best of both worlds: a comprehensive inventory of entailment relations that includes representations of both semantic containment and semantic exclusion.

Following Sánchez Valencia, we proceed by analogy with set relations. In a universe U, the set of ordered pairs $\langle x, y \rangle$ of subsets of U can be partitioned into 16 equivalence classes, according to whether each of the four sets $x \cap y$, $x \cap \bar{y}$, $\bar{x} \cap y$, and $\bar{x} \cap \bar{y}$ is empty or non-empty.[3] Of these 16 classes, nine represent degenerate cases in which either x or y is either empty or universal. Since expressions having empty denotations (e.g., *round square cupola*) or universal denotations (e.g., *exists*) fail to divide the world into meaningful categories, they can be regarded as semantically vacuous. Contradictions and tautologies may be common in

---

[2]The first three RTE competitions used the binary formulation, while the three-way formulation was adopted for RTE4. The three-way formulation was also employed in the FraCaS test suite (Cooper et al. 1996) and has been investigated in depth by Condoravdi et al. (2003).

[3]We use $\bar{x}$ to denote the complement of set x in universe U; thus $x \cap \bar{x} = \emptyset$ and $x \cup \bar{x} = U$.

Table 1 The set $\mathfrak{B}$ of seven basic entailment relations

Symbol[a]	Name	Example	Set theoretic definition[b]
$x \equiv y$	equivalence	*couch* $\equiv$ *sofa*	$x = y$
$x \sqsubset y$	forward entailment	*crow* $\sqsubset$ *bird*	$x \subset y$
$x \sqsupset y$	reverse entailment	*European* $\sqsupset$ *French*	$x \supset y$
$x \mathbin{^\wedge} y$	negation	*human* $^\wedge$ *nonhuman*	$x \cap y = \emptyset \wedge x \cup y = U$
$x \mid y$	alternation	*cat* $\mid$ *dog*	$x \cap y = \emptyset \wedge x \cup y \neq U$
$x \smile y$	cover	*animal* $\smile$ *nonhuman*	$x \cap y \neq \emptyset \wedge x \cup y = U$
$x \mathbin{\#} y$	independence	*hungry* $\#$ *hippo*	(all other cases)

[a]Selecting an appropriate symbol to represent each relation is a vexed problem. We sought symbols which (a) are easily approximated by a single ASCII character, (b) are graphically symmetric iff the relations they represent are symmetric, and (c) do not excessively abuse accepted conventions. The $^\wedge$ symbol was chosen to evoke the logically similar bitwise XOR operator of the C programming language family; regrettably, it may also evoke the Boolean AND function. The $\mid$ symbol was chosen to evoke the Sheffer stroke commonly used to represent the logically similar Boolean NAND function; regrettably, it may also evoke the Boolean OR function. The $\sqsubset$ and $\sqsupset$ symbols were obviously chosen to resemble their set-theoretic analogs, but a potential confusion arises because some logicians use the horseshoe $\supset$ (with the *opposite* orientation) to represent material implication

[b]Each relation in $\mathfrak{B}$ obeys the additional constraints that $\emptyset \subset x \subset U$ and $\emptyset \subset y \subset U$ (i.e., x and y are non-vacuous)

logic textbooks, but they are rare in everyday speech. Thus, in a practical model of informal natural language inference, we will rarely go wrong by assuming the *non-vacuity* of the expressions we encounter.[4] We therefore focus on the remaining seven classes, which we designate as the set $\mathfrak{B}$ of *basic entailment relations*, shown in Table 1.

First, the semantic containment relations ($\sqsubset$ and $\sqsupset$) of the monotonicity calculus are preserved, but are factored into three mutually exclusive relations: equivalence ($\equiv$), (strict) forward entailment ($\sqsubset$), and (strict) reverse entailment ($\sqsupset$). Next, we have two relations expressing semantic exclusion: negation ($^\wedge$), or exhaustive exclusion, which is analogous to set complement; and alternation ($\mid$), or non-exhaustive exclusion. The next relation is cover ($\smile$), or non-exclusive exhaustion. Though its utility is not immediately obvious, it is the *dual under negation* of the alternation relation.[5] Finally, the independence relation (#) covers all other cases: it expresses non-equivalence, non-containment, non-exclusion, and non-exhaustion. Note that #

---

[4]Our model can easily be revised to accommodate vacuous expressions and relations between them, but then becomes somewhat unwieldy. The assumption of non-vacuity is closely related to the assumption of *existential import* in traditional logic. For a defense of existential import in natural language semantics, see (Böttner 1988).

[5]We describe relations R and S as *duals under negation* iff $\forall x, y : \langle x, y \rangle \in R \Leftrightarrow \langle \overline{x}, \overline{y} \rangle \in S$. Thus $\sqsubset$ and $\sqsupset$ are dual; $\mid$ and $\smile$ are dual; and $\equiv$, $^\wedge$, and # are self-dual. The significance of this duality will become apparent in Sect. 5.

is the least informative relation, in that it places the fewest constraints on its arguments.[6]

Following Sánchez Valencia, we define the relations in $\mathfrak{B}$ for all semantic types. For semantic types which can be interpreted as characteristic functions of sets,[7] the set-theoretic definitions can be applied directly. The definitions can then be extended to other types by interpreting each type as if it were a type of set. For example, propositions can be understood (per Montague) as denoting sets of possible worlds. Thus two propositions stand in the $|$ relation iff there is no world where both hold (but there is some world where neither holds). Likewise, names can be interpreted as denoting singleton sets, with the result that two names stand in the $\equiv$ relation iff they refer to the same entity, or the $|$ relation otherwise.

By design, the relations in $\mathfrak{B}$ are mutually exclusive, so that we can define a function $\beta(x, y)$ which maps every ordered pair of expressions[8] to the unique relation in $\mathfrak{B}$ to which it belongs.

3 Joining Entailment Relations

If we know that entailment relation R holds between x and y, and that entailment relation S holds between y and z, then what is the entailment relation between x and z? The *join* of entailment relations R and S, which we denote $R \bowtie S$,[9] is defined by:

$$R \bowtie S \stackrel{\text{def}}{=} \{\langle x, z \rangle : \exists y \, (\langle x, y \rangle \in R \wedge \langle y, z \rangle \in S)\}$$

Some joins are quite intuitive. For example, it is immediately clear that $\sqsubset \bowtie \sqsubset = \sqsubset$, $\sqsupset \bowtie \sqsupset = \sqsupset$, $\wedge \bowtie \wedge = \equiv$, and for any R, $(R \bowtie \equiv) = (\equiv \bowtie R) = R$. Other joins are less obvious, but still accessible to intuition. For example, $| \bowtie \wedge = \sqsubset$. This can be seen with the aid of Venn diagrams, or by considering simple examples: *fish* $|$ *human* and *human* $\wedge$ *nonhuman*, thus *fish* $\sqsubset$ *nonhuman*.

But we soon stumble upon an inconvenient truth: not every join yields a relation in $\mathfrak{B}$. For example, if $x \mid y$ and $y \mid z$, the relation between x and z is not determined. They could be equivalent, or one might contain the other. They might be independent

---

[6]Two sets selected uniformly at random from 2^U are overwhelmingly likely to belong to # (for large $|U|$).

[7]That is, all functional types whose final output is a truth value. If we assume a type system whose basic types are e (entities) and t (truth values), then this includes most of the functional types encountered in semantic analysis: $e \to t$ (common nouns, adjectives, and intransitive verbs), $e \to e \to t$ (transitive verbs), $(e \to t) \to (e \to t)$ (adverbs), $(e \to t) \to (e \to t) \to t$ (binary generalized quantifiers), and so on.

[8]Assuming the expressions are non-vacuous, and belong to the same semantic type.

[9]In Tarskian relation algebra, this operation is known as *relation composition*, and is often represented by a semi-colon: $R \, ; \, S$. To avoid confusion with semantic composition (Sect. 5), we prefer to use the term *join* for this operation, by analogy to the database JOIN operation (also commonly represented by $\bowtie$).

Table 2 The join table for the basic entailment relations

⋈	≡	⊏	⊐	^	|	⌣	#
≡	≡	⊏	⊐	^	|	⌣	#
⊏	⊏	⊏	≡⊏⊐|#	|	|	⊏^⌣#	⊏|#
⊐	⊐	≡⊏⊐⌣#	⊐	⌣	⊐^|⌣#	⌣	⊐⌣#
^	^	⌣	|	≡	⊐	⊏	#
|	|	⊏^⌣#	|	⊏	≡⊏⊐|#	⊏	⊏|#
⌣	⌣	⌣	⊐^|⌣#	⊐	⊐	≡⊏⊐⌣#	⊐⌣#
#	#	⊏⌣#	⊐|#	#	⊐|#	⊏⌣#	•

or alternative. All we can say for sure is that they are not exhaustive (since both are disjoint from y). Thus, the result of joining | and | is not a relation in $\mathfrak{B}$, but a *union* of such relations, specifically $\bigcup\{\equiv, \sqsubset, \sqsupset, |, \#\}$.[10]

We will refer to (non-trivial) unions of relations in $\mathfrak{B}$ as *union relations*.[11] Of the 49 possible joins of relations in $\mathfrak{B}$, 32 yield a relation in $\mathfrak{B}$, while 17 yield a union relation, with larger unions conveying less information. Union relations can be further joined, and we can establish that the smallest set of relations which contains $\mathfrak{B}$ and is closed under joining contains just 16 relations.[12] One of these is the total relation, which contains all pairs of (non-vacuous) expressions. This relation, which we denote •, is the black hole of entailment relations, in the sense that (a) it conveys zero information about pairs of expressions which belong to it, and (b) joining a chain of entailment relations will, if it contains any noise and is of sufficient length, lead inescapably to •.[13] This tendency of joining to devolve toward less-informative entailment relations places an important limitation on the power of the inference method described in Sect. 7.

A complete join table for relations in $\mathfrak{B}$ is shown in Table 2.[14]

In an implemented model, the complexity introduced by union relations is easily tamed. Every union relation which results from joining relations in $\mathfrak{B}$ contains #, and thus can safely be approximated by #. After all, # is already the least informative relation in $\mathfrak{B}$—loosely speaking, it indicates ignorance of the relationship between two expressions—and further joining will never serve to strengthen it. Our implemented model therefore has no need to represent union relations.

---

[10] We use this notation as shorthand for the union $\equiv \cup \sqsubset \cup \sqsupset \cup \mid \cup \#$. To be precise, the result of this join is not identical with this union, but is a subset of it, since the union contains some pairs of sets (e.g. $\langle U \setminus a, U \setminus a \rangle$, for any $|a| = 1$) which cannot participate in the | relation. However, the approximation makes little practical difference.

[11] Some union relations hold intrinsic interest. For example, in the three-way formulation of the NLI task described in Sect. 2, the three classes can be identified as $\bigcup\{\equiv, \sqsubset\}$, $\bigcup\{^, |\}$, and $\bigcup\{\sqsupset, \smile, \#\}$.

[12] That is, the relations in $\mathfrak{B}$ plus 9 union relations. Note that this closure fails to include most of the 120 possible union relations. Perhaps surprisingly, the unions $\bigcup\{\equiv, \sqsubset\}$ and $\bigcup\{^, |\}$ mentioned in footnote 11 do not appear.

[13] In fact, computer experiments show that if relations are selected uniformly at random from $\mathfrak{B}$, it requires on average just five joins to reach •.

[14] For compactness, we omit the union notation here; thus $\sqsubset|\#$ stands for $\bigcup\{\sqsubset, |, \#\}$.

4 Lexical Entailment Relations

Suppose x is a compound linguistic expression, and let $e(x)$ be the result of applying an *atomic edit* e (the deletion, insertion, or substitution of a subexpression) to x. The entailment relation which holds between x and $e(x)$, which we denote $\beta(x, e(x))$, will depend on (1) the *lexical entailment relation* generated by e, which we label $\beta(e)$, and (2) other properties of the context x in which e is applied (to be discussed in Sect. 5). For example, suppose x is *red car*. If e is SUB(*car, convertible*), then $\beta(e)$ is $\sqsupset$ (because *convertible* is a hyponym of *car*). On the other hand, if e is DEL(*red*), then $\beta(e)$ is $\sqsubset$ (because *red* is an intersective modifier). Crucially, $\beta(e)$ depends solely on the lexical items involved in e, independent of context.

How are lexical entailment relations determined? Ultimately, this is the province of lexical semantics, which lies outside the scope of this work. However, the answers are fairly intuitive in most cases, and we can make a number of useful observations.

Substitutions The entailment relation generated by a substitution edit is simply the relation between the substituted terms: $\beta(\text{SUB}(x, y)) = \beta(x, y)$. For open-class terms such as nouns, adjectives, and verbs, we can often determine the appropriate relation by consulting a lexical resource such as WordNet. Synonyms belong to the $\equiv$ relation (*sofa* $\equiv$ *couch, forbid* $\equiv$ *prohibit*); hyponym-hypernym pairs belong to the $\sqsubset$ relation (*crow* $\sqsubset$ *bird, frigid* $\sqsubset$ *cold, soar* $\sqsubset$ *rise*); and antonyms and coordinate terms generally belong to the $|$ relation (*hot* $|$ *cold, cat* $|$ *dog*).[15] Proper nouns, which denote individual entities or events, will stand in the $\equiv$ relation if they denote the same entity (*USA* $\equiv$ *United States*), or the $|$ relation otherwise (*JFK* $|$ *FDR*). Pairs which cannot reliably be assigned to another entailment relation will be assigned to the # relation (*hungry* # *hippo*). Of course, there are many difficult cases, where the most appropriate relation will depend on subjective judgments about word sense, topical context, and so on—consider, for example, the pair *system* and *approach*. And some judgments may depend on world knowledge not readily available to an automatic system. For example, plausibly *skiing* $|$ *sleeping*, but *skiing* # *talking*.

Closed-class terms may require special handling. Substitutions involving generalized quantifiers generate a rich variety of entailment relations: *all* $\equiv$ *every, every* $\sqsubset$ *some, some* $\wedge$ *no, no* $|$ *every, at least four* $\smile$ *at most six*, and *most* # *ten or more*.[16] Two pronouns, or a pronoun and a noun, should ideally be assigned to the $\equiv$ relation if it can determined from context that they refer to the same entity, though this may be difficult for an automatic system to establish reliably. Prepositions are somewhat problematic. Some pairs of prepositions can be interpreted as antonyms, and thus

---

[15]Note that most antonym pairs do *not* belong to the $\wedge$ relation, since they typically do not exclude the middle.

[16]Some of these assertions assume the non-vacuity (Sect. 2) of the predicates to which the quantifiers are applied.

assigned to the | relation (*above* | *below*), but many prepositions are used so flexibly in natural language that they are best assigned to the ≡ relation (*on* [*a plane*] ≡ *in* [*a plane*] ≡ *by* [*plane*]).

Generic Deletions and Insertions   For deletion edits, the default behavior is to generate the ⊏ relation (thus *red car* ⊏ *car*). Insertion edits are symmetric: by default, they generate the ⊐ relation (*sing* ⊐ *sing off-key*). This heuristic can safely be applied whenever the affected phrase is an intersective modifier, and can usefully be applied to phrases much longer than a single word (*car which has been parked outside since last week* ⊏ *car*). Indeed, this principle underlies most current approaches the RTE task, in which the premise p often contains much extraneous content not found in the hypothesis h. Most RTE systems try to determine whether p subsumes h: they penalize new content inserted into h, but do not penalize content deleted from p.

Special Deletions and Insertions   However, some lexical items exhibit special behavior upon deletion or insertion. The most obvious example is negation, which generates the ∧ relation (*didn't sleep* ∧ *did sleep*). Implicatives and factives (such as *refuse to* and *admit that*) constitute another important class of exceptions, but we postpone discussion of them to Sect. 6. Then there are non-intersective adjectives such as *former* and *alleged*. These have various behavior: deleting *former* seems to generate the | relation (*former student* | *student*), while deleting *alleged* seems to generate the # relation (*alleged spy* # *spy*). We lack a complete typology of such cases, but consider this an interesting problem for lexical semantics. Finally, for pragmatic reasons, we typically assume that auxiliary verbs and punctuation marks are semantically vacuous, and thus generate the ≡ relation upon deletion or insertion. When combined with the assumption that morphology matters little in inference,[17] this allows us to establish, e.g., that *is sleeping* ≡ *sleeps* and *did sleep* ≡ *slept*.

5 Entailment Relations and Semantic Composition

How are entailment relations affected by semantic composition? In other words, how do the entailment relations between compound expressions depend on the entailment relations between their parts? Say we have established the value of $\beta(x, y)$, and let f be an expression which can take x or y as an argument. What is the value of $\beta(f(x), f(y))$, and how does it depend on the properties of f?

The monotonicity calculus of Sánchez Valencia provides a partial answer. It explains the impact of semantic composition on entailment relations ≡, ⊏, ⊐, and # by assigning semantic functions to one of three monotonicity classes: UP, DOWN, and NON. If f has monotonicity UP (the default), then the entailment relation between x

---

[17]Indeed, the official definition of the RTE task explicitly specifies that tense be ignored.

and y is projected through f without change: $\beta(f(x), f(y)) = \beta(x, y)$. Thus *some parrots talk* $\sqsubseteq$ *some birds talk*. If f has monotonicity DOWN, then $\sqsubseteq$ and $\sqsupseteq$ are swapped. Thus *no carp talk* $\sqsupseteq$ *no fish talk*. Finally, if f has monotonicity NON, then $\sqsubseteq$ and $\sqsupseteq$ are projected as #. Thus *most humans talk* # *most animals talk*.

The monotonicity calculus also provides an algorithm for computing the effect on entailment relations of multiple levels of semantic composition. Although Sánchez Valencia's presentation of this algorithm uses a complex scheme for annotating nodes in a categorial grammar parse, the central idea can be recast in simple terms: propagate a lexical entailment relation upward through a semantic composition tree, from leaf to root, while respecting the monotonicity properties of each node along the path. Consider the sentence *Nobody can enter without pants*. A plausible semantic composition tree for this sentence could be rendered as (*nobody* (*can* ((*without pants*) *enter*))). Now consider replacing *pants* with *clothes*. We begin with the lexical entailment relation: *pants* $\sqsubseteq$ *clothes*. The semantic function *without* has monotonicity DOWN, so *without pants* $\sqsupseteq$ *without clothes*. Continuing up the semantic composition tree, *can* has monotonicity UP, but *nobody* has monotonicity DOWN, so we get another reversal, and find that *nobody can enter without pants* $\sqsubseteq$ *nobody can enter without clothes*.

While the monotonicity calculus elegantly explains the impact of semantic composition on the containment relations (chiefly, $\sqsubseteq$ and $\sqsupseteq$), it lacks any account of the exclusion relations ($\wedge$ and $|$, and, indirectly, $\smile$). To remedy this lack, we propose to generalize the concept of monotonicity to a concept of *projectivity*. We categorize semantic functions into a number of *projectivity signatures*, which can be seen as generalizations of both the three monotonicity classes of Sánchez Valencia and the nine implication signatures of Nairn et al. (see Sect. 6). Each projectivity signature is defined by a map $\mathfrak{B} \mapsto \mathfrak{B}$ which specifies how each entailment relation is projected by the function. (Binary functions can have different signatures for each argument.) In principle, there are up to 7^7 possible signatures; in practice, probably no more than a handful are realized by natural language expressions. Though we lack a complete inventory of projectivity signatures, we can describe a few important cases.

Negation   We begin with simple negation (*not*). Like most functions, it projects $\equiv$ and # without change (*not happy* $\equiv$ *not glad* and *isn't swimming* # *isn't hungry*). As a downward monotone function, it swaps $\sqsubseteq$ and $\sqsupseteq$ (*didn't kiss* $\sqsupseteq$ *didn't touch*). But we can also establish that it projects $\wedge$ without change (*not human* $\wedge$ *not nonhuman*) and swaps $|$ and $\smile$ (*not French* $\smile$ *not German* and *not more than 4* $|$ *not less than 6*). Its projectivity signature is therefore $\{\equiv:\equiv, \sqsubseteq:\sqsupseteq, \sqsupseteq:\sqsubseteq, \wedge:\wedge, |:\smile, \smile:|, \#:\#\}$.

Intersective Modification   Intersective modification has monotonicity UP, but projects both $\wedge$ and $|$ as $|$ (*living human* $|$ *living nonhuman* and *French wine* $|$ *Spanish wine*), and projects $\smile$ as # (*metallic pipe* # *nonferrous pipe*). It therefore has signature $\{\equiv:\equiv, \sqsubseteq:\sqsubseteq, \sqsupseteq:\sqsupseteq, \wedge:|, |:|, \smile:\#, \#:\#\}$.[18]

---

[18] At least for practical purposes. The projection of $\wedge$ and $|$ as $|$ depends on the assumption of non-vacuity, and $\smile$ is actually projected as $\bigcup\{\equiv, \sqsubseteq, \sqsupseteq, |, \#\}$, which we approximate by #, as described in Sect. 3.

Table 3 Projectivity signatures for various quantifiers

Quantifier	Projectivity for 1st argument							Projectivity for 2nd argument						
	≡	⊏	⊐	^	|	⌣	#	≡	⊏	⊐	^	|	⌣	#
some	≡	⊏	⊐	⌣†	#	⌣†	#	≡	⊏	⊐	⌣†	#	⌣†	#
no	≡	⊐	⊏	|†	#	|†	#	≡	⊐	⊏	|†	#	|†	#
every	≡	⊐	⊏	|‡	#	|‡	#	≡	⊏	⊐	|†	|†	#	#
not every	≡	⊏	⊐	⌣‡	#	⌣‡	#	≡	⊐	⊏	⌣†	⌣†	#	#

Quantifiers While semanticists are well acquainted with the monotonicity properties of common quantifiers, how they project the exclusion relations may be less familiar. Table 3 summarizes the projectivity signatures of the most common binary generalized quantifiers for each argument position.

A few observations:

- All quantifiers (like most other semantic functions) project ≡ and # without change.
- The table confirms well-known monotonicity properties: *no* is downward-monotone in both arguments, *every* in its first argument, and *not every* in its second argument.
- Relation | is frequently "blocked" by quantifiers (i.e., projected as #). Thus *no fish talk* # *no birds talk* and *someone was early* # *someone was late*. A notable exception is *every* in its second argument, where | is preserved: *everyone was early* | *everyone was late*. (Note the similarity to intersective modification.)
- Because *no* is the negation of *some*, its projectivity signature can be found by projecting the signature of *some* through the signature of *not*. Likewise for *not every* and *every*.
- Some results depend on assuming the non-vacuity of the other argument to the quantifier: those marked with † assume it to be non-empty, while those marked with ‡ assume it to be non-universal. Without these assumptions, # is projected.

Verbs Verbs (and verb-like constructions) exhibit diverse behavior. Most verbs are upward-monotone (though not all—see Sect. 6), and many verbs project ^, |, and ⌣ as # (*eats humans* # *eats nonhumans*, *eats cats* # *eats dogs*, and *eats mammals* # *eats nonhumans*). However, verbs which encode functional relations seem to exhibit the same projectivity as intersective modifiers, projecting ^ and | as |, and ⌣ as #.[19] Categorizing verbs according to projectivity is an interesting problem for lexical semantics, which may involve codifying some amount of world knowledge.

---

[19]Consider the verbal construct *is married to*: *is married to a German* | *is married to a non-German, is married to a German* | *is married to an Italian, is married to a European* # *is married to a non-German*. The AUCONTRAIRE system (Ritter et al. 2008) includes an intriguing approach to identifying such *functional phrases* automatically.

Table 4 Implicatives and factives

	Signature	$\beta(\mathrm{DEL}(\cdot))$	$\beta(\mathrm{INS}(\cdot))$	Example
implicatives (UP)	+/−	≡	≡	*he managed to escape* ≡ *he escaped*
	+/○	⊏	⊐	*he was forced to sell* ⊏ *he sold*
	○/−	⊐	⊏	*he was permitted to live* ⊐ *he lived*
implicatives (DOWN)	−/+	∧	∧	*he forgot to pay* ∧ *he paid*
	−/○	|	|	*he refused to fight* | *he fought*
	○/+	⌣	⌣	*he hesitated to ask* ⌣ *he asked*
factives (NON)	+/+	⊏	⊐	*he admitted that he knew* ⊏ *he knew*
	−/−	|	|	*he pretended he was sick* | *he was sick*
	○/○	#	#	*he wanted to fly* # *he flew*

6 Implicatives and Factives

In (Nairn et al. 2006), Nairn et al. offer an elegant account of inferences involving implicatives and factives[20] such as *manage to, refuse to,* and *admit that*. Their model classifies such operators into nine *implication signatures*, according to their implications—positive (+), negative (−), or null (○)—in both positive and negative contexts. Thus *refuse to* has implication signature −/○, because it carries a negative implication in a positive context (*refused to dance* implies *didn't dance*), and no implication in a negative context (*didn't refuse to dance* implies neither *danced* nor *didn't dance*).

Most of the phenomena observed by Nairn et al. can be explained within our framework by specifying, for each implication signature, the relation generated when an operator of that signature is deleted from (or inserted into) a compound expression, as shown in Table 4.

This table invites several observations. First, as the examples make clear, there is room for variation regarding the appearance of infinitive arguments, complementizers, passivization, and morphology. An implemented model must tolerate such diversity.

Second, some of the examples may seem more intuitive when one considers their negations. For example, deleting signature ○/− generates ⊐; under negation, this is projected as ⊏ (*he wasn't permitted to live* ⊏ *he didn't live*). Likewise, deleting signature ○/+ generates ⌣; under negation, this is projected as | (*he didn't hesitate to ask* | *he didn't ask*).

Third, a fully satisfactory treatment of the factives (signatures +/+, −/−, and ○/○) would require an extension to our present theory. For example, deleting signature +/+ generates ⊏; yet under negation, this is projected not as ⊐, but as | (*he*

---

[20]We use "factives" as an umbrella term embracing counterfactives and nonfactives along with factives proper.

didn't admit that he knew | he didn't know). The problem arises because the implication carried by a factive is not an entailment, but a presupposition.[21] As is well known, the projection behavior of presuppositions differs from that of entailments (van der Sandt 1992). It seems likely that our model could be elaborated to account for projection of presuppositions as well as entailments, but we leave this for future work.

We can further cement implicatives and factives within our model by specifying the monotonicity class for each implication signature: signatures $+/-$, $+/\circ$, and $\circ/-$ have monotonicity UP (*force to tango $\sqsubset$ force to dance*); signatures $-/+$, $-/\circ$, and $\circ/+$ have monotonicity DOWN (*refuse to tango $\sqsupset$ refuse to dance*); and signatures $+/+$, $-/-$, and $\circ/\circ$ (the propositional attitudes) have monotonicity NON (*think tangoing is fun # think dancing is fun*). We are not yet able to specify the complete projectivity signature corresponding to each implication signature, but we can describe a few specific cases. For example, implication signature $-/\circ$ seems to project $\wedge$ as | (*refuse to stay | refuse to go*) and both | and $\smile$ as # (*refuse to tango # refuse to waltz*).

7 Putting It All Together

We now have the building blocks of a general method to establish the entailment relation between a premise p and a hypothesis h. The steps are as follows:

1. Find a sequence of atomic edits $\langle e_1, \ldots, e_n \rangle$ which transforms p into h: thus $h = (e_n \circ \ldots \circ e_1)(p)$. For convenience, let us define $x_0 = p$, $x_n = h$, and $x_i = e_i(x_{i-1})$ for $i \in [1, n]$.
2. For each atomic edit e_i:

   a. Determine the lexical entailment relation $\beta(e_i)$, as in Sect. 4.
   b. Project $\beta(e_i)$ upward through the semantic composition tree of expression x_{i-1} to find an *atomic entailment relation* $\beta(x_{i-1}, x_i)$, as in Sect. 5.

3. Join atomic entailment relations across the sequence of edits, as in Sect. 3:

$$\beta(p, h) = \beta(x_0, x_n) = \beta(x_0, e_1) \bowtie \ldots \bowtie \beta(x_{i-1}, e_i) \bowtie \ldots \bowtie \beta(x_{n-1}, e_n)$$

However, this inference method has several important limitations, including the need to find an appropriate edit sequence connecting p and h;[22] the tendency of

---

[21]Of course, the implicatives may carry presuppositions as well (*he managed to escape $\rightarrow$ it was hard to escape*), but these implications are not activated by a simple deletion, as with the factives.

[22]The order of edits can be significant, if one edit affects the projectivity properties of the context for another edit. In practice, we typically find that different edit orders lead to the same final result (albeit via different intermediate steps), or at worst to a result which is compatible with, though less informative than, the desired result. But in principle, edit sequences involving lexical items with unusual properties—not exhibited, so far as we are aware, by any natural language expressions— could lead to incompatible results. Thus we lack any formal guarantee of soundness.

Table 5 An example inference involving semantic exclusion

i	e_i	$x_i = e_i(x_{i-1})$	$\beta(e_i)$	$\beta(x_{i-1}, x_i)$	$\beta(x_0, x_i)$
		Stimpy is a cat			
1	SUB(cat, dog)		$\mid$	$\mid$	$\mid$
		Stimpy is a dog			
2	INS(not)		$\wedge$	$\wedge$	$\sqsubset$
		Stimpy is not a dog			
3	SUB(dog, $poodle$)		$\sqsupset$	$\sqsubset$	$\sqsubset$
		Stimpy is not a poodle			

the join operation toward less informative entailment relations, as described in Sect. 3; and the lack of a general mechanism for combining information from multiple premises.[23] Consequently, the method has less deductive power than first-order logic, and fails to sanction some fairly simple inferences, including de Morgan's laws for quantifiers. But the method neatly explains many inferences not handled by the monotonicity calculus.

For example, while the monotonicity calculus notably fails to explain even the simplest inferences involving semantic exclusion, such examples are easily accommodated in our framework. We encountered an example of such an inference in Sect. 1: *Stimpy is a cat* $\models$ *Stimpy is not a poodle*. Clearly, this is a valid natural language inference. To establish this using our inference method, we must begin by selecting a sequence of atomic edits which transforms the premise p into the hypothesis h. While there are several possibilities, one obvious choice is first to replace *cat* with *dog*, then to insert *not*, and finally to replace *dog* with *poodle*. An analysis of this edit sequence is shown in Table 5. In this representation (of which we will see several more examples in the following pages), we show three entailment relations associated with each edit e_i, namely:

- $\beta(e_i)$, the lexical entailment relation generated by e_i,
- $\beta(x_{i-1}, x_i)$, the atomic entailment relation which holds across e_i, and
- $\beta(x_0, x_i)$, the cumulative join of all atomic entailment relations up through e_i. This can be calculated in the table as $\beta(x_0, x_{i-1}) \bowtie \beta(x_{i-1}, x_i)$.

In Table 5, x_0 is transformed into x_3 by a sequence of three edits. First, replacing *cat* with its coordinate term *dog* generates the lexical entailment relation $\mid$. Next, inserting *not* generates $\wedge$, and $\mid$ joined with $\wedge$ yields $\sqsubset$. Finally, replacing *dog* with its hyponym *poodle* generates $\sqsupset$. Because of the downward-monotone context created by *not*, this is projected as $\sqsubset$, and $\sqsubset$ joined with $\sqsubset$ yields $\sqsubset$. Therefore, premise x_0 entails hypothesis x_3.

---

[23] However, some inferences can be enabled by auxiliary premises encoded as lexical entailment relations. For example, *men* $\sqsubset$ *mortal* can enable the classic syllogism *Socrates is a man* $\sqsubset$ *Socrates is mortal*.

Table 6 An example inference involving an implicative

i	e_i	$x_i = e_i(x_{i-1})$	$\beta(e_i)$	$\beta(x_{i-1}, x_i)$	$\beta(x_0, x_i)$
		We were not permitted to smoke			
1	DEL(*permitted to*)		⊐	⊏	⊏
		We did not smoke			
2	DEL(*not*)		∧	∧	‖
		We smoked			
3	INS(*Cuban cigars*)		⊐	⊐		
		We smoked Cuban cigars			

For an example involving an implicative, consider the inference in Table 6. Again, x_0 is transformed into x_3 by a sequence of three edits.[24] First, deleting *permitted to* generates ⊐, according to its implication signature; but because *not* is downward-monotone, this is projected as ⊏. Next, deleting *not* generates ∧, and ⊏ joined with ∧ yields |. Finally, inserting *Cuban cigars* restricts the meaning of *smoked*, generating ⊐, and | joined with ⊐ yields |. So x_3 contradicts x_0.

Let's now look at a more complex example (first presented in (MacCartney and Manning 2008)) that demonstrates the interaction of a number of aspects of the model we've presented. The inference is:

p: *Jimmy Dean refused to move without blue jeans.*
h: *James Dean didn't dance without pants.*

Of course, the example is quite contrived, but it has the advantage that it compactly exhibits several phenomena of interest: semantic containment (between *move* and *dance*, and between *pants* and *jeans*); semantic exclusion (in the form of negation); an implicative (namely, *refuse to*); and nested inversions of monotonicity (created by *refuse to* and *without*). In this example, the premise *p* can be transformed into the hypothesis *h* by a sequence of seven edits, as shown in Table 7. This time we include even "light" edits yielding ≡ for the sake of completeness.

We analyze these edits as follows. The first edit simply substitutes one variant of a name for another; since both substituends denote the same entity, the edit generates the ≡ relation. The second edit deletes an implicative (*refuse to*) with implication signature −/∘. As described in Sect. 6, deletions of this signature generate the | relation, and ≡ joined with | yields |. The third edit inserts an auxiliary verb (*did*); since auxiliaries are more or less semantically vacuous, this generates the ≡ relation, and | joined with ≡ yields | again. The fourth edit inserts a negation, generating the ∧ relation. Here we encounter the first interesting join: as explained in Sect. 3, | joined with ∧ yields ⊏. The fifth edit substitutes *move* with its hyponym *dance*, generating the ⊐ relation. However, because the edit occurs within the scope of the newly-introduced negation, ⊐ is projected as ⊏, and ⊏ joined with ⊏ yields ⊏. The sixth edit deletes a generic modifier (*blue*), which generates the ⊏ relation by default. This

---

[24]We neglect edits involving auxiliaries and morphology, which simply yield the ≡ relation.

Table 7 Analysis of a more complex inference

i	e_i	$x_i = e_i(x_{i-1})$	$\beta(e_i)$	$\beta(x_{i-1}, x_i)$	$\beta(x_0, x_i)$
		Jimmy Dean refused to move without blue jeans			
1	SUB(*Jimmy Dean, James Dean*)		≡	≡	≡
		James Dean refused to move without blue jeans			
2	DEL(*refused to*)		|	|	|
		James Dean moved without blue jeans			
3	INS(*did*)		≡	≡	|
		James Dean did move without blue jeans			
4	INS(*n't*)		∧	∧	⊏
		James Dean didn't move without blue jeans			
5	SUB(*move, dance*)		⊐	⊏	⊏
		James Dean didn't dance without blue jeans			
6	DEL(*blue*)		⊏	⊏	⊏
		James Dean didn't dance without jeans			
7	SUB(*jeans, pants*)		⊏	⊏	⊏
		James Dean didn't dance without pants			

time the edit occurs within the scope of *two* downward-monotone operators (*without* and negation), so we have two inversions of monotonocity, and ⊏ is projected as ⊏. Again, ⊏ joined with ⊏ yields ⊏. Finally, the seventh edit substitutes *jeans* with its hypernym *pants*, generating the ⊏ relation. Again, the edit occurs within the scope of two downward-monotone operators, so ⊏ is projected as ⊏, and ⊏ joined with ⊏ yields ⊏. Thus p entails h.

Of course, the edit sequence shown in Table 7 is not the only sequence which can transform p into h. A different edit sequence might yield a different sequence of intermediate steps, but the same final result. Consider, for example, the edit sequence shown in Table 8. Note that the lexical entailment relation $\beta(e_i)$ generated by each edit is the same as before. But because the edits involving downward-monotone operators (namely, INS(*n't*) and DEL(*refused to*)) now occur at different points in the edit sequence, many of the atomic entailment relations $\beta(x_{i-1}, x_i)$ have changed, and thus the sequence of joins has changed as well. In particular, edits 3 and 4 occur within the scope of *three* downward-monotone operators (negation, *refuse*, and *without*), with the consequence that the ⊏ relation generated by each of these lexical edits is projected as ⊐. Likewise, edit 5 occurs within the scope of two downward-monotone operators (negation and *refuse*), and edit 6 occurs within the scope of one downward-monotone operator (negation), so that \| is projected as ⌣. Nevertheless, the ultimate result is still ⊏.

However, it turns out not to be the case that every edit sequence which transforms p into h will yield equally satisfactory results. Consider the sequence shown in Table 9. The crucial difference in this edit sequence is that the insertion of *not*, which generates lexical entailment relation ∧, occurs within the scope of *refuse*,

Table 8 An alternative analysis of the inference from Table 7

i	e_i	$x_i = e_i(x_{i-1})$	$\beta(e_i)$	$\beta(x_{i-1}, x_i)$	$\beta(x_0, x_i)$
		Jimmy Dean refused to move without blue jeans			
1	INS(*did*)		$\equiv$	$\equiv$	$\equiv$
		Jimmy Dean did refuse to move without blue jeans			
2	INS(*n't*)		$\wedge$	$\wedge$	$\wedge$
		Jimmy Dean didn't refuse to move without blue jeans			
3	DEL(*blue*)		$\sqsubset$	$\sqsupset$	$\vert$
		Jimmy Dean didn't refuse to move without jeans			
4	SUB(*jeans, pants*)		$\sqsubset$	$\sqsupset$	$\vert$
		Jimmy Dean didn't refuse to move without pants			
5	SUB(*move, dance*)		$\sqsupset$	$\sqsupset$	$\vert$
		Jimmy Dean didn't refuse to dance without pants			
6	DEL(*refuse to*)		$\vert$	$\smile$	$\sqsubset$
		Jimmy Dean didn't dance without pants			
7	SUB(*Jimmy, James*)		$\equiv$	$\equiv$	$\sqsubset$
		James Dean didn't dance without pants			

Table 9 A third analysis of the inference from Table 7

i	e_i	$x_i = e_i(x_{i-1})$	$\beta(e_i)$	$\beta(x_{i-1}, x_i)$	$\beta(x_0, x_i)$
		Jimmy Dean refused to move without blue jeans			
1	INS(*did*)		$\equiv$	$\equiv$	$\equiv$
		Jimmy Dean did refuse to move without blue jeans			
2	INS(*not*)		$\wedge$	$\vert$	$\vert$
		Jimmy Dean did refuse not to move without blue jeans			
3	DEL(*refuse to*)		$\vert$	$\vert$	$\equiv\sqsubset\sqsupset\vert\#$
		Jimmy Dean didn't move without blue jeans			
4	DEL(*blue*)		$\sqsubset$	$\sqsubset$	$\bullet$
		Jimmy Dean didn't move without jeans			
5	SUB(*jeans, pants*)		$\sqsubset$	$\sqsubset$	$\bullet$
		Jimmy Dean didn't move without pants			
6	SUB(*move, dance*)		$\sqsupset$	$\sqsupset$	$\bullet$
		Jimmy Dean didn't dance without pants			
7	SUB(*Jimmy Dean, James Dean*)		$\equiv$	$\equiv$	$\bullet$
		James Dean didn't dance without pants			

so that $\wedge$ is projected as atomic entailment relation $\vert$ (see Sect. 5). But the deletion of *refuse to* also produces atomic entailment relation $\vert$ (see Sect. 6), and $\vert$ joined with $\vert$ yields a relatively uninformative union relation, namely $\bigcup\{\equiv, \sqsubset, \sqsupset, \vert, \#\}$ (which could also be described as the NON-EXHAUSTION relation). The damage has been done: further joining leads directly to the "black hole" relation •, from which there is no escape. Note, however, that even for this infelicitous edit sequence, our inference method has not produced an *incorrect* answer (because the • relation includes the ⊏ relation), only an *uninformative* answer (because it includes all other relations in 𝕭 as well).

Additional examples are presented in (MacCartney 2009).

8 Implementation and Evaluation

The model of natural logic described here has been implemented in software as the NatLog system. In previous work (MacCartney and Manning 2008), we have presented a description and evaluation of NatLog; this section summarizes the main results. NatLog faces three primary challenges:

1. *Finding an appropriate sequence of atomic edits connecting premise and hypothesis.* NatLog does not address this problem directly, but relies instead on edit sequences from other sources. We have investigated this problem separately in (MacCartney et al. 2008).
2. *Determining the lexical entailment relation for each edit.* NatLog learns to predict lexical entailment relations by using machine learning techniques and exploiting a variety of manually and automatically constructed sources of information on lexical relations.
3. *Computing the projection of each lexical entailment relation.* NatLog identifies expressions with non-default projectivity and computes the likely extent of their arguments in a syntactic parse using hand-crafted tree patterns.

We have evaluated NatLog on two different test suites. The first is the FraCaS test suite (Cooper et al. 1996), which contains 346 NLI problems, divided into nine sections, each focused on a specific category of semantic phenomena. The goal is three-way entailment classification, as described in Sect. 2. On this task, NatLog achieves an average accuracy of 70 %.[25] In the section concerning quantifiers, which is both the largest and the most amenable to natural logic, the system answers all problems but one correctly. Unsurprisingly, performance is mediocre in four sections concerning semantic phenomena (e.g., ellipsis) not relevant to natural logic and not modeled by the system. But in the other five sections (representing about 60 % of the problems), NatLog achieves accuracy of 87 %. What's more, precision is uniformly high, averaging 89 % over all sections. Thus, even outside its areas of expertise, the system rarely predicts entailment when none exists.

The RTE3 test suite (Giampiccolo et al. 2007) differs from FraCaS in several important ways: the goal is binary entailment classification; the problems have much longer premises and are more "natural"; and the problems employ a diver-

---

[25] Our evaluation excluded multi-premise problems, which constitute about 44 % of the test suite.

sity of types of inference—including paraphrase, temporal reasoning, and relation extraction—which NatLog is not designed to address. Consequently, the NatLog system by itself achieves mediocre accuracy (59 %) on RTE3 problems. However, its precision is comparatively high, which suggests a strategy of hybridizing with a broad-coverage RTE system. We were able to show that adding NatLog as a component in the Stanford RTE system (Chambers et al. 2007) led to accuracy gains of 4 %.

9 Conclusion

The model of natural logic presented here is by no means a universal solution to the problem of natural language inference. Many NLI problems hinge on types of inference not addressed by natural logic, and the inference method we describe faces a number of limitations on its deductive power (discussed in Sect. 7). Moreover, there is further work to be done in fleshing out our account of projectivity, particularly in establishing the proper projectivity signatures for a broader range of quantifiers, verbal constructs, implicatives and factives, logical connectives, and other semantic functions.

Nevertheless, we believe our model of natural logic fills an important niche. While approximate methods based on lexical and syntactic similarity can handle many NLI problems, they are easily confounded by inferences involving negation, antonymy, quantifiers, implicatives, and many other phenomena. Our model achieves the logical precision needed to handle such inferences without resorting to full semantic interpretation, which is in any case rarely possible. The practical value of the model is demonstrated by its success in evaluations on the FraCaS and RTE3 test suites.

References

Bos, J., & Markert, K. (2005). Recognising textual entailment with logical inference. In *Proceedings of the conference on human language technology and empirical methods in natural language processing* (pp. 628–635). Vancouver: Association for Computational Linguistics.

Böttner, M. (1988). A note on existential import. *Studia Logica, 47*(1), 35–40.

Chambers, N., Cer, D., Grenager, T., Hall, D., Kiddon, C., MacCartney, B., de Marneffe, M.-C., Ramage, D., Yeh, E., & Manning, C. D. (2007). Learning alignments and leveraging natural logic. In *Proceedings of the ACL-07 workshop on textual entailment and paraphrasing* (pp. 165–170). Prague: Association for Computational Linguistics.

Condoravdi, C., Crouch, D., de Paiva, V., Stolle, R., & Bobrow, D. (2003). Entailment, intensionality and text understanding. In *Proceedings of the HLT-NAACL 2003 workshop on text meaning* (pp. 38–45). Morristown: Association for Computational Linguistics.

Cooper, R., et al. (1996). *Using the framework* (Technical Report LRE 62-051 D-16). The FraCaS Consortium.

Dagan, I., Glickman, O., & Magnini, B. (2006). The PASCAL recognising textual entailment challenge. In J. Quiñonero-Candela, C. E. Rasmussen, F. Sinz, O. Bousquet, & B. Schölkopf (Eds.), *Machine learning challenges. Evaluating predictive uncertainty, visual object classification, and recognising textual entailment* (Vol. 3944, pp. 177–190). Berlin: Springer.

Fyodorov, Y., Winter, Y., & Francez, N. (2000). A natural logic inference system. In *Proceedings of the 2nd international workshop on inference in computational semantics* (ICoS-2), Germany: Dagstuhl.

Giampiccolo, D., Magnini, B., Dagan, I., & Dolan, B. (2007). The third PASCAL recognizing textual entailment challenge. In *Proceedings of the ACL-07 workshop on textual entailment and paraphrasing* (pp. 1–9). Prague: Association for Computational Linguistics

Glickman, O., Dagan, I., & Koppel, M. (2005). Web based probabilistic textual entailment. In *Proceedings of the PASCAL challenges workshop on recognizing textual entailment.* http://u.cs.biu. ac.il/~nlp/RTE1/Proceedings/glickman_et_al.pdf.

Hickl, A., Williams, J., Bensley, J., Roberts, K., Rink, B., & Shi, Y. (2006). Recognizing textual entailment with LCC's GROUNDHOG system. In *Proceedings of the second PASCAL challenges workshop on recognizing textual entailment*, Venice, Italy, PASCAL (pp. 137–142).

Lakoff, G. (1970). Linguistics and natural logic. *Synthese, 22,* 151–271.

MacCartney, B. (2009). *Natural language inference.* Ph.D. thesis, Stanford University.

MacCartney, B., & Manning, C. D. (2008). Modeling semantic containment and exclusion in natural language inference. In *Proceedings of the 22nd international conference on computational linguistics* (COLING-08) (pp. 521–528). Manchester: Association for Computational Linguistics.

MacCartney, B., Grenager, T., de Marneffe, M.-C., Cer, D., & Manning, C. D. (2006). Learning to recognize features of valid textual entailments. In *Proceedings of the human language technology conference of the North American chapter of the Association of Computational Linguistics* (pp. 41–48). New York: Association for Computational Linguistics.

Nairn, R., Condoravdi, C., & Karttunen, L. (2006). Computing relative polarity for textual inference. In *Proceedings of the fifth international workshop on inference in computational semantics* (ICoS-5) (pp. 67–76).

MacCartney, B., Galley, M., & Manning, C. D. (2008). A phrase-based alignment model for natural language inference. In *Proceedings of the conference on empirical methods in natural language processing* (pp. 802–811). Honolulu: Association for Computational Linguistics.

Ritter, A., Downey, D., Soderland, S., & Etzioni, O. (2008). It's a contradiction—no, it's not: A case study using functional relations. In *Proceedings of the conference on empirical methods in natural language processing* (pp. 11–20). Honolulu: Association for Computational Linguistics.

Sánchez Valencia, V. (1991). *Studies on natural logic and categorial grammar.* Ph.D. thesis, Univ. Amsterdam.

Sukkarieh, J. (2001). Quasi-NL knowledge representation for structurally-based inferences. In *Proceedings of the 3rd international workshop on inference in computational semantics* (ICoS-3), Siena, Italy.

van Benthem, J. (1988). The semantics of variety in categorial grammars. In W. Buszkowski, W. Marciszewski, & J. van Benthem (Eds.), *Categorial grammar* (pp. 33–55). Amsterdam: Benjamins.

van Benthem, J. (1991). *Studies in logic: Vol. 130. Language in action: Categories, lambdas and dynamic logic.* Amsterdam: North-Holland.

van Benthem, J. (2008). *A brief history of natural logic* (Technical Report PP-2008-05). Institute for Logic, Language & Computation. http://www.illc.uva.nl/Publications/ResearchReports/ PP-2008-05.text.pdf.

van der Sandt, R. A. (1992). Presupposition projection as anaphora resolution. *Journal of Semantics, 9*(4), 333–377.

van Eijck, J. (2005). Natural logic for natural language. http://homepages.cwi.nl/~jve/papers/05/ nlnl/NLNL.pdf.

Designing Efficient Controlled Languages for Ontologies

Camilo Thorne, Raffaella Bernardi, and Diego Calvanese

Abstract We describe a methodology to recognize efficient controlled natural languages (CLs) that compositionally translate into ontology languages, and as such are suitable to be used in natural language front-ends to ontology-based systems. Efficiency in this setting is defined as the tractability (in the sense of computational complexity theory) of logical reasoning in such fragments, measured in the size of the data they aim to manage. In particular, to identify efficient CLs, we consider fragments corresponding to the DL-Lite family of description logics, known to underpin data intensive ontologies and systems. Our methodology exploits the link between syntax and semantics of natural language captured by categorial grammars, controlling the use of lexical terms that introduce logical structure outside the allowed fragments. A major role is played by the control of function words introducing logical operators in first-order formal semantics meaning representations. Finally, we conduct a preliminary analysis of semantically parsed English written corpora to show how empirical methods may be useful in identifying CLs that provide good trade-offs between coverage and efficiency.

1 Introduction

The attempts made in the 70s and 80s to build natural language interfaces (NLIs) to information systems and databases turned into disappointments towards the 90s (Androutsopoulos et al. 1995). One of the reasons were the challenges posed by structural and semantic ambiguity in arbitrary natural language input. As a way to overcome the ambiguity problem, the *controlled natural language* (CL) paradigm

C. Thorne (✉) · D. Calvanese
Free University of Bozen-Bolzano, Bolzano, Italy
e-mail: cthorne@inf.unibz.it

D. Calvanese
e-mail: calvanese@inf.unibz.it

R. Bernardi
University of Trento, Trento, Italy
e-mail: bernardi@disi.unitn.it

H. Bunt et al. (eds.), *Computing Meaning*, Text, Speech and Language Technology 47, 149
DOI 10.1007/978-94-007-7284-7_9,

was proposed (Huijsen 1998; Kittredge 2003), to build NLIs where only a restricted fragment of a natural language can be used. An important area of application of CLs is to provide front-ends to ontologies and ontology-based systems. In this setting, CLs allow the systems to parse efficiently user statements and questions. It is less clear however whether they can be understood as efficiently, in particular by ontology-based systems that need to *reason* over the semantic representations of user inputs. The present chapter intends to study the semantic complexity of CLs, together with the conditions under which reasoning with a CL can scale to very large ontologies and ontology-based systems.

By an *ontology* we mean here a conceptualization of a domain of interest, expressed as a set of logical assertions. Specifically, ontologies formulated in variants of description logics (DLs), which are fragments of first-order logics with well understood computational properties and for which logical reasoning (e.g., to detect inconsistencies in a specification) is decidable and in significant cases also computationally tractable (Baader et al. 2003). DLs provide the formal underpinning for the Web Ontology Language OWL (Horrocks et al. 2003), which is the ontology specification language standardized by the W3C.[1]

The present chapter specifically addresses the questions of (1) *which* should be the CL to be used to manage ontologies efficiently, and (2) *how* can it be defined. Concretely, our proposal is to determine a methodology for defining *exactly* those fragments with a *desirable computational complexity*. We use DLs as the starting point to answer Question (1), viz. which is the most suitable NL fragment, and we use categorial grammars (CGs) to provide an answer to Question (2), viz. how to capture the syntactic structures corresponding exactly to the semantic representations allowed by the chosen, efficient DL.

With respect to the kind of DL, we focus our attention on *DL-Lite*, which is a family of DLs studied in the context of ontology-based access to (relational) databases (Calvanese et al. 2007, 2011). When considering the well-known trade-off between expressive power and computational complexity of inference, *DL-Lite* is specifically optimized for efficient reasoning also in the presence of large datasets, taking into account that in ontology-based systems the size of the data (stored in relational databases or in possibly very large triple stores) largely dominates the size of the ontology's intensional descriptions. Indeed, in *DL-Lite*, reasoning is computationally tractable in general, and can actually be carried out by exploiting the query answering functionalities of the data storage layer. This can be contrasted with the computational properties of more expressive DLs, such as *SHOIN*, the DL underlying OWL, in which reasoning is computationally intractable also when the complexity is measured with respect to the size of the data only. With respect to the CG, we define a grammar that relies on the sub-categorization of syntactic constituents to capture exactly the intended logic.

We exploit the syntax-semantics interface as realized by CGs to obtain *DL-Lite* meaning representations compositionally while parsing (van Benthem 1987; Moortgat 1997). To this end we consider of particular value the studies carried out by Pratt

---

[1]http://www.w3.org/TR/owl2-primer/

and Third (2006), who have investigated the satisfiability of sets of sentences in fragments of natural language and their computational complexity, but start instead from the logic (viz., an OWL fragment) as do Kaljurand and Fuchs (2006).

The rest of the chapter is structured as follows. In Sect. 2, we provide an overview of controlled languages and semantic complexity, highlighting the open questions that motivate our contributions. In Sects. 3 and 4, we introduce respectively the DL and the grammar we work with. In Sect. 5, we describe in detail how CGs can capture exactly the desired fragments of natural language. In Sect. 6, we show how corpora analysis can be used to justify further CL design choices. In Sect. 7, we provide an overview of related work, in the form of related results on CLs obtained and published elsewhere by the authors, and in the form of other CLs for ontologies that have been proposed in the literature. Finally, in Sect. 8, we summarize our results and outline our ongoing work regarding the computational properties of controlled languages, both declarative and interrogative.

2 Controlled Languages and Semantic Complexity

A *controlled language* (CL) is a fragment of natural language such as English with a limited lexicon and a small set of grammar rules (Huijsen 1998; Kittredge 2003). Importantly, CLs are engineered to handle natural language ambiguity, so that their utterances "compile", via, e.g., a rule-based, symbolic and compositional syntax-directed translation algorithm (in a way similar to programming languages' compilation), in *unambiguous* logical axioms and/or queries, due to their restricted syntax and lexicon.

This tight integration with formal ontology and query languages gives rise to a more general phenomenon: the property of *semantic complexity* as defined and investigated by Pratt and Third (2006). They show that each (controlled) fragment of English generates a logic fragment: the set of its *meaning representations* (MRs); semantic complexity is then naturally defined as the computational complexity of reasoning with its MRs (i.e., the computational complexity of the associated satisfiability problem). Furthermore, they show that semantic complexity correlates with coverage by considering the impact that particular combinations of English constructs (negation, relatives, transitive verbs, etc.) have on semantic complexity, pinpointing combinations that are: (i) tractable (**PTime** semantic complexity), (ii) intractable (**NP**-hard semantic complexity), or (iii) undecidable.

In our work, we extend both their methodology and their results: their methodology, by using categorial grammars to "reverse engineer" English controlled fragments from logics that exhibit desirable computational properties; their results, by considering semantic *data complexity*, viz., the semantic complexity of CLs for ontologies measured only in the size of the (typically very large) data repositories they are meant to manage as opposed to the size of the complete logical specification derived from the natural language utterances. More precisely, we (i) consider logic constructs that give rise to tractable data complexity, (ii) pinpoint those structures

Table 1 Fragments of English studied by Pratt and Third (2006)

Fragment	Coverage	Semantic complexity
COP	Copula, common, proper nouns, negation, universal and existential quantifiers	**PTime**
COP+TV+DTV	COP+transitive verbs ("reads") + ditransitive verbs ("gives")	**PTime**
COP+Rel	COP+relative pronouns ("who", "that", "which")	NP-complete
COP+Rel+TV	COP+Rel+transitive verbs	**ExpTime**-complete
COP+Rel+TV+DTV	COP+Rel+TV+ditransitive verbs	**NExpTime**-complete
COP+Rel+TV+RA	COP+Rel+TV+restr. anaphora ("him", "she", "itself" with *bounded* anaphoric co-references)	**NExpTime**-complete
COP+Rel+TV+GA	COP+Rel+TV+gen. anaphora (*unbounded* anaphoric pronouns)	undecidable

of English that map (following Montagovian semantics) into those logic constructs, and (iii) propose grammars that generate such structures. In this way one can determine the best trade-off between coverage and tractability holding for NLIs to ontologies and ontology-based systems.

Pratt and Third's Fragments of English   The work of Pratt and Third provides hints on how to determine which fragments hold the right expressiveness for ontology-based systems, via their notion of semantic complexity. We give now a brief overview of their *controlled fragments of English* (cf., Pratt and Third 2006), which are subsets of standard English meant to capture some simple, albeit for our purpose important, structures of English.

The fragments of Pratt and Third are built incrementally, starting with copula, nouns, negation, and the universal and existential quantifiers, and extending later coverage to larger portions of English—relative constructions, ditransitive verbs, and anaphora, as summarized in Table 1. The fragments are named after such combinations, COP if their sentences contain only the copula, COP+TV if they contain in addition transitive verbs, and COP+TV+DTV if they contain both transitive and ditransitive verbs. Further differences are due to the presence in the lexicon of the relative pronoun (Rel) and of anaphora in a general (GA) or restricted form (RA).

Each NL construct has a MR introducing an n-ary predicate or a logical operation in First Order Logic (FO): The MRs of relatives (e.g., "who") introduce conjunction ($\wedge$); negations (e.g., "no", "not") introduce logical negation ($\neg$); intransitive verbs (e.g., "runs") and nouns (e.g., "man") correspond to unary predicates; transitive verbs (e.g., "loves") correspond to binary predicates, and ditransitive verbs (e.g., "sells to") to ternary predicates; universal quantifiers ("every", "all", "everyone") to universal quantification ($\forall$), and existentials ("some", "someone") to existential quantification ($\exists$).

Example 1 COP and COP+TV+DTV generate English utterances such as:

(1) Some people are weak.

$$[\exists x\,(People(x) \wedge Weak(x))]$$

(2) Every husband has a wife.

$$[\forall x\,(Husband(x) \to \exists y\,(Wife(y) \wedge Has(x, y)))]$$

(3) Every salesman sells some item to some customer.

$$[\forall x\,(Salesman(x) \to \exists y\,(Customer(y) \wedge \exists z\,(Item(z) \wedge Sells(x, z, y))))]$$

Note that in (2) and (3) above, other translations might be possible due to NL ambiguity. However, these are discarded by the grammar, which follows only the surface order of constituents.

Boolean- and Non-Boolean-Closed Fragments As shown in Table 1, where we report the results of Pratt and Third (2006), the most expressive fragment of English they consider is undecidable. As a matter of fact, only the first two fragments, COP and COP+TV+DTV, are tractable, i.e., have **PTime** semantic complexity. Notice that as soon as we add rules dealing with the relative clause we lose tractability. COP+Rel (i.e., COP with relative clauses) is already **NP**-hard. This is because relatives express conjunctions which, together with negation, generate logics (i.e., fragments of FO) that contain the propositional calculus (for which reasoning is **NP**-complete). In other words, COP+Rel and all the fragments containing it are "Boolean-closed", and allow negation to be freely combined with conjunction and relatives. Instead, COP and COP+TV+DTV are "non-Boolean-closed". The challenge that we face here is to develop a methodology for defining tractable, "non-Boolean-closed" CLs that capture tractable ontology languages.

3 *DL-Lite* and Its Computational Properties

Description logics (DLs) (Baader et al. 2003) are the logics, typically fragments of FO, that provide the formal underpinning to ontologies and the Semantic Web (Horrocks et al. 2003). They allow one to structure the domain of interest by means of *concepts*, denoting sets of objects, and *roles*, denoting binary relations between (instances of) concepts. Complex concept and role expressions are constructed starting from a set of atomic concepts and roles by applying suitable constructs. The domain of interest is then represented by means of a DL knowledge base, consisting of a TBox (for "terminological box"), storing intensional information, and an ABox (for "assertional box"), storing extensional information about individual objects of the domain of interest.

We focus our attention on *DL-Lite* (Calvanese et al. 2007, 2011), a family of DLs specifically tailored to manage large amounts of data efficiently. Specifically, we consider variants of *DL-Lite* in which the TBox is constituted by a set of *inclusion assertions* of the form

$$Cl \sqsubseteq Cr$$

$$MScStudent \sqsubseteq Student$$
$$MScStudent \sqsubseteq Works$$
$$MScStudent \sqsubseteq \neg BScStudent$$
$$\exists Reads \sqsubseteq Works$$
$$Student \sqsubseteq \exists Reads$$

$$Student \sqcap Busy \sqsubseteq Works$$
$$Student \sqcap \exists Reads \sqsubseteq Works$$
$$\exists Reads \sqcap \exists Writes \sqsubseteq Works$$
$$Student \sqsubseteq \exists Reads.Book$$

Fig. 1 An example $DL\text{-}Lite_{core}$ TBox (*left part*), and some additional $DL\text{-}Lite_{R,\sqcap}$ assertions (*right part*)

where Cl and Cr denote concepts that may occur respectively on the left and right-hand side of inclusion assertions. The form of such concepts depends on the specific variant of $DL\text{-}Lite$. Here, we consider two variants, called $DL\text{-}Lite_{core}$ and $DL\text{-}Lite_{R,\sqcap}$, which we define below. In fact, $DL\text{-}Lite_{core}$ represents a core part shared by all logics of the $DL\text{-}Lite$ family.

Definition 1 ($DL\text{-}Lite_{core}$ and $DL\text{-}Lite_{R,\sqcap}$) In $DL\text{-}Lite_{core}$, Cl and Cr are defined as follows:[2]

$$Cl \longrightarrow B \mid \exists R \qquad Cr \longrightarrow B \mid \neg B \mid \exists R \mid \neg \exists R$$

where B denotes an atomic concept, and R denotes an atomic role. In $DL\text{-}Lite_{R,\sqcap}$, in addition to the clauses of $DL\text{-}Lite_{core}$, we have also:

$$Cl \longrightarrow Cl_1 \sqcap Cl_2 \qquad Cr \longrightarrow \exists R.B$$

where R denotes again an atomic role.

The $\sqcap$ construct denotes conjunction, and $\neg$ negation (or complement). The $\exists R$ construct is called *unqualified existential quantification*, and intuitively denotes the *domain* of role R, i.e., the set of objects that are connected through role R to some (not further specified) object.[3] Finally, the $\exists R.Cr$ construct, called *qualified existential quantification*, allows one to further qualify the object connected through role R as an instance of concept Cr.

As an example, consider the $DL\text{-}Lite_{core}$ TBox depicted in the left part of Fig. 1, which makes use of various concepts (*Student, MScStudent, BScStudent, Works*) and roles (*Reads, Writes*) to express some simple knowledge about the student domain. Specifically, the TBox assertions state that every MSc-student is a student, that MSc-students work, and that no MSc-student is a BSc-student, i.e., the two concepts are *disjoint*. Note that in $DL\text{-}Lite$, negation is used only to express disjointness, as in the statement in Fig. 1. Additionally, making use of unqualified existential quantification, we can express that everyone who reads something (i.e., is in the domain of the *Reads* role) works, and that every student reads something. The latter is also called

---

[2]We have omitted *inverse* roles R^- from the DLs to simplify the presentation of the main idea we are investigating.

[3]Instead, $\exists R^-$, for an inverse role R^-, denotes the *range* of role R.

a *participation constraint*, since it forces instances of *Student* to participate in the *Reads* role. In the right part of Fig. 1, we have shown also some *DL-Lite*$_{R,\sqcap}$ inclusion assertions, which make use of conjunction in the left-hand side to express that busy students work, that students who read something work, and that everyone who reads something and writes something works. Finally, to express that every student reads some book, we can make use of qualified existential quantification (allowed to appear only in the right-hand side of inclusion assertions).

To formally specify the semantics of *DL-Lite*, we provide its standard translation to FO. Specifically, we map each concept C (we use C to denote an arbitrary concept, constructed applying the rules above) to a FO formula $\varphi(C, x)$ with one free variable x (i.e., a unary formula), and each role R to a binary formula $\varphi(R, x, y)$ as follows:

$$\varphi(B, x) = \mathsf{B}(x) \qquad\qquad \varphi(R, x, y) = \mathsf{R}(x, y)$$
$$\varphi(\neg C, x) = \neg\varphi(C, x) \qquad\qquad \varphi(\exists R, x) = \exists y\varphi(R, x, y)$$
$$\varphi(C_1 \sqcap C_2, x) = \varphi(C_1, x) \wedge \varphi(C_2, x) \qquad \varphi(\exists R.C, x) = \exists y(R(x, y) \wedge \varphi(C, y))$$

In the translation of $\exists R.C$, the variable y is considered to be a fresh variable. An inclusion assertion $Cl \sqsubseteq Cr$ of the TBox corresponds then to the universally quantified FO sentence $\forall x(\varphi(Cl, x) \to \varphi(Cr, x))$.

We observe that the above translation actually generates a formula in the guarded fragment of FO. This holds not only for *DL-Lite* but for many other expressive DLs as well, and accounts for the good computational properties of such logics (Baader et al. 2003).

Finally, in *DL-Lite*, an ABox is constituted by a set of *assertions on individuals*, of the form $B(a)$ or $R(a, b)$, where B and R denote respectively an atomic concept and role, and a, b denote constants. As in FO, each constant is interpreted as an element of the interpretation domain. The above ABox assertions correspond to the analogous FO facts, or, by resorting to the above mapping, to $\varphi(B, x)(a)$ and $\varphi(R, x, y)(a, b)$, respectively. A *DL-Lite knowledge base* is simply a pair (*Tbox, Abox*), where *Tbox* is a TBox and *Abox* an ABox. A *model* of such knowledge base is a FO interpretation in which the (closed) FO formulae resulting from the translation of all assertions in *Tbox* ∪ *Abox* evaluates to true.

To study efficiency we consider the computational reasoning problems relevant to DL ontologies and knowledge bases. The key problem, to which most other ones can be reduced, is the problem of *knowledge base consistency*, in which, given a knowledge base (*Tbox, Abox*), we ask whether it has a model. Following Vardi (1982), when we consider the computational complexity measured only in terms of the *size* of the ABox (defined as the number of constants the ABox contains), we speak about *data complexity*. When instead the complexity is measured in terms of the size of the whole input, we speak of *combined complexity*. A DL can be considered as "efficient" for ontology-based data management, whenever such complexity is *tractable* (in **PTime**).

It turns out that *DL-Lite*, and in particular *DL-Lite*$_{core}$ and *DL-Lite*$_{R,\sqcap}$, are "optimally efficient", in the sense that their data complexity is even lower. Indeed, rela-

Table 2 Combined complexity and data complexity of consistency in different DLs

DL	Combined complexity	Data complexity
$DL\text{-}Lite_{core}$	in **NLogSpace**	$\mathbf{AC}^0$
$DL\text{-}Lite_{R,\sqcap}$	**PTime**-complete	$\mathbf{AC}^0$
ALC	**ExpTime**-complete	**coNP**-complete
$SHOIN$	**NExpTime**-hard	**coNP**-hard

tively to consistency, the problem we are interested in this chapter, they are in $\mathbf{AC}^0$ [4] in data complexity and in **PTime** in combined complexity.[5] The DLs in the *DL-Lite* family are essentially the maximal DLs that exhibit such nice computational properties (Calvanese et al. 2013; Artale et al. 2009). This is a consequence of suitable syntactic restrictions that have been imposed in such logics:

- Concepts are not closed under Boolean operations: negation is restricted to basic concepts within the scope of a *right Cr*, and the use of disjunction is ruled out.
- Value restriction, a typical DL construct corresponding to a form of universal quantification, is not allowed, and the use of qualified existential quantification is restricted to the right-hand side of inclusion assertions.

These restrictions ensure that the *DL-Lite* logics are contained in the Horn fragment of FO. The *DL-Lite* constructs are nevertheless sufficiently expressive to cover the main features of conceptual modeling languages such as UML class diagrams and of concept hierarchies in ontologies and ontology-based systems. This is important, since it implies that in practice reasoning does indeed scale to very large ontologies that can capture several naturally arising domains of interest. This has to be compared with the much higher computational complexity of more expressive DLs. For illustration, consider in Table 2 the complexity of the DL *ALC*, which is the smallest logic containing the *DL-Lite* logics that we have considered here[6] and closed under Boolean operations. Both for *ALC* and for *SHOIN*, the DL that underpins OWL DL, reasoning is **coNP**-hard in data complexity, and provably exponential in combined complexity. Notice that as soon as a DL becomes closed under Boolean operations, it is intractable, and hence reasoning does not really scale well with data growth.

We are interested in studying the linguistic structures that correspond to the *DL-Lite* constructs. In what follows (Sect. 5 below), we will look at straightforward ways to express them in natural language.

---

[4]The class $\mathbf{AC}^0$, is a complexity class strictly contained in (and hence easier than) **PTime**. SQL query evaluation in relational databases is in $\mathbf{AC}^0$ in data complexity, which accounts for the efficiency of database management systems in dealing with large amounts of data.

[5]Notice that Pratt and Third's complexity results do not distinguish between data and combined complexity.

[6]All *DL-Lite* logics include also the *inverse role* constructor, which cannot be captured in *ALC*. Moreover, some *DL-Lite* variants use (complex) role inclusions, which also would lead the logic outside the scope of *ALC*.

4 Categorial Grammars

As most of the linguistically motivated formal grammars currently in use, categorial grammars (CGs) are a class (or family of classes) of lexicalized grammars, i.e., grammars where the lexicon carries most of the information about how words can be assembled to form grammatical structures. In this framework, syntactic categories are seen as *formulas* and their category forming operators as connectives, i.e., *logical constants*. In addition, the Curry-Howard correspondence ensures the Montagovian homomorphism, a.k.a. syntax-semantics interface, between the (logical) calculus of syntactic categories and FO MRs (van Benthem 1987).

The peculiarity of CGs is that word assembly is carried out by natural deduction logical rules (that take care of natural language syntax); such natural deduction rules are coupled with (via the Curry-Howard correspondence) λ-calculus operations dealing with the FO meaning assembly, via the intermediate λ-FO formalism, viz., FO extended with (typed) λ-calculus λ-abstractions and λ-applications. In so doing, CGs capture better and more elegantly the tight correspondence between syntax and semantics of NL and its fragments than other equivalent grammatical formalisms such as semantically-enriched context-free grammars or some simple kinds of definite clause grammars.

This aspect of the formalism significantly simplifies the implementation task, since one has to focus only on the construction of the lexicon and can rely on any existing parser for the calculus. Information both about the syntactic structure where the word could occur and its meaning are stored in the lexicon. As derivation or logical deduction rules, we use the product free version of the (non-associative) Lambek calculus (Lambek 1958; Moortgat 1997).[7]

Definition 2 (Term labeled lexicon, categorial grammar) A (syntactic) *category* A is defined as follows

$$A \longrightarrow np \mid n \mid s \mid A_1 \backslash A_2 \mid A_2/A_1$$

where np (*noun phrases*), n (*nouns*) and s (*complete sentences*) are *atomic* categories. Complex categories are built out of atomic categories by means of the directional *left* and *right* functional connectives \ and / ($A_1 \backslash A_2$, resp. A_2/A_1, applied to a category A_1 situated to its left, resp. its right, yield category A_2). We denote by CAT the set of all such categories and by ATOM the set $\{np, n, s\}$.

We map each syntactic category A to a (semantic) *type* $typ(A)$ as follows:

$$typ(np) = e; \qquad typ(s) = t; \qquad typ(n) = (e, t),$$
$$typ(A_1/A_2) = (typ(A_2), typ(A_1)); \qquad typ(A_2 \backslash A_1) = (typ(A_2), typ(A_1)).$$

where the atomic types are e (*entities*) and t (*Booleans*), and (τ, τ') denotes the *functional* type (the type of functions from τ into τ').

---

[7]The lexicon we present in this chapter has been tested using the GRAIL parser (Moot 1998), based on the Lambek calculus.

Given a set Σ of natural language basic expressions (i.e., a natural language vocabulary), a *term labeled categorial lexicon* is a relation,

$$\text{LEX} \subseteq \Sigma \times (\text{CAT} \times \text{TERM}) \quad \text{s.t.,} \quad \text{if } (w, (A, \alpha)) \in \text{LEX, then } \alpha \in \text{TERM}_{typ(A)}$$

where TERM is the set of all lambda terms and $\text{TERM}_{typ(A)}$ denotes the set of lambda terms whose type is mapped to the category A.

Given a term labeled lexicon LEX, a *categorial grammar* is any finite subset $G \subsetneq \text{LEX}$.

This constraint on lexical entries categories and terms enforces the following requirement: if the expression (or word) w is assigned the syntactic category A and the term α, then the term α must be of a type appropriate for the category A. We assign lambda terms whose body is a FO formula, viz., λ-FO terms. We look at the determiner *every*, by means of example, since it has a crucial role in our grammar. The reader is referred to work by Keenan and Faltz (1985) and van Eijck (1985) for an in-depth explanation of this example in particular and the relationships between CGs and λ-FO in general.

Example 2 (Determiner) The meaning of "every NOUN" (e.g., "every man") is the set of those properties that "every NOUN" (e.g., "man") has

$$[\![\text{every NOUN}]\!] = \{X \mid [\![\text{NOUN}]\!] \subseteq X\}.$$

In a functional perspective, the determiner "every" is seen as a two-argument function taking a noun and a verb phrase (a property) as arguments. The syntactic category expressing this functional view as well as word order is the following

$$(s/(np \backslash s))/n$$

where the n is the first argument that must occur to the right of "every" and $np \backslash s$, i.e., a verb phrase, the second argument to occur to the right of "every NOUN" (viz. "every NOUN VERB_PHRASE"). The typed lambda term (according to generalized quantifier theory, see Barwise and Cooper (1980)) corresponding to this syntactic category is: $\lambda Y_{(e,t)}.\lambda X_{(e,t)}.\forall x_e(Y(x) \rightarrow X(x))$. In the following, we will not use types on lambda terms unless necessary.

An important feature of CGs is their "parsing as deduction" approach, which reduces the problem of checking whether a linguistic string is grammatical to the problem of proving that the string is of a certain syntactic category. More precisely, instead of directly recognizing linguistic word strings $w_1 \cdots w_n$, we work on the corresponding set of Lambek calculus formulas: to each lexicon entry $(w_i, (A_i, \alpha_i))$, for $i \in \{1, \ldots, n\}$ we associate a (Lambek calculus) *sequent* $A_i \vdash A_i : \alpha_i$; thereafter, following the inference rules of the calculus, a proof (a tree-shaped derivation) of a sequent $\Gamma \vdash s : \phi$, with ϕ of type t (a λ-FO formula) is constructed. More formally:

Definition 3 (Recognized language) Given a categorial grammar G the *language recognized by* G, denoted $L(G)$ is the set of all word strings $w_1 \cdots w_n$ such that the sequent $\Gamma \vdash s : \phi$, has a proof in the Lambek calculus; where Γ consists of a set $\{A_1 : \alpha_1, \ldots, A_n : \alpha_n\}$ of pairs of categories and terms as defined in the term labeled lexicon $\{(w_i, (A_i, \alpha_i)) \mid i = 1, \ldots, n\}$, and ϕ is a λ-FO formula (a term of type t).

As by-product of the derivation one derives also the MR of the structure assigned to the string, i.e., the λ-FO term ϕ which after reduction gives rise to a FO closed formula or sentence. As such, NLs (and fragments thereof) recognized by a CG that does not cover purely higher-order NL constructs such as, e.g., the second-order determiner "most", can induce (in a way similar, though more general, to Pratt and Third's fragments) a fragment of FO: the set of all the first-order MRs associated with its (grammatical) complete sentences. We will exploit this particular feature of the formalism to define a CL in the next section that generates the *DL-Lite* logics.

5 Lite English and Its Grammar CG-Lite

As mentioned above, the goal of our methodology is to define CLs for ontologies that are *efficient*, i.e., tractable w.r.t. semantic data complexity. We propose to this end to define them vis-à-vis those ontology constructs that give rise to tractable data complexity. More precisely, we propose to identify English syntactic categories that lexically control the restrictions imposed by the *DL-Lite* constructs. Such categories will naturally induce a CG (i.e., a term-labeled categorial lexicon) expressing *exactly* the *DL-Lite* family of logics as described earlier. In this section we outline such syntactic categories and how they were obtained. We proceed in three steps. Firstly, we outline the key constraints to be satisfied for a CL to induce *DL-Lite*. Secondly, we provide a sample CG (a finite term-labeled lexicon). Thirdly, we describe the main features of the fragment thus generated. Notice also that the methodology proposed is not, per se, grammar dependent, since our CLs can be equally, although less succinctly and not as elegantly, defined using semantically-enriched context-free grammars as we did in some previous work (Thorne 2010, Chap. 4). We call Lite-English the resulting CL, and CG-lite its CG.[8]

5.1 Fragment of Natural Language for DL-Lite

The constraints expressed in the TBox are universally quantified FO sentences. They are of the form $Cl \sqsubseteq Cr$, which translates into FO as $\forall x (\varphi(Cl, x) \rightarrow \varphi(Cr, x))$ and can be expressed by the following NL sentence patterns:

---

[8]We refer the reader to Appendix for the formal proofs of the claims made in this section.

(a) [[Every NOUN] VERB_PHRASE]

         Cl   *Cr*

(b) [[Everyone [who VERB_PHRASE]] VERB_PHRASE]

               Cl   *Cr*

The determiner "every" and the quantifier phrase "everyone" play a crucial role in determining the linguistic structures that belong to the natural language fragment corresponding to a *DL-Lite* TBox. In the following, we zoom into the NOUN and VERB_PHRASE constituents. In other words, we spell out how *DL-Lite Cl* and *Cr* concepts can be expressed in English. In doing so, we follow Definition 1.

First of all, a *Cl* or a *Cr* could be an atomic concept A. An atomic concept A corresponds to a unary predicate, which following standard formal semantic theory can be expressed either by a noun such as "student" (see (4) below), or an intransitive verb such as "work" (see (5) below).

The introduction of negation $\neg A$ on atomic concepts A, however, can occur only in a *Cr* and can thus be expressed only by a *predicate* VERB_PHRASE such as "is not a BSc-student" (6), or "does not work" (7).

The introduction of the $\exists R$ in a *Cl* can be performed by means of the quantifier phrase "everyone" followed by the relative pronoun "who" (9) (or by the conjunction that would correspond to the use of $\sqcap$ on the *Cl* part allowed in the *DL-Lite*$_{R,\sqcap}$ fragment, see (16) below).

(4) Every MSc-student is a student.   [*MScStudent* $\sqsubseteq$ *Student*]

(5) Every MSc-student works.   [*MScStudent* $\sqsubseteq$ *Works*]

(6) Every MSc-student is not a BSc-student.   [*MScStudent* $\sqsubseteq \neg$*BScStudent*]

(7) Every BSc-student does not work.   [*BScStudent* $\sqsubseteq \neg$*Works*]

(8) Everyone who learns works.   [*Learns* $\sqsubseteq$ *Works*]

(9) Everyone who reads something works.   [$\exists$*Reads* $\sqsubseteq$ *Works*]

On the other hand, the introduction of $\exists R$ on the *Cr* part corresponds to the use of a transitive verb followed by an existential quantifier phrase, "something" (10), and its negation to the use of "does not" to negate such construction (11).

(10) Every student reads something.   [*Student* $\sqsubseteq \exists$*Reads*]

(11) Every student does not read something.   [*Student* $\sqsubseteq \neg\exists$*Reads*]

Note that, as the *DL-Lite* clause shows, the only reading of the ambiguous sentence in (11) is the one with *every* having wide scope and *something* being in the scope of *not*.[9]

Also, the VERB_PHRASE in (a) and the second VERB_PHRASE in (b) (i.e., the VERB_PHRASE of the main clause expressing a *DL-Lite Cr* concept) can be of any of the structures in (4)–(11). On the other hand, the first VERB_PHRASE in (b) (i.e.,

---

[9]For ease of explanation we do not consider the distinction between *something* and the negative polarity item *anything*. This distinction could be incorporated into the fragment, as studied by Bernardi (2002).

the VERB_PHRASE of the relative clause expressing a *DL-Lite Cl* concept) cannot contain negation: for it only the cases 5–4 above hold.

When we move to *DL-Lite$_{R,\sqcap}$*, the addition of the conjunction in the *Cl* corresponds to the use of the adjective (12), or relative clauses modifying the noun quantified by "every" (13)–(15), or the "and" coordinating two VPs (16).

(12) Every nice student works.   [*Student* ⊓ *Nice* ⊑ *Works*]
(13) Every student who learns works.   [*Student* ⊓ *Learns* ⊑ *Works*]
(14) Every student who is a BSc-student works.   [*Student* ⊓ *BScStudent* ⊑ *Works*]
(15) Every student who reads something works.   [*Student* ⊓ ∃*Reads* ⊑ *Works*]
(16) Everyone who reads something and writes something works.

[∃*Reads* ⊓ ∃*Writes* ⊑ *Works*]

Furthermore, the introduction of the qualified existential on the *Cr* is performed by the determiner "a" (17).

(17) Every student reads a book.   [*Student* ⊑ ∃*Reads.Book*]

Non-Boolean-Closedness (Tractability) of the Fragment   An important point to emphasize is the presence of the relative pronoun in the above fragment of sentences. Pratt and Third have shown how the uncontrolled use of such expression leads to **NP**-complete fragments when allowing the use only of the copula, or even to **ExpTime**-completeness when adding transitive verbs. Below, we will show how relative pronouns can be used in a controlled grammar while preserving tractability of inferences.

5.2 Expressing DL-Lite$_{core}$

We start again by looking at the main syntactic constraints over *DL-Lite$_{core}$* concepts and consider, in particular, the two constraints regarding the use of negation:

1. negation of atomic concepts can occur in a *Cr* but not in a *Cl*: *Cl* ⟶ *B*, *Cr* ⟶ *B* | ¬*B*;
2. an unqualified existential can occur both in a *Cl* and a *Cr*, but its negation can occur only in *Crs*: *Cl* ⟶ ∃*R*, *Cr* ⟶ ∃*R* | ¬∃*R*.

As we anticipated before, *Cl* and *Cr* concepts correspond respectively to the so-called "restrictive scope" (the subject NOUN constituent), and "nuclear scope" (the predicate VERB_PHRASE constituent) of the sentence-building DET *every*. We need to constrain the linguistic structures that occur within them. In particular, we need to block the occurrences of negation within *Cls* and express the fact that NOT cannot outscope any VERB_PHRASE that occurs within the restrictive scope of the determiner *every*. As emphasized by Bernardi (2002), in CGs scope is determined by the sentential categories *s* that arise from complex CG syntactic categories. Different (possibly mutually exclusive) scope distributions can be enforced by multiplying sentential categories via *sentential levels*, and exploiting the derivability relations (and restrictions) among CG categories. It suffices to provide the intuition behind the proposed solution without going into its details: a complex category $A_1 \backslash A_2$, can be applied to either category A_1 or to a category A_3 that derives A_1 ($A_3 \Rightarrow A_1$). In our case, $\Rightarrow$ is the *derivability* relation of the logical grammar we use.

We mark the structures that express *DL-Lite Cls* and *Crs* and those that are negative or positive, by means of the four *sentential levels* s_{cl}, s_{cr}, $s_{\neg}$, and s, respectively, and establish the derivability relation below (we rule out any other derivability relations between atomic categorial formulas).[10] These sentential levels state that a negated sentence can be in the *Cr* construct ($s_{\neg} \Rightarrow s_{cr}$) while it cannot be in the *Cl* part ($s_{\neg} \nRightarrow s_{cl}$) and a positive sentence can be in both ($s \Rightarrow s_{cl}$, $s \Rightarrow s_{cr}$):

$$s_{\neg} \nRightarrow s_{cl}, \qquad s_{\neg} \Rightarrow s_{cr}, \qquad s \Rightarrow s_{cl}, \qquad s \Rightarrow s_{cr}, \quad \text{and} \quad s_{cl} \nLeftrightarrow s_{cr}.$$

Note that this induces a derivability relation between complex categories built with or containing these atomic sentential categories; for instance, from $s \Rightarrow s_{cr}$ it follows that $np \backslash s \Rightarrow np \backslash s_{cr}$. Besides these sentential levels, as we will show below, we use two other sentential levels: one to mark TBox sentences (s_{tb}) and one to mark constituents built by the relative pronoun who (s_{who}). All the constraints on these sentential levels are lexically anchored by means of the lexical assignments below.

Example 3 (Lexicon for *DL-Lite$_{core}$*) The lexicon entries to use are as below.[11] The content words (intransitive verbs and nouns) are only given by way of example.

- Every $\in (s_{tb}/(np \backslash s_{cr}))/n$: $\lambda X.\lambda Y.\forall x.(X(x) \to Y(x))$
- is a $\in (np \backslash s)/n$: $\lambda X.\lambda z.X(z)$
- is not a $\in (np \backslash s_{\neg})/n$: $\lambda X.\lambda z.\neg X(z)$
- does not $\in (np \backslash s_{\neg})/(np \backslash s)$: $\lambda X.\lambda z.\neg X(z)$
- works $\in np \backslash s$: $\lambda z.\text{Works}(z)$
- learns $\in np \backslash s$: $\lambda z.\text{Learns}(z)$
- student $\in n$: $\lambda z.\text{Student}(z)$
- MSc-student $\in n$: $\lambda z.\text{MScStudent}(z)$
- BSc-student $\in n$: $\lambda z.\text{BScStudent}(z)$
- everyone $\in (s_{tb}/(np \backslash s_{cr}))/(np \backslash s_{who})$: $\lambda X.\lambda Y.\forall x.(X(x) \to Y(x))$
- who $\in (np \backslash s_{who})/(np \backslash s_{cl})$: $\lambda P.\lambda z.P(z)$
- something $\in ((np \backslash s_{\exists})/np) \backslash (np \backslash s)$: $\lambda Z.\lambda y.\exists x.Z(y, x)$
- reads $\in (np \backslash s_{\exists})/np$: $\lambda x.\lambda z.\text{Reads}(z, x)$

A. Using Universal Quantification to Express Concept Subsumption   Notice that in Example 3 the categories assigned to *every* and *everyone* rule out the possibility for them to occur in object position—they can only be in subject position.

---

[10]We actually use residuated unary operators to carry out these derivability relations (Kurtonina and Moortgat 1995) exploiting their logical properties: $\Diamond_j \Box_j s \Rightarrow s \Rightarrow \Box_i \Diamond_i s$ etc. Examples of residuated unary operators are "possibility in the past" and "necessity in the future".

[11]Notice, in the present work we do not handle features of any sort (morphological etc.). Their usage will make the lexical entries more complex but won't have any effect on the main idea we are presenting.

Moreover, since they are the only entries yielding a TBox sentence (s_{tb}), only sentences starting with them will be considered as grammatical. The negation brings sentences to the negative sentential level, and once they are there, they are blocked from occurring in the restrictive scope of *every* and *everyone*.

B. Using Existential Quantification, Relatives, and Conjunction to Express Existentially Qualified Roles and Their Conjunctions Since in the fragment described by Example 3, we do not have the $\sqcap$ on the *Cl*, the introduction of the unqualified existential $\exists R$ in it can be performed only by means of the quantifier *everyone* followed by the relative pronoun "who" and a transitive verb composed with *something*. The introduction of $\exists R$ on the *Cr* corresponds to the use of a transitive verb followed by an existential quantifier, *something*. The lexical entries for *everyone*, *who*, *something*, and *reads* above account for these facts. The need of the s_{who} categories is due to the fact that *everyone* must be followed by a relative clause, i.e., sentences like *everyone left* or *everyone walks and speaks* cannot be part of the grammar. Similarly, transitive verbs can occur on the *Cr* part but only if followed by *something*, hence we use the category $s_\exists$ to guarantee this requirement.[12] Finally, the category assigned to "something" is such that it can occur only in object position.

C. Controlling the Behavior of Negation As the reader can see, negation in Example 3 can only occur within a VERB_PHRASE expressing a *Cr*. The reader can gain a better understanding of the mechanisms involved by checking how our sample lexicon, combined with the constraints CG-lite imposes over its sentential levels, ensures the ungrammaticality of the sentences below (blocked by $s_\neg \not\Rightarrow s_{cl}$). Such sentences generate MRs that are not *DL-Lite* expressible:

(18) Everyone who does not read something works $[\neg \exists Reads \sqsubseteq Works]$
(19) Everyone who is not a BSc-student works. $[\neg BScStudent \sqsubseteq Works]$

D. Expressing ABoxes The fragment of sentences whose meaning representation belongs to a *DL-Lite$_{core}$* ABox is rather easy to build since an ABox consists of a conjunction of (ground) unary and binary logical atoms. In other words, the lexicon is built only with nouns, intransitive verbs, the copula (i.e., unary predicates), transitive verbs (i.e., binary predicates), individual names and adjectives.

5.3 Expressing DL-Lite$_{R,\sqcap}$

We now move to *DL-Lite$_{R,\sqcap}$*, and account for the following additions

1. conjunctions are allowed in *Cl*s: $Cl \longrightarrow Cl_1 \sqcap Cl_2$;
2. the qualified existential can occur in *Cr*s: $Cr \longrightarrow \exists R.B$.

---

[12]Since we have neither *np* nor *np/n* entries we could also avoid the use of this extra sentential level $s_\exists$ in the example we are considering.

Example 4 (Lexicon extension for *DL-Lite*$_{R,\sqcap}$) In order to move to *DL-Lite*$_{R,\sqcap}$, we need to add into the lexicon the following lexical entries. The (intersective, qualitative) adjective *nice* is given only by way of example.

- nice $\in n_{cl}/n_{cl}$, $\lambda X.\lambda z.(X(z) \wedge \texttt{Nice}(z))$
- who $\in (n_{cl}\backslash n_{cl})/(np\backslash s_{cl})$: $\lambda X.\lambda Y.\lambda z.(X(x) \wedge Y(z))$
- and $\in ((np\backslash s_{cl})\backslash(np\backslash s_{cl}))/(np\backslash s_{cl})$: $\lambda X.\lambda Y.\lambda z.(X(z) \wedge Y(z))$
- a $\in (((np\backslash s_{\exists})/np)\backslash(np\backslash s_{cr}))/n$: $\lambda Y.\lambda Z.\lambda y.\exists x.(Z(y,x) \wedge Y(x))$

Again, we use sentential levels to control the occurrence of these constructs. The extended lexicon accounts also for the structures in (12)–(17).

A. Controlling the Interaction of Conjunction and Negation   Notice the need of having a conjunction operating at the sentential level s_{cl}: this blocks the composition of negation (*does not*) with a verb phrase built with an *and* that would wrongly give or recognize: *does not walk and speak* with *not* outscoping *and*; such constituent would yield the MR $\lambda z.\neg(\texttt{Walk}(z) \wedge \texttt{Speak}(z))$ that is not *DL-Lite* expressible, and would moreover give rise to intractable data complexity (Calvanese et al. 2013). For similar reasons we have to block the composition of *is not a* with a noun phrase built using an intersective adjective. The resulting NOUN_PHRASE constituent would yield non-*DL-Lite*-expressible λ-FO formulas where negation outscopes conjunction; e.g., a phrase like *is not a nice student* with MR $\lambda z.\neg(\texttt{Nice}(z) \wedge \texttt{Student}(z))$. The introduction of the category n_{cl} with $n \Rightarrow n_{cl}$ makes such phrases ungrammatical.

B. Qualified Existential Restrictions and Recursive Constituents   We have considered a DL, *DL-Lite*$_{R,\sqcap}$, with qualified existentials of the form $\exists R.A$. Hence the argument taken by the determiner *a* can only be a bare noun *n*. Finally, notice that the lexical entries for the adjective, conjunction, and qualified existential bring recursion into the language.

6 Distribution of Boolean- and Non-Boolean-Closed Fragments

As we have shown, reverse-engineering efficient CLs from ontologies is a promising path. Further, as shown by Thorne (2010), our methodology can be easily extended to define interrogative CLs with tractable data complexity. The question however remains as to how to identify CLs that, while enjoying the properties we desire them to have (express ontology and query languages, give rise to at most **PTime** data complexity), remain appealing to users.

In this section we propose a distributional methodology which may help in identifying desirable English constructs by focusing on their frequency in both interrogative and declarative English corpora. We believe that this method can yield techniques to pinpoint, in particular, CLs that may offer good trade-offs between coverage and semantic complexity. The intuition behind being that when we trade-off language coverage for performance (i.e., to attain tractable data complexity) in

Table 3 Corpora analyzed in this chapter

Corpus	Size	Domain	Sentence type
Brown corpus subset	19,741 sentences	Open (news)	Declarative[17]
Geoquery corpus	364 questions	Geographical	Interrogative
Clinical questions	12,189 questions	Clinical	Interrogative
TREC 2008	436 questions	Open	Interrogative

CLs, it makes sense to cover constructs that are frequently used and thus preferred by speakers. Specifically, we study the co-occurrence of crucial (for semantic complexity) logic constructs: negations, conjunctions, disjunctions, and universal and existential quantification, in English questions and sentences.

To obtain a representative sample we considered corpora of multiple domains and with sentences of arbitrary type (declarative and interrogative), since, when managing an ontology and/or an ontology-based system, users are required not only to assert but also to update and query (intensional and extensional) information belonging to different domains. We thus considered: (i) a subset (A: press articles) of the Brown corpus;[13] (ii) a subset of one (Geoquery880) of the Geoquery corpora;[14] (iii) a corpus of clinical questions;[15] and (iv) a sample from the TREC 2008 corpus.[16] Table 3 summarizes their main features.

To this end we exploited the availability of wide-coverage (statistical) deep semantic parsers such as Boxer, by Bos (2008), which output first-order MRs. We checked, for each such MR, the co-occurrence of a subset of the set $\{\forall, \exists, \neg, \wedge, \vee\}$ of FO operators (and only of that subset). Each such subset identifies MRs belonging, modulo logical equivalence, to a distinct fragment of FO. For instance, the combination $\{\forall, \exists, \wedge, \vee\}$ identifies MRs from the so-called positive fragment of FO. But it also identifies the class of corpora sentences that give rise to such MRs, and approximates the (controlled) fragment whose formal semantics may induce such FO fragment. Finally, with these considerations in mind, we observed the distribution of:

1. "Boolean-closed" fragments, viz.: $\{\exists, \wedge, \neg\}$, $\{\exists, \wedge, \neg, \forall\}$, $\{\exists, \wedge, \neg, \forall, \vee\}$, $\{\neg, \forall\}$, $\{\exists, \wedge, \forall\}$, and $\{\exists, \wedge, \forall, \vee\}$.
2. "Non-Boolean-closed" fragments, viz.: $\{\exists, \wedge\}$ and $\{\exists, \wedge, \vee\}$.

By "Boolean-closed", we recall, we mean fragments expressive enough to encode Boolean satisfiability and which give rise to intractable semantic complexity. A "non-Boolean-closed" combination, by contrast, cannot express Boolean functions and gives rise only to tractable semantic complexity.

---

[13] http://nltk.googlecode.com/svn/trunk/nltk_data/index.xml

[14] http://www.cs.utexas.edu/users/ml/nldata/geoquery.html

[15] http://clinques.nlm.nih.gov/

[16] http://trec.nist.gov/

[17] The sample contained only 36 questions.

Distribution of FO fragments

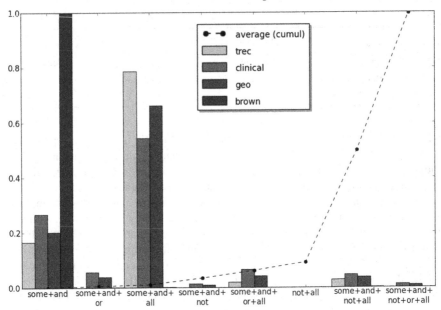

Fig. 2 Relative frequency of *co-occurring* FO operators in sample corpora. Notice the distribution of "non-Boolean-closed" sentences

The pipeline of Boxer consists of the following three basic steps: (i) each part of speech in a sentence is annotated with its most likely (categorial grammar) syntactic category; (ii) the most likely of the resulting possible combinatorial categorial grammar derivations (or proofs) is computed and returned; and (iii) a neo-Davidsonian semantically weakened[18] FO meaning representation is computed using discourse representation theory (DRT).

Example 5 When parsing Wh-questions from the TREC 2008 corpus such as "What is one common element of major religions?", Boxer outputs a FO semantic representation of the form

$$\exists y \exists z \exists e \exists u (\texttt{card}(y, u) \wedge \texttt{c1num}(u) \wedge \texttt{nnumeral1}(u) \wedge$$
$$\texttt{acommon1}(y) \wedge \texttt{nelement1}(y) \wedge \texttt{amajor1}(z) \wedge \texttt{nreligions1}(z) \wedge$$
$$\texttt{nevent1}(e) \wedge \texttt{rof1}(y, z))$$

where $\wedge$ and $\exists$ co-occur, but not $\vee$, $\neg$, or $\rightarrow$.

Figure 2 shows the co-occurrence distribution obtained, expressed in terms of relative frequency (i.e., number of MRs per class/total number of MRs per corpus).

---

[18]In this settings, the semantics of verbs is represented in terms of events connected via thematic roles to verb arguments (agents, themes, etc.). In addition, the semantics of non-FO constructs such as "most" is weakened to some FO representation.

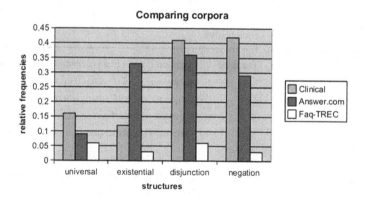

Fig. 3 Relative frequency of FO operators in question corpora (Bernardi et al. 2007)

As the figure shows, positive existential, $\{\exists, \wedge\}$ and $\{\exists, \wedge, \vee\}$, MRs occur quite frequently. Also, it seems that the same holds for sentences expressing universal quantification whereas the opposite is true for negation (low frequency overall).

This analysis can be compared to the more linguistics-based methodology followed by (Bernardi et al. 2007), in which we analyzed the distribution in (solely) interrogative corpora of classes of *logical words* which express FO operators, e.g., "all", "both", "each", "every", "everybody", "everyone", "any", "none", "nothing". See Fig. 3.

These results suggest that, while users use negation or disjunction words as frequently as conjunction and existential words, and all these more than universal words, when combining them *within* sentences "non-Boolean-closed" combinations are preferred.

7 Related Work

The work described in this chapter has been complemented by related results obtained by the authors and published elsewhere. In particular, we have applied and generalized the methodology defined in this chapter to determine which are the fragments of ACE-OWL that are tractable (i.e., at most **PTime**) and those that are intractable (i.e., **coNP**-hard) in data complexity (see Thorne and Calvanese 2012). Table 4 summarizes what these results mean in terms of language coverage, viz., which *maximal* combinations of (English) function and content words give rise to *tractable* ("non-Boolean closed") controlled fragments, and which *minimal* combinations give rise to *intractable* ("Boolean closed") controlled fragments.

Intractability arises with any combination capable of expressing full Boolean negation ("not") and full Boolean conjunction (conjunction, relative pronouns). Note that the good computational properties of Lite-English depend ultimately on the fact that, while expressing Boolean conjunction, it cannot express full Boolean

Table 4
Non-"Boolean-closed" and
"Boolean-closed" controlled
English constructs

Data complexity	Constructs
Tractable	Negation ("not") in a predicate VERB_PHRASE
	Relatives ("who", "which") everywhere
	Conjunction ("and") everywhere
	Transitive verbs ("loves") everywhere
	Existential quantification ("some") everywhere
Intractable	Negation ("not") in a subject NOUN
	Universal quantification ("only") in a subject NOUN
	Disjunction ("or") in predicate VERB_PHRASE

negation, but rather a very limited form of it. We observe that a similar analysis carried out on Pratt and Third's fragments (and extending their own) by Thorne (2010) yielded similar results.

We have also applied the methodology used in this chapter to study controlled fragments of English *questions* for which the data complexity of reasoning (or evaluation) against an ontology, authored using any of their fragments, is tractable (see Thorne 2010, Chap. 5). This work shows that positive questions (questions built with "some", relative pronouns, conjunction and eventually, disjunction) and restricted to proper and common nouns, and intransitive and transitive verbs as content words, give rise to tractability. It also shows that they can be enriched with so-called *aggregate determiners*, i.e., English constructs such as "the total number of", "the number of", "the average of", etc., that express *aggregate functions*,[19] in formal query languages without negatively impacting on the semantic complexity of the controlled fragments.

As we hinted in the introduction, several CLs, most of which are equipped with a compositional semantics, have been proposed to provide NLIs to ontologies and ontology-based systems. In particular, to provide English front ends to (i) ontology authoring systems, specifically, semantic web ontologies in the form of OWL DL ontologies (for which its fragment ACE-OWL was engineered) and (ii) controlled English querying to such ontologies. Table 5 provides an overview of the best known and used, viz., PENG (Schwitter et al. 2003), Rabbit (Schwitter et al. 2008) and OWL CNL (Schwitter and Tilbrook 2006), which are to a big extent siblings and/or children of the main two: Attempto Controlled English (ACE) and its fragment ACE-OWL (Fuchs et al. 2006; Kaljurand 2007).

While the coverage of ACE, ACE-OWL and its relatives is way greater than of any of the CLs defined in this chapter, they suffer from our perspective from the fact of being too expressive. Query evaluation over OWL DL (viz., *SHOIN*) ontologies and a fortiori in ACE-OWL NLIs is **coNP**-hard in the size of the data,

---

[19]That is, second-order functions such as, resp., $sum(\cdot)$, $\#(\cdot)$, $avg(\cdot)$, defined over *sets* of individuals or data values.

Table 5 An overview of some CLs; DCG stands for "definite clause grammar", the other acronyms for known English parsers or parser APIs such as GATE, and "comp." for "compositional"

CL (English)	Comp.	Maps to	Parser	Goal
ACE (Fuchs et al. 2006)	yes	FO	APE	Knowledge repr.
ACE-OWL (Kaljurand 2007)	yes	OWL DL	APE	Ontology mgmt
PENG (Schwitter et al. 2003)	yes	OWL DL	ECOLE	Ontology mgmt
OWL CNL (Schwitter and Tilbrook 2006)	yes	OWL DL	DCG parser	Ontology mgmt
Rabbit (Schwitter et al. 2008)	no	OWL Full	GATE	Ontology mgmt

and hence intractable and unsuited for managing large data repositories. In more expressive CLs such as Rabbit or (full) ACE, reasoning is undecidable.[20] However ACE-OWL and kindred CLs contain (grammatically correct) fragments which may exhibit better computational properties, which we believe can be defined using our methodology.

In addition to NLIs to OWL ontologies (Schwitter and Tilbrook 2006; Kaljurand and Fuchs 2006), systems have been proposed that, e.g., guide the user to formulate his/her natural language (NL) question via an ontology that incrementally shows the possible concepts that could be involved in the question (Franconi et al. 2010; Dongilli and Franconi 2006). Others guide the user via an incremental parser (Bernstein et al. 2006; Damljanovic 2010), or engage the user in clarification dialogs (Gunning et al. 2010).

8 Conclusions

In this chapter we have outlined a methodology for defining controlled fragments (CLs) of English for NLIs to ontology-based systems, which scale to very large ontologies. In addition to their scalability, such CLs can express key ontology language constructs via a symbolic translation formally underpinned by formal semantics in the Montagovian tradition.

We have argued that this can be achieved as follows: (i) On the one hand, by focusing on semantic complexity, viz., the computational complexity of logical reasoning in such CLs, which can be studied via the FO fragment induced by their formal, compositional semantics. We have stressed that a key requirement is for semantic complexity to be at most polynomial in the size of the ontology (or ontology-based system), and in AC^0 in the size of the data stored therein, that is, to have effi-

---

[20]Reasoning on OWL Full or FO is undecidable (cf., Baader et al. 2003).

cient semantic data complexity. (ii) On the other hand, by considering English constructs that express ontology languages with efficient data complexity. (iii) Finally, by putting together those English constructs via CGs to build a CL that expresses such low complexity ontology languages and that possesses appropriate semantic data complexity while expressing key ontology language constructs.

Following our methodology, we have identified the fragment of English that corresponds to an ontology language suitable for specifying and querying ontologies with optimal data complexity, namely *DL-Lite*; and based on this we have defined an efficient CL, Lite English, using CGs (via the CG-lite grammar).

We have also performed a preliminary corpus analysis regarding the distribution of relevant English constructs. We believe that this methodology could, if further developed, help the CL community in identifying suitable CLs that provide good trade-offs between coverage and tractability.

Acknowledgements   This research has been partially supported by the EU under the large-scale integrating project (IP) Optique (Scalable End-user Access to Big Data), grant agreement n. FP7-318338.

Appendix

In this appendix we sketch how CG-lite formally captures $DL\text{-}Lite_{R,\sqcap}$ (and a fortiori $DL\text{-}Lite_{core}$). That is, we show that for every $DL\text{-}Lite_{R,\sqcap}$ TBox assertion $Cl \sqsubseteq Cr$, there exists a CG-lite derivation D rooted in $s_{tb} \vdash s_{tb} : \forall x(\varphi(Cl, x) \to \varphi(Cr, x))$.

Remark 1 (Cl and Cr vs. λ-FO) Recall that Cl and Cr concepts are defined as below.

$$Cl \longrightarrow B \mid \exists R \mid Cl_1 \sqcap Cl_2 \quad \text{and} \quad Cr \longrightarrow B \mid \neg B \mid \exists R \mid \neg \exists R \mid \exists R.B.$$

Left concepts correspond to: (i) B, i.e., $\lambda x.(B(x))$ (in λ-FO), (ii) $\exists R$, i.e., $\lambda x.\exists y.R(x, y)$ (in λ-FO), and (iii) $Cl_1 \sqcap Cl_2$, i.e., $\lambda x.(\varphi(Cl, x) \wedge \varphi(Cl, x))$ (in λ-FO). Regarding right concepts, the new concepts that are not Cls are: (i') $\neg B$, i.e., $\lambda x.\neg B(x)$ (in λ-FO), (ii') $\neg \exists R$, i.e., $\lambda x.\neg \exists y.R(x, y)$ (in λ-FO), and (iii') $\exists R.B$, i.e., $\lambda x.\exists y.(R(x, y) \wedge B(y))$ (in λ-FO).

Remark 2 In a CG-lite derivation of $\Gamma \vdash A : \alpha$, the resulting category A will match a subcategory A' occurring in a positive position within the categories occurring in Γ. This means that, when expressing left and right concepts we are interested in derivations where (Cl_1) $A = n$, (Cl_2) $A = np \backslash s_{cl}$, (Cl_3) $A = np \backslash s_{who}$ and (Cr) $A = np \backslash s_{cr}$.

Lemma 1 (Left Cl concepts) *For every $DL\text{-}Lite_{R,\sqcap}$ left concept Cl, there exists a CG-lite derivation D satisfying Remarks 1 and 2 that expresses it.*

Proof (Sketch) We show, by (structural) induction on left concepts Cl, that there exists a CG-lite derivation D rooted in either of the following three Lambek sequents:

(1) $n \vdash n : \lambda x.\varphi(Cl, x)$ or (2) $np\backslash s_{cl} \vdash np\backslash s_{cl} : \lambda x.\varphi(Cl, x)$ or (3) $\vdash np\backslash s_{who} \vdash np\backslash s_{who} : \lambda x.\varphi(Cl, x)$, with categories found in or derived from CG-lite's lexicon CAT_{lex}.

- Base cases: Cl is an atomic concept B or a qualified existential $\exists R$.

    1. Consider the lexicon entry $n \vdash n : \lambda x.\texttt{Student}(x)$; (1) holds.
    2. Consider the lexicon entry $np\backslash s \vdash np\backslash s : \lambda x.\texttt{Left}(x)$; (2) holds.
    3. Consider the two entries $((np\backslash s_\exists)/np)\backslash(np\backslash s) \vdash ((np\backslash s_\exists)/np)\backslash(np\backslash s) : \lambda Z.\lambda y.\exists x.Z(y, x)$ and $(np\backslash s_\exists)/np \vdash (np\backslash s_\exists)/np : \lambda x.\lambda z.\texttt{Reads}(z, x)$. By applying one to each other, we derive $np\backslash s \vdash np\backslash s : \lambda x.\exists y \texttt{Reads}(x, y)$. Since $s \Rightarrow s_{cl}$, (1) holds.

- Inductive cases: Cl is a complex concept $Cl_1 \sqcap Cl_2$. By I.H. the property holds for Cl_1 and Cl_2. There are several cases. As they are similar, we deal only with one.

    1. Consider the lexicon entry $((np\backslash s_{cl})\backslash(np\backslash s_{cl}))/(np\backslash s_{cl}) : \lambda X.\lambda Y.\lambda z.(X(z) \wedge Y(z))$, expressing conjunction. By I.H., we may combine it in turn with the (derived) sequents $np\backslash s_{cl} \vdash np\backslash s_{cl} : \lambda x.\varphi(Cl_1, x)$ and $np\backslash s_{cl} \vdash np\backslash s_{cl} : \lambda x.\varphi(Cl_2, x)$ (i.e., verifying (2)). This results in a derivation rooted in $np\backslash s_{cl} \vdash np\backslash s_{cl} : \lambda x.(\varphi(Cl_1, x) \wedge \varphi(Cl_2, x))$, which satisfies (2). $\quad\square$

Lemma 2 (Right Cr concepts) *For every DL-Lite$_{R,\sqcap}$ right concept Cr, there exists a CG-lite derivation D satisfying Remarks 1 and 2 that expresses it.*

Proof (Sketch) The claim can be proven by case analysis on Cr as in the preceding lemma (there is no inductive clause in the Cr definition), viz., by showing that a derivation D rooted in (4) $np\backslash s_{cr} \vdash np\backslash s_{cr} : \lambda x.\varphi(Cr, x)$ exists. $\quad\square$

Theorem 1 *For every DL-Lite$_{R,\sqcap}$ TBox assertion $Cl \sqsubseteq Cr$, there exists a CG-lite derivation D satisfying Remarks 1 and 2 that expresses it.*

Proof The proof follows from the two Lemmas above and by the fact that the only two lexical entries with s_{tb} in a positive position are those for:

1. "every", i.e., $(s_{tb}/(np\backslash s_{cr}))\backslash n_{cl} \vdash (s_{tb}/(np\backslash s_{cr}))\backslash n_{cl} : \lambda X.\lambda Y.\forall x.(X(x) \rightarrow Y(x))$; and, on the other hand,
2. "everyone", i.e., $(s_{tb}/(np\backslash s_{cr}))/(np\backslash s_{cl}) \vdash (s_{tb}/(np\backslash s_{cr}))/(np\backslash s_{cl}) : \lambda X.\lambda Y.\forall x. (X(x) \rightarrow Y(x))$.

Now, by Lemmas 1 and 2, we know that left concepts Cl and right concepts Cr are CG-lite-expressible, i.e., that there exist derivations for them rooted in $np\backslash s_{cl} \vdash np\backslash s_{cl} : \lambda x.\varphi(Cl, x)$ and $np\backslash s_{cr} \vdash np\backslash s_{cr} : \lambda x.\varphi(Cr, x)$, resp.

When we combine such sequents with the entry for "every", we obtain immediately $s_{tb} \vdash s_{tb} : \forall x(\varphi(Cl, x) \rightarrow \varphi(Cr, x))$. In the case of "everyone", we need to combine them with the entry for "who", viz., $(np\backslash s_{who})/(np\backslash s_{cl}) \vdash$

$(np\backslash s_{who})/(np\backslash s_{cl}) : \lambda P.\lambda z.P(z)$, and we again derive $s_{tb} \vdash s_{tb} : \forall x(\varphi(Cl, x) \rightarrow$
$\varphi(Cr, x))$. $\square$

For reasons of space, we omit the proof of the converse, viz., that every (complete) sentence w in Lite-English expresses a $DL\text{-}Lite_{R,\sqcap}$ assertion. It can be constructed in a manner similar to Theorem 1, by induction on CG-lite derivations, i.e., by showing how every CG-lite constituent of category n or $np\backslash s_{cr}$ (resp. n or $n\backslash s_{cl}$) gives rise to a right (resp. left) concept. Such constituents are then combined together into a sentence expressing an assertion via the function words "every" or by "everyone who". The sentential levels and the derivability relations that ensue (see Sects. 5.2 and 5.3) prevent over-generation.

References

Androutsopoulos, I., Ritchie, G. D., & Thanish, P. (1995). Natural language interfaces to databases—An introduction. *Journal of Natural Language Engineering, 1*, 29–81.

Artale, A., Calvanese, D., Kontchakov, R., & Zakharyaschev, M. (2009). The *DL-Lite* family and relations. *Journal of Artificial Intelligence Research, 36*, 1–69.

Baader, F., Calvanese, D., McGuinness, D., Nardi, D., & Patel-Schneider, P. F. (Eds.) (2003). *The description logic handbook: Theory, implementation and applications.* Cambridge: Cambridge University Press.

Barwise, J., & Cooper, R. (1980). Generalized quantifiers and natural language. *Linguistics and Philosophy, 4*(2), 159–219.

Bernardi, R. (2002). *Reasoning with polarity in categorial type logic.* Ph.D. thesis, UiL, OTS, Utrecht University.

Bernardi, R., Bonin, F., Carbotta, D., Calvanese, D., & Thorne, C. (2007). English querying over ontologies: E-QuOnto. In *Proc. of the 10th congress of the Italian association for artificial intelligence* (AI*IA 2007).

Bernstein, A., Kaufmann, E., Kaiser, C., & Kiefer, C. (2006). Ginseng: A guided input natural language search engine for querying ontologies. In *2006 Jena user conference.*

Bos, J. (2008). Wide-coverage semantic analysis with Boxer. In *Proc. of the 2008 conf. on semantics in text processing* (STEP 2008).

Calvanese, D., De Giacomo, G., Lembo, D., Lenzerini, M., & Rosati, R. (2007). Tractable reasoning and efficient query answering in description logics: The *DL-Lite* family. *Journal of Automated Reasoning, 39*(3), 385–429.

Calvanese, D., De Giacomo, G., Lembo, D., Lenzerini, M., Poggi, A., Rodriguez-Muro, M., Rosati, R., Ruzzi, M., & Savo, D. F. (2011). The Mastro system for ontology-based data access. *Journal of Web Semantics, 2*(1), 43–53.

Calvanese, D., De Giacomo, G., Lembo, D., Lenzerini, M., & Rosati, R. (2013). Data complexity of query answering in description logics. *Artificial Intelligence, 195*, 335–360.

Damljanovic, D. (2010). Towards portable controlled natural languages for querying ontologies. In *Proc. of the 2nd workshop on controlled natural languages* (CNL 2010).

Dongilli, P., & Franconi, E. (2006). An intelligent query interface with natural language support. In *Proc. of the 19th int. Florida artificial intelligence research society conf.* (FLAIRS 2006).

Franconi, E., Guagliardo, P., & Trevisan, M. (2010). Quelo: NL-based intelligent query interface. In *Proc. of the 2nd workshop on controlled natural languages* (CNL 2010).

Fuchs, N. E., Kaljurand, K., & Schneider, G. (2006). Attempto Controlled English meets the challenges of knowledge representation, reasoning, interoperability and user interfaces. In *Proc. of the 19th int. Florida artificial intelligence research society conf.* (FLAIRS 2006).

Gunning, D., Chaudhri, V. K., Clark, P., Barker, K., Chaw, S., Greaves, M., Grosof, B., Leung, A., McDonald, D., Mishra, S., Pacheco, J., Porter, B., Spaulding, A., Tecuci, D., & Tien, J. (2010). Project Halo update—Progress toward digital Aristotle. *AI Magazine, 31*(3), 33–58.

Horrocks, I., Patel-Schneider, P. F., & van Harmelen, F. (2003). From *SHIQ* and RDF to OWL: The making of a Web Ontology Language. *Journal of Web Semantics, 1*(1), 7–26.

Huijsen, W. O. (1998). Controlled language—An introduction. In *Proc. of the 2nd int. workshop on controlled language applications* (CLAW 1998).

Kaljurand, K. (2007). *Attempto Controlled English as a Semantic Web language*. Ph.D. thesis, University of Tartu. Available at http://attempto.ifi.uzh.ch/site/pubs/.

Kaljurand, K., & Fuchs, N. E. (2006). Birectional mapping between OWL-DL and Attempto Controlled English. In *Proc. of the 4th int. workshop on principles and practice of Semantic Web reasoning* (PPSWR 2006).

Keenan, E., & Faltz, L. (1985). *Boolean semantics for natural language*. Dordrecht: Reidel.

Kittredge, R. I. (2003). Sublanguages and controlled languages. In R. Mitkov (Ed.), *The Oxford handbook of computational linguistics* (pp. 430–447). London: Oxford University Press.

Kurtonina, N., & Moortgat, M. (1995). Structural control. In P. Blackburn & M. de Rijke (Eds.), *Logic, structures and syntax*, Dordrecht: Kluwer Academic.

Lambek, J. (1958). The mathematics of sentence structure. *The American Mathematical Monthly, 65*, 154–170.

Moortgat, M. (1997). Categorial type logics. In J. van Benthem & A. ter Meulen (Eds.), *Handbook of logic and language* (pp. 93–178). Cambridge: MIT Press.

Moot, R. (1998). Grail: An automated proof assistant for categorial grammar logics. In *Proc. of the 1998 user interfaces for theorem provers conf.*

Pratt, I., & Third, A. (2006). More fragments of language. *Notre Dame Journal of Formal Logic, 47*(2), 151–177.

Schwitter, R., & Tilbrook, M. (2006). Let's talk in description logic via controlled natural language. In *Proc. of the 3rd int. workshop on logic and engineering of natural language semantics* (LENLS 2006).

Schwitter, R., Ljungberg, A., & Hood, D. (2003). ECOLE—A look-ahead editor for a controlled language. In *Proc. of the 8th int. workshop of the European association for machine translation and the 4th controlled language applications workshop* (EAMT/CLAW 2003).

Schwitter, R., Kaljurand, K., Cregan, A., Dolbear, C., & Hart, G. (2008). A comparison of three controlled natural languages for OWL 1.1. In *Proc. of the 4th int. workshop on OWL: Experiences and directions* (OWLED 2008).

Thorne, C. (2010). *Query answering over ontologies using controlled natural languages*. Ph.D. thesis, Faculty of Computer Science, Free University of Bozen-Bolzano.

Thorne, C., & Calvanese, D. (2012). Tractability and intractability of controlled languages for data access. *Studia Logica, 100*, 787–813.

van Benthem, J. (1987). Categorial grammar and lambda calculus. In D. Skordev (Ed.), *Mathematical logic and its applications* (pp. 39–60). New York: Plenum.

van Eijck, J. (1985). *Aspects of quantification in natural language*. Ph.D. thesis, University of Groningen.

Vardi, M. (1982). The complexity of relational query languages. In *Proc. of the 14th annual ACM symp. on theory of computing* (pp. 137–146).

Part III
Semantic Resources and Annotation

A Context-Change Semantics for Dialogue Acts

Harry Bunt

Abstract This chapter presents an update semantic for dialogue acts, defined in terms of combinations of 'elementary update functions'. This approach allows fine-grained distinctions to be made between related types of dialogue acts, and relations like entailment and exclusion between dialogue acts to be established. The approach is applied to the inventory of dialogue act types in the DIT^{++} taxonomy, using dialogue act representations as defined in the Dialogue Act Markup Language (DiAML), which is part of the recently established ISO standard 24617-2 for dialogue act annotation.

1 Introduction

The notion of a dialogue act plays a key role in studies of dialogue, in particular in the analysis of communicative behaviour and in the design of spoken dialogue systems and embodied conversational agents. In empirical studies of human conversation, dialogue acts are often used to characterize different types of communicative behaviour. In studies of utterance meaning, dialogue acts are used to relate utterances to information states and how these are changed by communication. In spoken dialogue systems, dialogue acts are used in dialogue management, i.e. in the processes of deciding how to continue an ongoing dialogue.

Over the years, a variety of dialogue act inventories and taxonomies has emerged, including the TRAINS inventory Allen et al. (1994); the MRDA annotation scheme (Dhillon et al. 2004); the DIT taxonomy (Bunt 1994); the HCRC Map Task scheme (Carletta et al. 1996); DAMSL (Allen and Core 1997), Switchboard-DAMSL (Jurafsky et al. 1997); COCONUT (Di Eugenio et al. 1998), the Verbmobil scheme (Alexandersson et al. 1998), the MALTUS tag set (Popescu-Belis 2004) and the AMI (2005) annotation scheme (http://corpus.amiproject.org). Each of these schemes has been used to build annotated dialogue corpora.

H. Bunt (✉)

Tilburg Center for Cognition and Communication (TiCC) and Department of Philosophy, Tilburg University, P.O. Box 90153, 5000 LE Tilburg, The Netherlands
e-mail: harry.bunt@uvt.nl

H. Bunt et al. (eds.), *Computing Meaning*, Text, Speech and Language Technology 47,   177
DOI 10.1007/978-94-007-7284-7_10,

In order to support the creation of *interoperable* annotated corpora, the International Organisation for Standards ISO has recently developed a standard for dialogue act annotation (ISO 24617-2 2012; see also Bunt et al. 2010, 2012), which is largely based on the DIT^{++} taxonomy, a comprehensive domain-independent schema which was constructed by adding to the DIT taxonomy a number of concepts from DAMSL and other schemes and dialogue studies (see Bunt 2009 and http://dit.uvt.nl).

DIT^{++} is based on the dynamic approach to utterance meaning of Dynamic Interpretation Theory (DIT), which views dialogue acts semantically as update operations on the information states of the dialogue participants; an approach that is also known as the 'information-state update' or 'context-change approach' to utterance meaning—see e.g. Bunt (2000), Traum and Larsson (2003). On this approach, the two most important components of a dialogue act are its semantic content, which describes the objects, properties, relations, or actions that the dialogue act is about, and its communicative function, which specifies how an addressee should update his information state with the semantic content.

Utterances are often multifunctional, i.e., they have more than one communicative function. Dialogue analysis and annotation frameworks are therefore often 'multidimensional' in the sense of allowing the assignment of multiple dialogue act tags to utterances; this is e.g. the case for DAMSL, COCONUT, and MRDA. The multifunctionality of utterances is due not just to the fact that an utterance may contain parts that have different functions, but also to the phenomenon that they may contain segments that have more than one communicative function (see Bunt 2011). In order to accurately describe the relation between dialogue acts and stretches of speech, text, or other forms of communicative behaviour, the notion of a *functional segment* has been introduced in the DIT^{++} annotation framework, defined as a minimal stretch of communicative behaviour that has at least one communicative function (Geertzen et al. 2007). Functional segments may be discontinuous, may overlap, may spread over multiple turns, and may contain parts contributed by different speakers. The following dialogue fragment illustrates some of these phenomena.

(1) 1. A: could you tell me what departure times there are for flights to Frankfurt on Saturday morning?
     2. B: sure, there's a Lufthansa flight at. . . let me see. . . 7.45, . . .
     3. A: yes,
     4. B: and a KLM flight at 08.15, . . .
     5. A: yes,
     6. B: and then there's a flight by Philippine airlines, . . .

The response to A's request includes an enumeration of items, which B communicates one by one in separate turns (of which the example shows the first two items and part of the third). B's first utterance consists of several functional segments, of which the first ("*sure*") has the functions of taking the turn and accepting A's request; the discontinuous second segment ("*there's a Lufthansa flight at [. . .] 7.45*") provides a part of the information that A requested while at the same time indicating that there's more to come; and the third segment that is embedded in the second ("*let me see*") has a time management function (Stalling). In fact, the dialogue act providing the information that A requested corresponds to a discontinuous, multi-turn functional segment formed by *"there's a Lufthansa flight at [...] 7.45"*, utterance 4, utterance 6, and subsequent utterances containing further parts of B's answer. A's utterance 3 *"yes"*, has (by virtue of its intonation) both the function of indicating positive feedback (viz. that A has understood what B said and accepted the information provided) and of giving the turn back to B, encouraging him to go on.

The multidimensional annotation schemes mentioned above use an implicitly defined notion of dimension as a set of mutually exclusive tags. By contrast, Bunt (2006) based the design of the DIT^{++} scheme on a notion of dimension which reflects the observation that participation in a dialogue involves, beyond activities strictly related to performing a certain task, also other types of communicative activity such as a sharing information about understanding and accepting each other's utterances; monitoring contact and attention; managing the use of time; taking turns; and correcting a speaking error made by oneself or by another speaker. A dimension in dialogue act analysis is defined as corresponding to such a type of communicative activity. Dialogue acts belonging to different dimensions are thus concerned with different types of semantic content: feedback acts with the success of processing previous utterances; turn management acts with the allocation of the speaker role, task-related acts with the dialogue task; and so on. Dimensions thus classify the semantic contents of dialogue acts.

Petukhova and Bunt (2009a,b) formulate criteria for distinguishing dimensions, and apply these in the analysis of the structure of 18 existing annotation schemes. They show that the DIT^{++} taxonomy has a well-founded set of ten dimensions (nine of which have been retained in ISO standard 24617-2); namely:

(2) 1. Task/Activity: dialogue acts for performing the task or activity underlying the dialogue;
     2. Auto-Feedback: dialogue acts providing information about the speaker's processing of previous utterances;
     3. Allo-Feedback: dialogue acts expressing opinions or eliciting information about the addressee's processing of previous utterances;
     4. Contact Management: dialogue acts for establishing and maintaining contact;
     5. Turn Management: dialogue acts concerned with grabbing, keeping, giving, or accepting the speaker role;
     6. Time Management: dialogue acts indicating that the speaker needs some time to formulate his contribution;
     7. Discourse Structuring: dialogue acts for explicitly structuring the conversation;
     8. Own Communication Management: dialogue acts for editing the speaker's current utterance;
     9. Partner Communication Management: dialogue acts to assists or correct the current speaker;
    10. Social Obligations Management: dialogue acts that take care of social conventions such as greetings, apologies, and expressions of gratitude.

Some communicative functions are specific for a particular dimension; for instance *Turn Accept* and *Turn Release* are specific for turn management; *Stalling* and *Pausing* for time management. Other functions can be applied in any dimension; for instance a *Check Question* can be used with task-related semantic content, but also for checking correct understanding (feedback). More generally, all types of question and inform can be used in any dimension, and the same is true of directive acts such as *Suggest, Request, Instruct,* and *Accept Offer,* and of commissive acts such as *Offer, Promise,* and *Accept Request.* These functions are called *general-purpose* functions—see Fig. 1 in the Appendix, and http://dit.uvt.nl for the taxonomy of general-purpose communicative functions of ISO 24617-2 and DIT^{++}.

The *dimension-specific* communicative functions, which can only be used with a particular type of semantic content to form a dialogue act in that particular dimension, also form a set with a hierarchical organization. The DIT^{++} and ISO 24617-2 taxonomies thus consist of two parts: a taxonomy of *general-purpose functions* and one of *dimension-specific functions*. Figure 2 in the Appendix shows the taxonomies of dimension-specific communicative functions in ISO 24617-2 and DIT^{++}. There are some differences between the two, since ISO 24617-2 does not have the Contact Management dimension, lacks communicative functions for different levels of processing for feedback, and lacks a few other fine-grained distinctions that are made in DIT^{++}.

This chapter describes a computational semantics for dialogue acts formed with a communicative function of the DIT^{++} taxonomy. This description takes the form of the definition of the semantics of the annotation language DiAML (Dialogue Act Markup Language), which forms part of the ISO 24617-2 standard. Expressions in DiAML describe dialogue act information, associated with a functional segment. This information consists for each dialogue act of its communicative function; the type of semantic content; the speaker and the addressee(s); semantic relations of various kinds to other dialogue acts or functional segments; communicative function qualifiers (if any); and the functional segment by which the dialogue act is expressed (verbally, nonverbally, or with a combination of modalities). Section 2 describes the DiAML language, with the way its semantics is organized, using operations that update the dialogue participants' information states. Section 3 discusses the notion of information state, or 'dialogue context'. Section 4 describes in some detail the semantics of the DIT^{++} communicative functions. Section 5 draws general conclusions and indicates perspectives for future work.

2 DiAML: Dialogue Act Markup Language

The Dialogue Act Markup Language (DiAML) has been designed in accordance with the ISO Linguistic Annotation Framework,[1] which makes a distinction between *annotation* and *representation*. The term 'annotation' refers to the linguistic information that is added to segments of language data, independent of format; 'rep-

---

[1] ISO 24612:2012; see also Ide and Romary (2004).

resentation' refers to the format in which an annotation is rendered, independent of content. Annotation standards are required to be defined not at the level of a representation formats, but at the more abstract level of annotations.

This distinction has been implemented in the DiAML definition by applying a multilevel design methodology, called CASCADES (Bunt 2010, 2013a,b), which defines an annotation language by means of a syntactic component that specifies, besides a class of XML-based *representation structures*, also a class of set-theoretical structures called *annotation structures*. These two parts of the definition are called the *concrete* and the *abstract syntax* of the language, respectively.

2.1 Abstract Syntax

An abstract syntax consists of: (a) a specification of the elements from which annotation structures are built up, called a 'conceptual inventory', and (b) a specification of the possible ways of constructing annotation structures using these elements.

a. Conceptual Inventory The conceptual inventory of DiAML consists of six finite sets:

1. a set of dimensions (ten in the case of DIT^{++}; nine in ISO 24617-2);
2. a set of communicative functions;
3. a set of qualifiers, that can be associated with communicative functions; this set is partitioned into subsets for different aspects of qualification, such as certainty, conditionality, and sentiment;
4. a set of rhetorical relations, that can hold between dialogue acts or their content;
5. a set of dialogue participants;
6. a set of functional segments of primary data.

The set of functional segments is specific for a particular annotation task; since annotation means associating linguistic information with segments of primary data, an annotation language must have elements for identifying relevant segments, which in the case of dialogue act annotation correspond to functional segments. The set of dialogue participants is also specific for a particular annotation task, and is assumed to be specified in the metadata of the dialogue under consideration. The four other sets of concepts in the conceptual inventory are independent of any particular annotation task.

b. Annotation Structures An annotation structure is a set of two kinds of elements, called *entity structures* and *link structures*. An entity structure contains semantic information about a functional segment; a link structure describes a semantic relation between segments. Formally, an annotation structure is a set $\{\epsilon_1, \ldots, \epsilon_k, L_1, \ldots, L_m\}$ of one or more entity structures ϵ_i and zero or more link structures L_j.

An entity structure in DiAML is a nested pair

(3) $\epsilon = \langle s, \langle \alpha, \Delta \rangle \rangle$

consisting of a functional segment s, a 'dialogue act structure' α, which character-izes a single dialogue act without the relations that it might have to other dialogue units, and a 'dependence structure' Δ, which describes the semantic dependence relations between the dialogue act α and other dialogue units.

A 'dialogue act structure' is a sixtuple

(4) $\alpha = \langle S, A, H, d, f, q \rangle$

where S is the sender of the dialogue act; A is a non-empty set of addressees; H is a (possibly empty) set of other dialogue participants (such as overhearers or side-participants; see Clark 1996); d is a dimension; f is a communicative function; and q is a (possibly empty) set of qualifiers. In order to avoid details which are irrelevant to the purpose of this chapter, we will only consider cases where the set H of participants who are neither speakers nor addressees is empty, and where there is only a single addressee—we will use A to indicate this addressee, rather than the set consisting of this lone addressee.

A 'dependence structure' is a pair consisting of a (possibly empty) set of entity structures E, whose members α has a dependence relation with, and the element δ which specifies the nature of a dependence relation (functional or feedback—see below):

(5) $\Delta = \langle E, \delta \rangle$

The other kind of component of an annotation structure besides entity structures, a link structure, is a triple consisting of an entity structure ϵ, a non-empty set E of entity structures, and a rhetorical relation ρ, which relates the dialogue act α in ϵ to the entity structures in E.

(6) $L = \langle \epsilon, E, \rho \rangle$

The 'dependence structures' that an entity structure may contain[2] and that make entity structures potentially recursive, are semantic relations between a dialogue act and one or more other units in dialogue that must be taken into account in order to determine its semantic content. Two such relations are distinguished in DiAML, called 'functional dependence' and 'feedback dependence'.

A functional dependence relation occurs when a dialogue act is semantically de-pendent on one or more dialogue acts that occurred earlier in the dialogue, due to having a communicative function which is responsive in nature. This is for example the case for answers, whose meaning is partly determined by the question which is being answered, as is immediately obvious for an answer like "*No*", whose meaning depends almost entirely on the question that is answered. Similarly for the accep-tance or rejection of offers, suggestions, requests (where "*Yes*" may illustrate the point), and acceptance of apologies and thankings.

Feedback-providing and eliciting acts provide or elicit information about the pro-cessing of something that was said earlier in the dialogue, such as its perception or

---

[2] If the set E in a dependence structure $\Delta = \langle E, \delta \rangle$ is empty, then this amounts to there being no dependences. We will designate a dependence structure $\Delta = \langle \emptyset, \delta \rangle$ by $\emptyset$.

its interpretation, and their meaning often depends on that (or those) earlier contribution(s) to the dialogue. Positive feedback utterances like *"OK"* and *"Yes"*, and negative ones like *"What?"* and *"Excuse me?"* illustrate this phenomenon.

Responsive dialogue acts and feedback acts are semantically incomplete without the specification of functional and feedback dependence relations, which are therefore part of the entity structures that are used to annotate such acts.

A dialogue act may, finally, also be related to other dialogue acts through rhetorical relations, as in (7).

(7) 1. A: it ties you on in terms of the technology and the complexity that you want
    2. A: like for example voice recognition
    3. A: because you might need to power a microphone and other things

In this example, from the AMI corpus,[3] we see three functional segments, where the second segment is related to the first through an *Exemplification* relation, and the third through an *Explanation* relation.

Different from functional and feedback dependence relations, rhetorical relations are not part of the meaning of a dialogue act, but add semantic information to the way a self-contained dialogue act is related to other dialogue acts (or how their semantic contents are related—see Petukhova et al. 2010). They therefore turn up in a different way in annotation structures, namely in link structures.

2.2 Concrete Syntax

The concrete syntax defines a rendering of annotation structures in a particular format, such as XML. It is defined in accordance with the methodology for defining semantic annotation languages described in Bunt (2010, 2013a), which introduces the notion of an *ideal representation format*, defined as one where (1) every annotation structure defined by the abstract syntax can be represented, and (2) every representation represents one and only one annotation structure. The semantics of the language is defined for the structures defined by the *abstract* syntax. This has the effect that any two 'ideal' representation formats are semantically equivalent; every representation in one such format can be converted by a meaning-preserving mapping into any other such format.[4] The representation format defined by the concrete syntax of DiAML is illustrated in (8). P2's utterance is segmented into two overlapping functional segments: one (fs2.1) in the Auto-Feedback dimension and one (fs2.2) in the Task dimension (TA), with value 'answer' qualified as 'uncertain'.

---

[3] http://corpus.amiproject.org

[4] See Bunt (2010) for formal definitions and proofs relating to alternative representation formats sharing the same abstract syntax, and Bunt (2013a) for a procedure to derive a concrete syntax from an abstract syntax.

(Values with a "#" prefix are defined outside the XML element in which they occur; either in the metadata or in another layer of annotation.)

(8)   a.   Segmented dialogue fragment:

1.	P1:	*What time does the next train to Utrecht leave?*
	TA:	fs1: What time does the next train to Utrecht leave?
2.	P2:	*The next train to Utrecht leaves I think at 8:32.*
	AuFB	fs2.1: The next train to Utrecht leaves
	TA	fs2.2: The next train to Utrecht leaves I think at 8:32.

b. DiAML annotation structure:

$$AS = \langle \{\epsilon_1, \epsilon_2, \epsilon_3\}, \emptyset \rangle, \text{ where}$$

- $\epsilon_1 = \langle \text{fs1}, \langle \alpha_1, \emptyset \rangle \rangle$;
- $\epsilon_2 = \langle \text{fs2.1}, \langle \alpha_2, \langle \{\text{fs1}\}, \text{feedback} \rangle \rangle \rangle$;
- $\epsilon_3 = \langle \text{fs2.2}, \langle \alpha_3, \langle \{\alpha_1\}, \text{functional} \rangle \rangle \rangle$

c. DiAML representation:

```
<diaml xmlns:"http://www.iso.org/diaml/">
<dialogueAct xml:id="da1" target="#fs1"
   sender="#p1" addressee="#p2" dimension="task"
   communicativeFunction="setQuestion"/>
<dialogueAct xml:id="da2" target="#fs2.1"
   sender="#p2" addressee="#p1"
   communicativeFunction="inform"
   dimension="autoFeedback"
   feedbackDependence="#fs1"/>
<dialogueAct xml:id="da3" target="#fs2.2"
   sender="#p2" addressee="#p1" dimension="task"
   communicativeFunction="answer"
   certainty="uncertain"
   functionalDependence="#da1"/>
</diaml>
```

2.3 DiAML Semantics

A dialogue act structure captures the *functional* part of a dialogue act; it does not include the full semantic content but only a dimension which classifies the content. The semantics of a dialogue act structure is therefore defined as a function that can be applied to a given semantic content to form the interpretation of a full-blown dialogue act. For a dialogue act without functional or feedback dependences this is expressed by (9), which defines the interpretation $I_a(\langle s, \alpha, \emptyset \rangle)$ of the entity structure that associates the dialogue act structure α with the functional segment s. This interpretation is a function applied to the semantic content $\kappa_1(s)$ of that segment.

(9) $\quad I_a(\epsilon) = I_a(\langle s, \langle \alpha, \emptyset \rangle \rangle) = I_a(\alpha)(\kappa_1(s))$

The interpretation $I_a(\epsilon)$ of a dialogue act structure without function qualifiers is defined as the interpretation of its communicative function, applied to the interpretations of the other components of the dialogue act structure, where the function F assigns values to the constants of DiAML:

(10) $\quad I_a(\langle S, A, d, f \rangle) = I_a(f)(F(S), F(A), F(d))$

To the sender and an addressee of a dialogue act (S and A) the function F assigns certain individuals, identified in the metadata of the dialogue; to the dimension argument d, a component is assigned of an Information State (IS) to be updated. The interpretation of a dialogue act with communicative function qualifiers is discussed in Sect. 4.2; if the communicative function f has no qualifiers, then $I_a(f) = F(f)$; see Sect. 4.1 for the definition of $F(f)$.

A link structure $L = \langle \epsilon, E, \rho \rangle$ is interpreted semantically as a set of updates that create rhetorical links between the representations of the dialogue acts in ϵ and E in the participants' ISs. This assumes that the dialogue acts that occur in a dialogue are represented as such in an IS, an assumption that is commonly made in proposals for dialogue context modelling (see Sect. 3). More specifically, the assumption is that an IS has a part (the 'Dialogue History'), where a record is kept of the communicative events in the dialogue, typically in the form of a transcription of what was said, with an interpretation in terms of dialogue acts. The updates corresponding to link structures then come down to the addition of rhetorical links between these representations.

The semantics of an annotation structure $\{e_1, \ldots, e_n, L_1, \ldots, L_k\}$, consisting of the entity structures $\{e_1, \ldots, e_n\}$ and the link structures $\{L_1, \ldots, L_k\}$, is defined as the sequential application of the update functions corresponding to the constituent entity and link structures, following the textual order $<_T$ of their functional segments, where the update operations corresponding to textually coinciding ('$=_T$') entity structures are unified rather than sequenced. This is expressed in (11), where the notation '$\alpha ; / \sqcup \beta$' is used to indicate that the operation α should be followed ('$;$') by the operation β if $\alpha <_T \beta$, and should be unified ($\sqcup$) if $\alpha =_T \beta$.

(11)
$$I_a(\{e_1, \ldots, e_n, L_1, \ldots, L_k\})$$
$$= I_a(e_1); / \sqcup \ldots; / \sqcup I_a(e_n); / \sqcup I_a(L_1); / \sqcup \ldots; / \sqcup I_a(L_k)$$

The semantics of an entity structure with dependence relations is defined as follows, where s_ϵ is the functional segment of entity structure ϵ; f_α is the communicative function of α; κ_{2a} computes the semantic content of a dependent dialogue act from its local content $\kappa_1(s_{\epsilon_1})$ and the contents of the dialogue acts that α, depends on (given the communicative function f_α and the nature of the dependence relation δ).

(12) $\quad I_a(\langle s, \alpha, \langle E, \delta \rangle \rangle) = I_a(\alpha)(\kappa_{2a}(\kappa_1(s), \{\kappa_1(s_\epsilon)|\epsilon \in E\}, f_\alpha, \delta))$

3 Context Model Structure and Content

3.1 Types of Context Information

As the proposed semantics of dialogue acts is in terms of IS updates, the question arises as to what exactly is an information state in this context; what information does it contain, and how is it structured. The dialogue act semantics described in this chapter does not make any assumptions about a particular formalism that is used to represent information states; proposals in the literature include Discourse Representation Structures (Poesio and Traum 1997); Constructive Type Theory (Ahn 2001); Modular Partial Models (Bunt 2000); Record Types (Cooper 2004) and typed feature structures (Keizer et al. 2011; Petukhova et al. 2010). An IS is assumed to have a number of components that contain different kinds of information, such as a dialogue history and a representation of the state of the underlying task or activity.

The details of an IS update semantics depend on whether only the information state of an *addressee* is considered to be updated by dialogue acts, or also that of the *sender*, and on whether these updates involve nested or mutual beliefs (as e.g. argued in Bunt 1989). In this chapter we consider only the updates of a single addressee's information state; approaches involving multiple ISs and mutual beliefs are readily extrapolated from this. In DIT, it is customary to speak of 'contexts' or 'context models', rather than 'information states', and this terminology will also be used in the rest of this chapter.

A requirement for an adequate notion of context model is that, for a given range of dialogue act types, it contains the kinds of information that can be updated by a dialogue act. For the dialogue acts of the DIT^{++} taxonomy, we require the context models to include the following kinds of information: properties of the dialogue task (and task domain); success/problems in processing previous utterances; allocation of the speaker role; allocation of time; presence and contact; structuring of the discourse; success/problems in utterance production; social obligations and interactive pressures. It can be argued (see Bunt 2000) that an agent's context model does not need to have a separate component for each dimension of the taxonomy, but that it is convenient to distinguish the following five components:

(13) 1. Linguistic Context, which contains a record of the dialogue history, information about discourse plans (if any), and preferences concerning the occupation of the speaker role;
   2. Task Context, which contains the agent's information and goals relating to the dialogue task, as well as his assumptions about the dialogue partner's task-related goals and beliefs;
   3. Cognitive Context, which contains information about the agent's cognitive processes concerned with the processing and production of dialogue utterances, including time estimates for these processes;
   4. Physical/Perceptual Context, which contains information about physical and perceptual properties of the interactive situation;
   5. Social Context, which contains information relevant for interpreting and generating 'social' acts like greetings, apologies, expressions of gratitude.

Versions of such a 5-component context model have been implemented in the PARADIME dialogue manager (Keizer and Bunt 2006, 2007; Keizer et al. 2011) and for theoretical studies by Petukhova et al. (2010).

A context-update semantics has to take into account that update operations should not undermine the consistency of the context model. A dialogue participant may for example change his mind on something in the course of a dialogue, possibly as an effect of receiving new information which contradicts something that the participant believed. Updates are therefore not simply additions of information. Rather then building consistency checks into the semantics of each dialogue act, we exploit the DIT distinction of several levels of utterance processing: (1) attending, (2) perceiving, (3) understanding, (4) evaluating, and (5) executing. The level of *understanding* determines the meaning of a dialogue segment in terms of dialogue acts. The *evaluation* level checks whether the corresponding updates would keep the current context model consistent. If so, the updates are performed. One way to implement this approach is to add to a context model a part called the *pending context*, which serves as a buffer for items to be inserted in the main context once their consistency with the current content of the main context has been established.[5] Updating the pending context is then simply a matter of adding items to it. For convenience we will assume the pending context $A*$ of an agent A's context model to be structured in the same way as the main context; a piece of information which is found to be consistent with the main context can then simply be moved from its pending context component to the corresponding component of the main context. The notation (14) will be used to designate the operation of adding the information z to component $A*_i$ of A's pending context:

(14) $A*_i =+z$

3.2 Semantic Primitives

The definitions of the communicative functions in the DIT^{++} and ISO 24617-2 taxonomies make use of a number of formal concepts needed to describe update effects. This involves such concepts as an agent believing something, an agent wanting to know something, and an agent being committed to do something. Table 1 lists the basic concepts that are required for formulating the update semantics of dialogue acts with a general-purpose function, with the terms used to designate them in the rest of this chapter.

For convenience, we introduce the following abbreviations: **Bel**(S, p) abbreviates **Bel**(S, p, firm); **Wk-Bel**(S, p) abbreviates **Bel**(S, p, weak); **Assumes**(S, p) abbreviates **Bel**$(S, p) \vee$ **Wk-Bel**(S, p). In all action-related attitude operators we suppress the argument $\top$ representing the 'empty' condition, hence **WilDo**(S, α) abbreviates **WilDo**$(S, \alpha, \top)$, and so on. These semantic primitives are similar to

---

[5]This approach has been implemented in the multimodal DenK dialogue system; see Kievit et al. (2001).

Table 1 Semantic primitives for the interpretation of general-purpose communicative functions. (C_α may be the universally true condition $\top$.)

Description	Notation	Meaning
believes that	**Bel**(S, p, σ)	S believes that p; σ indicates the strength of this belief ($\sigma =$ 'firm' or $\sigma =$ 'weak')
knows value of	**Know-val**(S, z)	S possesses the information z
has goal	**Want**(S, p)	S has the goal that p
is able to do	**CanDo**(S, α)	S is able to perform the action α
is willing to do	**WilDo**(S, α, C_α)	S is willing to perform the action α if the condition C_α is satisfied
is committed to do	**CommitDo**(S, α, C_α)	S is committed to perform the action α if the condition C_α is satisfied
is committed to refrain from doing	**RefrainDo**(S, α, C_α)	S is committed to refrain from performing the action α if the condition C_α is satisfied
is considering	**ConsidDo**(X, α, Y, C_α)	X is considering the performance of action α by agent Y, if condition C_α is satisfied
is in the interest of	**Interest**(Y, α)	action α is in the interest of agent Y

Table 2 Dimension-specific semantic primitives

Dimension	Primitives
Auto- and Allo-Feedback	**Attended, Perceived, Understood, Accepted, Executed, Success-Processing**
Turn Management	**Current-Speaker, Next-Speaker**
Time Management	**Time-Need, small, substantial**
Contact Management	**Present**
Discourse Structuring	**Ready, Available, Start-Dialogue, Close-Dialogue**
Own and Partner Communication Man.	**Delete, Replace, Append**
Social Obligations Management	**Available, Thankful, Regretful, Knows-id, Final**

those proposed by Poesio and Traum in their axiomatization of dialogue acts (Poesio and Traum 1997), which is however limited to a small set of general-purpose functions and positive auto-feedback functions, and does not consider the other dimensions, nor communicative function qualifiers.

Since dimension-specific communicative functions are concerned with a specific kind of semantic content, certain specific semantic primitives are required for representing their semantics; these are listed in Table 2.

For expressing the semantics of a feedback act, we must distinguish between feedback functions which indicate a certain *level of processing*, and those that do not. The taxonomy of dimension-specific communicative functions for feedback in DIT^{++} is based on the distinction of five levels of processing that a feedback act may address: attending, perceiving, understanding, evaluating and executing. At each of these levels, positive auto-feedback reports that the sender believes his processing of one or more previous utterances to be sufficiently successful to go on, not requiring a repetition or clarification; negative feedback reports that the sender does not believe that. Similarly, positive allo-feedback reports that the sender believes that the addressee did process one or more utterances successfully, and negative allo-feedback that this is not the case. The semantics of feedback acts which are specific about the level of processing that they refer to, requires the semantic primitives mentioned in Table 2.

Since feedback acts are often not specific for a particular level of processing, DIT^{++} also has level-unspecific feedback functions: one for level-unspecific positive auto-feedback, one for negative auto-feedback, one for positive allo-feedback, one for negative allo-feedback, and one for feedback elicitation. The ISO 24617-2 standard has only these level-unspecific functions. A study reported in Bunt (2012) shows that the dialogue participants interpret level-unspecific feedback acts in different ways depending on the interactive setting, and therefore introduces a semantic primitive **Success-Processing** whose interpretation is context-dependent, one common interpretation being "Well understood and possibly also accepted and executed successfully"—see Bunt (2012) for details. This primitive has therefore been added to the level-specific primitives in Table 2.

4 Dialogue Act Interpretation

The definition of the semantics of the communicative functions in the DIT^{++} and ISO 24617-2 taxonomies is organized in a way that exploits the hierarchical structure of these taxonomies, which reflects the phenomenon that some communicative functions are specializations of others. For example, a confirmation is a special kind of answer, and an answer is a special kind of inform (namely an inform in response to a question); this is reflected in the taxonomy by the communicative function Inform dominating the Answer function, which in turn dominates the Confirm function.

An update semantics of dialogue acts with an Inform, an Answer, or a Confirm function should bring this out by having in common that in all three cases (1) the speaker wants to make certain information available to the addressee, and (2) the speaker assumes that this information is correct. These are (minimally) the updates of an Inform act. An Answer act has additional update effects, reflecting that (3) the speaker believes that the addressee wanted to obtain this information; and (4) the addressee assumed that the speaker possessed the requested information. A Confirm act has a further additional update effect, reflecting that (5) the speaker believes that the addressee had an uncertain belief that this information was correct. The DiAML semantics described below therefore makes use of so-called *elementary update functions*, which update an information state with a single information item, such as (1) or (2) in this example.

Table 3 Update semantics for information-providing and information-seeking communicative functions

$F(\text{Inform})$	$= \lambda s.\lambda X.\lambda Y.\lambda D_i.\lambda p.U_1(X, Y, D_i, p, s) \sqcup U_2(X, Y, D_i, p, s)$
$F(\text{Agreement})$	$= \lambda s.\lambda X.\lambda Y.\lambda D_i.\lambda p.U_1(X, Y, D_i, p, s) \sqcup U_2(X, Y, D_i, p, s)$ $\sqcup U_5(X, Y, D_i, p)$
$F(\text{Disagreement})$	$= \lambda s.\lambda X.\lambda Y.\lambda D_i.\lambda p.U_1(X, Y, D_i, \neg p, s) \sqcup U_2(X, Y, D_i, \neg p, s)$ $\sqcup U_5(X, Y, D_i, p)$
$F(\text{Correction})$	$= \lambda s.\lambda X.\lambda Y.\lambda D_i.\lambda p.U_1(X, Y, D_i, p_1, s) \sqcup U_2(X, Y, D_i, \neg p_1, s)$ $\sqcup U_6(X, Y, D_i, p_2)$
$F(\text{Answer})$	$= \lambda s.\lambda X.\lambda Y.\lambda D_i.\lambda p.U_1(X, Y, D_i, p, s) \sqcup U_2(X, Y, D_i, p, s)$ $\sqcup U_9(X, Y, D_i, p) \sqcup U_7(X, Y, D_i, p)$
$F(\text{Confirm})$	$= \lambda s.\lambda X.\lambda Y.\lambda D_i.\lambda p.U_1(X, Y, D_i, p, s) \sqcup U_2(X, Y, D_i, p, s)$ $\sqcup U_8(X, Y, D_i, p) \sqcup U_9(X, Y, D_i, p, s) \sqcup U_7(X, Y, D_i, p)$
$F(\text{Disconfirm})$	$= \lambda s.\lambda X.\lambda Y.\lambda D_i.\lambda p.U_1(X, Y, D_i, \neg p, s) \sqcup U_2(X, Y, D_i, \neg p, s)$ $\sqcup U_8(X, Y, D_i, p, s) \sqcup U_9(X, Y, D_i, p) \sqcup U_7(X, Y, D_i, p)$
$F(\text{Question})$	$= \lambda X.\lambda Y.\lambda D_i.\lambda z.U_{10}(X, Y, D_i, z) \sqcup U_{11}(X, Y, D_i, z)$
$F(\text{Prop.Question})$	$= \lambda X.\lambda Y.\lambda D_i.\lambda p.U_{10}(X, Y, D_i, p) \sqcup U_{11}(X, Y, D_i, p) \sqcup U_{12}(X, Y, D_i, p)$
$F(\text{CheckQuestion})$	$= \lambda X.\lambda Y.\lambda D_i.\lambda p.U_{10}(X, Y, D_i, p) \sqcup U_{11}(X, Y, D_i, p) \sqcup U_4(X, Y, D_i, p)$
$F(\text{SetQuestion})$	$= \lambda X.\lambda Y.\lambda D_i.\lambda z.U_{10}(X, Y, D_i, z) \sqcup U_{11}(X, Y, D_i, z) \sqcup U_{13}(X, Y, D_i, z)$
$F(\text{ChoiceQuestion})$	$= \lambda X.\lambda Y.\lambda D_i.\lambda p.U_{15a}(X, Y, D_i, p) \sqcup U_{15}(X, Y, D_i, p) \sqcup U_{16}(X, Y, D_i, p)$

Table 4 Elementary update functions used in the semantics of information-transfer functions

$U_1(X, Y, D_i, p, s)$	$Y *_i = +\textbf{Bel}(Y, \textbf{Want}(X, \textbf{Bel}(Y, p, s)))$
$U_2(X, Y, D_i, p, s)$	$Y *_i = +\textbf{Bel}(Y, \textbf{Bel}(X, p, s))$
$U_3(X, Y, D_i, p)$	$Y *_i = +\textbf{Bel}(Y, \textbf{Assume}(X, p))$
$U_4(X, Y, D_i, p)$	$Y *_i = +\textbf{Bel}(Y, \textbf{Wk-Bel}(X, p))$
$U_5(X, Y, D_i, p)$	$Y *_i = +\textbf{Bel}(Y, \textbf{Bel}(X, \textbf{Assume}(Y, p)))$
$U_6(X, Y, D_i, p)$	$Y *_i = +\textbf{Bel}(Y, \textbf{Assume}(X, \textbf{Assume}(Y, p)))$
$U_7(X, Y, D_i, P)$	$Y *_i = +\textbf{Bel}(Y, \textbf{Bel}(X, \textbf{Assume}(Y, \textbf{Know-val}(X, P))))$
$U_8(X, Y, D_i, p)$	$Y *_i = +\textbf{Bel}(Y, \textbf{Assume}(X, \textbf{Wk-Bel}(Y, p)))$
$U_9(X, Y, D_i, P)$	$Y *_i = +\textbf{Bel}(Y, \textbf{Bel}(X, \textbf{Want}(Y, \textbf{Know-val}(Y, P))))$
$U_{10}(X, Y, D_i, P)$	$Y *_i = +\textbf{Bel}(Y, \textbf{Want}(X, \textbf{Know-val}(X, P)))$
$U_{11}(X, Y, D_i, P)$	$Y *_i = +\textbf{Bel}(Y, \textbf{Assume}(X, \textbf{Know-val}(Y, P)))$
$U_{12}(X, Y, D_i, p)$	$Y *_i = +\textbf{Bel}(Y, \textbf{Bel}(X, p \vee \neg p))$
$U_{13}(X, Y, D_i, P)$	$Y *_i = +\textbf{Bel}(Y, \textbf{Assume}(X, \exists x.P(x)))$
$U_{14}(X, Y, D_i, P)$	$Y *_i = +\textbf{Bel}(Y, \textbf{Want}(X, \textbf{Know-val}(X, P)))$
$U_{15}(X, Y, D_i, p)$	$Y *_i = +\textbf{Bel}(Y, \textbf{Assume}(X, p_1 \; xor \; p_2))$
$U_{15a}(X, Y, D_i, p)$	$Y *_i = +\textbf{Bel}(Y, \textbf{Want}(X, \textbf{Bel}(X, p_1) \vee \textbf{Bel}(X, p_2)))$
$U_{16}(X, Y, D_i, p)$	$Y *_i = +\textbf{Bel}(Y, \textbf{Assume}(X, \textbf{Bel}(Y, p_1) \vee \textbf{Bel}(Y, p_2)))$

The update semantics of the Inform function, as specified in Table 3, is defined as the combination of the elementary update functions U_1 and U_2 (defined in Table 4), which perform the updates illustrated by (1) and (2). The update semantics of the

Answer function shares the use of U_1 and U_2 with that of the Inform function, and adds to that the effects of the elementary update functions U_7 and U_9 (defined in Table 4); the semantics of the Confirm function further adds to that the update defined by U_8.

4.1 The Semantics of Communicative Functions

4.1.1 General-Purpose Communicative Functions

The class of general-purpose communicative functions in ISO 24617-2 and DIT^{++} falls apart into *information-transfer functions* and *action-discussion functions*, further subdivided into information-providing and information-seeking functions, and commissives and directives, respectively (see Appendix). We first consider the class of information-transfer functions.

a. Information-Providing and Information-Seeking Functions   The hierarchy of information-providing functions has the function *Inform* as the mother of all information-providing functions; all other functions are specializations of this function, and therefore have in common that the speaker wants the addressee to possess certain information which the speaker assumes to be correct.

Using the epistemic operators introduced in Sect. 3.2, these conditions can be formalized as sown in (15), where (15.b) says that the speaker S believes that the content p is true, with certainty σ and (15a) says that S wants the addressee A to also have that belief.

(15) a. **Want**$(S, \mathbf{Bel}(A, p, \sigma))$
     b. **Bel**(A, p, σ)

When addressee A understands an utterance by S as an *Inform* with the content denoted by p, then the update effects on the pending context part of A's IS will be that A believes that the two conditions in (15) hold.

If a speaker is uncertain about the content of an *Answer* or an *Inform* ($\sigma = weak$), then his goal cannot be that the addressee believes for sure that the content is true; if, on the other hand, the speaker is certain, then it would be strange if he would want the addressee to be uncertain. The argument σ should therefore have the same value in both conditions in (15). The semantics of the Inform function, specified in Table 3, has this effect. (See also below, Sect. 4.2, on certainty qualifiers.)

As an illustration of the update semantics of information-providing functions, consider the case of the answer in (16.2).

(16) 1. *D*: twenty-five euros, how much is that in pounds?
     2. *C*: twenty-five euros is something like 20 pounds

Applying the semantics of the Answer function (see Table 3) to the participants C and D and the semantic content of (16.2), we obtain:

Table 5 Update semantics for commissive and directive functions (selection)

$F(\text{Offer})$	$= \lambda C_\alpha.\lambda X.\lambda Y.\lambda D_i.\lambda\alpha.U_{25a}(X, Y, D_i, \alpha) \sqcup U_{20}(X, Y, D_i, \alpha, C_\alpha)$
$F(\text{AddressRequest})$	$= \lambda C_\alpha.\lambda X.\lambda Y.\lambda D_i.\lambda\alpha.U_{17a}(X, Y, D_i, \alpha, C_\alpha) \sqcup U_{18}(X, Y, D_i, \alpha)$
	$\sqcup U_{26b}(X, Y, D_i, \alpha)$
$F(\text{AcceptRequest})$	$= \lambda C_\alpha.\lambda X.\lambda Y.\lambda D_i.\lambda\alpha.U_{17}(X, Y, D_i, \alpha, C_\alpha) \sqcup U_{18}(X, Y, D_i, \alpha)$
	$\sqcup U_{26b}(X, Y, D_i, \alpha)$
$F(\text{DeclineRequest})$	$= \lambda C_\alpha.\lambda X.\lambda Y.\lambda D_i.\lambda\alpha.U_{27}(X, Y, D_i, \alpha, C_\alpha) \sqcup U_{18}(X, Y, D_i, \alpha)$
	$\sqcup U_{26b}(X, Y, D_i, \alpha)$
$F(\text{Request})$	$= \lambda C_\alpha.\lambda X.\lambda Y.\lambda D_i.\lambda\alpha.U_{23}(X, Y, D_i, \alpha, C_\alpha) \sqcup U_{26}(X, Y, D_i, \alpha)$
$F(\text{Instruct})$	$= \lambda C_\alpha.\lambda X.\lambda Y.\lambda D_i.\lambda\alpha.U_{24}(X, Y, D_i, \alpha, C_\alpha) \sqcup U_{26}(X, Y, D_i, \alpha)$
	$\sqcup U_{25}(X, Y, D_i, \alpha)$
$F(\text{AddressOffer})$	$= \lambda C_\alpha.\lambda X.\lambda Y.\lambda D_i.\lambda\alpha.U_{17b}(X, Y, D_i, \alpha, C_\alpha) \sqcup U_{25}(X, Y, D_i, \alpha)$
	$\sqcup U_{25b}(X, Y, D_i, \alpha)$
$F(\text{AcceptOffer})$	$= \lambda C_\alpha.\lambda X.\lambda Y.\lambda D_i.\lambda\alpha.U_{24}(X, Y, D_i, \alpha) \sqcup U_{25}(X, Y, D_i, \alpha)$
	$\sqcup U_{25b}(X, Y, D_i, \alpha)$

$$
\begin{aligned}
& F(\text{Answer})(C, D, \text{Task}, \text{€}25 = \text{£}20) \\
& = U_1(C, D, \text{TaskC}, \text{€}25 = \text{£}20) \\
& \quad \sqcup U_2(C, D, \text{Task}, \text{€}25 = \text{£}20) \\
& \quad \sqcup U_9(C, D, \text{Task}, \text{€}25 = \text{£}20) \\
(17) & \quad \sqcup U_7(C, D, \text{Task}, \text{€}25 = \text{£}20) \\
& = D*_{TaskC} = +\mathbf{Bel}(D, \mathbf{Want}(C, \mathbf{Bel}(D, \text{€}25 = \text{£}20))); \\
& \quad D*_{TaskC} = +\mathbf{Bel}(D, \mathbf{Bel}(C, \text{€}25 = \text{£}20)); \\
& \quad D*_{TaskC} = +\mathbf{Bel}(D, \mathbf{Bel}(C, \mathbf{Want}(D, \mathbf{Know\text{-}val}(D, \text{€}25 = \text{£}20)))); \\
& \quad D*_{TaskC} = +\mathbf{Bel}(D, \mathbf{Bel}(C, \mathbf{Assume}(D, \mathbf{Know\text{-}val}(C, \text{€}25 = \text{£}20))))
\end{aligned}
$$

Hence the following beliefs are added to D's pending Task Context:

(18) (1) C wants D to know that $\text{€}25 = \text{£}20$;
    (2) C believes that $\text{€}25 = \text{£}20$;
    (3) C believes that $\overset{.}{D}$ wants to know whether $\text{€}25 = \text{£}20$;
    (4) C believes that D assumes C to know whether $\text{€}25 = \text{£}20$.

b. Commissive and Directive Functions   Table 5 specifies the semantics of a representative selection of the commissive and directive communicative functions; Table 6 defines the elementary update functions used in the semantics of these functions.

As an example of the interpretation of a directive dialogue act, consider the request in (19.2):

(19) 1. B: (...)
    2. A: Please repeat that

Applied to the participants A and B and the semantic content Repeat($u1$), which situates the Request act in the Auto-Feedback dimension, the definition of the Request semantics in Table 5 leads to the update (20) (where 'CC' stands for Cognitive Context):

Table 6 Elementary update functions used in the semantics of action-discussion functions

$U_{17}(X, Y, D_i, \alpha, C_\alpha)$	$Y*_i =+\mathbf{Bel}(Y, \mathbf{CommitDo}(X, \alpha, C_\alpha))$
$U_{17a}(X, Y, D_i, \alpha, C_\alpha)$	$Y*_i =+\mathbf{Bel}(Y, \mathbf{ConsidDo}(X, \alpha, X, C_\alpha))$
$U_{17b}(X, Y, D_i, \alpha, C_\alpha)$	$Y*_i =+\mathbf{Bel}(Y, \mathbf{ConsidDo}(X, \alpha, Y, C_\alpha))$
$U_{18}(X, Y, D_i, \alpha)$	$Y*_i =+\mathbf{Bel}(Y, \mathbf{Bel}(X, \mathbf{Want}(Y, \mathbf{CommitDo}(X, \alpha, C_\alpha))))$
$U_{20}(X, Y, D_i, \alpha, C_\alpha)$	$Y*_i =+\mathbf{Bel}(Y, \mathbf{WilDo}(X, \alpha, C_\alpha))$
$U_{21}(X, Y, D_i, \alpha)$	$Y*_i =+\mathbf{Bel}(Y, \mathbf{Bel}(X, \mathbf{Interest}(\alpha, Y)))$
$U_{23}(X, Y, D_i, \alpha)$	$Y*_i =+\mathbf{Bel}(Y, \mathbf{Want}(X, [\mathbf{WilDo}(Y, \alpha, C_\alpha) \to \mathbf{CommitDo}(Y, \alpha, C_\alpha)]))$
$U_{24}(X, Y, D_i, \alpha)$	$Y*_i =+\mathbf{Bel}(Y, \mathbf{Want}(X, \mathbf{CommitDo}(Y, \alpha)))$
$U_{25}(X, Y, D_i, \alpha, C_\alpha)$	$Y*_i =+\mathbf{Bel}(Y, \mathbf{Bel}(X, \mathbf{WilDo}(Y, \alpha, C_\alpha)))$
$U_{25a}(X, Y, D_i, \alpha, C_\alpha)$	$Y*_i =+\mathbf{Bel}(Y, \mathbf{Want}(X, \mathbf{Bel}(Y, \mathbf{WilDo}(X, \alpha, C_\alpha))))$
$U_{25b}(X, Y, D_i, \alpha, C_\alpha)$	$Y*_i =+\mathbf{Bel}(Y, \mathbf{Bel}(X, \mathbf{Want}(Y, \mathbf{Bel}(X, \mathbf{WilDo}(Y, \alpha, C_\alpha)))))$
$U_{26}(X, Y, D_i, \alpha)$	$Y*_i =+\mathbf{Bel}(Y, \mathbf{Assume}(X, \mathbf{CanDo}(Y, \alpha)))$
$U_{26b}(X, Y, D_i, \alpha)$	$Y*_i =+\mathbf{Bel}(Y, \mathbf{Bel}(X, \mathbf{Assume}(Y, \mathbf{CanDo}(X, \alpha))))$
$U_{27}(X, Y, D_i, \alpha, C_\alpha)$	$Y*_i =+\mathbf{Bel}(Y, \mathbf{CommitRefrain}(X, \alpha, C_\alpha))$

$$F(\text{Request})(A, B, \text{Auto-Feedback}, \langle\text{Repeat}(u1), \text{unconditional}\rangle)$$
$$= \lambda C_\alpha.\lambda X.\lambda Y.\lambda D_i.\lambda\alpha.U_{23}(X, Y, D_i, \alpha, C_\alpha)$$
$$\sqcup U_{26}(X, Y, D_i, \alpha)(A, B, \text{Auto-Feedback}, \text{Repeat}(u1), \top)$$
(20)
$$= U_{23}(A, B, CC, \text{Repeat}(u1), \top) \sqcup U_{26}(A, B, CC, \text{Repeat}(u1))$$
$$= B*_{CC} =+\mathbf{Bel}(B, \mathbf{Want}(A, [\mathbf{WilDo}(A, \text{Repeat}(u1) \to \mathbf{CommitDo}(B, \text{Repeat}(u1))]));$$
$$B*_{CC} =+\mathbf{Bel}(B, \mathbf{Assume}(A, \mathbf{CanDo}(B, \text{Repeat}(u1))))$$

In words, B's pending cognitive context is extended with two beliefs: (1) that A wants B to commit himself to repeating the previous utterance, if he is willing to do so; (2) that A assumes B is able to repeat that utterance.

4.1.2 Dimension-Specific Communicative Functions

Feedback Functions   The communicative functions for providing and eliciting feedback in DIT^{++} fall apart in those concerned with the speaker's own processing of previous utterances (Auto-Feedback) and those concerned with the addressee's processing, as perceived by the speaker (Allo-Feedback). The elementary update functions for these two dimensions are nearly identical, differing only in whose processing is concerned. Tables 7 and 8 show the update semantics of a small, representative subset of the (altogether twenty-five) DIT^{++} communicative functions for providing and eliciting feedback.

Turn Management Functions   The communicative functions for turn management serve to decide who has or will have the speaker role. The functions for taking, accepting, grabbing, keeping, releasing, or assigning the turn are therefore all defined in terms of who currently occupies the speaker role and who wants or should

Table 7 Elementary update functions for the semantics of auto- and allo-feedback functions (selection)

$U_{31}(X, Y, z)$	$Y*_{CC} =+$**Bel**$(Y,$ **Want**$(X,$ **Bel**$(Y,$ **Success-Processing**$(X, z))))$
$U_{33}(X, Y, z)$	$Y*_{CC} =+$**Bel**$(Y,$ **Want**$(X,$ **Bel**$(Y,$ **Perceived**$(X, z))))$
$U_{35}(X, Y, z)$	$Y*_{CC} =+$**Bel**$(Y,$ **Want**$(X,$ **Bel**$(Y,$ **Accepted**$(X, z))))$
$U_{79}(X, Y, z)$	$Y*_{CC} =+$**Bel**$(Y,$ **Want**$(X,$ **Bel**$(Y,$ **Perception-Problem**$(Y, z))))$
$U_{76}(X, Y, z)$	$Y*_{CC} =+$**Bel**$(Y,$ **Want**$(X,$ **Bel**$(Y,$ **Execution-Problem**$(Y, z))))$
$U_{61}(X, Y, z)$	$Y*_{CC} =+$**Bel**$(Y,$ **Bel**$(X,$ **Success-Processing**$(X, z)))$
$U_{62}(X, Y, z)$	$Y*_{CC} =+$**Bel**$(Y,$ **Bel**$(X,$ **Perceived**$(X, z)))$
$U_{64}(X, Y, z)$	$Y*_{CC} =+$**Bel**$(Y,$ **Bel**$(X,$ **Accepted**$(X, z)))$
$U_{67}(X, Y, z)$	$Y*_{CC} =+$**Bel**$(Y,$ **Bel**$(X,$ **Perception-Problem**$(X, z)))$
$U_{85}(X, Y, z)$	$Y*_{CC} =+$**Bel**$(Y,$ **Bel**$(X,$ **Execution-Problem**$(Y, z)))$

Table 8 Semantics of feedback functions (selection)

F(AutoPositive)	$= \lambda X.\lambda Y.\lambda z.U_{31}(X, Y, z) \sqcup U_{61}(X, Y, z)$
F(AlloPerceptionNegative)	$= \lambda X.\lambda Y.\lambda z.U_{33}(X, Y, z) \sqcup U_{62}(X, Y, z)$
F(AutoEvaluationPositive)	$= \lambda X.\lambda Y.\lambda z.U_{35}(X, Y, z) \sqcup U_{64}(X, Y, z)$
F(AlloExecutionNegative)	$= \lambda X.\lambda Y.\lambda z.U_{76}(X, Y, z) \sqcup U_{85}(X, Y, z)$

have it next. Table 9 defines the semantics of these functions, using the elementary update functions defined in Table 10.

For example, assigning the turn to a dialogue partner (using a Turn Assign function) means that the participant who currently occupies the speaker role wants the indicated other participant to occupy the speaker role next. This is expressed in the form of a combination of elementary update functions as shown in (21):

$$
\begin{aligned}
& F(\text{TurnAssign})(A, B) \\
& = \lambda X.\lambda Y.[U_{101}(X, Y) \sqcup U_{102}(X, Y)](A, B) \\
(21) \quad & = U_{101}(A, B, \text{TurnM}) \sqcup U_{102}(A, B) \\
& = B*_{LiC} =+\textbf{Bel}(B, \textbf{Bel}(A, \textbf{Current-Speaker}(A))) \\
& \quad\ B*_{LiC} =+\textbf{Bel}(B, \textbf{Want}(A, \textbf{Next-Speaker}(B)))
\end{aligned}
$$

In other words, the Linguistic Context component of B's pending context is updated to contain the beliefs that A is the current speaker and wants B to be the next speaker.

Time Management Functions   Time management acts are used by a speaker to indicate that he needs some time to compose his utterance, as signalled for instance by protracting (decreasing the speech tempo) or by filled pauses; or that he needs so much time that he suspends the dialogue as in *"Just a moment"*. The semantics of such acts requires a context model that contains information about

Table 9 Elementary update functions for the semantics of turn management functions

$U_{101}(X, Y)$	$Y *_{LiC} =+\mathbf{Bel}(Y, \mathbf{Bel}(X, \mathbf{Current\text{-}Speaker}(X)))$
$U_{102}(X, Y)$	$Y *_{LiC} =+\mathbf{Bel}(Y, \mathbf{Want}(X, \mathbf{Next\text{-}Speaker}(Y)))$
$U_{103}(X, Y)$	$Y *_{LiC} =+\mathbf{Bel}(Y, \mathbf{Bel}(X, \mathbf{Current\text{-}Speaker}(Y)))$
$U_{104}(X, Y)$	$Y *_{LiC} =+\mathbf{Bel}(Y, \mathbf{Wants}(X, \mathbf{Current\text{-}Speaker}(X)))$
$U_{105}(X, Y)$	$Y *_{LiC} =+\mathbf{Bel}(Y, \mathbf{Wants}(X, \mathbf{Next\text{-}Speaker}(X)))$
$U_{105}(X, Y)$	$Y *_{LiC} =+\mathbf{Bel}(Y, \mathbf{Want}(X, \neg\mathbf{Next\text{-}Speaker}(X)))$
$U_{107}(X, Y)$	$Y *_{LiC} =+\mathbf{Bel}(Y, \mathbf{Bel}(X, \neg\mathbf{Next\text{-}Speaker}(X) \wedge \neg\mathbf{Next\text{-}Speaker}(Y)))$
$U_{108}(X, Y)$	$Y *_{LiC} =+\mathbf{Bel}(Y, \mathbf{Bel}(X, \mathbf{Want}(Y, \mathbf{Next\text{-}Speaker}(X))))$

Table 10 Update semantics of turn management functions

$$
\begin{aligned}
F(\text{TurnAccept}) &= \lambda X.\lambda Y.U_{103}(X, Y) \sqcup U_{105}(X, Y) \sqcup U_{107}(X, Y) \\
F(\text{TurnAssign}) &= \lambda X.\lambda Y.U_{101}(X, Y) \sqcup U_{102}(X, Y) \\
F(\text{TurnGrab}) &= \lambda X.\lambda Y.U_{103}(X, Y) \sqcup U_{104}(X, Y) \\
F(\text{TurnKeep}) &= \lambda X.\lambda Y.U_{101}(X, Y) \sqcup U_{105}(X, Y) \\
F(\text{TurnRelease}) &= \lambda X.\lambda Y.U_{101}(X, Y) \sqcup U_{106}(X, Y) \\
F(\text{TurnTake}) &= \lambda X.\lambda Y.U_{105}(X, Y) \sqcup U_{107}(X, Y)
\end{aligned}
$$

Table 11 Elementary update functions for the semantics of time management functions

$U_{111}(X, Y, CC)$	$Y *_{CC} =+\mathbf{Bel}(Y, \mathbf{TimeNeed}(X, small))$
$U_{112}(X, Y, CC)$	$Y *_{CC} =+\mathbf{Bel}(Y, \mathbf{TimeNeed}(X, substantial))$

the amount of time needed by certain cognitive processes; the DIT context model therefore assumes the representation of estimates of amount of time to be represented in the Cognitive Context component, which also contains other information about the speaker's utterance processing and generation. In natural human communication such estimates are rough; an expression like "*Just a minute*" does not mean that the speaker thinks he needs one minute to process the utterance in question. The semantic primitives needed for the semantics of dimension-specific dialogue act (see Table 2) therefore include only the time estimates 'small' and 'substantial', which is adequate for interpreting the two time management functions in ISO 24617-2 and DIT^{++}: 'small' for *Stalling* and 'substantial' for *Pausing*.

Consider for example the update semantics of a *Stalling* act, which uses the elementary update scheme U_{111}, defined in Table 11:

$$
\begin{aligned}
(22) \quad & I_a(\langle Sys, Usr, \text{TimeM}, \text{Stalling}\rangle) \\
&= (\text{Stalling})(Sys, Usr, CC) \\
&= U_{111}(Sys, Usr, CC, \mathbf{Time\text{-}Need}(Sys, small)) \\
&= Usr'_{CC} =+\mathbf{Bel}(Usr, \mathbf{TimeNeed}(Sys, small))
\end{aligned}
$$

This update operation adds to the pending cognitive context of *Usr* the information that *Sys* needs a small amount of time.

Table 12 Specification of the semantics of communicative function qualifiers

$F(\text{certain})$	$= \text{'firm'}$
$F(\text{uncertain})$	$= \text{'weak'}$
$F(\text{conditional})$	$= \text{'cond'}$
$F(\text{unconditional})$	$= \top$ (the 'empty' condition)
$F(\text{sentiment}_k)$	$= \lambda X.\lambda Y.\lambda a.U_{500}(X, Y, SP_k, a)$

Other Communicative Functions   The semantics of the dimension-specific communicative functions for Contact Management, Discourse Structuring, Own Communication Management, Partner Communication Management, and Social Obligations Management is similar to that of the dimension-specific communicative functions considered above, and can be derived from their definitions as specified in ISO 24617-2 and at http://dit.uvt.nl; the most important difference is the use of other, dimension-specific semantic primitives.

4.2 Communicative Function Qualifiers

Communicative function qualifiers (Petukhova and Bunt 2010) make the IS updates of the communicative functions that they qualify more specific. Qualifiers come in two varieties, "restrictive" and "additive" ones. Restrictive qualifiers make the preconditions of a communicative function more elaborate, for instance specifying for an answer that there is some uncertainty about the correctness of its content. Additive qualifiers, by contrast, enrich a communicative function with additional information, for instance adding that an offer is accepted *happily*. ISO 24617-2 and DIT^{++} have two classes of restrictive qualifiers, for expressing uncertainty and conditionality, and one class of additive qualifiers, for expressing sentiment. Certainty qualifiers can apply only to information-providing functions; conditionality only to action-discussion functions. Sentiment qualifiers can apply to every communicative function.

The following clauses in the definition of the interpretation function I_a specify the semantic interpretation of a communicative function qualified by a restrictive qualifier, by an additive one, and by both a restrictive and an additive one, respectively:

(23)   a. $I_a(\langle f, q_r \rangle) = I_a(f)(F(q_r))$
       b. $I_a(\langle f, q_a \rangle) = \lambda S.\lambda z.[F(f)(S, z) \sqcup F(q_a)(S, z)]$
       c. $I_a(\langle f_i, q_r, q_a \rangle) = \lambda S.\lambda z.[((I_a(f_i))(F(q_r)))(S, z) \sqcup F(q_a)(S, z)]$

The semantics of each of the individual qualifiers is defined in Table 12, with the elementary update function U_{500} defined as in (24), where SP_k stands for a predicate that represents a particular sentiment (see Table 12, bottom line).

(24) $U_{500}(X, Y, SP_k, a) : Y *_{CC} =+\mathbf{Bel}(Y, SP_k(X, a))$

We consider two examples. The first concerns a restrictive qualifier, illustrating the semantics of an answer qualified as uncertain, as in (25) (where $tdp5$ abbreviates the proposition that the train to Tilburg leaves from platform 5):

(25)   1. A: Does the train to Tilburg leave from platform 5?
      2. B: I think so, probably yes.

$I_a(\langle$Answer, uncertain$\rangle)(B, A, \text{Task}, tdp5) =$
    $A *_{TaskC} = +\textbf{Bel}(A, \textbf{Want}(B, \textbf{Bel}(A, tdp5, \text{weak})));$
    $A *_{TaskC} = +\textbf{Bel}(A, \textbf{Bel}(B, tdp5, \text{weak}));$
    $A *_{TaskC} = +\textbf{Bel}(A, \textbf{Bel}(B, \textbf{Want}(A, \textbf{Know-val}(A, tdp5))));$
    $A *_{TaskC} = +\textbf{Bel}(A, \textbf{Bel}(B, \textbf{Assume}(A, \textbf{Know-val}(B, tdp5))))$

This means that A's pending task context is extended with the following pieces of information:

(26)   1. $\textbf{Bel}(B, tdp5, \text{weak})$, or equivalently: $\textbf{Wk-Bel}(B, tdp5)$; i.e., B holds the uncertain belief that $tdp5$;
    2. $\textbf{Want}(B, \textbf{Wk-Bel}(A, tdp5))$, i.e. B has the goal that A also holds this uncertain belief;
    3. $\textbf{Bel}(B, \textbf{Want}(A, \textbf{Know-val}(A, tdp5)))$, i.e. B believes that A wants to know whether $tdp5$;
    4. $\textbf{Bel}(B, \textbf{Assume}(A, \textbf{Know-val}(B, tdp5)))$: B believes that A assumes that B knows whether $tdp5$.

The second example concerns the use of both a restrictive and an additive qualifier, illustrated by the semantics (using (23c)) of an unconditional Accept Offer with a happy sentiment, as in (27).

(27)   1. A: How about a cup of coffee?
      2. B: Oh yes, that would be wonderful!

$I_a(\langle$AcceptOffer, unconditional, happy$\rangle)$

(28)
$= \lambda S.\lambda z.[[I_a(\text{AcceptOffer})(I_a(\text{unconditional}))](S, z) \sqcup [I_a(\text{happy})](S, z)]$
$= \lambda S.\lambda z.[[[\lambda X.\lambda Y.\lambda D_i.\lambda \alpha.\lambda C_\alpha.U_{24}(X, Y, D_i, \alpha) \sqcup U_{25}(X, Y, D_i, \alpha, C_\alpha)$
    $\sqcup U_{25b}(X, Y, D_i, \alpha, C_\alpha)](\top)](S, z) \sqcup U_{500}(X, Y, \text{HAPPY}, \alpha)(S, z)]$
$= \lambda S.\lambda z.\lambda Y.\lambda D_i.[U_{24}(S, Y, D_i, z) \sqcup U_{25}(S, Y, D_i, z, \top)$
    $\sqcup U_{25b}(S, Y, D_i, z, \top) \sqcup U_{500}(X, Y, \text{HAPPY}, z)]$

Applied to the participants A and B and the action of having coffee, we obtain:

(29)
$A *_{Task} = +\textbf{Bel}(A, \textbf{Want}(B, \textbf{CommitDo}(A, \text{have\_coffee})));$
$A *_{Task} = +\textbf{Bel}(A, \textbf{Bel}(B, \textbf{WilDo}(A, \text{have\_coffee})));$
$A *_{Task} = +\textbf{Bel}(A, \textbf{Bel}(B, \textbf{Want}(A, \textbf{Bel}(B, \textbf{WilDo}(A, \text{have\_coffee})))));$
$A *_{CC} = +\textbf{Bel}(A, \text{HAPPY}(B, \text{have\_coffee}))$

In other words, A's pending context is extended with the beliefs that B wants A to commit himself to arrange coffee; that A is willing to do so; that A wants B to believe that; and that B would be happy to get some coffee.

5 Conclusion

In this chapter we have provided a computational semantics of dialogue acts in the form of updates of an addressee's information state. We have formulated this in the form of a semantics for the annotation structures defined by the abstract syntax of the language DiAML, the Dialogue Act Markup Language for semantic annotation, which forms part of ISO standard 24617-2 for dialogue annotation. The semantics as described in this chapter abstracts away from many of the details concerning the 'information states' or 'context models' of dialogue participants, to which the update operations apply, but by way of example we have adopted some of the assumptions of Dynamic Interpretation Theory regarding the structure and content of context models, and we have shown how such a choice can be useful for implementing update operations for the interpretation of dialogue acts.

This semantics provides an essential part of the foundations of the ISO standard for dialogue annotation, as well as of the DIT^{++} taxonomy of dialogue acts, which slightly extends the ISO standard. Both the ISO 24617-2 and the DIT^{++} annotation schemes go beyond what is commonly done in dialogue act annotation in not just indicating the communicative functions of utterances but also certain ways in which these functions may be qualified for uncertainty, conditionality, or sentiment, and also indicating functional dependence relations, feedback dependence relations, and rhetorical relations between dialogue acts and other dialogue units. The semantics described in this chapter takes these extensions into account.

Future work includes computer implementation, testing and evaluation of context models and their use in dialogue act interpretation and dialogue act generation for the entire ISO 24617-2 and DIT^{++} taxonomies, extending the partial implementations of Petukhova et al. (2010) and Keizer et al. (2011).

Acknowledgements   I thank the members of the Tilburg Dialogue Club, who over the years have contributed to shaping Dynamic Interpretation Theory and the DIT^{++} annotation scheme, as well as PhD students and colleagues in related projects. This includes Volha Petukhova, Jeroen Geertzen, Simon Keizer, Roser Morante, Amanda Schiffrin, Ielka van der Sluis, Hans van Dam, Yann Girard, Rintse van der Weff, Elyon Dekoven, Paul Piwek, Robbert-Jan Beun, René Ahn, and Leen Kievit. Important contributions have also come from collaborative work in relation to ISO project 24617-2 "Semantic Annotation Framework, Part 2: Dialogue Acts", in particular with David Traum, Jan Alexandersson, Andrei Popescu-Belis, Laurent Prévot, Marcin Wlodarzcak, Jens Allwood, Jean Carletta, Jae-Woong Choe, Alex Fang, Kiyong Lee, Laurent Romary, Nancy Ide, Claudia Soria, Dirk Heylen, and David Novick.

Appendix: The DIT^{++}/ISO 24617-2 Taxonomies of Communicative Functions

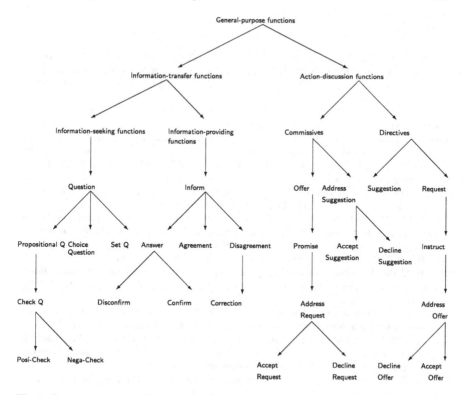

Fig. 1 General-purpose communicative functions in ISO 24617-2 and DIT++

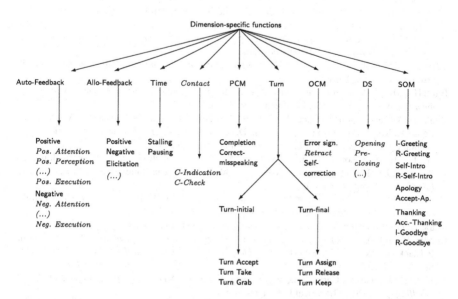

Fig. 2 Dimension-specific communicative functions in ISO 24617-2 and DIT++. Functions and dimensions in italics are defined only in DIT++

References

Ahn, R. (2001). *Agents, objects and events*. Ph.D. Thesis, Eindhoven University of Technology.

Alexandersson, J., Buschbeck-Wolf, B., Fujinami, T., Kipp, M., Koch, S., Maier, E., Reithinger, N., Schmitz, B., & Siegel, M. (1998). *Dialogue acts in VERBMOBIL-2* (2nd ed.) (Verbmobil Report No. 226). Saarbrücken: DFKI.

Allen, J., & Core, M. (1997). *DAMSL: Dialogue act markup in several layers (Draft 2.1)* (Technical Report). Rochester: University of Rochester.

Allen, J., Schubert, L., Ferguson, G., Heeman, P., Hwang, C. H., Kato, T., Light, M., Martin, N., Miller, B., Poesio, M., & Traum, D. (1994). *The TRAINS project: A case study in defining a conversational planning agent* (Technical Report No. 532). Computer Science Department, University of Rochester.

Augmented Multiparty Interaction Consortium (AMI) (2005). *Guidelines for dialogue act and addressee annotation*. Unpublished report, University of Edinburgh.

Bunt, H. (1989). Information dialogues as communicative action in relation to partner modelling and information processing. In M. Taylor, F. Néel, & D. Bouwhuis (Eds.), *The structure of multimodal dialogue* (pp. 47–74). Amsterdam: North-Holland.

Bunt, H. (1994). Context and dialogue control. *Think Quarterly, 3*(1), 19–31.

Bunt, H. (2000). Dialogue pragmatics and context specification. In H. Bunt & W. Black (Eds.), *Abduction, belief and context in dialogue. Studies in computational pragmatics* (pp. 81–150). Amsterdam: Benjamins.

Bunt, H. (2006). Dimensions in dialogue annotation. In *Proceedings of the 5th international conference on language resources and evaluation* (LREC 2006), Genova, Italy. Paris: ELRA.

Bunt, H. (2009). A framework for dialogue act specification. In D. Heylen, C. Pelachaud, & D. Traum (Eds.), *Proceedings of EDAML@AAMAS workshop "Towards a standard markup language for embodied dialogue acts"*, Budapest (pp. 13–24).

Bunt, H. (2010). A methodology for designing semantic annotation languages exploiting semantic-syntactic ISO-morphisms. In *Proceedings of the second international conference on global interoperability for language resources* (ICGL 2010), Hong Kong.

Bunt, H. (2011). Multifunctionality in dialogue and its interpretation. *Computer Speech & Language, 25*, 222–245.

Bunt, H. (2012). The semantics of feedback. In *Proceedings of SeineDial, 2012 workshop on the semantics and pragmatics of dialogue*, Paris.

Bunt, H. (2013a). *A methodology for designing semantic annotations* (TiCC Technical Report TR 2013-001). Tilburg University.

Bunt, H. (2013b). Annotations that effectively contribute to semantic interpretation. In *Computing meaning* (Vol. 4, pp. 49–69). Dordrecht: Springer. Chapter 4.

Bunt, H., Alexandersson, J., Choe, J.-W., Fang, A., Hasida, K., Lee, K., Petukhova, V., Popescu-Belis, A., Romary, L., Soria, C., & Traum, D. (2010). Towards an ISO standard for dialogue act annotation. In *Proceedings of LREC 2010*, Malta. Paris: ELDA.

Bunt, H., Alexandersson, J., Choe, J.-W., Fang, A., Hasida, K., Petukhova, V., Popescu-Belis, A., & Traum, D. (2012). A semantically-based standard for dialogue annotation. In *Proceedings of LREC 2012*, Istanbul. Paris: ELRA.

Carletta, J., Isard, S., Kowtko, J., & Doherty-Sneddon, G. (1996). *HCRC dialogue structure coding manual* (Technical Report HCRC/TR-82).

Clark, H. (1996). *Using Language*. Cambridge: Cambridge University Press.

Cooper, R. (2004). Information states, attitudes and dependent record types. In N. B. L. Cavedon, P. Blackburn, & A. Shimolina (Eds.), *Logic, language and computation* (Vol. 3, pp. 85–106). Stanford: CSLI.

Dhillon, R., Bhagat, S., Carvey, H., & Schriberg, E. (2004). *Meeting recorder project: Dialogue labelling guide* (ICSI Technical Report TR-04-002).

Di Eugenio, B., Jordan, P., & Pylkkaenen, L. (1998). *The COCONUT project: Dialogue annotation manual* (ISP Technical Report 98-1).

Geertzen, J., Petukhova, V., & Bunt, H. (2007). A multidimensional approach to utterance segmentation and dialogue act classification. In *Proceedings of the 8th SIGdial workshop on discourse and dialogue*, Antwerp (pp. 140–149).

Ide, N., & Romary, L. (2004). International standard for a linguistic annotation framework. *Natural Language Engineering, 10*, 211–225.

ISO (2012). *Language resource management—semantic annotation framework (SemAF)—Part 2: Dialogue acts*. International Organisation for Standardisation ISO. ISO International Standard 24617-2:2012(E).

Jurafsky, D., Schriber, E., & Biasca, D. (1997). Switchboard SWBD-DAMSL shallow-discourse-function annotation coders manual.

Keizer, S., & Bunt, H. (2006). Multidimensional dialogue management. In *Proceedings of the SIGdial workshop on discourse and dialogue*, Sydney, Australia (pp. 37–45).

Keizer, S., & Bunt, H. (2007). Evaluating combinations of dialogue acts for generation. In *Proceedings of the SIGdial workshop on discourse and dialogue*, Antwerp, Belgium (pp. 158–165).

Keizer, S., Bunt, H., & Petukhova, V. (2011). Multidimensional dialogue management. In A. van den Bosch & G. Bouma (Eds.), *Interactive multimodal question answering* (pp. 118–145). Berlin: Springer.

Kievit, L., Piwek, P., Beun, R.-J., & Bunt, H. (2001). Multimodal cooperative resolution of referential expressions in the DenK system. In H. Bunt & R.-J. Beun (Eds.), *LNAI: Vol. 2155. Revised selected papers from the second international conference on cooperative multimodal communication* (pp. 197–214). Berlin: Springer.

Petukhova, V., & Bunt, H. (2009a). The independence of dimensions in multidimensional dialogue act annotation. In *Proceedings NAACL HLT conference*, Boulder, Colorado.

Petukhova, V., & Bunt, H. (2009b). *Dimensions in communication* (TiCC Technical Report TR 2009-003). Tilburg University.

Petukhova, V., & Bunt, H. (2010). Introducing communicative function qualifiers. In *Proceedings second international conference on global interoperability for language resources* (ICGL-2), Hong Kong (pp. 123–133).

Petukhova, V., Bunt, H., & Malchanau, A. (2010). Empirical and theoretical constraints on dialogue act combinations. In *Proceedings 14th workshop on the semantics and pragmatics of dialogue* (PozDial), Poznán, Poland.

Poesio, M., & Traum, D. (1997). Conversational actions and discourse situations. *Computational Intelligence, 13*(3), 309–347.

Popescu-Belis, A. (2004). *Dialogue act tagsets for meeting understanding: An abstraction based on the DAMSL, Switchboard and ICSI-MR tagsets* (Technical report, IM2.MDM-09, v1.2).

Traum, D., & Larsson, S. (2003). The information state approach to dialogue management. In J. van Kuppevelt & R. Smith (Eds.), *Current and new directions in discourse and dialogue* (pp. 325–345). Dordrecht: Kluwer.

VerbNet Class Assignment as a WSD Task

Susan Windisch Brown, Dmitriy Dligach, and Martha Palmer

Abstract The VerbNet lexical resource classifies English verbs based on semantic and syntactic regularities and has been used for numerous NLP tasks, most notably, semantic role labeling. Since, in addition to thematic roles, it also provides semantic predicates, it can serve as a foundation for further inferencing. Many verbs belong to multiple VerbNet classes, with each class membership corresponding roughly to a different sense of the verb. A VerbNet token classifier is essential for current applications using the resource and could provide the basis for a deep semantic parsing system, one that made full use of VerbNet's extensive syntactic and semantic information. We describe our VerbNet classifier, which uses rich syntactic and semantic features to label verb instances with their appropriate VerbNet class. It achieves an accuracy of 88.67 % with multiclass verbs, which is a 49 % error reduction over the most frequent class baseline.

1 Introduction

Rich verb representations are central to deep semantic parsing, requiring the identification of not only a verb's meaning but also how it connects the participants in the sentence. Disambiguating verbs using a lexicon that has already been enriched with syntactic and semantic information, rather than a more traditional lexicon, can bring end systems a step closer to accurate knowledge representation and reasoning. One such lexical resource, VerbNet, groups verbs into classes based on commonalities

S.W. Brown
Universita degli Studi di Firenze, Florence, Italy
e-mail: susanwbrown@att.net

D. Dligach
Boston Children's Hospital, Harvard Medical School, 300 Longwood Avenue, Boston, MA 02115, USA
e-mail: dmitriy.dligach@childrens.harvard.edu

M. Palmer (✉)
Department of Linguistics, University of Colorado at Boulder, Boulder, CO 80309-0295, USA
e-mail: martha.palmer@colorado.edu

H. Bunt et al. (eds.), *Computing Meaning*, Text, Speech and Language Technology 47, DOI 10.1007/978-94-007-7284-7_11,

in their semantic and syntactic behavior. It is widely used for a number of semantic processing tasks, including semantic role labeling (Swier and Stevenson 2004), the creation of conceptual graphs (Hensman and Dunnion 2004), and the creation of semantic parse trees (Shi and Mihalcea 2005). In addition, the detailed semantic predicates associated with each VerbNet class have the potential to contribute to text-specific semantic representations and, thereby, to inferencing tasks. However, application of VerbNet's semantic and syntactic information to specific text requires first identifying the appropriate VerbNet class of each verb token. This is equivalent to a word sense disambiguation task.

Studies that have made use of VerbNet have dealt with the issue of multiclass verbs in different ways. When deciding on the class for a particular token of a verb in text, Zapirain et al. (2008) simply assigned the most frequent class for the verb rather than attempt to disambiguate. Their data consisted of any sentences in the Semlink corpus (Loper et al. 2007) in which the thematic roles mapped completely between PropBank and VerbNet, which resulted in a corpus that contained about 56 % of the original. For the data in their study, the most frequent class label was accurate 97 % of the time. Multiclass verbs throughout the entire Semlink corpus, however, have a most frequent class baseline of 73.8 %.

Other systems seem to have set aside the problem of multiclass verbs. For example, Bobrow et al. (2007) describe using VerbNet's semantic predicates in the PARC's question-answering system to derive pre- and post-conditions of events, such as the change of location of entities. For a verb like *leave*, the system attempts to use the semantic predicates provided by the VerbNet Leave-51.2 class:

MOTION(DURING(E), THEME)
LOCATION(START(E), THEME, SOURCE)
NOT(LOCATION(END(E), THEME, SOURCE))
DIRECTION(DURING(E), FROM, THEME, SOURCE)

to show that an entity was located in one place before the event and was in another location after the event. However, *leave* has multiple usages, not all of them involving physical change of location.

Table 1 shows its VerbNet classes and their semantic predicates. The PARC system would need to identify only those instances in their data where *leave* has the change of location meaning.

Zaenen et al. (2008) explain that the problem of automatically selecting only those instances that fit the desired class remains to be solved, especially in terms of dividing metaphorical from literal tokens of a verb: "We ignore the problem of metaphorical extensions for the relevant verbs. Resources other than VerbNet will need to be exploited to insure that these non-physical interpretations are excluded." Although they do not state which ones are the relevant verbs, for many verbs this problem could be alleviated by disambiguating the class assignment for a specific verb instance. To continue our example, *leave* has six VerbNet classes: Escape, Fulfilling, Future_having, Keep, Leave and Resign. Only the Leave class and the Resign class have the START location and END location information they are looking for, and, for the Resign class, the CHANGE OF LOCATION is metaphorical. Therefore,

Table 1 VerbNet classes and semantic predicates for the verb *leave*

VerbNet class	Example	VerbNet semantics
Escape-51.1	The students left.	MOTION(DURING(E), THEME) DIRECTION(DURING(E), PREP_DIR, THEME)
Leave-51.2	Elvis has left the building.	MOTION(DURING(E), THEME) LOCATION(START(E), THEME, SOURCE) NOT(LOCATION(END(E), THEME, SOURCE)) DIRECTION(DURING(E), FROM, THEME, SOURCE)
Resign-10.11	He left Microsoft in 2008.	CAUSE(AGENT, E) LOCATION(START(E), SOURCE) NOT(LOCATION(END(E), SOURCE))
Fulfilling-13.1.4	He left the tenant with his business card.	HAS_POSSESSION(START(E), AGENT, THEME) HAS_POSSESSION(END(E), RECIPIENT, THEME) TRANSFER(DURING(E), THEME) CAUSE(AGENT, E)
Future_having-13.3	He left Sam his stamp collection.	HAS_POSSESSION(START(E), AGENT, THEME) FUTURE_POSSESSION(END(E), RECIPIENT, THEME) CAUSE(AGENT, E)
Keep-15.2	She left the papers in her desk.	PREP(DURING(E), THEME, LOCATION) CAUSE(AGENT, E)

the Leave class is the only class for this verb that suits their purposes. Classifying instances with the appropriate VerbNet class would enable them to apply the Location predicate to only those instances that are relevant. For the Semlink corpus, applying a most frequent class heuristic for *leave* would result in only 59 % accuracy. This is only one example of how an accurate, automatic VerbNet classifier would be useful.

2 Related Work

We know of only two previous efforts to create a VerbNet class disambiguator for verb tokens, those of Girju et al. (2005) and Abend et al. (2008). Girju et al. used a supervised machine learning methodology, with features from the words within three positions of the verb. These features included lemma, part of speech tag, phrase type from a syntactic chunker and named entity information. First, however, they faced the problem of creating a training set tagged with VerbNet class labels. They automatically constructed one by mapping from PropBank roleset labels to VerbNet classes, choosing to label only those verb instances in which the PropBank roleset mapped to only one VerbNet class. This methodology resulted in a set of target verbs in which 96 % belonged to only one VerbNet class. The high most-frequent-class baseline of 96.5 % reflects the predominance of monosemous verbs and explains the low level of improvement over it: only 2 %. Because our classifier uses only multiclass verbs and a gold standard corpus with VerbNet class labels, it is not comparable to the Girju classifier.

The disambiguator developed by Abend et al. (2008) supports a much closer comparison. They also approach the task as a supervised machine learning problem, training and testing on the Semlink corpus. Polysemous verbs account for 58 % of their data, and they report results for all verbs and for just polysemous verbs. The Semlink corpus has annotated the verbs in the Wall Street Journal corpus with VerbNet classes. They selected instances that had been labeled with a VerbNet class, disregarding those verb instances that had been labeled as having no appropriate VerbNet class. Their system achieved 96.4 % accuracy, which was a 2.9 % increase over the 93.7 % baseline. The high baseline can also be attributed to the large number of monosemous verbs in their data. Considering only the polysemous verbs and the model using an automatic parser, the scenario most closely resembling our experimental setup, the most frequent class baseline was 88.6 % and the system accuracy was 91.9 %, which represents an error reduction of 28.95 %.

The results of the Abend et al. study suggest that automatic disambiguation of VerbNet classes is a reasonable line of research, and a possible method for verb sense disambiguation. The classifier relies on lexical and syntactic features, such as part of speech and heads of phrases. The classifier we describe is similar in several ways, although it adds several unique syntactic and semantic features and trains and tests only on multiclass verbs. The following sections will include comparisons of features and results where appropriate.

3 Method

To achieve verb token classification with VerbNet classes, we use a supervised machine learning approach. Using a corpus annotated with VerbNet class labels, we create a feature vector for each verb instance. A learning algorithm is then applied to generate a classifier. The following sections describe the data, the features and the experimental setup.

3.1 The Data

The training and test data are drawn from the Semlink corpus (Loper et al. 2007), which consists of the Penn Treebank portions of the Wall Street Journal corpus. A combination of automatic and manual techniques was used to label each verb instance with the appropriate VerbNet class. The resulting corpus is the largest repository of VerbNet token classification available. The corpus contains 113 K verb instances, 97 K of which are verbs represented in at least one VerbNet class (i.e., 86 %). Semlink includes 495 verbs that have instances labeled with more than one class (including verbs labeled with a single VerbNet class and None). We have

Table 2 Classifier features

Lexical	All open class words from target sentence and the surrounding sentences
	The two words preceding the target and their POS tags
	The two words following the target and their POS tags
Syntactic	The path through the parse tree from the target verb to its arguments
	Whether the target has a subj or obj and their head wds and POS
	Whether the target has a subordinate clause
	Whether the target has a PP adjunct
	The subcategorization frame
	The verb's voice (active or passive)
Semantic	Named-entity tags of the target's arguments
	WN hypernyms of the target's arguments
	WN synonyms of the target's arguments
	Dynamic Dependency Neighbors (DDNs)

trained and tested with all of these verbs that have 10 or more instances, resulting in a set of 344 verbs. The average number of classes for these verbs is 2.7, and the average number of instances was 133. All instances in the corpus for each verb were used, which created a dataset of 45,584 instances.

3.2 Features

We use a wide variety of features, including lexical, syntactic and semantic features, all derived automatically. Previous work has focused on lexical and syntactic features possibly because of the strong association of a VerbNet class to its syntactic alternations. However, a verb's membership in different classes also depends on its meaning, making the inclusion of semantic features a possible benefit. As mentioned earlier, multiple class memberships usually correlate with different senses of the verb, making VerbNet class disambiguation much like verb sense disambiguation. For this reason, we thought it was appropriate to treat the task as a verb sense disambiguation task. Some of the features are fairly standard ones used for general word sense disambiguation, but we have added some rich syntactic and semantic features that have proven useful for sense disambiguation of verbs. All features, which were previously also shown to be useful for WSD (Dligach and Palmer 2008) are summarized in Table 2 and explained more fully in the sections that follow.

3.2.1 Lexical Features

The lexical features include all open class words drawn from the target sentence and the sentence directly before and the sentence directly after it. In addition, we use a feature that pairs each of the two words before and the two words after the target verb with their respective part-of-speech tag.

3.2.2 Syntactic Features

The syntactic features are drawn from syntactic parses automatically created with the Bikel Parser (Bikel et al. 1999). These features focus on the type of patterns that often distinguish one verb sense from another and that help delineate Verb-Net classes. These include whether the target verb is in an active or passive form, whether it has a subject, an object, a subordinate clause, or a prepositional phrase adjunct. For each of these dependent items, the head word and its part of speech are included as features.

We also implement several unusual syntactic features that seem particularly well suited for VerbNet class disambiguation. The first is the path through the parse tree from the target verb to the verb's arguments, and the second is the sentence's subcategorization frame, as used in semantic role labeling. Because syntactic alternations, or patterns of subcategorization frames, play a large role in the organization of VerbNet classes, we expect these final two features to be particularly useful.

3.2.3 Semantic Features

Our use of semantic features is motivated by the work of Patrick Hanks (1996), who proposed that sense distinctions in verbs often rely on the membership of the verb's arguments in narrowly defined verb-specific semantic classes that he called lexical sets. A lexical set could consist, for example, of such nouns as *fist, finger, hand*, etc. (but not all body-parts); its members, when used as objects of *shake*, form instances of the communicative act sense of *shake*. This view corroborates our motivation that states the necessity of capturing the semantics of the verb's arguments and semantic similarities among them.

To illustrate with an example from our data, the verb *fix* falls into two VerbNet classes: (1) Preparing-26.3, (e.g., *He fixed lunch for the team; My mom fixed me a peanut butter and bacon sandwich*) and (2) Price-54.4, with the sense of "establish" (e.g., *They fixed the interest rate at 3 %; The lawyers fixed the terms of the agreement at their last meeting*). These two senses can be distinguished largely on the basis of the objects *lunch, sandwich, rate* and *terms*, the first two indicating the Preparing-26.3 class and the latter two indicating the Price-54.4 class. Not surprisingly, semantic features drawn from a target verb's arguments have been shown to improve verb sense disambiguation above and beyond lexical and syntactic features (Dligach and Palmer 2008).

Another study that reinforces a similar idea was reported by Federici et al. (1999). They describe their SENSE system that relies on inter-contextual analogies between tagged and untagged instances of a word to infer that word's sense. For example, if a verb's sense is preserved when used with two different objects, it is often possible

Table 3 Semantic features for one sense of the verb *fix*

Object	NE tag	WN synset	WN hypernyms	Sample DDNs
price	n/a	price, terms, damage	cost	raise, bring, increase, put, reduce, cut, have, offer, set
terms	n/a	price, terms, damage	cost	reduce, cut, have, offer, set
rate	n/a	charge per unit	cost	raise, bring, increase, put, reduce, cut, have, offer, set
number	n/a	figure	amount	raise, bring, increase, put, reduce, cut, have, offer, set

to conclude by analogy that the sense of another verb is also preserved when it is used with the same two objects.

In word sense disambiguation, the existing approaches to extracting semantic features are often based on obtaining lexical knowledge about the target verb's arguments from electronic dictionaries such as WordNet (Fellbaum 1998). WordNet synonyms and hypernyms are often used as semantic features (Dang and Palmer 2002; Dligach and Palmer 2008). Named entity tags, another source of lexical knowledge, can be obtained from the output of a named-entity tagger such as IdentiFinder (Bikel et al. 1999).

Four types of semantic features are used, all derived from the arguments of the target verb: (1) named entity tags for all of the arguments of the target verb, extracted using IdentiFinder; (2) synonyms of the arguments as listed in their synonym sets in WordNet; (3) hypernyms of the arguments, also taken from WordNet; and (4) dynamic dependency neighbors (DDNs) (Dligach and Palmer 2008), which connect objects of the verb based on the type of verbs they frequently occur with in object position. In this paper we utilized object-based DDNs to capture the semantics of the target verb's object. Elsewhere (citation below) we also experimented with subject-based DDNs in the context of verb sense disambiguation. We discovered that subject-based DDNs do not improve the performance over and above object-based DDNs. For these experiments the DDNs were calculated from the verbs' and objects' occurrence in the English Gigaword corpus, parsed with the dependency MaltParser (Nivre et al. 2007).

This last feature finds similarities between objects that can be missed by the other three, as can be seen in Table 3. The similarity in the first two objects, *price* and *terms*, is captured by the WordNet synset. The third object, *rate*, can be grouped with these via the WordNet hypernym. The fourth object, however, has none of these features in common with the others. Even moving up the WN hypernym hierarchy, *number* does not connect to the others until the very general category of Abstract Entity. However, objects with very different hypernyms or named entity tags may still be common objects of the same verbs. Objects grouped in this way can often help identify the particular sense of a verb (Dligach and Palmer 2008). Comparing lists of the top 50 verbs that each object occurs with shows a great deal of overlap and notably draws the noun number into a group with the other three.

3.3 Experimental Setup

Like all supervised word sense disambiguation, each verb required the training and testing of its own classifier. We classified using support vector machines (Chang and Lin 2001). Accuracy and error rates were computed with 5-fold cross validation. Baselines were established for each target verb type by calculating the accuracy that would be achieved if all instances of a verb were labeled with its most frequent VerbNet class. The average baseline for our verb set was 77.78 %.

4 Results

The average accuracy of the system with the target verbs was 88.67 %, which represents an error reduction of 49 % over the baseline of 77.78 %. The closest comparison to the Abend et al. classifier is to their results based on only polysemous verbs and using features drawn from an automatic parser. In this scenario, their classifier had an accuracy of 91.9 %, with an error reduction of 28.95 % over their baseline of 88.6 %.

In order to assess the contribution of the features we use to the performance of the classifier, we developed several different models composed of various combinations of our features. In addition we created a dedicated test set using 30 % of the Semlink corpus so that each model would be evaluated on identical training and test sets, assuring consistent comparisons. Using this test set, the overall performance of our classifier (the model with all features) was 84.64 %. This result is somewhat lower than the classifier accuracy using 5-fold cross-validation described above, possibly because of the smaller amount of training data used for this method. Compared to the most frequent class baseline, this figure still represents an error reduction of 31 %.

Lexical features are generally the most standard in supervised WSD systems and seem to contribute the most to the accuracy. Therefore, we used a model containing only the lexical features as our most stripped-down model. This model had an accuracy of 83.07 %. The second model added syntactic features to that, and achieved an accuracy of 84.44 %. Adding semantic features brought the accuracy to 84.65 %. We were particularly interested in assessing the contribution of the DDN feature, given that it can be generated automatically and requires no manually built lexical resource. For that reason, we also created a model with all the features but the DDN and a model with all the features but the non-DDN semantic features, which resulted in accuracies of 84.12 % and 84.89 % respectively, validating the efficacy of the DDN feature. See Table 4 for a summary of these results, along with error reduction figures.

5 Discussion

The accuracy of our VerbNet classifier approaches 90 %, the level that several researchers have indicated is needed for useful WSD (Sanderson 2000; Ide and Wilks

Table 4 Accuracy and error reduction of models using various features

Model	Baseline (%)	Accuracy (%)	Error reduction (%)
Lexical features only	77.78	83.07	23.81
Lexical + syntactic	77.78	84.44	29.97
Lexical + semantic	77.78	83.75	26.87
All but DDN	77.78	84.12	28.53
Lexical + syntactic + DDN	**77.78**	**84.89**	**32.00**
All features	77.78	84.65	30.92

2006). Using VerbNet classes as sense distinctions makes available sets of semantic predicates that can be used for deeper analysis. WSD is not an end in itself; it is only useful in so far as it improves more complex applications. By substituting VerbNet classification for verb sense disambiguation, we would gain both a coarse-grained sense of the verb and direct mappings to VerbNet's class-specific syntactic and semantic information. With the goal of improving future VerbNet classifiers, we discuss several pertinent issues in the following sections.

5.1 Contributions of the Features

The difference between the model with only lexical features and that with both lexical and syntactic features was statistically significant (p = .0005), suggesting that our syntactic features were a notable improvement to the model. Given the strong basis of VerbNet classes on syntactic alternations, we expected that syntactic features focused on argument structure would improve the system, and this comparison supports that hypothesis.

The semantic features showed a more complex pattern. A model with lexical and semantic features achieved an accuracy of 83.75 %. Compared to the accuracy of the lexical-only model, this was a significant improvement (p = .0182), although less strongly so than the syntactic features. Interestingly, when the lexical+syntactic model (no semantic features) was compared to one with lexical, syntactic and semantic features, the difference in accuracy was not significant (p = .6982), suggesting that the small improvement we saw with the semantic features was only replicating some of the information the system was gaining from the syntactic features.

When the semantic features were tested separately, however, we found that the DDN feature substantially improved the system, while the other semantic features did not help the system. A model with all the features but the DDN feature showed no significant improvement over the lexical+syntactic model. This suggests that the named entity, WordNet synset, and WordNet hypernym features added nothing to the model. In a head-to-head comparison between the model with all features but the DDN and one with lexical, syntactic, and only DDNs, we found that the DDN feature significantly improved the system (p < .05). With an error reduction of 32 %, the lexical + syntactic + DDN model performed the best of all those we tested.

These results suggest that the system could be streamlined by removing the named entity tag, WordNet synset, and WordNet hypernym features and leaving the DDNs as the only semantic features. This would reduce the system's dependence on other resources with no loss of accuracy. In addition, the DDN feature is created dynamically, and can be done with any corpus, increasing the portability of this system to new domains.

5.2 Semlink Annotation

A couple of matters came to light during a close examination of some of the Semlink annotation in our dataset. First, for some of the verbs, the mapping from PropBank to VerbNet that was the basis of the semiautomatic labeling inappropriately mapped some VerbNet classes. For example, the verb *fix* belongs to the Preparing class, which primarily describes events of food preparation. The thematic roles and semantic predicates for this class indicate the creation of some entity, such as *He fixed me a sandwich*. This class was used in the Semlink data to label such instances, but also to label instances of *fix* as a repair event, such as *We had to fix his car*, a usage that is currently not covered by any VerbNet class. Accuracy for this verb was still high at 89 %, possibly because the feature patterns were still consistent when these instances were labeled with the Preparing class.

The consequences of inappropriate labeling in this case are mixed. If thematic roles were assigned based on this label, they would likely still be correct. Both senses of *fix* call for an Agent and a Patient. The subject in *We had to fix his car* would be correctly labeled as an Agent and the object would be correctly labeled as a Patient. For semantic role labeling, this sort of error should have little negative effect. Any inferences based on the semantic predicates, however, would be misleading. In a Repair event, such as *We had to fix his car* no new entity is created, but the Preparing class label would incorrectly imply that the car is a newly created entity. It is not clear whether such inappropriate mapping is an isolated problem or not. In Sect. 7 we discuss some methods for assessing the existing annotation and for efficiently augmenting it.

5.3 Metaphorical Interpretations

A more common issue concerns the extension of VerbNet classes to metaphorical or figurative usages of a verb. Although some classes include metaphorical usages of the member verbs, such as the Amalgamate-22.2 class, others restrict the uses to literal events. For example, the Bump-18.4 class describes events of contact between a Theme and a Location, such as *The grocery cart hit the wall*. The class restricts both the Theme and Location to [+concrete] arguments. A natural extension of this sense of *hit* would apply to abstract arguments and metaphorical events of contact, such as *The Bank of England was hit hard by the financial slump*. This usage of *hit* would not strictly fit the Bump-18.4 class because the financial slump (the Theme) is not a concrete entity and the Bank of England would not qualify as a concrete location, at least as it is used in this sentence. There is currently no VerbNet class, however, that would accommodate this usage of *hit*.

For several verbs in our set, including *hit* and *pay*, class labels were applied to metaphorical sense extensions. It is unclear whether this affected the accuracy of the classifier; for these two examples, the accuracy for *hit* was 75 %, whereas for *pay*, it was 97 %. More importantly, in terms of applying the labeled data to further semantic processing, metaphorical extensions should have little detrimental effect. Any thematic roles assigned based on the class label would be correct, although the semantic restrictions on the roles (e.g., +concrete) would not. The semantic predicates would also be correct, as long as they were interpreted metaphorically as well.

6 Conclusion

The VerbNet class disambiguator we present in this paper achieves 89 % accuracy with polysemous verbs, which is a 49 % error reduction over the most frequent class baseline. Given that most applications that currently use verb mappings to VerbNet classes rely on a most-frequent-class heuristic (or hand-selected data), this classifier should improve the functioning of these applications.

In addition, we have demonstrated that VerbNet class disambiguation often corresponds to coarse-grained verb sense disambiguation. However, unlike sense disambiguation with more traditional lexicons, VerbNet class disambiguation would not only help disambiguate the senses of verbs in context, it would automatically connect that context to detailed information about likely thematic roles, semantic representations, and related verbs. In combination with a syntactic parse of the sentence, knowing the appropriate VerbNet class could help select a semantic representation of the events in the sentence. By choosing VerbNet as a sense inventory, the next steps in complex knowledge representation and reasoning tasks could be facilitated.

7 Future Work

Some additional steps can be taken to improve the usefulness of VerbNet class labeling. The coverage of verbs and verb senses could be improved, both in the Semlink corpus and in VerbNet itself: 25 % of the verb tokens in the Semlink corpus have no VerbNet class label. However, Semlink is based on version 2.1 of VerbNet. The current version, 3.1, incorporates over 700 new verb senses, many of which introduce very common verbs, such as *seem*, *involve*, and *own*. Updating the corpus with annotations for these new verbs and verb senses would improve coverage. A more long-term goal is to annotate data from other types of corpora than the WSJ, which would likely improve any VerbNet classifier's portability to new domains.

We plan to increase VerbNet annotation in the Semlink corpus using methods that take advantage of existing mappings between PropBank and VerbNet and efficient manual annotation (Dligach 2011). Semlink expansion can be accomplished in two ways. First, more data can be labeled using some form of active learning (Settles 2010) (e.g., batch mode uncertainty sampling). Once more annotated data has been acquired, it may be a good idea to double annotate all or parts of the data, leading to a more error-free labeled corpus. Various error detection techniques can be used to reduce the amount of the second round of annotation (Dligach 2011). These methods can also be used to judge the reliability of the semiautomatic annotation that has already been done, which should indicate how widespread mislabeling is (such as with the verb *fix*, see Sect. 5.2).

The question of metaphorical extensions in the VerbNet annotation is currently being addressed by the VerbNet team. Plans are underway to enhance VerbNet classes with metaphorical information, where appropriate. These enhancements will indicate any changes in thematic role restrictions with a metaphoric usage, and any changes necessary for a semantic predicate to be interpreted correctly.

Given the success of the DDN feature, we would like to see if expanding its contribution would further enhance our classifier. Currently, the DDN feature is only calculated for objects of the verb, but the feature could be encoded for the subject of the verb as well.

We see this classifier as an important step toward using VerbNet for deep semantic analysis. We have shown that verbs in multiple VerbNet classes can be disambiguated with close to 90 % accuracy. Another related task, semantic role labeling, has made great strides lately (Palmer et al. 2010). Using the output from both these tasks should enable us to identify the specific VerbNet frame and semantic predicate for the sentence. For example, VerbNet class disambiguation and semantic role labeling would identify the sentence *He left Sam his stamp collection* as

Agent V(class:Future-having-13.3) Recipient Theme.

Only one frame in the Futurehaving13.3 class has that pattern: the NP V NPdative NP frame. Its semantic predicates are

HAS_POSSESSION(START(E), AGENT, THEME)
FUTURE_POSSESSION(END(E), RECIPIENT, THEME)
CAUSE(AGENT, E).

Given the argument labels from the semantic role labeling, it is straightforward to map from the original sentence to the semantic representation:

HAS_POSSESSION(START(E), HE, THE STAMP COLLECTION)
FUTURE_POSSESSION(END(E), SAM, THE STAMP COLLECTION)
CAUSE(HE, E).

Recent work in coreference resolution (Haghighi and Klein 2009) and implicit argument resolution (Gerber and Chai 2010) suggest how this representation could be enriched by identifying the referent of *he* from the surrounding text. All of these pieces of the semantic puzzle have the potential to fit together into a richer and deeper semantic representation of text. To further this goal, we intend to develop our classifier for all of the verbs in VerbNet and release the system to the public, along with an expanded version of the Semlink corpus.[1]

References

Abend, O., Reichart, R., & Rappoport, A. (2008). A supervised algorithm for verb disambiguation into verbnet classes. In *Proceedings of the 22nd international conference on computational linguistics – Volume 1* (pp. 9–16). Stroudsburg: Association for Computational Linguistics.

Bikel, D. M., Schwartz, R., & Weischedel, R. M. (1999). An algorithm that learns what's in a name. *Machine Learning, 34*(1–3), 211–231.

Bobrow, D., Cheslow, B., Condoravdi, C., Karttunen, L., King, T., Nairn, R., de Paiva, V., Price, C., & Zaenen, A. (2007). PARC's bridge and question answering system. In *Grammar engineering across frameworks* (pp. 46–66).

Chang, C.-C., & Lin, C.-J. (2001). LIBSVM: A library for support vector machines.

Dang, H. T., & Palmer, M. (2002). Combining contextual features for word sense disambiguation. In *Proceedings of the ACL-02 workshop on word sense disambiguation*, Morristown, NJ, USA (pp. 88–94). Stroudsburg: Association for Computational Linguistics.

Dligach, D. (2011). *High-performance word sense disambiguation with less manual effort*. Ph.D. thesis, University of Colorado at Boulder.

Dligach, D., & Palmer, M. (2008). Novel semantic features for verb sense disambiguation. In *HLT '08: Proceedings of the 46th annual meeting of the Association for Computational Linguistics on human language technologies*, Morristown, NJ, USA (pp. 29–32). Stroudsburg: Association for Computational Linguistics.

Federici, S., Montemagni, S., & Pirrelli, V. (1999). Sense: An analogy-based word sense disambiguation system. *Natural Language Engineering, 5*(2), 207–218.

Fellbaum, C. (1998). *WordNet: An electronic lexical database*. Cambridge: MIT Press.

Gerber, M., & Chai, J. (2010). Beyond nombank: A study of implicit arguments for nominal predicates. In *Proceedings of the 48th annual meeting of the Association for Computational Linguistics* (pp. 1583–1592). Stroudsburg: Association for Computational Linguistics.

Girju, R., Roth, D., & Sammons, M. (2005). Token-level disambiguation of verbnet classes. *Urbana, 51*, 61801.

Haghighi, A., & Klein, D. (2009). Simple coreference resolution with rich syntactic and semantic features. In *Proceedings of the 2009 conference on empirical methods in natural language processing: Volume 3* (pp. 1152–1161). Stroudsburg: Association for Computational Linguistics.

Hanks, P. (1996). Contextual dependency and lexical sets. Dépendance contextuelle et ensembles lexicaux. *International Journal of Corpus Linguistics, 1*(1), 75–98.

Hensman, S., & Dunnion, J. (2004). Automatically building conceptual graphs using verbnet and wordnet. In *Proceedings of the 2004 international symposium on information and communication technologies* (pp. 115–120). Dublin: Trinity College.

Ide, N., & Wilks, Y. (2006). Making sense about sense. In *Word sense disambiguation* (pp. 47–73).

Loper, E., Yi, S., & Palmer, M. (2007). Combining lexical resources: Mapping between propbank and verbnet. In *Proceedings of the 7th international workshop on computational linguistics*, Tilburg, the Netherlands.

---

[1] This expanded corpus is now available at https://verbs.colorado.edu/wiki/index.php/Main_Page.

Nivre, J., Hall, J., Nilsson, J., Chanev, A., Eryigit, G., Kübler, S., Marinov, S., & Marsi, E. (2007). MaltParser: A language-independent system for data-driven dependency parsing. *Natural Language Engineering, 13*(02), 95–135.

Palmer, M., Gildea, D., & Xue, N. (2010). Semantic role labeling. *Synthesis Lectures on Human Language Technologies, 3*(1), 1–103.

Sanderson, M. (2000). Retrieving with good sense. *Information Retrieval, 2*(1), 49–69.

Settles, B. (2010). *Active learning literature survey.* Madison: University of Wisconsin.

Shi, L., & Mihalcea, R. (2005). Putting pieces together: Combining framenet, verbnet and wordnet for robust semantic parsing. In *Computational linguistics and intelligent text processing* (pp. 100–111).

Swier, R., & Stevenson, S. (2004). Unsupervised semantic role labelling. In *Proceedings of the 2004 conference on empirical methods in natural language processing* (pp. 95–102).

Zaenen, A., Condoravdi, C., & Bobrow, D. (2008). The encoding of lexical implications in verbnet predicates of change of locations. 716/922 EF 8.

Zapirain, B., Agirre, E., & Màrquez, L. (2008). Robustness and generalization of role sets: Propbank vs. verbnet. In *Proc. of ACL.*

Annotation of Compositional Operations with GLML

James Pustejovsky, Anna Rumshisky, Olga Batiukova, and Jessica L. Moszkowicz

Abstract In this paper, we introduce a methodology for annotating compositional operations in natural language text and describe the Generative Lexicon Mark-up Language (GLML), a mark-up language inspired by the Generative Lexicon model, for identifying such relations. While most annotation systems capture surface relationships, GLML captures the "compositional history" of the argument selection relative to the predicate. We provide a brief overview of GL before moving on to our proposed methodology for annotating with GLML. There are three main tasks described in the paper. The first one is based on atomic semantic types and the other two exploit more fine-grained meaning parameters encoded in the Qualia Structure roles: (i) Argument Selection and Coercion Annotation for the SemEval-2010 competition; (ii) Qualia Selection in modification constructions; (iii) Type selection in modification constructions and verb-noun combinations involving dot objects. We explain what each task comprises and include the XML format for annotated sample sentences. We show that by identifying and subsequently annotating the typing and

J. Pustejovsky (✉) · J.L. Moszkowicz
Department of Computer Science, Brandeis University, 415 South Street, Waltham, MA 02454, USA
e-mail: jamesp@cs.brandeis.edu

J.L. Moszkowicz
e-mail: jlittman@cs.brandeis.edu

A. Rumshisky
Department of Computer Science, University of Massachusetts, One University Avenue, Lowell, MA 01854, USA

A. Rumshisky
Computer Science and Artificial Intelligence Laboratory, Massachusetts Institute of Technology, Cambridge, MA, USA
e-mail: arum@csail.mit.edu

O. Batiukova
Department of Spanish Philology, Autonomous University of Madrid, Ciudad Universitaria Cantoblanco, Carretera de Colmenar, km. 15, 28049 Cantoblanco, Madrid, Spain
e-mail: volha.batsiukova@uam.es

H. Bunt et al. (eds.), *Computing Meaning*, Text, Speech and Language Technology 47,
DOI 10.1007/978-94-007-7284-7_12,
© Springer Science+Business Media Dordrecht 2014

subtyping shifts in these constructions, we gain an insight into the workings of the general mechanisms of composition.

1 Introduction: Motivation and Previous Work on Semantic Annotation

In recent years, a number of annotation schemes that encode semantic information have been developed and used to produce data sets for training machine learning algorithms. Semantic markup schemes initially focused on annotating entity types and, more generally, word senses, have been extended to include semantic relationships between sentence elements, such as the semantic role (or label) assigned to the argument by the predicate (see Palmer et al. 2005, Ruppenhofer et al. 2006, Kipper 2005, Burchardt et al. 2006, Subirats 2004).

The Generative Lexicon Markup Language (GLML) takes one step further and attempts to capture the "compositional history" of the argument selection relative to the predicate, and the modifier interpretation relative to the head noun. The emphasis here will be on identifying the nature of the compositional operation rather than merely annotating the surface types of the entities involved in argument selection.

Consider the well-known example below. The distinction in semantic types appearing as subject in (1) is captured by entity typing (HUMAN versus ORGANIZATION), but not by any sense tagging from, e.g., FrameNet (Ruppenhofer et al. 2006) or PropBank (Palmer et al. 2005).

(1) a. *Mary* called yesterday.
    b. *The Boston office* called yesterday.

While this has been treated as *type coercion* or *metonymy* in the literature (Hobbs et al. 1993; Pustejovsky 1991; Nunberg 1979; Egg 2005), the point here is that an annotation using frames associated with verb senses should treat the sentences on par with one another. Yet this is not possible if the entity typing given to the subject in (1a) is HUMAN and that given for (1b) is ORGANIZATION.

The SemEval Metonymy task (Markert and Nissim 2007) was a good attempt to annotate such metonymic relations over a larger data set. This task involved two types with their metonymic variants:

(2) i. **Categories for Locations**: literal, place-for-people, place-for-event, place-for-product;
    ii. **Categories for Organizations**: literal, organization-for-members, organization-for-event, organization-for-product, organization-for-facility.

One of the limitations with this approach, however, is that, while appropriate for these specialized metonymy relations, the annotation specification and resulting corpus are not an informative guide for extending the annotation of argument selection more broadly.

In fact, the metonymy example in (1) is an instance of a much more pervasive phenomenon of type shifting and coercion in argument selection. For example, in

(3) below, the sense annotation for the verb *enjoy* should arguably assign similar values to both (3a) and (3b).

(3) a. Mary enjoyed *drinking her beer.*
  b. Mary enjoyed *her beer.*

The consequence of this, however, is that, under current sense and role annotation strategies, the mapping to a syntactic realization for a given sense is made more complex, and as a result, proves challenging for machine learning algorithms operating over subcategorization types for the verb.

The goal of the present work is to: (a) create a broadly applicable specification of the compositional operations involved in argument selection; (b) apply this specification over a corpus of natural language texts, in order to encode the selection mechanisms implicated in the compositional structure of the language.

The creation of a corpus that explicitly identifies the "compositional history" associated with argument selection will be useful to computational semantics in several respects: (a) the actual contexts within which type coercions are allowed can be more correctly identified and perhaps generalized; (b) machine learning algorithms can take advantage of an enriched feature set for deeper semantic interpretation, in the training phase; and (c) some consensus might emerge on the general list of type-changing operations involved in argument selection, as the tasks are revised and enriched.

The rest of this chapter proceeds as follows: after reviewing the theoretical assumptions from GL in Sect. 2, in Sect. 3 we present the general methodology and architecture for GL annotation, which was tested in the Argument Selection and Coercion task within the SemEval-2010 evaluation exercise. We briefly describe the task and go through the different phases of corpus development. Section 4 gives an overview of a more sophisticated qualia-based annotation in adjectival modification constructions and nominal compounds headed by natural and artifactual types (in Sects. 4.1.1 and 4.1.2, respectively). Section 4.2 deals with complex types in both modification constructions and verb-noun combinations.[1]

2 Theoretical Preliminaries: Modes of Composition in the Generative Lexicon Theory

Generative Lexicon (hereafter GL) introduces a knowledge representation framework which offers a rich and expressive vocabulary for lexical information. The motivations for this are twofold. Overall, GL is concerned with explaining the creative use of language; we consider the lexicon to be the key repository holding much of the information underlying this phenomenon. More specifically, however, it is the notion of a constantly evolving lexicon that GL attempts to emulate. This is in contrast to views of static lexicon design, where the set of contexts licensing the use of words is determined in advance, and no formal mechanisms are offered for expanding this set.

---

[1]A complete overview of the GLML specification as well as updates on the annotation effort can be found at www.glml.org.

One of the most difficult problems faced by theoretical and computational semantics is defining the representational interface between linguistic and non-linguistic knowledge. GL was initially developed as a theoretical framework for encoding selectional knowledge in natural language. This in turn required making some changes in the formal rules of representation and composition. Perhaps the most controversial aspect of GL has been the manner in which lexically encoded knowledge is exploited to construct interpretations for linguistic utterances.

The theoretical foundations for compositional operations within the sentence have long been developed in considerable detail. Type shifting and type coercion operations have been recognized as playing an important role in many formal descriptions of language, in order to maintain compositionality (cf. Partee and Rooth 1983; Chierchia 1998; Groenendijk and Stokhof 1989; Egg 2005; Pinkal 1999; Pustejovsky 1995, and many others). The novelty of the approach to composition within GL is that it is based on a rich type system, ultimately derived from fine-grained lexical features of the predicate arguments (cf. Pustejovsky 2006a and Asher and Pustejovsky 2006).

These lexical features constitute the *qualia structure*, which specifies four essential aspects of a word's meaning (cf. Pustejovsky 1991):

(4) a. FORMAL: that which distinguishes it within a larger domain;
    b. CONSTITUTIVE: the relation between an object and its constituent parts;
    c. TELIC: the purpose or function of the object, if there is one;
    d. AGENTIVE: the factors involved in the object's origins or "coming into being".

Pustejovsky (2001) separates the domain of individuals into three distinct type levels according to which roles are prominent in each case:

(5) a. NATURAL TYPES: Natural kind concepts consisting of reference only to formal and constitutive qualia roles (e.g. *tree, woman*; *arrive, rain*; *red, big*).
    b. ARTIFACTUAL TYPES: Concepts making reference to purpose or function (e.g. *violin, dancer*; *spoil, repair*; *useful, broken*).
    c. COMPLEX TYPES: Concepts making reference to an inherent relation between types (e.g. *lunch* is typed as both PHYSICAL OBJECT and EVENT).

The mechanisms mediating the information required by a predicate and that encoded by its arguments are type-sensitive. Pustejovsky (2006a) and Asher and Pustejovsky (2006) distinguish the following modes of composition in natural language (cf. Pustejovsky (2011) for the most recent discussion of this model).

(6) a. PURE SELECTION (Type Matching): the type a function requires is directly satisfied by the argument;
    b. ACCOMMODATION: the type a function requires is inherited by the argument;
    c. TYPE COERCION: the type a function requires is imposed on the argument type. This is accomplished by either:

    i. *Exploitation*: taking a part of the argument's type;

    ii. *Introduction*: wrapping the argument with the required type.

Let us consider the artifactual predicate *spoil* as an example. Nouns denoting arti-facts satisfy it directly, as in *the food spoiled*. When combined with complex types, such as *lunch*, it takes advantage of one of its types by the rule of EXPLOITATION: *my lunch spoiled* refers to spoiled food, not to a "spoiled" event. Finally, when a natural type is in the subject position (as in *the water spoiled*), it acquires functional interpretation by the rule of INTRODUCTION: 'the water was going to be used for something, and now it cannot fulfill the intended function'.

3 Verb-Based Annotation. Methodology of Annotation in the Argument Selection and Coercion Task

This section focuses on the data preparation for the task *Argument Selection and Co-ercion* (hereafter ASC), included in the SemEval-2010 competition. The SemEval tasks are intented to test automatic systems for semantic analysis of text in any aspect relevant to particular NLP applications (machine translation, information re-trieval, and information extraction).

3.1 MATTER

Before introducing the specifics of the ASC task, we will briefly review our assump-tions regarding the role of annotation in computational linguistic systems.

    We assume that the features we use for encoding a specific linguistic phe-nomenon are rich enough to capture the desired behavior. These linguistic descrip-tions are typically distilled from extensive theoretical modeling of the phenomenon. The descriptions in turn form the basis for the annotation values of the specification language, which are themselves the features used in a development cycle for train-ing and testing a labeling algorithm over a text. Finally, based on an analysis and evaluation of the performance of a system, the model of the phenomenon may be revised.

    These steps follow the MATTER methodology, as described in Pustejovsky (2006b), Pustejovsky and Stubbs (2012) and diagrammed in Fig. 1.

Model: Structural descriptions provide theoretically informed attributes derived from empirical observations over the data;

Annotate: Annotation scheme assumes a feature set that encodes specific structural descriptions and properties of the input data;

Train: Algorithm is trained over a corpus annotated with the target feature set;

Test: Algorithm is tested against held-out data;

Evaluate: Standardized evaluation of results;

Fig. 1 The MATTER
methodology

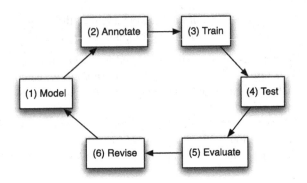

Revise: Revisit the model, annotation specification, or algorithm, in order to make
the annotation more robust and reliable.

Some of the current and completed annotation efforts that have undergone such a
development cycle include PropBank (Palmer et al. 2005), NomBank (Meyers et al.
2004), and TimeBank (Pustejovsky et al. 2005).

3.2 Task Description

The ASC task involves identifying the selectional mechanism used by the predicate
over a particular argument. For the purposes of this task, the possible relations between the predicate and a given argument were restricted to *selection* (as in (7)) and
coercion (as in (8)).

The task is defined as follows: for each argument of a predicate, identify whether
the entity in that argument position satisfies the type expected by the predicate. If
not, then identify how the entity in that position satisfies the typing expected by the
predicate; that is, identify the source and target types in a type-shifting or *coercion*
operation.

(7) a. The spokesman denied the *statement* (PROPOSITION).
    b. The child threw the *stone* (PHYSICAL OBJECT).
    c. The audience didn't believe the *rumor* (PROPOSITION).

Coercion encompasses all cases when a type-shifting operation (e.g. exploitation
or introduction, cf. Sect. 2) must be performed on the complement NP in order to
satisfy selectional requirements of the predicate. In the examples (8) below, the
event nominal *attack* has to be interpreted as PROPOSITION in order to match the
selectional requirements of *deny; the White House* changes from the type LOCATION
to HUMAN in order to be compatible with *deny; update*, another event nominal,
acquires the type INFORMATION imposed by *call*. Note that coercion operations
may apply to any argument position in a sentence, including the direct object, as in
(8a), the subject, as in (8b), and prepositional object, as in (8c).

(8) a. The president denied the *attack* (EVENT → PROPOSITION).

    b. *The White House* (LOCATION → HUMAN) denied this statement.

    c. The Boston office called with *an update* (EVENT → INFO).

In order to determine whether type-shifting has taken place, the classification task must then involve (1) identifying the verb sense and the associated syntactic frame, (2) identifying selectional requirements imposed by that verb sense on the target argument, and (3) identifying the semantic type of the target argument.

3.3 The Type System for Annotation

The type system we have chosen for annotation is purposefully shallow, but we also aimed to include those types that would ease the complexity of the annotation task. The type system is not structured in a hierarchy, but rather is presented as a set of types. For example, HUMAN is a subtype of both ANIMATE and PHYSICAL OBJECT, but annotators and system developers were instructed to choose the most relevant type (e.g., HUMAN) and to ignore inheritance. The types used for annotation were the following:

(9) ABSTRACT ENTITY, ANIMATE, ARTIFACT, ATTITUDE, DOCUMENT, DRINK, EMOTION, ENTITY, EVENT, FOOD, HUMAN, HUMAN GROUP, IDEA, INFOR- MATION, LOCATION, OBLIGATION, ORGANIZATION, PATH, PHYSICAL OB- JECT, PROPERTY, PROPOSITION, RULE, SENSATION, SOUND, SUBSTANCE, TIME PERIOD, VEHICLE

These types were taken from the Brandeis Shallow Ontology (BSO), which is a shallow hierarchy of types developed as a part of the CPA effort (Hanks 2009; Pustejovsky et al. 2004; Rumshisky et al. 2006). Types were selected for their prevalence in manually identified selection context patterns developed for several hundred English verbs. That is, they capture common semantic distinctions associated with the selectional properties of many verbs.

3.4 Corpus Development

We prepared the data for this task in two phases: the *data set construction phase* and the *annotation phase* (see Fig. 2). The first phase consisted of (1) selecting the target verbs to be annotated and compiling a sense inventory for each target, and (2) data extraction and preprocessing. The prepared data was then loaded into the annotation interface. During the annotation phase, the annotation judgments were entered into the database and an adjudicator resolved disagreements. The resulting database was then exported in an XML format.

The English data set for the task was created using the following steps:

1. The verbs were selected by examining the data from the BNC (BNC 2000) using the Sketch Engine (Kilgarriff et al. 2004) as described in Rumshisky and

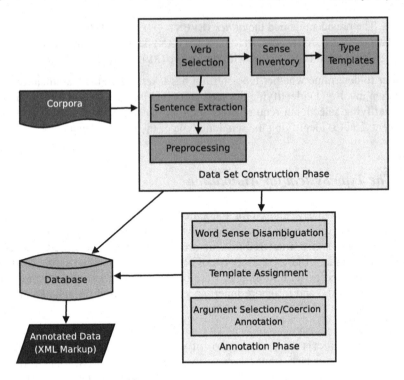

Fig. 2 Corpus development architecture

Batiukova (2008). Verbs that consistently impose semantic typing on one of their arguments in at least one of their senses (strongly coercive verbs) were included in the final data set: *arrive* (*at*), *cancel, deny, finish,* and *hear.*

2. Sense inventories were compiled for each verb, with the senses mapped to OntoNotes (Pradhan et al. 2007) whenever possible. For each sense, a set of type templates was compiled using a modification of the CPA technique (Hanks and Pustejovsky 2005; Pustejovsky et al. 2004): every argument in the syntactic pattern associated with a given sense was assigned a type specification. The coercive senses of the chosen verbs were associated with the following type templates:

   a. *Arrive* (*at*), sense 'reach a destination or goal': HUMAN arrive at LOCATION
   b. *Cancel,* sense 'call off': HUMAN cancel EVENT
   c. *Deny,* sense 'state or maintain that something is untrue': HUMAN deny PROPOSITION
   d. *Finish,* sense 'complete an activity': HUMAN finish EVENT
   e. *Hear,* sense 'perceive physical sound': HUMAN hear SOUND

3. A set of sentences was randomly extracted for each target verb from the BNC. The extracted sentences were parsed automatically and subsequently organized according to the grammatical relation the target verb was involved in. Sentences were excluded from the set if the target argument was expressed as an anaphor

or was not present in the sentence. The semantic head for the target grammatical relation was identified in each case.

4. Word sense disambiguation of the target predicate was performed manually on each extracted sentence, matching the target against the sense inventory and the corresponding type templates as described above. The appropriate senses were then saved into the database along with the associated type template.

5. For the annotation phase, the sentences containing coercive senses of the target verbs were loaded into the Brandeis Annotation Tool (Verhagen 2010). Annotators were presented with a list of sentences and asked to determine whether the argument in the specified grammatical relation to the target belongs to the type associated with that sense in the corresponding template. Disagreements were resolved by adjudication.

6. To guarantee robustness of the data, two additional steps were taken. First, only the most recurrent coercion types were selected, up to a total of six. Preference was given to cross-domain coercions, where the source and the target types are not related ontologically:

   a. EVENT → LOCATION (*arrive at*)
   b. ARTIFACT → EVENT (*cancel, finish*)
   c. EVENT → PROPOSITION (*deny*)
   d. ARTIFACT → SOUND (*hear*)
   e. EVENT → SOUND (*hear*)
   f. DOCUMENT → EVENT (*finish*)

   Second, the distribution of selection and coercion instances were skewed to increase the number of coercions. The final English data set contains about 30 % coercions.

7. Finally, the data set was randomly split in half into a training set and a test set. The training data included 1032 instances, 311 of which were coercions, and the test data included 1039 instances, 314 of which were coercions.

3.5 The Data Format

The test and training data were provided in XML. The relation between the predicate (viewed as a function) and its argument was represented by composition link elements (CompLink), as shown below. The test data differed from the training data in the omission of CompLink elements.

In case of *coercion*, there is a mismatch between the source and the target types, and both types need to be identified; e.g., *The State Department repeatedly denied the attack*:

```
The State Department repeatedly
<SELECTOR sid="s1">denied</SELECTOR>
the <TARGET id="t1">attack</TARGET>.
<CompLink cid="cid1"
          compType="COERCION"
```

```
selector_id="s1"
relatedToTarget="t1"
sourceType="EVENT"
targetType="PROPOSITION"/>
```

When the compositional operation is *selection*, the source and target types must match; e.g., *The State Department repeatedly denied the statement*:

```
The State Department repeatedly
<SELECTOR sid="s2">denied</SELECTOR>
the <TARGET id="t2">statement</TARGET>.
<CompLink cid="cid2"
          compType="SELECTION"
          selector_id="s2"
          relatedToTarget="t2"
          sourceType="PROPOSITION"
          targetType="PROPOSITION"/>
```

The results of the participating systems are summed up in Pustejovsky et al. (2010).

4 Noun-Based Annotation. Exploiting the Qualia

The verb-noun annotation as it was described in the previous section is based on atomic semantic types. A more fine-grained annotation can refer to the particular parameter of meaning acted on by the predicate. As mentioned in Sect. 2, these meaning parameters are the Qualia Structure roles in the GL model.

The following sentences illustrate qualia selection in verb-noun contexts; the qualia of the noun being activated by the verb is shown in parentheses.

(10) a. Antonio Stradivari finished the *violin*. (AGENTIVE)
      b. John bought a *violin*. (FORMAL)
      c. The audience enjoyed the *violin*. (TELIC)
      d. Mary heard the *violin*. (TELIC)

Note that the verbs *finish* and *hear* were associated with the type coercions ARTIFACT → EVENT and ARTIFACT → SOUND in the ASC task, respectively (as described in Sect. 3.4). A qualia-based approach explains why these coercions are possible and identifies the semantic nature of the link between the argument and the verb selecting it. In the example above, *violin* can be interpreted as the EVENT of building this musical instrument because this information is encoded in the lexical entry of the noun (in its agentive role). Similarly, *hear* selects for the type SOUND, encoded in the telic role of *violin*. All the cases above are instances of *exploitation*, a specific kind of coercion whereby a part of the argument's type satisfies the selectional requirements of the predicate.

In what follows we will present several kinds of constructions involving nouns, which tap into sub-lexical aspects of nominal semantics. We will show that, by identifying and subsequently annotating the qualia roles acted on in these constructions, we gain insight into the workings of the general mechanisms of composition.

4.1 Qualia Selection in Modification Constructions

In these tasks, the annotation identifies the manner in which the modifying expression semantically relates to the target element, typically a noun. We follow Bouillon (1997) in distinguishing different modification relations of an adjective over a head as cases of distinct qualia selection.

4.1.1 Adjectival Modification

This task involves annotating how particular noun qualia values are bound by the adjectives. Following Pustejovsky (2000), we assume that the properties grammatically realized as adjectives "bind into the qualia structure of nouns, to select a narrow facet of the noun's meaning." The different types of binding of the adjectival modification can be better understood if we examine the modification structure of *large carved wooden useful arrow* in (11):

(11)

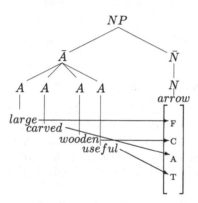

Large refers to the arrow as a physical object, its FORMAL type, so that the adjective is associated with that quale. Similarly, *carved* is associated with the creation of the arrow (AGENTIVE), *wooden* is associated with a material part of the arrow (CONSTITUTIVE), and *useful* is associated with how the arrow is used (TELIC).

Many adjectives are specialized with respect to the qualia they bind and, in these cases, they identify the concrete value of the relevant quale. See the examples in (12)–(15).

(12) CONSTITUTIVE
    a. wooden house
    b. wrinkled face
    c. mountainous region

(13) FORMAL heavy, red, large, sweet, raw, rough, hard, simple, responsible, happy, short, narrow, poor, bitter, new

(14) TELIC useful, effective, good (knife/table/teacher)

(15) AGENTIVE
   a. carved figure
   b. hand-made shoes
   c. synthetic material
   d. natural light

The task begins with sense disambiguation of the target nouns. Questions are then used to help the annotator identify which relations are selected. For example, the TELIC question for the noun *woman* would be "Is the verb associated with a specific role of woman?" These questions will change according to the type associated with the noun. That is, for PHYSICAL OBJECT-denoting nouns, the question corresponding to the AGENTIVE role involves "making or destroying" the object, while the EVENT-denoting nouns elicit a question involving the "beginning or ending" of the event. QLinks are then created based on the annotator's answers, as in the following example:

The walls and the wooden table had all been lustily scrubbed.

```
<SELECTOR sid="s1">wooden</SELECTOR>
<NOUN nid="n1">table</NOUN>
<QLink qid="qid1" sID="s1" relatedToNoun="n1" qType="CONST"/>
```

4.1.2 Nominal Compounds

This task explores the semantic relationship between elements in nominal compounds. The general relations presented in Levi (1978) are a useful guide for beginning a classification of compound types, but the relations between compound elements quickly proves to be too coarse-grained. Warren's comprehensive work (Warren 1978) is a valuable resource for differentiating relation types between compound elements.

The class distinction in compound types in language can be broken down into three forms (cf. Spencer 1991):

(16) a. ENDOCENTRIC COMPOUNDS: One element in the construction functions as the head, e.g. *taxi driver, pastry chef*;
   b. EXOCENTRIC COMPOUNDS (BAHUVRIHI): Neither element in the construction functions as the head, i.e. neither is the hyponym of the head: e.g. *houndstooth* is a textile pattern, not a *hound* or a *tooth*;
   c. DVANDVA compounds: a simple conjunction of two elements, without a dependency holding between them, e.g. *hunter-gatherer*.

Following Bisetto and Scalise (2005), however, it is possible to distinguish three slightly differently constructed classes of compounds, each exhibiting endocentric and exocentric behavior:

(17) a. SUBORDINATING: the head acts functionally over N_1, incorporating it as an argument;
   b. ATTRIBUTIVE: a general modification relation;
   c. COORDINATE: the dvandva construction mentioned above.

We will focus on the two classes of *subordinating* and *attributive* compounds. Within each of these, we will distinguish between *synthetic* and *non-synthetic* compounds. The former are deverbal nouns, and when acting functionally (subordinating), they take the sister noun as an argument, as in *bus driver* and *window cleaner*. The non-synthetic counterparts of these include *pastry chef* and *bread knife*, where the head is not deverbal in any obvious way. While Bisetto and Scalise's distinction is a useful one, it does little to explain how non-relational sortal nouns such as *chef* and *knife* act functionally over the accompanying noun in the compound, as above.

This construction has been examined within GL by Johnston and Busa (1999). We will assume much of that analysis in our definition of the task described here. Our basic assumption regarding the nature of the semantic link between both parts of compounds is that it is generally similar to the one present in adjectival modification. The only difference is that in nominal compounds, for instance, the qualia of a head noun are activated or exploited by a different kind of modifier, a noun.

Following Johnston and Busa (1999), consider the following $[N_1\ N_2]$ constructions in English and the corresponding $[N_2\ P\ N_1]$ constructions in Italian.

(18) a. coltello da pane
        'bread knife'
     b. bicchiere da vino
        'wine glass'
     c. foro di pallottola
        'bullet hole'
     d. succo di limone
        'lemon juice'
     e. porta a vetri
        'glass door'

In compounds (18a,b), the relation between N_1 and N_2 can be identified as the Telic role for the heads, *knife* and *glass*, while in (18c,d), the relation can be identified with the Agentive of the respective heads, *hole* and *juice*. In (18e), on the other hand, *glass* is the Constitutive of the head *door*. Interestingly, Johnston and Busa (1999) illustrate how in Italian, the choice between *da* and *di* in compounds is not in free variation, but is rather conditioned by the semantic relation between the nouns.[2]

Using the strategy of qualia selection outlined above by Johnston and Busa (1999), we can identify a broad range of semantic relations in noun compound constructions as qualia-based. As illustration, consider the attributive compounds in (19)–(20).

(19) $[N_1\ N_2]$: N_1 is the TELIC of N_2:
     a. fishing rod
     b. magnifying glass

---

[2]Specifically, they argue that it is the particular quale binding the two nouns that determines the choice. They correlate the use of *da* with the Telic quale while *di* can be associated with either Agentive or Constitutive.

   c. swimming pool
   d. shopping bag
   e. drinking water

(20) $[N_1\ N_2]$: N_1 is the CONSTITUTIVE of N_2:
   a. paper napkins
   b. metal cup
   c. gold filling

Synthetic subordinating compounds may also be characterized as qualia relations, even though they are acting functionally. The examples in (21) are both subordinating and AGENTIVE-selecting compounds:

(21) $[N_1\ N_2]$: N_1 is the AGENTIVE of N_2:
   a. food infection
   b. heat shock

Interestingly, there are corresponding non-synthetic compounds, which also act functionally and are AGENTIVE-selecting:

(22) $[N_1\ N_2]$: N_1 is the AGENTIVE of N_2:
   a. university fatigue
   b. automobile accident
   c. sun light

The annotation for this task is performed just as it is for the adjectival modification task, given their similarity. A QLink is created as in the following example:

Our guest house stands some 100 yards away.

```
<SELECTOR sid="s1">guest</SELECTOR>
<NOUN nid="n1">house</NOUN>
<QLink qid="qid1" sID="s1" relatedToNoun="n1" qType="TELIC"/>
```

4.2 Type Selection Involving Dot Objects

This task involves annotating how particular types within dot objects are exploited in adjectival and nominal modification constructions as well as verb-noun combinations. *Dot objects* or *complex types* (Pustejovsky 1995) are defined as the product of a type constructor • ("dot"), which creates dot objects from any two types a and b, creating $a • b$. Complex types are unique because they are made up of seemingly conflicting types such as FOOD and EVENT for *lunch*, for example (see Sect. 2).

   Given a complex type $c = a • b$, there are three possible options:

1. the modifier/verbal predicate applies to both a and b
2. the modifier/verbal predicate applies to a only
3. the modifier/verbal predicate applies to b only

Option 1 is illustrated by the following examples of modification and argument selection:

(23) a. good book (+INFO, +PHYSOBJ)
        purchase the book (+INFO, +PHYSOBJ)
     b. long lecture (+INFO, +EVENT)
        prepare the lecture (+INFO, +EVENT)
     c. new appointment (+EVENT, +HUMAN)
        welcome the appointment (+EVENT, +HUMAN)

Options 2 and 3 can be illustrated by:[3]

(24) a. lunch (EVENT • FOOD):
        delicious lunch (FOOD) vs. long lunch (EVENT)
        share lunch (FOOD) vs. skip lunch (EVENT)
     b. book (INFO • PHYSOBJ):
        boring book (INFO) vs. heavy book (PHYSOBJ)
        illustrate the book (INFO) vs. close the book (PHYSOBJ)
     c. rumor (ACTIVITY • PROPOSITION):
        false rumor (PROPOSITION) vs. persistent rumor (ACTIVITY)
        spread the rumor (PROPOSITION) vs. trigger the rumor (ACTIVITY)
     d. lecture (EVENT • INFO):
        morning lecture (EVENT) vs. interesting lecture (INFO)
        miss the lecture (EVENT) vs. write the lecture (INFO)
     e. concert (EVENT • INFO):
        open-air concert (EVENT) vs. orchestral concert (INFO)
        host the concert (EVENT) vs. record the concert (INFO)
     f. lamb (ANIMAL • FOOD):
        roast lamb (FOOD) vs. newborn lamb (ANIMAL)
        eat lamb (FOOD) vs. sacrifice the lamb (ANIMAL)
     g. construction (PROCESS • RESULT):
        wooden construction (RESULT) vs. road construction (PROCESS)
        admire the construction (RESULT) vs. supervise the construction (PROCESS)
     h. appointment (EVENT • HUMAN):
        urgent appointment (EVENT) vs. troubled appointment (HUMAN)
        arrange an appointment (EVENT) vs. see the (next) appointment (HUMAN)

The sense inventory for the collection of dot objects chosen for this task includes only homonyms. That is, only contrastive senses such as the *river bank* versus *financial institution* for *bank* will need to be disambiguated. Complementary senses such as "the financial institution" itself versus "the building where it is located" are not included.

In order to create the appropriate CompLink, the annotator will select which type from a list of component types for a given dot object is exploited in the sentence. The resulting GLML is:

---

[3] See Pustejovsky (2005), Rumshisky et al. (2007) for an expanded listing of dot objects.

After a while more champagne and a delicious lunch was served.

```
<SELECTOR sid="s1">delicious</SELECTOR>
<NOUN nid="n1">lunch</NOUN>
<CompLink cid="cid1" sID="s1" relatedToNoun="n1" gramRel="mod"
compType="SELECTION" sourceType="[PHYS_OBJ,EVENT]"
targetType="PHYS_OBJ" />
```

5 Conclusion

In this chapter, we approach the problem of annotating the relation between a predicate and its argument as one that encodes the compositional history of the selection process. This allows us to distinguish surface forms that directly satisfy the selectional (type) requirements of a predicate from those that are accommodated or coerced in context. We described a specification language for selection, GLML, based largely on the type selective operations in GL, and three annotation tasks using this specification to identify argument selection behavior.

There are clearly many compositional operations in language that have not been addressed here. The framework is general enough, however, to describe a broad range of type selective behavior. As the tasks become more refined, the extensions will also become clearer. Furthermore, as other languages are examined for annotation, new tasks will emerge reflecting perhaps language-specific constructions.

Acknowledgements   The idea for annotating a corpus according to principles of argument selection within GL arose during a discussion at GL2007 in Paris, between one of the authors (James Pustejovsky) and Nicoletta Calzolari and Pierrette Bouillon. The authors would like to thank the members of the GLML Working Group and the organizers of the ASC task at SemEval-2010 for their fruitful feedback. In particular, we would like to thank Nicoletta Calzolari, Elisabetta Jezek, Alessandro Lenci, Valeria Quochi, Jan Odijk, Tommaso Caselli, Claudia Soria, Chu-Ren Huang, Marc Verhagen, and Kiyong Lee. The contribution by Olga Batiukova was partially financed by the Ministry of Economy and Competitiveness of Spain under Grant No. FFI2009-12191 (Subprogram FILO).

References

Asher, N., & Pustejovsky, J. (2006). A type composition logic for Generative Lexicon. *Journal of Cognitive Science, 6*, 1–38.

Bisetto, A., & Scalise, S. (2005). The classification of compounds. *Lingue e Linguaggio, 2*, 319–332.

BNC (2000). The British National Corpus. The BNC Consortium, University of Oxford. http://www.natcorp.ox.ac.uk/.

Bouillon, P. (1997). *Polymorphie et semantique lexical: le cas des adjectifs*. PhD dissertation, Paris VII, Paris.

Burchardt, A., Erk, K., Frank, A., Kowalski, A., Pado, S., & Pinkal, M. (2006). The SALSA corpus: A German corpus resource for lexical semantics. In *Proceedings of LREC*, Genoa, Italy.

Chierchia, G. (1998). Reference to kinds across language. *Natural Language Semantics, 6*(4), 339–4015.

Egg, M. (2005). *Flexible semantics for reinterpretation phenomena.* Stanford: CSLI.

Groenendijk, J., & Stokhof, M. (1989). *Type-shifting rules and the semantics of interrogatives* (Vol. 2, pp. 21–68). Dordrecht: Kluwer.

Hanks, P. (2009). Corpus pattern analysis. CPA Project Page. Retrieved April 11, 2009, from http://nlp.fi.muni.cz/projekty/cpa/.

Hanks, P., & Pustejovsky, J. (2005). A pattern dictionary for natural language processing. *Revue Française de Linguistique Appliquée, X,* 63–82.

Hobbs, J. R., Stickel, M., & Martin, P. (1993). Interpretation as abduction. *Artificial Intelligence, 63,* 69–142.

Johnston, M., & Busa, F. (1999). The compositional interpretation of compounds. In E. Viegas (Ed.), *Breadth and depth of semantic lexicons* (pp. 167–187). Dordrecht: Kluwer.

Kilgarriff, A., Rychly, P., Smrz, P., & Tugwell, D. (2004). The sketch engine. In *Proceedings of EURALEX,* Lorient, France (pp. 105–116).

Kipper, K. (2005). *VerbNet: A broad-coverage, comprehensive verb lexicon.* PhD dissertation, University of Pennsylvania, PA.

Levi, J. N. (1978). *The syntax and semantics of complex nominals.* New York: Academic Press.

Markert, K., & Nissim, M. (2007). Metonymy resolution at SemEval I: Guidelines for participants. In *Proceedings of the ACL 2007 conference.*

Meyers, A., Reeves, R., Macleod, C., Szekely, R., Zielinska, V., Young, B., & Grishman, R. (2004). The NomBank project: An interim report. In *HLT-NAACL 2004 workshop: Frontiers in corpus annotation* (pp. 24–31).

Nunberg, G. (1979). The non-uniqueness of semantic solutions: Polysemy. *Linguistics and Philosophy, 3,* 143–184.

Palmer, M., Gildea, D., & Kingsbury, P. (2005). The proposition bank: An annotated corpus of semantic roles. *Computational Linguistics, 31*(1), 71–106.

Partee, B., & Rooth, M. (1983). *Generalized conjunction and type ambiguity* (pp. 361–383). Berlin: de Gruyter.

Pinkal, M. (1999). On semantic underspecification. In H. Bunt & R. Muskens (Eds.), *Proceedings of the 2nd international workshop on computational semantics (IWCS 2),* January 13–15, The Netherlands: Tilburg University.

Pradhan, S., Hovy, E., Marcus, M., Palmer, M., Ramshaw, L., & Weischedel, R. (2007). Ontonotes: A unified relational semantic representation. In *ICSC 2007, International conference on semantic computing* (pp. 517–526).

Pustejovsky, J. (1991). The Generative Lexicon. *Computational Linguistics, 17*(4), 409–441.

Pustejovsky, J. (1995). *Generative Lexicon.* Cambridge: MIT Press.

Pustejovsky, J. (2000). Events and the semantics of opposition. In C. Tenny & J. Pustejovsky (Eds.), *Events as grammatical objects* (pp. 445–482). Stanford: CSLI.

Pustejovsky, J. (2001). Type construction and the logic of concepts. In *The syntax of word meaning,* Cambridge: Cambridge University Press.

Pustejovsky, J. (2005). *A survey of dot objects* (Technical report). Brandeis University.

Pustejovsky, J. (2006a). Type theory and lexical decomposition. *Journal of Cognitive Science, 6,* 39–76.

Pustejovsky, J. (2006b). Unifying linguistic annotations: A TimeML case study. In *Proceedings of TSD 2006,* Brno, Czech Republic.

Pustejovsky, J. (2011). Coercion in a general theory of argument selection. *Journal of Linguistics, 49*(6), 1401–1431.

Pustejovsky, J., Hanks, P., & Rumshisky, A. (2004). Automated induction of sense in context. In *COLING 2004,* Geneva, Switzerland (pp. 924–931).

Pustejovsky, J., Knippen, R., Littman, J., & Sauri, R. (2005). Temporal and event information in natural language text. *Language Resources and Evaluation, 39*(2), 123–164.

Pustejovsky, J., Rumshisky, A., Plotnick, A., Jezek, E., Batiukova, O., & Quochi, V. (2010). Semeval-2010 task 7: Argument selection and coercion. In *Proceedings of the 5th international workshop on semantic evaluation,* Uppsala, Sweden (pp. 27–32). Stroudsburg: Association for Computational Linguistics.

Pustejovsky, J., & Stubbs, A. (2012). *Natural language annotation for machine learning*. Sebastopol: O'Reilly Publishers.

Rumshisky, A., & Batiukova, O. (2008). Polysemy in verbs: Systematic relations between senses and their effect on annotation. In *COLING workshop on human judgement in computational linguistics (HJCL-2008)*, Manchester, England.

Rumshisky, A., Grinberg, V., & Pustejovsky, J. (2007). Detecting selectional behaviour of complex types in text. In *4th international workshop on Generative Lexicon*, Paris.

Rumshisky, A., Hanks, P., Havasi, C., & Pustejovsky, J. (2006). Constructing a corpus-based ontology using model bias. In *The 19th international FLAIRS conference, FLAIRS 2006*, Melbourne Beach, Florida, USA.

Ruppenhofer, J., Ellsworth, M., Petruck, M., Johnson, C., & Scheffczyk, J. (2006). *FrameNet II: Extended theory and practice*. Berkeley: California International Computer Sciences Institute.

Spencer, A. (1991). *Morphological theory: An introduction to word structure in generative grammar*. Oxford, UK and Cambridge, USA: Blackwell Textbooks in Linguistics.

Subirats, C. (2004). FrameNet Español. Una red semántica de marcos conceptuales. In *VI international congress of Hispanic linguistics*, Leipzig.

Verhagen, M. (2010). The Brandeis annotation tool. In *Language resources and evaluation conference, LREC 2010*, Malta.

Warren, B. (1978). *Semantic patterns of noun-noun compounds*. Göteborg: Acta Universitatis Gothoburgensis.

Incremental Recognition and Prediction of Dialogue Acts

Volha Petukhova and Harry Bunt

Abstract This chapter is concerned with the incremental understanding of utterances in spoken dialogue, with a focus on how their intended (possibly multiple) communicative functions can be recognized in a data-oriented way on the basis of observable features of communicative behaviour. An incremental, token-based approach is described which combines the use of local classifiers, that exploit local utterance features, and global classifiers that use the outputs of local classifiers applied to previous and subsequent tokens. This approach is shown to result in excellent dialogue act recognition scores for unsegmented spoken dialogue. This can be seen as a significant step forward towards the development of fully incremental, on-line methods for computing the meaning of utterances in spoken dialogue.

1 Introduction

When reading a sentence in a text, a human language understander obviously does not wait trying to understand what he is reading until he has come to the end of the sentence. Similarly for trying to understand what is said in a spoken conversation; evidence from the examination of transcripts of spoken conversations and from psycholinguistic experiments suggests that interpretation starts long before a complete utterance is constructed. Psycholinguistic studies provide further support for this view, for example, eye-tracking experiments reported by Tanenhaus et al. (1995), Sedivy et al. (1999) and Sedivy (2003) show that definite descriptions are resolved incrementally when the referent is visually accessible. Other evidence suggests that understanding involves parallel generation of multiple hypothesis. It has

V. Petukhova (✉)
Department of Spoken Language Systems, Saarland University, Building C7 1, PO Box 151150, 66041 Saarbrücken, Germany
e-mail: v.petukhova@lsv.uni-saarland.de

H. Bunt
Tilburg Center for Cognition and Communication (TiCC) and Department of Philosophy, Tilburg University, P.O. Box 90153, 5000 LE Tilburg, The Netherlands
e-mail: harry.bunt@uvt.nl

H. Bunt et al. (eds.), *Computing Meaning*, Text, Speech and Language Technology 47, DOI 10.1007/978-94-007-7284-7_13,
© Springer Science+Business Media Dordrecht 2014

been shown, e.g. for processing ambiguous words by Swinney (1979) and Simpson (1994), for definite expression resolution (Tanenhaus et al. 1995), and for pronoun interpretation (Corbett and Chang 1983), that all possible hypotheses are activated in parallel until it is possible to identify a single candidate, or at least reduce their number.

Observations of natural dialogue behaviour show that humans process dialogue contributions *incrementally*, and are often able to anticipate the end of the utterance (see e.g. de Ruiter et al. 2006). People are also able to predict turn endings with high accuracy using semantic, syntactic, pragmatic, prosodic and visual features (Ford and Thompson 1996; Grosjean and Hirt 1996; Barkhuysen et al. 2008, among others). Dialogue phenomena such as backchannelling (providing feedback while someone else is speaking), the completion of a partner utterance, and requests for clarification that overlap the utterance of the main speaker, illustrate this. Studies of nonverbal behaviour in dialogue show that participants start to perform certain body movements that are perceived and interpreted by others as dialogue acts while someone else is still speaking, see e.g. Petukhova and Bunt (2009). All these observations provide evidence for the incremental nature of human dialogue understanding.

Traditional models of language understanding for dialogue systems are pipelined and modular, and operate on complete utterances. Typically, such systems have a speech recognition module, a language understanding module responsible for syntactic and semantic analysis, an interpretation manager, a dialogue manager, a natural language generation module, and a module for speech synthesis. The output of each module is the input for another. The language understanding module typically performs the following tasks:

1. segmentation: identification of relevant segments in the input, such as sentences;
2. lexical analysis: lexical lookup, possibly supported by morphological processing, and by additional resources such as WordNet, VerbNet, or lexical ontologies;
3. parsing: construction of syntactic interpretations;
4. semantic analysis: computation of propositional, referential, or action-related content;
5. pragmatic analysis: determination of speaker intentions.

Of these tasks, lexical analysis, being concerned with local information at word level, can be done for each word as soon as it has been recognized, and is naturally performed as an incremental part of utterance processing, but syntactic, semantic and pragmatic analysis are traditionally performed on complete utterances. Tomita's pioneering work in left-to-right syntactic parsing has shown that incremental parsing can be much more efficient and of equal quality as the parsing of complete utterances (Tomita 1986). Computational approaches to incremental semantic and pragmatic interpretation have been less successful (see e.g. Haddock 1989; Milward and Cooper 2009), but work in computational semantics on the design of underspecified representation formalisms has shown that such formalisms, developed originally for the underspecified representation of quantifier scopes, can also be applied in situations where incomplete input information is available (see e.g. Bos 2002; Bunt 2007; Hobbs 1985; Pinkal 1999) and as such hold a promise for incremental semantic interpretation.

Pragmatic interpretation is primarily based on the recognition of the speaker's intentions. The recognition of the intentions encoded in user utterances is one of the most important aspects of language understanding for a dialogue system. Computational modelling of dialogue behaviour in terms of dialogue acts aims to capture speaker intentions in the communicative functions of dialogue acts, and offers an effective integration with semantic content analysis through the information state update approach (Poesio and Traum 1998; Bunt 2000; Traum and Larsson 2003). In this approach, a dialogue act is viewed as having as its main components a communicative function and a semantic content, where the semantic content is the referential, propositional, or action-related information that the dialogue act addresses, and the communicative function defines how an understander's information state is to be updated with that information.

Evaluation of a non-incremental dialogue system and its incremental counterpart reported in Aist et al. (2007) showed that the latter is faster overall than the former due to the incorporation of pragmatic information in early stages of the understanding process. Since users formulate utterances incrementally, partial utterances may be available for a substantial amount of time and may be interpreted by the system. An incremental interpretation strategy may allow the system to respond more quickly, by minimizing the delay between the time the user finishes and the time the utterance is interpreted (DeVault and Stone 2003).

Although human language processing is largely incremental, some decisions need to be postponed. In some cases, a hypothesis cannot be resolved immediately, because there is insufficient evidence for disambiguation. Some semantic phenomena cannot be resolved incrementally, e.g. scope assignment; here, partial interpretations may initially be constructed and refined later. In this chapter we present the results of a series of experiments carried out in order to assess the automatic incremental segmentation and classification of dialogue acts, investigating the automatic recognizability of multiple communicative functions on the basis of observable features such as linguistic cues, intonation properties and dialogue history. We will show that in order to arrive at the best output prediction two different classification strategies are needed: (1) local classification that is based on features observed in dialogue behaviour and that can be extracted from the annotated data; and (2) global classification that takes the locally predicted context into account. The first strategy corresponds with *Fine-Grained Incremental Interpretation*, where each small portion of an utterance is analyzed immediately when it is encountered, such as each token either word or vocal signal. The second strategy corresponds with *Coarse-Grained Incremental Interpretation*, the processor having fine-grained results waits until larger chunks of an utterance are encountered (cf. Chater et al. 1995).

This chapter is structured as follows. Section 2 discusses approaches and results of studies of automatic dialogue act recognition. In Sect. 3 we outline the experiments we performed, describing the data, tag set, features, algorithms and evaluation metrics that were used. Section 4 reports on the experimental results, applying a variety of machine learning techniques and feature selection algorithms, to assess the automatic recognition and classification of dialogue acts using simultaneous incremental segmentation and dialogue act classification.

2 Related Work

The state of the art in dialogue act recognition is to use all available information sources from multiple modalities. These sources include: (1) linguistic information, that can be derived from the surface form of an utterance: lexical, collocational and syntactic information; (2) perceptual information from multiple channels available for dialogue participants, including acoustic and prosodic properties of utterances as well as information from visual and other modalities; (3) contextual information obtained from the preceding dialogue context and dialogue structure, as well as global context properties like dialogue setting, knowledge about dialogue participants, and so on.

Various machine learning techniques have been applied successfully to natural-language based dialogue analysis. For example, techniques based on n-gram language modelling were applied by Reithinger and Klesen (1997) to the Verbmobil corpus, with a reported tagging accuracy of 74.7 %. Hidden Markov Models (HMM) have been tried for dialogue act classification in the Switchboard corpus (Stolcke et al. 2000), achieving a tagging accuracy of 71 % on word transcripts. Another approach that has been applied to dialogue act recognition by Samuel et al. (1998), uses transformation-based learning; they achieved an average tagging accuracy of 75.12 % for the Verbmobil corpus. Keizer (2003) used Bayesian Networks applying a slightly modified version of DAMSL with an accuracy of 88 % for backward-looking functions and 73 % for forward-looking functions in the SCHISMA corpus.[1] Lendvai et al. (2004) adopted a memory-based approach, based on the k-nearest-neighbour algorithm, and report a tagging accuracy of 73.8 % for the OVIS data.[2]

Apart from using different techniques, these approaches also differ with respect to feature selection strategies. Some approaches rely solely on the wording of an input utterance, using n-gram models or cue-phrase, e.g. Reithinger and Klesen (1997) and Webb et al. (2005). Others successfully integrate prosodic features that facilitate accurate dialogue act recognition, e.g. Shriberg et al. (1998), Jurafsky et al. (1998), Fernandez and Picard (2002), Stolcke et al. (2000). Again others combine the predictions derived from the utterance and its context, e.g. Keizer (2003), Stolcke et al. (2000), Samuel et al. (1998), Lendvai et al. (2004). None of these approaches deals with the possible multifunctionality of dialogue segments; Stolcke et al. (2000) for example use dialogues from the Switchboard as segmented into 'slash-units' (Meteer and Taylor 1995), which has been shown to preclude an accurate characterization of utterances in terms of multiple communicative functions (Bunt et al. 2013).

Nakano et al. (1999) proposed a method for incremental understanding of user utterances whose boundaries are not known. The *Incremental Sentence Sequence*

---

[1]The SCHISMA corpus consists of 64 dialogues in Dutch collected in Wizard-of-Oz experiments, has keyboard-entered utterances within the information exchange and transaction task domain, where users can make inquiries about theatre performances scheduled and make ticket reservations.

[2]*O*penbare *V*ervoer *I*nformatie *S*ysteem (Public Transport Information System), see http://www. let.rug.nl/~vannoord/Ovis/.

Search (ISSS) algorithm finds plausible boundaries of utterances, called 'significant utterances' (SUs), that can be a full sentence or a subsentential phrase, such as a noun phrase or a verb phrase. Any phrase that can change the belief state is defined as SU. In this sense an SU corresponds more or less with what we call a functional segment. ISSS maintains multiple possible belief states, and updates those belief states when a word hypothesis is input (i.e. word-by-word). The ISSS approach does not deal with the multifunctionality of segments, however, and does not allow segments to overlap.

Lendvai and Geertzen (2007) proposed *token-based* dialogue act segmentation and classification, worked out in more detail in (Geertzen 2009). This approach takes dialogue data that is not segmented into syntactically or semantically complete units, but operates on the transcribed speech as a stream of words and other vocal signs (e.g. laughs or breathing), including disfluent elements (e.g. abandoned or interrupted words) for each dialogue participant. Segmentation and classification of dialogue acts are performed simultaneously in one step. Geertzen (2009) reports on classifier performance on this task for the DIAMOND data[3] using DIT^{++} labels; *F*-scores range from 47.7 to 81.7. It was shown that performing segmentation and classification together results in better segmentation performance, but affects the dialogue act classification negatively.

The incremental dialogue act recognition method as proposed here takes the token-based approach for building classifiers for the recognition of multiple dialogue acts for each input token.

3 Set-Up of Classification Experiments

3.1 Tag Set

The data used in the experiments was annotated with the DIT^{++} Release 4 tag set.[4] The DIT^{++} taxonomy distinguishes 10 dimensions, addressing information about: the domain or task (*Task*), feedback on communicative behaviour of the speaker (*Auto-Feedback*) or other interlocutors (*Allo-Feedback*), managing difficulties in the speaker's contributions (*Own-Communication Management*) or those of other interlocutors (*Partner Communication Management*), the speaker's need for time to continue the dialogue (*Time Management*), establishing and maintaining contact (*Contact Management*), who should have the next turn (*Turn Management*), the way the speaker is planning to structure the dialogue, introducing, changing or closing a topic (*Dialogue Structuring*), and conditions that trigger dialogue acts by social convention (*Social Obligations Management*), see Table 1.

---

[3] The **DIAMOND** corpus (Geertzen et al. 2004) contains human-machine and human-human Dutch dialogues that have an assistance-seeking nature. The dialogues were video-recorded in a setting where the subject could communicate with a help desk employee using an acoustic channel and ask for explanations on how to configure and operate a fax machine.

[4] For more information about the tag set and the dimensions that are identified, please visit http://dit. uvt.nl/ or see Bunt (2009).

For each dimension, a functional segment can be assigned at most one communicative function (not counting implied functions, see Bunt 2011), which is either a function that can occur in this dimension only (a *dimension-specific* (DS) function) or a function that can occur in any dimension (a *general-purpose* (GP) function). Dialogue acts with a DS communicative function can only be concerned with a particular type of information, such as a Turn Grabbing act, which is concerned with the allocation of the speaker role, or a Stalling act, which is concerned with the timing of utterance production. GP functions, by contrast, are not specifically related to any dimension in particular, e.g. one can ask a question about any type of semantic content, provide an answer about any type of content, or request the performance of any type of action (such as *Could you please close the door* or *Could you please repeat that*). These communicative functions include Question, Answer, Request, Offer, Inform, and many other familiar core speech acts.

The tag set used in these studies contains 38 dimension-specific functions and 44 general-purpose functions. A tag consists either of a pair consisting of a communicative function (*CF*) and the addressed dimension (*D*), or (in the case of a DS function), of just a communicative function.

3.2 Features and Data Encoding

We used data selected from the AMI meeting corpus[5] and the Map Task corpus.[6] For training we used three annotated AMI meetings that contain 17,335 tokens which form 3,897 functional segments. The Map Task training set contains 6 dialogues consisting of 5,941 tokens that form 2,589 functional segments. Table 1 shows the distribution of annotated dialogue acts over the DIT^{++} dimensions for both corpora, indicating the percentage of identified functional segments per dimension. Table 2 presents the percentage of functional segments with general-purpose functions. Note that for better recognition of pragmatic and semantic distinctions between different types of Inform acts they are divided into two categories: Informs *tout court* and Informs that are rhetorically related to previous dialogue acts, e.g. elaborating, justifying, or explaining them.

Features extracted from the data considered here relate to *dialogue history*: functional tags of the 10 previous turns; *timing*: token *duration* and *floor-transfer off-*

---

[5]The *A*ugmented *M*ulti-party *I*nteraction http://www.amiproject.org/ corpus contains human-human multi-party interactions in English. Meeting participants (mostly four) play different roles in a fictitious design team that takes a new project from kick-off to completion over the course of a day. The *AMI corpus* contains manually produced orthographic transcriptions for each individual speaker, including word-level timings that have been derived using a speech recogniser in forced alignment mode. The meetings are video-recorded and each dialogue is also provided with sound files (for our analysis we used recordings made with close-talking microphones to eliminate noise).

[6]Detailed information about the Map Task project can be found at http://www.hcrc.ed.ac.uk/maptask/. The corpus contains so-called instruction dialogues, where one participant plays the role of an instruction-giver and another that of instruction-follower, who navigates through the map following the instructions of the instruction-giver. The Map Task corpus contains orthographic transcriptions for each individual speaker, including word-level timings.

Table 1 Distribution of functional segments across dimensions for AMI and Map Task corpora

Dimension	AMI corpus	Map Task corpus
Task	31.8	52.4
Auto-Feedback	20.5	15.7
Allo-Feedback	0.7	4.7
Turn Management	50.2	24.3
Social Obligation Management	0.5	0.1
Discourse Structuring	2.8	0.5
Own Communication Management	10.3	2.8
Time Management	26.7	13.4
Partner Communication Management	0.3	0.3
Contact Management	0.1	1.7

Table 2 Distribution of functional tags for general-purpose communicative functions for the AMI and Map Task corpora (in %)

General-purpose function	AMI corpus	Map Task corpus
Propositional Question	5.8	7.1
Set Question	2.3	2.9
Check Question	3.3	7.1
Propositional Answer	9.8	4.3
Set Answer	3.9	2.4
Inform	11.7	7.8
Inform (Rhetorical)	21.9	13.4
Instruct	0.3	26.8
Suggest	10.1	0

set[7] computed in milliseconds; *prosody*: minimum, maximum, mean, and standard deviation for pitch (F0 in Hz), energy (RMS), voicing (fraction of locally unvoiced frames and number of voice breaks) and speaking rate (number of syllables per second);[8] and *lexical information*: each token is coded as a feature, and bi- and tri-gram models were constructed and used as lexical features. For the AMI data, being multi-party dialogues, we also include the speaker (A, B, C, D) and the addressee (other participants individually or the group as a whole) as features.

---

[7] Difference between the time that a turn starts and the moment the previous turn ends.

[8] These features were computed using the PRAAT tool, see http://www.praat.org. We examined both raw and normalized versions of these features. Speaker-normalized features were obtained by computing z-scores ($z = $ (X-mean)/standard deviation) for the feature, where mean and standard deviation were calculated from all functional segments produced by the same speaker in the dialogues. We also used normalizations by first speaker turn and by previous speaker turn.

Speaker	Token	Task	Auto-F.	Allo-F.	TurnM.	TimeM.	ContactM.	DS	OCM	PCM	SOM
B	it	B:inf	O	O	O	O	O	O	O	O	O
B	has	I:inf	O	O	O	O	O	O	O	O	O
B	to	I:inf	O	O	O	O	O	O	O	O	O
B	look	I:inf	O	O	O	O	O	O	O	O	O
B	you	O	O	B:check	O	O	O	O	O	O	O
B	know	O	O	E:check	O	O	O	O	O	O	O
B	cool	I:inf	O	O	O	O	O	O	O	O	O
D	mmhmm	O	BE:positive	O	O	O	O	O	O	O	O
B	and	I:inf	O	O	BE:t_keep	O	O	O	O	O	O
B	gimmicky	E:inf	O	O	O	O	O	O	O	O	O

Fig. 1 Encoding of segment boundaries and communicative functions in different dimensions

For classification experiments based on complete segments, word occurrence is represented by a bag-of-words vector[9] indicating the presence or absence of words in the segment. In total, 1,668 features are used for the AMI data and 829 features for the Map Task data.

To be able to identify segment boundaries, we assign to each token its communicative function label and indicate whether a token starts a segment (B), is inside a segment (I), ends a segment (E), is outside a segment (O), or forms a functional segment on its own (BE). Thus, the class labels consist of a segmentation prefix (IBOE) and a communicative function label, see example in Fig. 1.

3.3 Classifiers and Evaluation Metrics

A wide variety of machine-learning techniques has been used for NLP tasks with various instantiations of feature sets and target class encodings. For dialogue processing, it is still an open issue which techniques are the most suitable for which task. We used two types of classifier to test their performance on our data: a probabilistic one and a rule inducer.

As a probabilistic classifier we used *Bayes Nets*. This classifier estimates probabilities rather than produce predictions, which is often more useful because this allows us to rank predictions. Bayes Nets estimate the conditional probability distribution on the values of the class attributes given the values of the other attributes.

As a rule induction algorithm we chose *Ripper* (Cohen 1995). The advantage of a rule inducer is that the regularities discovered in the data are represented as human-readable rules.

The results of all experiments were obtained using 10-fold cross-validation.[10] As a baseline it is common practice to use the majority class tag, but for our data sets

[9]With a size of 1,640 entries for AMI data and 802 entries for the Map Task data.

[10]In order to reduce the effect of imbalances in the data, it is partitioned ten times. Each time a different 10 % of the data is used as test set and the remaining 90 % as training set. The procedure is repeated ten times so that in the end every instance has been used exactly once for testing, and the scores are averaged. The cross-validation was stratified, i.e. the 10 folds contained approximately the same proportions of instances with relevant tags as the entire dataset.

such a baseline is not very useful because of the relatively low frequencies of the tags in some dimensions. Instead, we use a baseline that is based on a single feature, namely, the tag of the previous dialogue utterance, unless specified differently.

Several metrics have been proposed in the literature for the evaluation of classifier performance. For assessing the performance of the joint segmentation and classification of dialogue acts, a word-based and a dialogue act-based metric are used. The word-based metric has been introduced in (Ang et al. 2005). It measures the percentage of words that were placed in a segment perfectly identical to that in the reference. In other words, if an output segment perfectly matches a corresponding reference segment on the word level, each word in that segment is counted as correct. All other placements of words are counted as incorrect. A dialogue act-based metric (DER) was proposed in (Zimmermann et al. 2005), which considers a word to be correctly classified if and only if it has been assigned the correct dialogue act type and it lies in exactly the same segment as the corresponding word of the reference. Thus, the DER metric not only requires a dialogue act candidate to have exactly matching boundaries but also to be tagged with the correct dialogue act type. We use the combined DER_{sc} metric to evaluate joint segmentation (s) and classification (c):

$$DER_{sc} = \frac{tokens\ with\ wrong\ boundaries\ and/or\ wrong\ function\ class}{total\ number\ of\ tokens} \times 100.$$

The most commonly used performance metrics are accuracy, precision, recall and F-scores. The overall success rate (*accuracy*) is computed by dividing the number of correct classifications by the total number of classifications. A common metric which represents the balance between precision and recall is the *F-score*:

$$F\text{-}score = \frac{2 \cdot recall \cdot precision}{recall + precision} = \frac{2 \cdot tp}{2 \cdot tp + fp + fn}.$$

We will use these standard metrics when evaluating classification results.

4 Classification Results

4.1 Joint Segmentation and Classification

We performed token-based machine-learning experiments on the AMI and Map Task data. The results for joint segmentation and classification for different classifiers are presented in Table 3 for the AMI data.

The results show that both classifiers outperform the baseline by a broad margin. The BayesNet classifier marginally outperforms the Ripper rule-inducer, showing no significant differences in overall performance. Comparing our results with those reported in (Geertzen 2009) for the DIAMOND data, we see that the F-scores obtained in our experiments are slightly higher. This may be due to the fact that our

Table 3 Overview of F-scores and DER_{sc} for joint segmentation and classification in each DIT^{++} dimension for AMI data. (Best scores indicated by numbers in bold face.)

Classification	BL		BayesNet		Ripper	
Dimension	F_1	DER_{sc}	F_1	DER_{sc}	F_1	DER_{sc}
Task	32.7	51.2	52.1	48.7	**66.7**	42.6
Auto-Feedback	43.2	84.4	**62.7**	33.9	60.1	45.6
Allo-Feedback	70.2	59.5	**73.7**	35.1	71.3	49.1
Turn Management: initial	34.2	95.2	**57.0**	58.4	54.3	81.3
Turn Management: final	33.3	92.7	**54.2**	46.9	49.3	87.3
Time management	43.7	96.5	**64.5**	46.1	61.4	53.1
Discourse Structuring	41.2	35.1	**72.7**	19.9	50.2	30.9
Contact Management	59.9	53.2	71.4	49.9	**83.3**	37.2
OCM	36.5	87.9	**68.3**	51.3	58.3	76.8
PCM	49.5	59.0	**58.5**	45.5	51.4	58.7
SOM	34.5	47.5	**86.5**	35.9	83.3	44.3

Table 4 Overview of F- and DER_{sc}-scores for joint segmentation and classification in each DIT^{++} dimension for Map Task data. (Best scores indicated by numbers in bold face.)

Classification task	BL		BayesNet		Ripper	
Dimension	F_1	DER_{sc}	F_1	DER_{sc}	F_1	DER_{sc}
Task	43.8	70.2	**79.7**	41.9	77.7	58.5
Auto-Feedback	64.6	60.6	65.4	55.2	**80.1**	43.9
Allo-Feedback	30.7	91.2	59.3	54.0	**72.7**	51.8
Turn Management	50.3	47.5	70.8	40.9	**81.4**	36.2
Time management	54.2	28.4	72.1	20.3	**83.6**	10.4
Discourse Structuring	33.2	95.1	62.5	44.3	**66.7**	43.5
Contact Management	24.7	93.2	**57.0**	79.5	11.0	93.5
OCM	11.2	97.4	**42.9**	64.7	28.6	92.1
PCM	14.3	95.2	61.5	55.2	**66.7**	50.1
SOM	08.8	96.2	40.0	71.8	**85.7**	21.4

training set is three times larger. For better comparison, we decided to perform the same experiments using Map Task dialogues. Table 4 shows the overall performance of the classifiers for joint segmentation and classification for these data.

The classifiers perform better on the Map Task data than on the AMI data, for the five most frequently occurring dimensions: Task, Auto- and Allo-Feedback, Turn Management and Time Management. This is because the classifiers need to deal with less complex phenomena in these data.

Although the results are encouraging, the performance for joint segmentation and classification does not outperform the two-step segmentation and classification

Table 5 Overview of F-scores on the baseline (BL) and the classifiers on two-step segmentation and classification tasks. (Best scores indicated by numbers in bold face.)

Classification	BL	NBayes	Ripper	IB1
Task	66.8	71.2	**72.3**	53.6
Auto-Feedback	77.9	86.0	**89.7**	85.9
Allo-Feedback	79.7	**99.3**	99.2	98.8
Turn M.: initial	93.2	92.9	93.2	88.0
Turn M.: final	58.9	85.1	**91.1**	69.6
Time management	69.7	99.2	**99.4**	99.5
Discourse Structuring	69.3	**99.3**	**99.3**	99.1
Contact Management	89.8	99.8	99.8	99.8
OCM	89.6	90.0	**94.1**	85.6
PCM	99.7	99.7	99.7	99.7
SOM	99.6	99.6	99.6	99.6

scores reported in (Geertzen et al. 2007) and summarized in Table 5. It was noticed that lower F-scores are due to lower recall. Beginnings and endings of segments were often not found. For example, the beginnings of Set Questions are identified with perfect precision (100 %), but about 60 % of the cases were not found. The reason that classifiers still show reasonable performance is that most tokens occur inside segments and were better classified, e.g. inside-tokens of Set Questions were classified with high precision (83 %) and reasonably high recall scores (76 %). In general, the correct identification of the start of a relevant segment is crucial for further decisions.

4.2 Fine-Grained Incremental Interpretation: Local Classification

Dialogue utterances are often multifunctional, having a function in more than one dimension (see e.g. Bunt 2011). This makes dialogue act recognition a complex task. Splitting up the learning task may make the task more manageable. A widely used strategy is to split a multi-class learning task into several binary learning tasks. Learning multiple classes, however, allows a learning algorithm to exploit interactions among classes. We split the classification task in such a way that a classifier needs to learn (1) communicative functions in isolation; (2) semantically related functions together, e.g. all information-seeking functions (questions) or all information-providing functions (all answers and all informs). We have built in total 64 classifiers for dialogue act recognition for the AMI data and 43 classifiers for the Map Task data. The difference in the number of classifiers is due to the fact that there are fewer general-purpose functions in the Map Task dialogues (9 comparing to 16 in the AMI corpus). Some of the tasks were defined as binary ones, e.g. the dimension recognition task, others are multi-class learning tasks.

Table 6 Overview of F-scores and DER_{sc} for the baseline (BL) and the classifiers upon joint segmentation and classification for each DIT^{++} communicative function or cluster of functions for AMI data. (Best scores indicated by numbers in bold face.)

Classification	BL		BayesNet		Ripper	
Communicative function	F_1	DER_{sc}	F_1	DER_{sc}	F_1	DER_{sc}
General-purpose functions						
Propositional Questions	47.0	39.1	**94.9**	3.9	75.8	23.5
Check Questions	43.8	56.4	**68.5**	19.6	61.3	33.1
Set Questions	44.8	52.1	74.1	18.6	**76.3**	17.7
Choice Question	41.8	54.2	68.6	15.7	**73.1**	21.4
Inform	45.8	39.9	**79.8**	18.7	66.5	30.5
Inform (Elaborate)	37.2	38.9	**69.1**	13.4	68.7	23.9
Inform (Justify)	46.3	35.2	**80.5**	11.2	75.7	31.6
Inform (Conclude)	43.2	48.5	**66.7**	13.5	59.0	37.2
Inform (Remind)	47.5	38.6	**63.3**	21.4	56.2	22.7
(Dis-)Agreement	41.3	79.1	**72.1**	12.6	71.6	60.2
PropositionalAnswer	32.0	77.8	**66.8**	26.1	52.2	53.8
(Dis-)Confirm	25.0	87.3	**47.3**	30.3	46.5	47.2
Set Answer	44.3	54.2	**77.5**	13.2	57.3	44.1
Suggest	45.8	38.4	**65.6**	17.3	48.8	35.6
Request	45.8	49.3	**75.8**	14.5	50.3	36.9
Instruct	46.3	49.3	**60.5**	14.5	46.3	36.9
Address Request	34.8	74.8	**79.0**	15.3	54.2	42.1
Offer	25.0	93.7	**65.3**	23.9	45.6	34.3
Dimension-specific functions						
Auto-Feedback	57.1	23.5	**78.8**	13.2	66.7	15.5
Allo-Feedback	89.3	4.4	**95.1**	2.9	94.3	3.9
Turn Management	24.8	21.9	**72.8**	7.4	46.3	10.7
Time management	68.3	32.3	82.4	13.7	**92.8**	11.4
Discourse Structuring	40.7	13.6	72.6	2.5	**74.5**	1.7
Contact Management	21.4	48.6	89.2	5.7	**92.3**	3.6
Own Communication Management	26.7	48.6	**78.0**	11.6	68.1	20.0
Partner Communication Management	33.4	18.2	77.8	8.5	**88.9**	6.5
Social Obligation Management	60.0	18.7	88.9	8.3	**90.1**	5.5

We trained a classifier for each general-purpose and dimension-specific function defined in the DIT^{++} taxonomy, and observed that this has the effect that the various classifiers perform significantly better. These functions were learned (1) in isolation; (2) as semantically related functions together. Both the recognition of communicative functions and that of segment boundaries improves significantly. Table 6 gives an overview of the overall performance (best obtained scores) of the trained classi-

Table 7 Overview of F-scores and DER_{sc}-scores for the baseline (BL) and the classifiers upon joint segmentation and classification for each DIT^{++} communicative function or cluster of functions for Map Task data. (Best scores indicated by numbers in bold face.)

Classification	BL		BayesNet		Ripper	
Communicative function	F_1	DER_{sc}	F_1	DER_{sc}	F_1	DER_{sc}
General-purpose functions						
Propositional Questions	29.5	73.9	**87.8**	13.5	71.6	27.1
Check Questions	25.0	73.2	**59.8**	63.6	52.8	57.9
Set Questions	24.8	72.6	**69.3**	42.2	69.0	43.1
Choice Question	23.5	73.4	**66.7**	48.9	67.1	45.7
Inform	24.1	72.7	**69.3**	50.9	59.8	60.7
Inform (Clarify)	24.8	73.7	**65.0**	46.7	60.5	54.8
Inform (Elaborate/Explain)	16.3	71.7	47.8	62.7	**62.2**	60.9
Propositional Answer	19.6	70.7	63.3	58.2	**76.0**	41.7
Set Answer	24.8	73.0	61.5	38.9	**63.8**	40.6
Instruct	36.0	66.3	**74.3**	26.7	69.5	41.3
Dimension-specific functions						
Auto-Feedback	51.7	36.9	67.2	27.6	79.5	13.5
Turn Management	50.3	47.5	70.8	40.9	**81.4**	36.2
Time management	54.2	28.4	72.1	20.3	**83.6**	10.4
Discourse Structuring	65.3	17.2	92.3	10.4	93.2	8.9
Contact Management	33.3	34.6	54.6	26.2	70.5	12.2
Own Communication Management	11.2	97.4	**42.9**	64.7	28.6	92.1
Partner Communication Management	14.3	95.2	61.5	55.2	**66.7**	50.1
Social Obligation Management	08.8	96.2	40.0	71.8	**85.7**	21.4

fiers after splitting the learning task for the AMI data and Table 7 for the Map Task data.

Both the recognition of communicative function and that of segment boundaries is fairly accurate. In general, classifiers performed well on this task. F-scores achieved are much higher than baseline scores. The recognition of some acts was not so successful, for example, (Dis-)Confirm acts were often confused with Propositional Answers because they share the same vocabulary. Since (Dis-)Confirm acts entail Propositional Answer acts, this would have only marginal consequences for an interactive system that makes use of online dialogue act understanding.

The realization of dimension-specific functions is highly conventional: dialogue participants use certain formulae to take or keep the turn, to open or close the dialogue, to move from one topic to another, to signal positive or negative feedback, and so on. Both corpora do not have dimension-specific functions for the Task dimension, which is why this dimension is left out. The Map Task data does not have dimension-specific functions in the Allo-Feedback dimension.

Table 8 Overview of F-scores and DER_{sc} for complex label classification (boundary+communicative function+dimension) in AMI data. (Best scores indicated by numbers in bold face.)

Classification	BL		BayesNet		Ripper	
Dimension	F_1	DER	F_1	DER	F_1	DER
Task	28.0	83.2	**62.0**	78.2	48.0	77.8
Auto-Feedback	31.2	85.7	**45.3**	68.3	33.3	69.1
Allo-Feedback	23.3	96.2	**37.6**	80.3	24.7	83.6
Discourse Structuring: delimitation	24.5	93.9	**32.9**	87.1	29.4	91.6
Discourse Structuring: topic organization	13.3	87.1	**23.0**	63.8	20.1	69.5

Segments having a general-purpose functions may address any of the ten DIT^{++} dimensions. The task of dimension recognition can be approached in two ways. One approach is to learn segment boundaries, communicative function label and dimension in one step (e.g. the class label *B:task;inform*). This task is very complicated, however. First, it leads to data which are high-dimensional and sparse, which will have a negative influence on the performance of the trained classifiers. Second, in many cases the dimension can be recognized reliably only with some delay; for the first few segment tokens it is often impossible to say what the segment is about. For example:

(1) 1. What do you think who we're aiming this at?
2. What do you think we are doing next?
3. What do you think Craig?

The three Set Questions in (1) start with exactly the same words, but they address different dimensions: Question 1 is about the Task (in AMI—the design the television remote control); Question 2 serves the purpose of discourse structuring; and Question 3 elicits feedback.

Another approach is to first recognize segment boundaries and communicative function, and define dimension recognition as a separate classification task.

We tested both strategies. The F-scores for the joint learning of complex class labels range from 23.0 ($DER_{sc} = 68.3$) to 45.3 ($DER_{sc} = 63.8$) (see Table 8). The results are reported only for those dimensions that are addressed in our data by general purpose functions in a substantial number of cases. We have no or only very few examples of general-purpose functions used for Turn, Time, Contact, Own/Partner Communication and Social Obligation Management.

For dimension recognition as a separate learning task the F-scores are significantly higher, ranging from 70.6 to 97.7 (see Table 9). The scores for joint segmentation and function recognition in the latter case are those listed in Table 6. Figure 2 gives an example of predictions made by five classifiers for the input *What you guys have already received um in your mails*. Hypotheses about the type of semantic content are generated for each token. The probability score for the first segment tokens are, however, lower than for the other tokens belonging to the same segment.

Table 9 Overview of F-scores for dimension recognition for general-purpose functions in AMI data

Classification	GP functions		Dimension recognition for GP functions			
Communicative function	F_1	DER_{sc}	Task	Auto-F.	Allo-F.	Dial. Struct.
Propositional Question	94.9	3.9	99.0	84.4	91.0	81.6
Set Question	74.1	18.6	94.8	79.6	na	87.5
Check Question	68.5	19.6	94.1	76.5	80.6	86.8
Inform	79.8	18.7	93.8	76.6	na	86.5
Inform (Elaborate)	69.1	13.4	94.6	na	58.3	86.9
Inform (Justify)	80.5	11.2	94.2	76.8	na	86.6
Inform (Conclude)	66.7	13.5	94.3	na	na	86.9
Inform (Remind)	63.3	21.4	94.1	na	na	86.9
(Dis-)Agreement	72.1	12.6	94.1	76.8	57.9	86.8
Propositional Answer	66.8	26.1	94.0	76.8	58.1	86.9
(Dis-)Confirm	47.3	30.3	94.1	76.7	58.0	na
Set Answer	77.5	13.2	94.1	76.7	na	86.8
Suggest	65.6	17.3	96.1	77.1	na	97.1
Request	75.8	14.5	99.1	na	na	86.8
Instruct	60.5	14.5	99.4	na	na	96.8
Address Request	79.0	15.3	99.0	na	na	86.2
Offer	65.3	23.9	96.1	na	na	78.3

Tokens	SetQuestion		Task		Auto-F.		TurnM.		Complex label (BIOE:D;CF)	
	label	p	label	p	label	p	label	p	label	p
what	B:setQ	0.85	O	0.71	O	1	O	0.68	O	0.933
you	I:setQ	1	task	0.985	O	1	B:give	0.64	O	0.869
guys	I:setQ	1	task	0.998	O	1	E:give	0.66	O	0.937
have	I:setQ	1	task	0.997	O	1	O	1	I:task;setQ	0.989
already	I:setQ	1	task	0.996	O	1	O	0.99	I:task;setQ	0.903
received	I:setQ	1	task	0.987	O	1	O	1	I:task;setQ	0.813
um	O	0.93	O	0.89	O	1	BE:keep	0.99	O	0.982
in	I:setQ	1	task	0.826	O	1	O	0.89	I:task;setQ	0.875
your	I:setQ	1	task	0.996	O	1	O	0.99	I:task;setQ	0.948
mails	E:setQ	0.99	task	0.987	O	1	O	1	E:task;setQ	0.948

Fig. 2 Predictions with indication of confidence scores (highest p class probability selected) for each token assigned by five trained classifiers simultaneously

4.3 Managing Local Classifiers: Global Classification and Global Search

As was shown in the previous section, given a certain input all possible output predictions (hypotheses) were obtained from *local classifiers*. Some predictions made

Table 10 Overview of F-scores and DER_{sc} when global classifiers are used for AMI and Map Task data, based on added predictions of local classifiers for five previous tokens. (Best scores indicated by numbers in bold face.)

Classification	AMI data				Map Task data			
	BayesNet		Ripper		BayesNet		Ripper	
Dimension	F_1	DER_{sc}	F_1	DER_{sc}	F_1	DER_{sc}	F_1	DER_{sc}
Task	65.3	14.9	**79.1**	21.8	81.6	17.8	**82.4**	14.1
Auto-Feedback	72.9	8.1	**77.8**	7.2	77.2	26.5	**81.3**	17.6
Allo-Feedback	67.7	10.9	**74.2**	9.5	68.3	35.4	**74.3**	20.6
Turn Management: initial	**72.2**	11.5	69.5	11.4	**82.9**	11.4	81.4	18.4
Turn Management: close	82.7	5.0	**83.0**	4.9	**72.9**	29.1	67.2	28.9
Time Management	70.0	3.0	**73.5**	2.1	**91.3**	8.7	75.8	19.3
Discourse Structuring	**72.3**	4.9	63.7	3.6	78.1	19.3	**81.3**	17.3
Contact Management	79.1	4.5	**84.3**	4.6	**79.5**	17.9	78.5	18.9
OCM	66.0	2.4	**68.3**	2.3	**80.4**	17.6	67.3	28.9
PCM	**63.2**	7.8	59.5	11.4	**72.7**	33.2	66.7	29.1
SOM	**88.4**	0.9	81.6	1.7	**95.7**	6.3	**95.7**	6.4

by local classifiers are false, but once a local classifier has made a decision it is never revisited. Humans, by contrast, may revise their previous decisions while interpreting utterances, as illustrated for example by the well-known 'garden-path' phenomena (see e.g. Bever 1970; Frazier and Rayner 1982). It is therefore important to base a decision not only on local features of the input, but to take *outputs of all local classifiers* into account as well. Thus, broader contextual information should be combined with a variety of local information to guide dialogue act recognition over time. For example, making use of the partial output predicted so far, i.e. of the history of previous predictions, and taking this as features into the next classification step, would help to discover and correct errors and make more accurate predictions. This is known as the 'recurrent sliding window strategy' (see Dietterich 2002) when the true values for previous predictions are used as features. However, this suffers not only from the label bias problem when a classifier overestimates the importance of certain features, but also depicts an unrealistic situation, since this information is not available to a classifier in real time. A solution proposed by Van den Bosch (1997) is 'adaptive training', when the actual predicted output of previous processing steps are used as features.

We trained higher-level classifiers (often referred to as 'global') that have, along with features extracted locally from the input data as described above, the partial output predicted so far from all local classifiers. We used five previously predicted class labels, assuming that long distance dependencies may be important, and taking into account that the average length of a functional segment in our data is 4.4 tokens. Table 10 gives an overview of the results. We can observe an improvement of about 10–15 % on average (cf. Tables 3 and 4). The classifiers still make some incorrect predictions, because the decision is sometimes based on incorrect previous

Table 11 Overview of F-scores and DER_{sc} when global classifiers are used for AMI and Map Task data, based on added predictions of local classifiers for five previous and five next tokens. (Best scores indicated by numbers in bold face.)

| Classification | AMI data | | | | Map Task data | | | |
| | BayesNet | | Ripper | | BayesNet | | Ripper | |
Dimension	F_1	DER_{sc}	F_1	DER_{sc}	F_1	DER_{sc}	F_1	DER_{sc}
Task	82.6	9.5	**86.1**	8.3	**85.8**	12.2	80.8	9.1
Auto-Feedback	81.9	1.9	**95.1**	0.6	84.4	15.0	**93.0**	7.6
Allo-Feedback	**96.3**	0.6	95.7	0.5	**95.3**	4.6	94.6	6.9
Turn Management: initial	**85.7**	1.5	81.5	1.6	89.5	8.2	**91.0**	8.0
Turn Management: close	90.9	3.8	**91.2**	3.6	**82.9**	17.1	77.2	18.9
Time management	90.4	2.4	**93.4**	1.7	**94.9**	5.5	92.8	6.1
Discourse Structuring	**82.1**	1.7	78.3	1.8	85.7	12.4	**87.4**	8.2
Contact Management	87.9	1.2	**94.3**	0.6	87.4	9.9	**88.3**	7.4
OCM	78.4	2.2	**81.6**	2.0	87.2	9.8	**87.4**	7.6
PCM	**71.8**	2.4	70.0	4.6	86.7	11.1	**86.8**	9.8
SOM	98.6	0.4	98.6	0.5	**97.9**	1.1	**97.9**	1.2

predictions. An optimized global search strategy may lead to further improvements of these results.

A strategy to optimize the use of output hypotheses is to perform a global search in the output space looking for best predictions. Our classifiers do not just predict the most likely class for an instance, but also generate a distribution of output classes. Class distributions can be seen as confidence scores of all predictions that led to a certain state. Our confidence models are based on token-level information given the dialogue left-context (i.e. dialogue history, wording of the previous and currently produced functional segment). This is particular useful for dialogue act recognition because the recognition of intentions should be based on the understanding of discourse and not just on the interpretation of an isolated utterance. Searching the (partial) output space for the best predictions is not always the best strategy, however, since the highest-ranking predictions are not always correct in a given context. A possible solution to this is to postpone prediction until some (or all) future predictions have been made for the rest of the segment. For training, the classifier then uses not only previous predictions as additional features, but also some or all future predictions of local classifiers (till the end of the current segment or to the beginning of the next segment, depending on what is recognized). This forces the classifier to not immediately select the highest-ranking predictions, but to also consider lower-ranking predictions that could be better in the context of the rest of the sequence.

Table 11 gives an overview of the global classification results based on added previous and next predictions of local classifiers. We can observe a further improvement in terms of high F-scores and quite low error rate. Both classifiers performed very well on this task. The results show the importance of optimal global classification for finding the best output prediction. The use of local classifiers only is outperformed by a broad margin (see Tables 3 and 4 for AMI and Map Task data respectively). For instance, using global classifiers for the important Task dimension an F-score was reached of 86.1, while the best obtained F-score using only local classifiers is 79.7. F-scores for communicative function recognition by local classifiers range from 54.2 to 86.5, while the F-scores using global classifiers range from 71.8 to 97.9 (statistically significant, $p < .05$, one-tailed z-test). The performance of global classifiers is very close to the performance of classifiers upon two-step segmentation and classification reported in Table 5. Global classifiers perform significantly better for recognizing the Task dimension (F-score of 86.1 compared to 72.3 for AMI data using Ripper) and the Auto-Feedback dimension (95.1 compared to 89.7), which are the most important and frequently occurring categories of dialogue acts. It may be noted that the overall performance of global classifiers reported here is generally substantially better than the results of other approaches that have been reported in the literature (see the introduction to this chapter).

To summarize, we have shown that a token-based approach combining the use of local classifiers, which exploit local utterance features, with the use of global classifiers that exploit the outputs of local classifiers applied to previous and subsequent tokens, results in excellent dialogue act recognition scores for unsegmented spoken dialogue. This may be seen as a significant step forward towards the development of fully incremental, on-line methods for computing the meaning of utterances in spoken dialogue.

5 Conclusions and Future Research

This chapter presented a machine learning-based approach to the incremental understanding of dialogue utterances, with a focus on the recognition of their communicative functions. We discussed various strategies in the automatic recognition of dialogue acts. Not only word-level features are taken into account but also word N-grams, prosodic and acoustic features, and features calculated from speaker's and partner's previous utterances. The latter is particularly useful for communicative function recognition, because the recognition of a speaker's intention should be based on the understanding of the preceding discourse, and not just on understanding an utterance in isolation.

One of the main conclusions is that the commonly used strategy to first determine segment boundaries and subsequently perform dialogue act classification has serious theoretical and practical disadvantages. The identification of dialogue unit boundaries heavily depends on how a dialogue unit is defined (see Traum and Heeman 1997). The definition of a functional segment is based on the criterion of carrying a communicative function: a functional segment is a minimal stretch of behaviour that has at least one communicative function. As a consequence, the identification of boundaries cannot precede the recognition of communicative functions.

Incremental dialogue act recognition is a complex task. Splitting up the output structure may make the task more manageable. Sometimes, however, learning of multiple classes allows a learning algorithm to exploit the interactions among classes. Combining these two strategies resulted in building a number of classifiers that show substantial improvement both in communicative function recognition and in segment boundary detection, and result in excellent dialogue act recognition scores.

The incremental construction of input interpretation hypotheses has the effect that the understanding of an input segment is already nearly ready when the last token of the segment is received; viewing a dialogue act as a recipe for updating an information state, this means that the specification of the update operation is almost ready at that moment. It may even happen that the confidence score of a partially processed input segment is that high, that the system may decide to go forward and update its information state without waiting until the end of the segment, and prepare or produce a response based on that update. Of course, full incremental understanding of dialogue utterances includes not only the recognition of communicative functions, but also that of semantic content. However, many dialogue acts have no or only marginal semantic content, such as turn-taking acts, backchannels (*m-hm*) and other feedback acts (*okay*), time management acts (*Just a moment*), and in general dialogue acts with a dimension-specific function; for these acts the proposed strategy can work well without semantic content analysis, and will increase the system's interactivity significantly. Moreover, given that the average length of a functional segment in our data is no more than 4.4 tokens, the semantic content of such a segment tends not to be very complex, and its construction therefore does not seem to require very sophisticated computational semantic methods, applied either in an incremental fashion (see e.g. Aist et al. 2007; DeVault and Stone 2003) or to a segment as a whole.

Interactivity is however not the sole motivation for incremental interpretation. The integration of pragmatic information obtained from the dialogue act recognition module, as proposed here, at early processing stage can be beneficially used by an incremental semantic parser as well as by a syntactic parser module. For instance, information about the communicative function of the incoming segment at an early stage of processing can defuse a number of ambiguous interpretations, e.g. used for the resolution of anaphoric expressions. A challenge for future work is to integrate the incremental recognition of communicative functions with incremental automatic speech recognition, and incremental syntactic and semantic parsing, and to exploit the interaction of prosodic, lexical, syntactic, semantic and pragmatic hypotheses in order to understand incoming dialogue segments incrementally in an optimally efficient manner.

Acknowledgements This research was conducted within the project 'Multidimensional Dialogue Modelling', sponsored by the Netherlands Organisation for Scientific Research (NWO), under grant reference 017.003.090.

References

Aist, G., Allen, J., Campana, E., Gomez Gallo, C., Stoness, S., Swift, M., & Tanenhaus, M. K. (2007). Incremental understanding in human-computer dialogue and experimental evidence for advantages over nonincremental methods. In R. Arstein & L. Vieu (Eds.), *Proceedings of the 11th workshop on the semantics and pragmatics of dialogue*, Trento, Italy (pp. 149–154).

Ang, J., Liu, Y., & Shriberg, E. (2005). Automatic dialog act segmentation and classification in multiparty meetings. In *Proceedings of the international conference on acoustics, speech and signal processing* (ICASSP), Philadelphia, USA (Vol. *1*, pp. 1061–1064).

Barkhuysen, P., Krahmer, E., & Swerts, M. (2008). The interplay between auditory and visual cues for end-of-utterance detection. *Journal of the Acoustical Society of America, 123*(1), 354–365.

Bever, T. (1970). The cognitive basis for linguistic structure. In I. Hayes (Ed.), *Cognitive development of language*, New York: Wiley.

Bos, J. (2002). *Underspecification and resolution in discourse semantics*. PhD Thesis, Saarbrücken: Saarland University.

Bunt, H. (2000). Dialogue pragmatics and context specification. In H. Bunt & W. Black (Eds.), *Abduction, belief and context in dialogue; studies in computational pragmatics* (pp. 81–105). Amsterdam: John Benjamins.

Bunt, H. (2007). Semantic underspecification: Which techniques for what purpose? In H. Bunt & R. Muskens (Eds.), *Computing meaning* (Vol. *3*, pp. 55–85). Dordrecht: Springer.

Bunt, H. (2009). The DIT++ taxonomy for functional dialogue markup. In H. Heylen, C. Pelachaud, R. Catizone, & D. Traum (Eds.), *Proceedings of the AAMAS 2009 workshop 'Towards a standard markup language for embodied dialogue acts'* (EDAML 2009), Budapest (pp. 13–25).

Bunt, H. (2011). Multifunctionality in dialogue. *Computer, Speech and Language, 25*, 222–245.

Bunt, H., Fang, A., Cao, J., Liu, X., & Petukhova, V. (2013). Issues in the addition of ISO standard annotations to the switchboard corpus. In *Proceedings ninth joint ISO – ACL SIGSeM workshop on interoperable semantic annotation* (ISA-9), Potsdam (pp. 59–70).

Chater, N., Pickering, M., & Milward, D. (1995). What is incremental interpretation? *Edingburg Working Papers in Cognitive Science, 11*, 1–23.

Cohen, W. (1995). Fast effective rule induction. In *Proceedings of the 12th international conference on machine learning* (ICML'95) (pp. 115–123).

Corbett, A., & Chang, F. (1983). Pronoun disambiguating: Accessing potential antecedents. *Memory and Cognition, 11*, 283–294.

de Ruiter, J., Mitterer, H., & Enfield, N. (2006). Projecting the end of a speaker's turn: A cognitive cornerstone of conversation. *Language, 82*, 515–535.

DeVault, D., & Stone, M. (2003). Domain inference in incremental interpretation. In *Proceedings of the workshop on inference in computational semantics*, INRIA Lorraine, Nancy, France (pp. 73–87).

Dietterich, T. (2002). Machine learning for sequential data: A review. In T. Caelli, A. Amin, R. Duin, M. Kamel, & D. Ridder (Eds.), *Proceedings of the joint IAPR international workshop on structural, syntactic, and statistical pattern recognition* (pp. 15–30).

Fernandez, R., & Picard, R. W. (2002). Dialog act classification from prosodic features using support vector machines. In *Proceedings of speech prosody 2002*, Aix-en-Provence, France.

Ford, C., & Thompson, S. (1996). Interactional units in conversation: Syntactic, intonational, and pragmatic resources for the management of turns. In E. Schegloff & S. Thompson (Eds.), *Interaction and grammar* (pp. 135–184). Cambridge: Cambridge University Press.

Frazier, L., & Rayner, K. (1982). Making and correcting errors during sentence comprehension: Eye movements in the analysis of structurally ambiguous sentences. *Cognitive Psychology, 14*, 178–210.

Geertzen, J. (2009). *Dialogue act recognition and prediction: Exploration in computational dialogue modelling*. PhD Thesis, The Netherlands: Tilburg University.

Geertzen, J., Girard, Y., & Morante, R. (2004). The DIAMOND project. In *Poster at the 8th workshop on the semantics and pragmatics of dialogue* (CATALOG 2004), Barcelona, Spain.

Geertzen, J., Petukhova, V., & Bunt, H. (2007). A multidimensional approach to utterance segmentation and dialogue act classification. In *Proceedings of the 8th SIGdial workshop on discourse and dialogue*, Antwerp, Belgium (pp. 140–149). Stroudsburg: Association for Computational Linguistics.

Grosjean, F., & Hirt, C. (1996). Using prosody to predict the end of sentences in English and French: Normal and brain-damaged subjects. *Language and Cognitive Processes*, *11*, 107–134.

Haddock, N. (1989). Computational models of incremental semantic interpretation. *Language and Cognitive Processes*, *14*(3), SI337–SI380.

Hobbs, J. (1985). Ontological promiscuity. In *Proceedings 23rd annual meeting of the ACL*, Chicago (pp. 61–69).

Jurafsky, D., Shriberg, E., Fox, B., & Curl, T. (1998). Lexical, prosodic, and syntactic cues for dialogue acts. In M. Stede, L. Wanner, & E. Hovy (Eds.), *Discourse relations and discourse markers: Proceedings of the workshop on discourse relations and discourse markers*, Somerset, New Jersey, USA (pp. 114–120). Stroudsburg: Association for Computational Linguistics.

Keizer, S. (2003). *Reasoning under uncertainty in natural language dialogue using Bayesian networks*. PhD Thesis, The Netherlands: Twente University.

Lendvai, P., Bosch, v. d. A., Krahmer, E., & Canisius, S. (2004). Memory-based robust interpretation of recognised speech. In *Proceedings of the 9th international conference on speech and computer* (SPECOM '04), St. Petersburgh, Russia (pp. 415–422).

Lendvai, P., & Geertzen, J. (2007). Token-based chunking of turn-internal dialogue act sequences. In *Proceedings of the 8th SIGdial workshop on discourse and dialogue*, Antwerp, Belgium (pp. 174–181).

Meteer, & Taylor, R. A. (1995). Dysfluency annotation stylebook for the switchboard corpus. ftp://ftp.cis.upenn.edu/pub/treebank/swbd/doc/DFL-book.ps.

Milward, D., & Cooper, R. (2009). Incremental interpretation: Applications, theory, and relationship to dynamic semantics. In *Proceedings COLING 2009*, Kyoto, Japan (pp. 748–754).

Nakano, M., Miyazaki, N., Hirasawa, J., Dohsaka, K., & Kawabata, T. (1999). Understanding unsegmented user utterances in real-time spoken dialogue systems. In *Proceedings of the 37th annual conference of the Association of Computational Linguistics, ACL* (pp. 200–207).

Petukhova, V., & Bunt, H. (2009). Who's next? Speaker-selection mechanisms in multiparty dialogue. In *Proceedings of the workshop on the semantics and pragmatics of dialogue*, Stockholm (pp. 19–26).

Pinkal, M. (1999). On semantic underspecification. In H. Bunt & R. Muskens (Eds.), *Computing meaning* (Vol. *1*, pp. 33–56). Dordrecht: Kluwer.

Poesio, M., & Traum, D. (1998). Towards an axiomatization of dialogue acts. In *Proceedings of the Twente workshop on the formal semantics and pragmatics of dialogue* (pp. 309–347). The Netherlands: University of Twente.

Reithinger, N., & Klesen, M. (1997). Dialogue act classification using language models. In *Proceedings of EuroSpeech-97* (pp. 2235–2238).

Samuel, K., Carberry, S., & Vijay-Shanker, K. (1998). Dialogue act tagging with transformation-based learning. In *Proceedings of the 36th annual meeting of the Association for Computational Linguistics and 17th international conference on computational linguistics*, Montreal (Vol. 2, pp. 1150–1156).

Sedivy, J. (2003). Pragmatic versus form-based accounts of referential contrast: Evidence for effects of informativity expectations. *Journal of Psycholinguistic Research*, *32*(1), 3–23.

Sedivy, J., Tanenhaus, M., Chambers, C., & Carlson, G. (1999). Achieving incremental semantic interpretation through contextual representation. *Cognition*, *71*, 109–147.

Shriberg, E., Bates, R., Stolcke, A., Taylor, P., Jurafsky, D., Ries, K., Coccaro, N., Martin, R., Meteer, M., & van Ess-Dykema, C. (1998). Can prosody aid the automatic classification of dialog acts in conversational speech? *Language and Speech (Special Issue on Prosody and Conversation)*, *41*(3–4), 439–487.

Simpson, G. (1994). Context and the processing of ambiguous words. In M. Gernsbacher (Ed.), *Handbook of psycholinguistics* (pp. 359–374). San Diego: Academic Press.

Stolcke, A., Ries, K., Coccaro, K., Shriberg, E., Bates, R., Jurafsky, D., Taylor, P., Martin, R., van Ess-Dykema, C., & Meteer, M. (2000). Dialogue act modeling for automatic tagging and recognition of conversational speech. *Computational Linguistics*, *26*(3), 339–373.

Swinney, D. (1979). Lexical access during sentence comprehension: (Re)consideration of context effects. *Journal of Verbal Learning and Verbal Behaviour*, *18*, 545–567.

Tanenhaus, M., Spivey-Knowlton, M., Eberhard, K., & Sedivy, J. (1995). Integration of visual and linguistic information in spoken language comprehension. *Science, 268,* 1632–1634.

Tomita, M. (1986). *Efficient parsing for natural language.* Dordrecht: Kluwer.

Traum, D., & Heeman, P. (1997). Utterance units in spoken dialogue. In *Proceedings of ECAI workshop on dialogue processing in social language systems,* London, UK (pp. 125–140).

Traum, D., & Larsson, S. (2003). The information state approach to dialogue acts. In R. Smith & J. van Kuppevelt (Eds.), *Current and new directions in discourse and dialogue* (pp. 325–353). Dordrecht: Kluwer.

Van den Bosch, A. (1997). *Learning to pronounce written words: A study in inductive language learning.* PhD thesis, The Netherlands: Maastricht University.

Webb, N., Hepple, M., & Wilks, Y. (2005). Error analysis of dialogue act classification. In *Proceedings of the 8th international conference on text, speech and dialogue,* Karlovy Vary, Czech Republic (Vol. *3658,* pp. 451–458).

Zimmermann, M., Lui, Y., Shriberg, E., & Stolcke, A. (2005). Toward joint segmentation and classification of dialog acts in multiparty meetings. In *Proceedings of the multimodal interaction and related machine learning algorithms workshop* (MLMI-05) (pp. 187–193). Berlin: Springer.

Index